# Reasons *to* Believe

*Also by John Marks*

# Reasons | to

# Believe

*One Man's Journey*

*Among the Evangelicals*

*and the Faith He Left Behind*

## john marks

*An Imprint of HarperCollinsPublishers*

HarperCollins books may be purchased for educational, business, or sales
promotional use. For information, please write: Special Markets Department,
HarperCollins Publishers, 10 East 53rd Street, New York, NY 10022.

FIRST EDITION

*Designed by Nicola Ferguson*

Library of Congress Cataloging-in-Publication Data is available upon request.
ISBN: 978-0-06-083276-6

08   09   10   11   12      ID/RRD      10   9   8   7   6   5   4   3   2   1

*For Mom and Dad, Tolbert and Molly, with love and gratitude*

# Acknowledgments

I owe so much to so many people in the making of this book. Thanks to Dan Halpern at Ecco for taking it on, and thanks to Emily Takoudes for helping me to shape it and hone it for readers. Thanks to the wonderful Joe Regal for being such a friend and supporter right from the start, and to all the folks at Regal Literary who helped me figure out how to tackle this subject matter. Thanks to Courtney Hodell for seeing its potential.

And for the years of research on the book, thanks to all of the Christians around the country who opened their homes, lives, offices, and churches to me, who made time on weekends and on week nights during the school year, during hard times and holidays. I couldn't have worked without such generosity. I am especially indebted to Don and Lillie McWhinney, without whom this book would never have come into existence, and want to pause a moment to remember their son Tedd. In equal measure, I'm grateful to Craig Detweiler, who opened his life and world to me, and who taught me patience and joy in word and deed, as he has done since we first met more than two decades ago. Thanks also to his wife, Caroline, who seemed always to welcome my presence even during times of great difficulty. I benefited hugely from the insights of so many pastors: the Reverends Tommy Nelson, John Brown, Mike Scheer, Bob Russell, Dave Stone, Dino Rizzo, Rodney Pearce, Steve Parelli, and Brent Alderman Sterste, among others.

When it came to the political side, David Barton was always ready to take a phone call, have me pay a visit or come along for the national tour. Special thanks to his Wall Builders team, especially his wife Cheryl, for all their help. My trip to Prague would not have been possible without Charles Thaxton. My trip to Frontier Ranch in Colorado would not have been possible without the help of the folks at Young Life. I am grateful for the hour that Carrie McDonnall gave me to talk about her life, and for the days that Joanne Brokaw spent shepherding me around the music scene in Nashville and Darien Lakes.

And the list goes on. Thanks to the members of the Priddy family: John and Terry, Ed and Mark, for hosting me and putting up with me; to the International Mission Board of the Southern Baptist Convention, to congregations of churches in Kingston, Massachusetts; Northampton, Massachusetts; Plano, Texas; York, Pennsylvania; Baton Rouge, Louisiana; Denton, Texas; Louisville, Kentucky; Gonzalez, Louisiana; and Nashville, Tennessee. Thanks to the folks at Focus on the Family for allowing me to participate in a session of the Truth Project. Thanks to the Berryhills and the ladies of Mission Messiah for opening their doors. Thanks to Rodney and a very pregnant Erin Pearce for a delicious Sunday meal a few days before election day 2006 and her due date. Thanks to Jack and Sue Crans and the folks at Chester County Prison, to Debra Childrers at Southeast Christian Church, Marc Cleary at Healing Place Church, to Davidson College, and to Biola University and its wonderful students, to Morley Safer at *60 Minutes*, who gave me the chance to produce a piece on the Left Behind books, to Beverly at Tyndale, and to Tim LaHaye and Jerry Jenkins. Thanks to Professor James Borland for assisting me in attendance of the annual meeting of the Evangelical Theological Society.

Finally, thanks to all my family members and friends, who spoke honestly with me about the past and their beliefs and everything else: Thanks to Bobby McCreless, Chris Busbee, and Julie Knisley for helping me to recall my high school self. Thanks to Murphy Martin and Jack Simons, whose friendships permeate this book, even though they themselves are not in it. For all of their love and support over the years, and their part in this story, thanks to Aunt Fay, Uncle Bill, and Aunt Esther. Special thanks to Scott and Michele Birdwell for giving me their insights into family and faith and for helping me with contacts in their circle. And special thanks to Aunt Margaret for introducing me to so many of her friends in Odessa and Midland; and to Ricky and Nancy Marks and Delinda Gillham for helpful conversations. To Doug Wright and Jim Hynes for advice and friendship for as long as I can remember. Thanks to Aunt Nene, Aunt Di, Uncle Dale, Aunt Gina, Sharilyn, Sharon, Mark, Reba, Steven, and Scott for hints, help, and encouragement along the way. Finally, I owe so much to Debra and Joe for putting up with the months and months that I spent on the road, for helping me through lots of ups and downs, for loving me every day. I couldn't have made it without them.

A good man out of the good treasure of the heart bringeth forth good things: and an evil man out of the evil treasure bringeth forth evil things. But I say unto you, That every idle word that men shall speak, they shall give account thereof in the day of judgment. For by thy words thou shalt be justified, and by thy words, thou shalt be condemned.

—*Matthew 12:35–37*

# Contents

## book 1: the way

## book 2: the truth

# book 1

## *The Way*

## First Things

*In* the fall of 2003, on assignment for the CBS news show
*60 Minutes*, I went home to Dallas, Texas, in search of
interview candidates for a segment on evangelical Christians. I made the
decision casually. My hometown had more than its share of evangelicals. I
didn't expect to find a lost piece of myself there.

As a producer for Morley Safer, I had begun work on a story about a
series of novels inspired by the Christian version of the end of the world,
and one of the authors, the Reverend Tim LaHaye, had agreed to appear
at a Prophecy Conference in the Dallas suburb of Garland. For the story, I
wanted to find fans of the books who could talk with enthusiasm about what
the novels had meant to them—the assumption being that these books, unlike
most popular fiction, had an appeal that went well beyond entertainment.

Pastors at several churches gave me names and phone numbers. I found
Don and Lillie McWhinney through a church in Denton, Texas, and they
agreed to meet me for lunch at a prime rib restaurant among a twist of free-
ways and toll roads in north Dallas. At the time, I had no earthly idea how
important they would become to me, or this book, but I was struck by their
presence immediately. Don, a former oil executive, had dressed in a dark
blue business suit, Lillie in a beige pantsuit. They were both trim, good-

looking people. Don had the bigger personality. A man in his midsixties, with snow white hair and beetling white eyebrows, with a sonorous voice to match, Don looked and sounded like a local anchorman. He often began a thought with my first name, "You see, John," and when the words came out of his mouth, they had a stylized flair. They sounded like scripted lines. Don told me that he often worked as a chaplain in the Dallas area, making visits to corporate offices and patients in hospice care, and it made sense. You could hear him delivering an impromptu message in an elevator, at the water cooler, in a cubicle during lunch hour, or in the afternoon quiet of a house where someone slowly passed away. When he stopped talking, the silence dropped like a barbell.

Lillie, a small, attractive woman in her fifties, with big eyes and a sly smile, was less imposing. She wasn't at all shy, but her manner and physical presence conveyed a certain fragility that seemed, at first, to be at odds with her robust sense of spiritual urgency. She listened closely to Don and never interrupted, but he would often turn to her and say, "Lillie, tell him what you told me just the other day."

The McWhinneys ordered the prime rib, and for an hour I quizzed them about their faith. The lunch was an audition. I asked them if they liked the Left Behind books, and Don praised them. The Left Behind books were works of history, he maintained, set in the future rather than the past, and he compared them to fictionalized accounts of the story of the *Titanic*. Lillie liked them too, but Don was the enthusiast. They both believed that events recounted in the novels would one day come to pass. They believed in the Rapture, when Jesus would come and spirit away his people. They believed in the Tribulation, when God would allow the Antichrist to govern those people on earth who had been left behind. And they certainly believed in God's final retribution, when all nonbelievers would be destroyed. Lillie said that she sometimes liked to imagine what the Rapture would feel like; she gazed at the sky above her backyard and imagined some mundane morning when she would look out of her kitchen window and see spirits flying beyond the roofs of homes into the sunlight. And yet, as Don and Lillie described the historical inevitability of the annihilation of most of the human race, they did so without the slightest trace of malevolence. They were almost sweet about it. By the end of an hour, I had decided that Don McWhinney would make an ideal interview candidate.

Typically, the meeting would have ended there, but just as the couple were finishing their meals, it became clear that Don had something else on his mind. He peered at me across the table. I was struck again by those looks. With those bushy white eyebrows, with his blue eyes and snowy hair, he seemed the Hollywood ideal of benevolent goodness come to life. When God called, Don McWhinney would go to heaven, and the belief had transformed his very flesh.

"You've asked us a lot of questions," Don said. I nodded. "May I ask you a question?" A stillness settled on the table. I knew what was coming. Lillie watched my face. I braced for it.

"Will you be left behind?"

WOULD I BE left behind? In other words, had I been saved by the grace of Jesus Christ? Or would I be left to face the torments of hell, or the violence of hell on earth, should the end come during my lifetime? It struck me as the most remarkable question imaginable, and at the same time, maybe the most American. According to the preeminent pollster in the evangelical world, George Barna, the United States has more born-again Christians than any other country in the world, some 100 million people who are "assured of eternal salvation solely because they have confessed their sins and accepted Jesus Christ as their savior." And a majority of these believers told the pollster they had shared their faith with a non-Christian. They had posed the Don McWhinney question, in effect. The proper verb for that is "witness": to witness is to share or impart a sense of one's own faith to another. Scripture calls believers to do so as often as possible—to become a living witness to their own redemption, testifying of the event. Black and Hispanic believers are more likely to witness to nonbelievers than whites. These figures, the pollster informs, have remained the same for about a decade, which means, if the poll is even roughly correct, that within the previous year more than 50 million Americans had posed a question like the one Don McWhinney posed to me to a fellow American. In my lifetime, hundreds of millions had been put on the spot.

Would I be left behind? The question should have been easy to dismiss. On the face of it, the words were offensive and ludicrous, the kind of thing that so often invites scorn toward evangelical Christians. But I didn't dismiss the question. I didn't laugh or condescend.

In fact, I took Don's words very seriously. They hadn't startled me. I had half expected them. But they took on a bizarre force in the banal atmosphere of the prime rib restaurant, amid the click of fork against plate, as the knife of a carver whispered through a haunch of beef. This wasn't a dream. The question leapt off the pages of a work of fiction and into that small corner of the real world.

Would I be left behind? Because we had been discussing the Left Behind books, Don had framed the question in this way. But there are countless ways to ask. The word choice can be poetically beautiful or bluntly ridiculous. It can be sung on a radio station, signed on a highway, sighed by a lover in or out of bed, or couched in utter and impressive silence, understood by the hearer implicitly, in the form of what is called "lifestyle evangelism." This is when believers demonstrate behavior in their lives that will make nonbelievers question their own beliefs. I have seen the question in a Bible verse painted in bright red ink on the side of a golf ball—"Read John 3:16–17"—meant to be hit into a sand trap and found by a lost and seeking soul. I have seen it in the form of a simple child's game, a kind of Rubik's Cube called the Evangecube, made of a series of plastic squares and covered in images that tell the story of Christian redemption, meant to wordlessly unfold in the hands of the damned, used as a tool of conversion by 1.5 million believers since the year 2000, or so claims the website. I have heard the message scored to electric guitars at rock concerts, confessed from the mouth of a contrite Hollywood movie star, from countless preachers and close friends, and once, memorably, on a T-shirt in Central Asia, "For God so loved Kazakhstan . . ."

On that day, Don went for maximum dramatic effect. But the effect was not all—he believed in the words. The possible end of the prime rib–scented world came to life right then and there, and the restaurant dimmed a bit in its shadow. Don and Lillie truly believed that these biblical events might be approaching. The Rapture might come soon.

There would be no time for explanations or apologies. Their confidence appalled me.

"I will definitely be left behind," I told him.

"Why?" asked Lillie.

"Because I don't believe."

Once, though, I had. That was the most unsettling thing about the question. Don and Lillie McWhinney sounded utterly familiar to me. As infuriating as it was, the question posed by this upper-middle-class north Dallas man was oddly comforting, like words spoken in the voice of a grandparent long passed away. Nothing had changed in my hometown. I might have left these people far behind, but they had remained where they were, rock solid, unmoved by politics, culture, or society, or so I thought at the time, a force of immovable belief. I knew them so well that I almost wanted to accommodate them, answer in the negative just to acknowledge the old bond: "No, Don, of course I won't be left behind." But that was impossible. I had left the fold for good.

"I don't find Jesus Christ, as savior, to be a convincing or even compelling idea," I told them, rather glibly. "He was a great human being. His teachings have endured. But the world is complete without him. Its sheer plentitude dwarfs the idea that one man, born more than 2 billion years after its creation, is the key that fits all locks. He's just not necessary."

I was getting heated as I spoke, could feel my blood pressure rising. My words made no impression at all on Lillie. "What about sin?" she asked me.

She had told me earlier in the lunch that she led a Bible study for young married women, many of whom were in bad and even abusive marriages. With the help of Christ, she had convinced most of these women to stay in their marriages and try to work things out. She was not one to surrender a point. Nor was I.

"Sin is just another word for death," I replied. "As one way of looking at death, it's interesting, but it's not adequate to the task of explaining evil or suffering in the world."

"No," she corrected me. "I mean your own sin."

This was incredibly presumptuous. I was a television producer here to interview her, after all. What was she thinking? But I also felt self-conscious, like a teenager caught smoking a cigarette in the school bathroom. I also felt that I owed them a few answers. After all, they had sat and answered mine about their personal beliefs for an hour.

"I have my struggles," I told her.

"In my case, for instance," she went on in her pleasurable drawl, more or less ignoring my reply, "my great sin is fear. I am a person who is very afraid of the world. I couldn't overcome that fear without the Lord. I tried and tried, but it wasn't until I fell on my knees and let Christ take over that I was healed."

Her confession moved me. Much later, I found out why, but at that moment, this fragile woman looked afraid. With her big, soft eyes, pale skin, and tentative manner, she looked like someone who had been hiding in the dark for a long time. Maybe she was afraid of Don, I thought, though it didn't seem so; on the contrary, in a subtle way, he seemed to defer to her. Maybe she feared her own shadow. Certainly she was afraid of death, and Jesus allayed her fear. I could relate to that. I was afraid, too. I had been in New York City on September 11 and rode in a subway to work every morning, or drove across a bridge or through a tunnel. I feared terrorism. I feared for my wife and son. I feared death. But why should her newfound courage in Christ depend upon the obliteration of others? Why should my son and wife have to suffer endless torment for her peace of mind?

Lillie backed off. She and Don told me I was a thoughtful person and thanked me for being honest. There were no hard feelings. A few weeks later, after Don did the interview with Morley Safer, he handed me a gift to give to my son Joe, a box of Hot Wheel cars, and I took them back to my hotel room. On the face of it, the gesture had the same sweetness as their conversation. The McWhinneys have boys of their own, all grown-up, and I'm certain that they meant the Hot Wheels as a sincere token of affection. But I couldn't get it out of my mind that they were gifts for a boy doomed to cosmic incineration. A day later, when I checked out of the hotel, I left the Hot Wheels in the room.

IF THE MCWHINNEYS had known, I doubt they would have understood, but I had my reasons, which I will now try to explain. On the day of that lunch, I withheld crucial information. I didn't tell the couple that my wife and son were Jewish. It certainly wasn't shame or guilt. The McWhinneys would not have minded the idea of my having a Jewish mate. On the contrary, I believe they would have been spiritually titillated by the news. For evangelicals, Jews are the closest thing to hard evidence in this life of the truth of the Christian message. It's a paradox. Jews have become, in the last half century, the living fulfillment of end-time prophecies, their status as God's chosen people confirmed by their longevity, by their prosperity, and by their immense suffering. In this scenario, even the inexplicable horror of the Holocaust has a specific meaning and purpose—6 million men, women, and children subjected to atrocious death in German concentration camps as part of a divine plan that would underscore God's displeasure with his people's rejection of Christ and hasten the day to their final redemption in the land of their forefathers. Similarly, the birth of the state of Israel in 1948 told evangelicals that this final redemption lay at hand. The countdown had begun. The Bible had predicted that, before the end, the Jews would return to the Holy Land, and they had. Next they must rebuild the Temple of Solomon, and when that happens, prophecy says, the end is come. Without the Jews in Jerusalem, everything would look like coincidence. As it is, everything looks inevitable.

What does this have to do with my wife and son? For me, Debra and Joe are the most precious creatures on earth, and they have nothing to do with faith or prophecy or religious truth. They are as immediate, as elemental, as sunlight, air, and water. But for Don and Lillie McWhinney and tens of millions of others, they become members of the prophetic race—markers, if you will—and God has a special plan for them. In my eyes, this doesn't elevate my wife and son in stature. It reduces them to a biblical statistic. For this reason, I didn't reveal the truth to Don and Lillie. It would have felt somehow like a conspiracy against my own family, a collusion with their version of the universe to unmask my wife and son as members of that holy race. In fact, Debra and Joe lay at the heart of my resistance to everything that Don and Lillie stood for: a reduction of the world in all its infinite mystery to a formula; human beings, in all their complexity, turned into fixed points on an ancient map. Forget the two thousand years of history that had occurred since the exile of the Jews from Palestine. Forget Spinoza, Mendelssohn, and Kafka. Forget Debra and Joe. All that was as the blink of an eye. The Jews had returned to Jerusalem. Jesus would come.

IT DIDN'T OCCUR to me, at the time, that I was reducing Don and Lillie to equally simplistic figures, that I robbed them of their human mystery and singularity in the same way they appeared to me to rob Debra and Joe. I left that lunch in a state of extreme agitation. In more ways than one, time had fallen away. Decades of my own life had collapsed, and the life of the race, too. Behind the infinite detail of daily life lay centuries in which nothing had occurred but the slow creep of immortal destiny. This wasn't just the case for Jews. Every vanished life was but a spark in the robe of God. I drove on the LBJ Freeway—the Lyndon Baines Johnson Freeway, named after the American president who had shepherded the Civil Rights Act of 1964 through Congress, who had committed tens of thousands of troops to the Vietnam War, who had stepped into the shoes of John F. Kennedy after he was assassinated in my hometown in 1963, but what did all of this matter in the vast tapestry of divinity? I was gripped by memories of a faith that I had left behind—there is more than one meaning to those words—and shaken by the fact that this faith, once safely abandoned, had now come to haunt me, politically and culturally. What had once been my personal struggle suddenly felt to me like the precursor to a much greater and larger struggle.

Who was I on the day when Don McWhinney asked me the question, which, he believed, came from a force outside of him, placed in his mouth with a cosmic purpose by a destiny to which he had dedicated his entire life? Who was the man to whom he addressed his urgent concern? A heterosexual white male, forty years old, husband and father of one, a resident of Brooklyn, the most diverse city in the United States, a producer for the top-rated news show on American television, *60 Minutes*, a published author of two critically acclaimed, commercially unsuccessful novels of war and revolution in Eastern Europe and the Balkans, a German speaker, a native Texan, a fanatical glutton for certain kinds of American pop culture, with an inordinate love of westerns and horror movies, a sloppy love for old-time country music, a child of the 1970s, a long-time admirer of the 1960s, whose oldest and closest male friend was a proud gay fellow son of Dallas and author of a Pulitzer Prize–winning play about an East German transvestite, a thoroughly contemporary man who had lived for five years in sin with his Jewish girlfriend before marrying her, who hadn't voted in an American presidential election until he was thirty, but since then had voted Republican twice, for Rudy Giuliani for mayor of New York, and otherwise for Democrats, a descendant of Methodists and Presbyterians, Creek Indians and English settlers, with hints and rumors of Jewish blood floating around, a pessimist, a hedonist, a committed, happy, straight-up pagan.

But from the age of sixteen, I had believed like Don and Lillie. It seems impossible now, but it was true. I marvel at the intensity of what gripped me. In high school, I had been a pretty good student. I had acted on the stage, written short stories that had nothing to do with faith, made friends who were serious drinkers and drug users. I had never stopped listening to rock and roll or loving zombie movies dripping with extreme gore. And yet during those same years, I had never touched alcohol or drugs. I had never slept with a girl. I had never even touched a girl's breast. I didn't take the Lord's name in vain. I read my Bible every morning and memorized verses that I carried around with me in my wallet. I prayed all the time. Who had I been? What was this belief?

By the time I met Debra, I felt as if a huge gulf separated me from those younger days. By then, among other sins against the old belief, I had lost my virginity and started to drink. I had tried pot and lived with a woman who was not my wife, and I saw those experiences as evidence of the slow inrush of sanity. I had studied history, philosophy, and theology and discovered that my belief had deep roots, a complicated genealogy. I had discovered that European thinkers had been grappling with the loss of the Christian faith for two centuries at least. At the same time, I hadn't stopped believing in God altogether. That happened five years later, in the Balkans, when I caught a small glimpse of the hell that human beings make for themselves on earth and could no longer reasonably believe in the existence of a sovereign being. From then on, it seemed inconceivable to me that a meaningful, not to speak of a loving god could be in charge of this world. It's an old story in the history of Christianity, this moment of negative revelation, and it had become mine.

†

MILLIONS OF BELIEVERS came to a different conclusion, of course. As I was leaving the faith, something profound was happening in the body of the faithful, a metamorphosis with great implications for the future. In the 1980s, a small group of activists, some with familiar names—Jerry Falwell, Pat Robertson, and Tim LaHaye—began to organize a loosely affiliated group of believers of all denominations into a potent political force that came to be known as the Moral Majority and claimed to speak for vast numbers of Christian Americans beleaguered by the social, cultural, and sexual transformations that had come out of the 1960s. The galvanizing political moment had occurred in 1973, with the Supreme Court decision in *Roe* v. *Wade*, upholding a woman's right to have an abortion, but the shock of that moment took years to build into a consensus, carrying with it waves of resentment over the changing roles of women, the frank sexuality on display in movies and music, the banning of prayer from schools, and new discoveries in molecular biology and other sciences that seemed to reduce religion to a form of backwater ignorance. Along with these developments came a rebellion against all authority, political and otherwise, that culminated in the impeachment of Richard Nixon but had its analogues in the community of churchgoers, too, where young people found it hard to accept the old hierarchies of religious obedience. My faith had not been political at all, but as my contemporaries grew up, those who continued to believe met a world that outraged them, and they began to feel like a people under attack. They responded by shaping a future more compatible with their vision of the world. For a long time, this meant withdrawal from the mainstream American experience, into homeschooling and private Christian schools and colleges, as well as a retreat from the culture of Hollywood and the morass of Washington, D.C., except as lobbyists. Now it means the opposite; it means engagement.

Once, when I returned to Dallas after college, I had coffee with one of my best friends from high school, a woman named Margaret. She had been one of the funniest people in our school. She had shiny red hair that fell straight to her shoulders, topped, most of the time, by a bright red or green bow. She had freckles and pale skin that made her seem an unlikely delivery system for pitiless judgments on the various phonies and fakes in high school. Her deadpan had no equal. Margaret had participated in church activities and camp, but had never struck me as dogmatic or preachy. But when we had coffee, and I told her I had been reading Nietzsche and other thinkers, and that I no longer believed in Jesus Christ as the son of God, she said, "See, that's the problem. You've been overeducated." Years later, sitting in a church in Denton, Texas, a less wealthy, less highfalutin northern cousin to Dallas, I would hear a preacher explicitly speak about that "Highland Park kid who fell in love with Hegel and Marx and fell out of love with Jesus," and the judgment awaiting him, and think of Margaret's assessment of me.

At the time, over that cup of coffee, I recognized a new language. She wasn't just talking about my own personal lapse. In her own way, using ideas that had begun to reverberate throughout Christian circles, she was referring to the state of the nation. "See," she'd said, grasping a wider pattern. Others, too, had been "overeducated." I was not alone in my heresy. And it wasn't just a surplus of intellectual activity; it was the content of that education. Margaret could have been a member of the Moral Majority. She wanted evolution out of textbooks and women out of abortion clinics. She worried about the decline of culture and the destruction of the American family. But what mattered, what lay behind it all, was her sense that the rising secular culture not only disdained her beliefs. It ruled them out. *I* ruled them out.

My politics swung sharply to the left during those years, but while most of my friends disliked evangelicals for their political positions, I had a more complicated reaction. I knew and liked plenty of evangelicals personally, but I also had a much deeper dread of them as a political force—an irrational dread, or so I thought. I feared the triumph of their worldview. I feared its constriction, its nihilism, its hatred of the world, and their theologically justified desire for a final act of destruction. I feared their belief that all meaning lay in one consecrated truth. And most of all I feared their belief that I had become, in my own beliefs, an ally of the devil. In the minds of Margaret and people like her, I was worse than lost. I had become the enemy.

Slowly, my own worldview expanded and I came to see these people and their beliefs with a little less dread. In my twenties, I began a long and difficult intellectual journey to find my own understanding of the world, my own gods, my own devils. My fear of evangelicals abated, and a curiosity grew. After college, I traveled to India to get a firsthand taste of the world's religions in one place, everything from animism and Hinduism to Islam, Buddhism, Jainism, and, of course, Christianity. While there, two experiences shaped my thought on evangelicals in deep ways.

First, while in Kashmir, I came upon the tomb of Jesus Christ. I initially thought that it was a kind of ancient hoax. My Muslim friends assured me that it wasn't. There had been a tradition for many centuries in Kashmir that Christ had been rescued from the cross and smuggled out of Palestine. Eventually, he made his way to Kashmir, where he became a favorite of the local prince and died with honors. The tomb sat in a dilapidated corner of Srinagar and couldn't possibly have been two thousand years old, but it didn't matter. All of a sudden, in the face of a completely different account of the life and death of Jesus, I came to see the historical underpinnings of religious belief, the way that local tradition and superstitions are shaped by politics, economics, and geography. The point wasn't that Jesus had actually died in Kashmir. The point was that people in Kashmir really believed that he had died and was buried there. For them, he wasn't the founder of a religion. He was a revered local saint. And that suggested the possibility of other, more historically accurate points of view on the subject.

More important, perhaps, I became friends with a devout Sufi who tried to convert me to Islam. And in his efforts to make me see his way, the light of his truth, I saw a mirror of the person I had been. In my friend Amin, who had a sincere and devout belief in Allah as well as a penchant for sleeping with Scandinavian girls who backpacked to Lake Dal, I understood that there were many faiths in this world, and most of them wanted adherents, and all of them centered upon an absolute truth that could admit of no other absolute claims. Amin told me that his greatest desire in this life was to disappear like a drop of sunlit water in the great sea of God's mercy and truth. To me, that thought was horrifying. I didn't want to disappear into anything. Amin listened to me and shook his head. I simply didn't understand. Had I still been a Christian, I would have tried to convince him that he was the one who didn't understand, but those days were past. And he didn't seem offended that I rejected his belief. It was a benign encounter.

Years later, on September 11, 2001, in New York City, I saw the smoke rising at the end of my island and thought of Amin. What did he now believe? Did he believe what the men in the airplanes believed? Surely not. He would have been as appalled as I was.

IN THE YEARS before September 11, I forgot about Margaret Williams, I forgot about being overeducated, and I worried less about the movement the more I grew away from my years as a believer. Now and then, my sister and I would laugh about it. She had gone through a similar experience. After scratching up my old Led Zeppelin albums and speaking in tongues in a Bible study with a popular cheerleader, she came out the other end, still a Christian, no longer militant, not much worse for the wear. I could even acknowledge some of the benefits of my evangelical period. Close readings of the Bible had influenced my secular reading and writing in positive ways. I had a serious knowledge of what is arguably the most important text in Western civilization. My experience of religion helped me to understand what was happening in the Balkans and elsewhere in the world, which made me a better reporter. But mostly, those years belonged to a distant past that no longer weighed on me.

In the meantime, close friends had remained in the faith, and family members had converted. These friends and family are Bible-believing Christians, homeschoolers, pro-life, anti-gay marriage, and I love them and respect them. I never asked them what they think of my family or me. I don't really care. My wife and I have raised our son in a relaxed way as a Jew, though we celebrate Christmas, too. My oldest friend, a gay man, served in our wedding, and gay couples danced at the reception. No one made an issue of this. But they don't have to. If they're traditional evangelical Christians, I know what they believe. They believe, as the McWhinneys do, that come the day of the Rapture, I and mine will be left behind. I will be destroyed, as will my wife, my son, and my gay friends. It's nothing personal. They love me, but salvation knows no loopholes.

Until recently, none of this would have bothered me. This is a free country, and we are all entitled to believe what we want, so long as it doesn't hurt anyone else. Even now, I would never suggest that my cousins, aunts, and uncles should lose the right to believe whatever they choose. Who am I to exercise such a judgment? But do they have the right to assert their belief as a national religion? Do they have the right to run a country filled with tens of millions of people, who will, according to their beliefs, be left behind? Can a pluralist democracy absorb and support an exclusive, nonpluralist religious belief at the heart of its system?

If so, who gets left behind? It occurred to me that, on the day of the Dallas lunch, Don and Lillie weren't just putting their question to me. They were putting it to the entire country. After a while, I began to feel they deserved a real answer.

THE *60 MINUTES* piece on the Left Behind books led the show on a Sunday night in February 2004. In addition to highlighting the popularity of the novels, the segment drew connections between the Christian fans of the book and the evangelical president, George W. Bush. A few days after the segment aired, Mel Gibson's movie *The Passion of the Christ* opened in theaters, quickly becoming one of the most popular films of all time, a fact that seemed to underscore the relevance of this group of people, these Christians. Friends and colleagues of mine in New York began to ask about them in worried tones. Who were they, exactly? What did they want? None of my answers reassured them, and that was partly because I didn't know myself how to respond. My years as a believer lay far behind me, and my few months of research for the *60 Minutes* segment barely scratched the surface of this community, which appeared to outsiders like cross-wielding armies running ambushes out of valleys where they had somehow hidden from view. It was a false but powerful impression that was reinforced by the 2004 elections several months later. After that, for a time, a rhythm was established. Every month or so, Christian energy burst again onto the national stage—the Terry Schiavo case, the marriage amendment, the nomination of Harriet Miers, the box office success of the first in the implicitly Christian series of Narnia movies—and I felt again the division in my life, in the country. I felt again the need to produce some kind of answer, a genuine response to the questions that now seem to come from everywhere.

Going into the 2008 elections, four years after I started work on this project, the political and cultural landscape seems to have changed dramatically for believers, and yet less has changed than meets the eye. George W. Bush has been tarnished in their eyes by his stance on immigration, his troubled war in Iraq, and his failure to deliver major victories for Christian values. Though he vigorously opposed an expansion of stem cell research, and appointed two conservative judges to the Supreme Court, many Christians came to believe that his administration considered them to be useful tools—but fools.

Major conservative Christian political figures have left the stage: Tom DeLay in the wake of corruption scandals, Senator Rick Santorum voted out of office in 2006 in Pennsylvania, and the late Reverend Jerry Falwell. Falwell's death last year, in particular, marked the end of an era in the relationship between Christians and Republican politics. That alliance, built in the 1980s and 1990s, faces real challenge as a new generation of Christians, baby boomers and their children, reassess the legacy of the Moral Majority.

The reassessment will not lead to a withdrawal from politics. On the contrary, these last few years have meant a new beginning. For the first time in decades, mainstream America has taken Christianity seriously as a social and cultural force. Evangelicals have made the covers of *Time* and *Newsweek*, and many believers now see Bono of the band U2 as representative of their role in the world. They want more influence where it counts—in mainstream media, in state houses and Congress, in the public square. Church is no longer home. The world is.

For these reasons, I have come to feel that Don and Lillie McWhinney, and every other Christian who asks, deserves a real answer to their question. For years, I asked it myself, but I have come to feel that it can no longer be ignored by anyone. Not answering, I believe, now constitutes a threat to the democracy. Not answering means a silence resulting in dreadful things that I don't even want to contemplate as yet. After all, the askers are my fellow Americans. They pay taxes as I do; they hold the same passport; they breathe the same air. They believe the salvation of my soul, the health of the nation, the future of the species, and the pleasure of God, depends upon the answer that I give. So here it is, from the bottom of my heart, using every ounce of my intellect and emotion, plumbing the depths of what I once believed, traveling the country and the world with my skills as a reporter, my attempt to respond fully and completely. Will I be left behind? You're holding the answer in your hands.

## chapter 1

# The Prodigal

*W*hat you're about to read is intended for two audiences: those who have ever asked the McWhinney question, and those who have ever, in one way or another, been asked. Those are two vast groups, comprising, I would guess, a large percentage of the American population. But at the outset, I need to define a few terms more closely. In any attempt to identify the askers, several terms present immediate problems: Christian, fundamentalist, evangelical, Pentecostal, born-again, believer. Each of these terms has multiple meanings that vary depending on context.

As a base line, my subjects are American Christians, but many in that category won't find themselves in these pages. The people I'm writing about, in my mind, are those whose faith leads them inevitably and primarily to spread their belief. Theologically speaking, as a matter of explicit identity, they feel compelled to ask other people if they believe or want to believe. That rules out a large spectrum of the so-called mainline church. Not that mainline Christians—and I am speaking here of Episcopalians, Presbyterians, Methodists, Lutherans, and others who have been deeply influenced by liberal forms of modernism—don't know about the injunction to spread the gospel. It's that these churches long ago deemphasized this aspect of the faith, as well as the more literal interpretations of the Bible that go along with it, in favor of an emphasis on social justice, on probing questions about the nature and identity of divinity, and on an ecumenism that often allows for transcendence and even salvation in other religions. In many cases, these Christians are in direct conflict with more conservative members of their own denominations over questions of homosexuality and the ordination of women, so they have a great stake in the questions raised by this book. They are not, however, its subject and don't figure heavily in its narrative.

I am going to spend a fair amount of time on trying to define the nature of this kind of Christianity, but at the outset, for purposes of clarification, I will divide the askers into three major categories, using the simple device of the Holy Trinity, the form of godhood accepted by most Christians around the world. The Trinity describes a single entity, God, possessed of a three-in-one nature: the Father, the Son, and the Holy Ghost. In American Christianity, among the asking believers, the body of the faithful divides into its own trinity, mirroring the divine, but making a much less perfect unity: fundamentalists, evangelicals, and charismatics, also known as pentecostals. I place each group according to what I see as an emphasis in its theology on one or the other aspect of the Trinity.

Fundamentalists, while upholding the strict belief in Jesus Christ as the only hope of redemption and salvation for humanity, also place a very great emphasis on God the Father, and therefore on the Old Testament, as a complete guide to life. The more fundamentalist a person tends to be, the more likely he or she will be to adopt what is called a "biblical worldview," in which every aspect of life conforms to principles laid out in the Old and New Testaments. Emphasis on the Father tends to favor rules, strict adherence to dates and times, and an extremely literal understanding of events in the Bible. Here you will find the largest number of people who profess to believe that creation happened exactly as written in Genesis, that the age of the earth can be counted in thousands of years rather than millions, that Israel as a modern state has a divine purpose, and that the world will end very much in line with prophecies in the book of Revelation. They fight to resist the allure of the secular culture and often deplore Christian contemporary music for its rock sound. Politically, they are overwhelmingly Republican. For a variety of reasons, their numbers have dwindled relative to the other two groups.

One reason for the shrinking numbers has to do with the term itself: the word "fundamentalism" has turned sour in meaning in the English language, with flavors of radical violence; even people who profess a fundamentalist faith will resist the description, particularly as it is used by nonbelievers. I would draw a loose parallel to the uses of the racial epithet *nigger*: if a white person uses it to refer to a black person, it tends to be a vile and degrading insult; used among blacks, it can be a term of endearment and a mark of authenticity. The same holds true, with less force, among the asking believers. From outside, it's an insult. Within the faith, however, it is often used to draw a distinction between real believers, who observe the fundamentals, and lax believers who fudge the details, that is, the evangelicals.

This latter word, which can include many people of a fundamentalist persuasion, has become the most common way of referring to people like Don and Lillie McWhinney. It, too, has developed a pejorative ring when used from outside, and so a new generation in the faith may come to look at it with as much suspicion as the term "fundamentalism." However, for purposes of my story, the evangelicals are that part of the American trinity placing the greatest emphasis on Jesus. The message of salvation takes center stage for evangelicals, and they tend to criticize the fundamentalists for being too "legalistic" and therefore like the Hebrew Pharisees in their insistence on form over content. Evangelicals much prefer to talk about love and "the heart." They believe in adapting to the secular culture in order to win over that culture, and so their churches increasingly favor casual dress on Sunday mornings, electric guitars and drums in services, and a strong impulse to universalize the Christian message and make it less forbidding. A burning hell and a living Satan have less prominence in the presentation, though they remain strong elements in the belief system. A quarter of evangelicals have polled as voting Democrats, and a new movement, called the "emerging church," tends to be at the progressive end of the political scale, taking a cue from mainline churches in their focus on social justice issues. In fact, I will argue here that a revolution in theology is occurring among this group, which is large and dynamic and conflicted in identity at its core, pulled between a fundamentalist, conservative past and a more socially liberal and progressive future.

That brings us to the third and, in terms of the fashion and style of worship, most influential of the three groups, the charismatics and pentecostals. In my trinity, they favor the Holy Spirit or the Holy Ghost. Among these believers, one may find a more or less fundamentalist take on scripture, but that's not the centerpiece of the experience. Charismatics live in an electric world, alive with the possibility of real-time encounter with God. They talk and teach of healing powers and spirits. They speak in tongues and perform versions of exorcism. They tend to see the corporeal shape of the devil more often than noncharismatics and fight that shape through prayer and spiritual struggle. Their dramatic, even melodramatic, beliefs have produced an infectious style of worship, bursting with ecstatic, eccentric utterance and gesture. These people quite often describe themselves to pollsters as "born-again," in keeping with their focus on the sensual experience of the faith. Most fundamentalists and evangelicals would also consider themselves born-again, but charismatics frequently define themselves by these words.

They used to carry the stigma of poverty and ignorance, and some rural and urban churches probably still do. Middle-class and upper-middle-class evangelicals have smiled at their antics in the past. Fundamentalists have seen them as satanically influenced. And yet their style of worship has become a mainstream norm. Now, go to any church of asking believers on a given Sunday, and you will find the entire congregation with hands in the air, eyes closed, bodies in movement, as they sing directly to God. This is a toned-down version of the pentecostal fire. Older members of more conservative churches may see this style of worship as showboating, as crass and vulgar, even an embarrassment. They may even suspect that the rhythmic beat of the music, the noise, opens the door to crude, ungodly forms of emotion or even to sexual abandon, but younger members, baby boomers in particular, want to allow their emotions free rein—they crave ecstasy in the divine encounter. They desire a connection to God that feels more authentic than sermons, hymns, and the collection plate. The charismatic style delivers.

My story is not about one member of this trinity, because the lines between them have begun to blur. The American megachurches, in particular, have become laboratory experiments in mixing the elements of each into a volatile brew: the biblical worldview of the fundamentalists, the evangelicals' heart for Jesus, and the holy-rolling fire of the charismatics. In this mix, races, classes, and sexes find it easier to mingle. Denominations have begun to fade in significance. At the same time, tensions have grown within the body of the church, as believers confront their own prejudices. Just as fundamentalists tend to see evangelicals as lax on the details, and evangelicals find fundamentalists legalistic, both of these find the charismatics to be on questionable ground with speaking in tongues, spiritual healing, and exorcism. Change in the American church, long in coming, is not a matter of set blueprints. It's happening pell-mell, growth and power and wealth all at once, and believers respond as best they can in the heat of a remarkable moment.

WHO AM I, the man who was asked—who am I now? I am certainly someone other than the man who sat down to lunch with the McWhinneys in Dallas, Texas. Between then and now, so much has changed. A time of personal and professional crisis informs much of this book's content.

For most of my professional life, ever since college, I have worked as a professional journalist: first at daily newspapers in Plano, Texas, and Iowa City, Iowa; later as a clerk for the *New York Times*. Eventually, I became a foreign correspondent for *U.S. News & World Report*, and finally, a *60 Minutes* producer. All in all, until recently, and with a few months' exception here and there, I have been in this business for twenty years. Leaving it was traumatic.

In the summer of 2005, as a result of dramatic upheaval in my workplace, I lost my job and my two decades in the profession came to an abrupt end. By the time I got the bad news, I was in terrible physical shape. For the first time in my life, a doctor told me that I had borderline high blood pressure and was in danger of heart disease. I had gained too much weight and gone through a time of physically corrosive stress.

My wife and I could no longer afford to live in New York City. She got a job in a quiet corner of western Massachusetts; we rented out our house in Brooklyn and moved to a part of the country that I never in my wildest dreams expected to call home. Overnight, I became a native Texan in

Massachusetts in the age of George W. Bush. There were happy aspects to the change. In these same years, my son went from being a toddler to a little boy, its own kind of wonder. As a result of leaving New York and its strains, I would have more time with him and with my wife. Life got easier. We made new friends. But these realizations came later.

In those first months of transition, my chief means of dealing with the crisis became Don McWhinney's question; I grappled with professional loss by taking up the ancient cosmic drama of answering the call to faith. I embarked on a literal quest. The question of belief is, among other things, the question of identity. Who am I and where do I belong?

IN JUNE 2005, right after finishing my last *60 Minutes* piece, I caught a plane for Texas, and that was the beginning of my journey through the world of American Christianity, a trip spanning two years and two thousand miles, from Checotah, Oklahoma, to Fort Collins, Colorado; from Donaldsonville, Louisiana, to Louisville, Kentucky; from Odessa, Texas, to La Mirada, California; from Kingston, Massachusetts, to Valley Forge, Pennsylvania. Every step along the way, the research defied any kind of journalism that I had ever done before. Right from the start, it amounted to an unexpected form of intimacy with my country and its people. I had spent seven years of my adult life abroad and lived the rest in New York City. It had been years since I returned to my roots in Texas and Oklahoma. I had never spent so much time talking to ordinary Americans about their lives and beliefs.

As with Don and Lillie, right away, there was a profound familiarity. Checotah and Odessa belonged to my childhood, but I had never been to most of the other cities. And yet none of them felt unfamiliar or unwelcoming, because the people were not strange to me. I once again became a member of a family in which my absence, it seemed, had been registered but not held against me. At the same time, I was always and at every moment put to the test. I had been a part of this family, but I had left, and as soon as I told of the loss of my faith, most everyone needed to know why. What could possibly have happened? And how could one simply lose a faith? Many didn't believe it possible. These questions became a matter of urgency for some of them, and most could see that it had become one for me. My rejection of the

Christian family called into question the very nature of the bond that I was invoking. But if I had rejected that bond, why had I come back? Why had I traveled across the country to talk to complete strangers?

There could be only one answer. God was calling. The prodigal was returning. Everyone interviewed in this book, to one extent or another, held this belief, whether they stated it or not. They saw an intimation of it in my eyes. They heard it in my voice. In a time of great crisis, the god of my youth was calling me back, and I wanted to be received. I was received joyfully, and found myself greeted time and again by that sensation of anticipation. They recognized me. Scripture told them that such things would come to pass. Such prodigals would happen along. I knew that scripture, too.

In my old King James Bible, with my own name emblazoned across the front, John Humphrey Marks III, in Luke, chapter 15, verses 11 to 32, I could read the story of my possible redemption as understood by most of the people to whom I spoke. "A certain man had two sons: And the younger of them said to his father, Father, give me the portion of goods that falleth to me. And he divided unto them his living. And not many days after the younger son gathered all together, and took his journey into a far country, and there wasted his substance with riotous living." That same son, when he falls upon hard times, recognizes that in leaving his father, he has "sinned against heaven." When he returns, he is welcomed with joy. "The father said to his servants, Bring forth the best robe, and put it on him; and put a ring on his hand, and shoes on his feet." In every conversation with a Christian for this book, I knew the full implication of such a scenario. Most of my conversations began with a prayer, most ended with one. Hundreds of people around the country have told me that they're praying for me, and for this book, by name. It's a wonderful feeling, and it's utterly terrifying.

What if, having returned, I say no to the old family on this final occasion? To God? The questions dogged me at every turn. The book came to feel an awesome weight. It felt like a coming act of treason. It felt, in the middle of the night, at 3:00 A.M., when my reason shook and every fear plagued me, like I had willfully chosen to spit in the face of God, and I would pay for it and my loved ones would pay for it if I didn't accede to the central demand, if I didn't bend my knee and bow my head. These terrors accompanied me every step of the way. They returned from hidden years to become a central tension of my life.

It should have come as no surprise to me, but it did. Perhaps I thought that the old faith would hold little or no sway over me. I thought that I would meet these people comfortably as a stranger and leave them as a stranger. Or maybe I was in denial. Maybe I knew that the opposite would be true, that I needed the internal ruse of diffidence to get me to see them at all, because I feared the seduction of this old and tenacious family. It is not the case that the life of the faith is a dark hole in which idiots and fools and charlatans connive to live like barbarians. On the contrary, I had remembered, and would experience again in these years, the beauty of the faith, its consolations in the form of fellowship, the word that Christians use for the exercise of the loving bond that joins them. When I was among them, time and again, I wanted to be one of them, but I wasn't. If I became one of them, I would cease to be someone else. If I accepted once again their idea of salvation, if I joined the family, I felt in my heart that I would lose my real family. I would lose everything I had become, too—a living repudiation of the life of the mind that had become the central pillar of my identity as a writer and a thinker. Jesus had said, after all, that we must lose our lives to gain our lives, and in my darkest nightmares, I lost my human love for Debra and Joe in exchange for this divine love. I might feel a betrayal of God in my resistance to his call, but I intuited an even deeper betrayal of myself in responding.

WHEN I TOLD a friend from high school days what I had undertaken, he looked at me as if I was crazy. He still lived in Dallas. "Oh my God," he told me with a grin of disbelief on his face, when I told him how I'd spent much of my time, "you've willingly subjected yourself to a living hell."

For him, as it would have been for me not long ago, the very notion of engagement with these people at a personal level was repugnant. He knew that, by willingly returning to the fold, even as a reporter, but not only as a reporter, I had submitted myself to countless hours of evangelization. I had sat through dozens of sermons, in megachurches, in homes, at funerals, and at concerts, in the wake of extreme sorrow over sudden unexpected death, in the presence of terrible storms, surrounded by strumming guitars, in summer camp, at 7:00 A.M. men-only Bible study or at 8:00 P.M. disciple-ship class, in conferences dedicated to every kind of theology, among blog-gers, scientists, filmmakers, members of Congress. I had listened to endless hours of Christian worship music, been in small rooms where people raised their arms, reaching out for their Lord, where I felt that I had to join the throng, even if I didn't feel it, trying to sing along to the words projected on one more screen, "May your kingdom come, May your will be done," or "He knows my name, He knows my every thought, He sees each tear that falls, He hears me when I talk," all of it scored to contemporary rock or folk, un-dergirded by the beat of grunge drums, occasions for rapture, if you believe, or for a feeling of dislocation and even repulsion, bordering on nausea, if you do not. Or did the devil bring on that latter sensation?

But I couldn't agree with my friend that it had been pure hell. If it was only hell, I never would have stayed the course. It also had to be heaven, and at times, it was. At other times, it was the sweetest kind of normal life. It was good conversation with real people, out in the American heartland, some-times intellectual in nature, more often very emotional and rich in amazing twists of fate. I have heard dozens of conversion stories. I've met criminals and the wives of criminals, people who sank to the lower depths of human experience before rising up again, reborn. I've met people who came from the hardest of hard luck, and millionaires and megachurch pastors, people who came to death's door and then walked back. I met a missionary who was shot twenty-two times in the desert of Iraq but survived, and returned to life while her husband, also shot, did not. I met a soldier who was in the Penta-gon on September 11, when a plane struck his office, killing his colleagues. He also wanted to die and came back, called back to life by God, led back, he says, in that enveloping silence that occurs when you have already given in to the reality of your own demise. I have talked to young women who slept with everything that moved, rich kids from the suburbs, poor folks from the rotten holes of the country. I have met people who claimed to have actually seen demons, and any number who feel themselves locked in a dark war with forces from the other side. I have spoken with black and white and Hispanic believers, have broken bread with the Christian fathers and mothers of gay Christian children, with pastors whose homosexuality destroyed their ministry, who still believe, despite everything, and wage their war to belong like everyone else. I have held the hands of some of these people as they have walked close to death. I have cried with them and laughed with them and shared one or two of the transcendent moments of my life.

It is not possible that I could come away from this journey unchanged. Asking a man or woman about faith is like asking about sex. It always means something. The same goes for faith. When one human being asks another about faith, faith itself, and the urgency of it, is in the room. I have been in that room for two years now and have just returned to the quiet place where I am now writing.

I write with the sense that my answer matters for myself. I write with the sense that how I answer will have consequences. I write with the sense that, if I answer incorrectly, I am risking my soul or my family or myself. One way or another, I lose. But I am also filled with a kind of strange excitement. I have been waiting all my life to write these words, it seems. There is the feel of destiny for me about what follows, even if my college German professor would roll his eyes at this notion and see every bit of his hard work to restrain my religious imagination undone.

IT'S NECESSARY TO say one last thing about these encounters: I have made three unexpected discoveries in my attempt to communicate across a great divide. First, and most important to establishing an initial trust, I discovered that believers were eager to meet a nonbeliever who didn't consider them de facto idiots or dullards. Most evangelical Christians in this country believe they are perceived negatively by other Americans, and while it is offensive to them, it's also painful and damaging in subterranean ways to a fragile sense of self-esteem. I would even say that there's a deep strain of self-loathing in many Christians, who reject vehemently on the surface all characterizations of them by the secular media but secretly harbor the inner conviction that these characterizations are true. A needling little voice inside them says, You are stupid. You are an idiot. Something is wrong with you. At Gospel Music Week in Nashville, Tennessee, I got to know a lovely woman named Paula, a homeschooler and a freelance journalist in the Christian music industry. After many hours of talk, late one night toward the end of my stay, she became emotional in the lobby of the hotel and said, "You must think we're all a bunch of idiots."

I assured her that I didn't, but that kind of promise carries a huge weight of responsibility. I had once believed these things about myself, and then I had believed them about these people. But I had come out the other side and discovered my own need to know in a deeper way the nature of this experience, and so I'd abandoned a lot, though not all, of my loathing for the evangelical. She was right, in her way, but it was exactly that impulse driving me to write the book. I intentionally waged war against my own preconceptions because I knew them to be wrong, and Paula was one more living proof. She, and others like her, could see at the very least an honest conflict within me; if not that, an honest appeal. I had sought them out because I wanted to understand. And for them, to find a desire to understand on the opposite side of the conversation, to have someone who wanted to hear them talk about themselves and their faith, struck a chord. They wanted to be included in a conversation from which they had felt excluded. They yearned for that experience, as I yearned for an honest conversation with them.

Even more surprising, often enough, I met Christians who were relieved that I was neither a complete stranger to their faith nor a believer. It was extremely important to many people that I did not share their worldview. At times, it was decisive, both because a lot of Christians now want to have conversations with people outside their faith, to heal an alarming breach, but also because an enormous pressure to conform now exists within the faith. I brought as little of my secular prejudices to bear as humanly possible, but I came as well without the preconceptions and judgments of a fellow believer. My questions didn't require a response in conformity with a biblical worldview. People could wrestle with their demons in the confidence that I wouldn't hold them accountable for thinking other than their pastor or Bible study group or fellow members in discipleship would require.

My last and greatest surprise in trying to grasp the truth of this life is that it is anything but uniform.

On the contrary, Christianity in the United States is now undergoing a massive and total transformation. In a generation, the faith as it has been practiced for decades in this country will be hard to recognize, as mainline denominations lose their memberships, independent Bible churches mushroom in size, and the faith fragments like the rest of the culture across dozens of different subcultures and venues. George Barna, the evangelical pollster, calls this a revolution, and he's onto something, though he seems less aware of the dangers of revolution than its virtues. We live in the aftermath of a century when revolution lined up hundreds of millions of people and gunned them down, and yet he uses that word as if it had no negative context at all; to my surprise, on one video, he even quotes Mao on the dangers of complacency.

Wherever I went, I encountered a volatility and conflict that appeared to me immensely fruitful and a little scary and very much in the spirit of revolution. At times, I could only wish upon the secular world an equal amount of fervor and ferment. In classrooms and lecture halls, churches and homes, in every walk of the faith, I found people in dispute about which way Christianity should turn in the twenty-first century. Even for those for whom biblical truth is immutable and unchanging, who subscribe to the doctrine of inerrancy, there is a vast challenge looming. How does God want the church to live?

In short, and in closing this opening, I arrived at a moment of earthquake. Without expecting to, as a by-product of my own obsessions and relationships, I have stumbled upon one of the great American dramas of our time. And in this hour of revolution, it is not possible for me to behave in a detached and analytical fashion. My entire life had been summoned forth to give an account. This is what Christians mean when they ask their question, ultimately: What, in your life, in your mind, in your heart and its short history, justifies a negative response to God's unmistakable call?

## chapter 2

# The Nation

O*n* the morning of February 29, 1704, a party of Mohawk Indians and French soldiers launched a surprise attack on the western Massachusetts hamlet of Deerfield, murdering forty-eight men, women, and children in the space of a few hours. Survivors were carried off to Canada. According to tradition, the remains of the dead lie buried to this day beneath a four-foot-high mound in the corner of the burying ground in Deerfield. It is the only mass grave I have ever seen in the United States, aside from the vast hole at the lower end of Manhattan, and in these places, the mortality of my country, the world's most powerful nation, becomes apparent, its amazing life and inevitable death folding into one thing, a piece of land embodying the boundary between systems of government, the divide between civilizations, even the line between heaven and hell. Most of the time, as Americans, we occupy a space without a past, thinking constantly of progress and optimism. In these burying grounds, the mood is otherwise; fear and sorrow and loss, a melancholy sense of futility, a sense of how things might have been different. Plenty of Christians today believe we lost our way as a nation long ago, when we ceased to make a direct connection between the bounty of the wilderness and the providence of the Lord. A whisper of betrayed providence still clings to the dead in Deerfield.

New England is ghost country, after all. The hills of western Massachusetts are full of odd tales and strange places. The writer H. P. Lovecraft, whose stories haunted me as a kid, set his tales in this part of the nation, in lost valleys beyond the roads. Those tales depicted a human world resting very lightly on a much more ancient existence, old Yankee families stumbling across the remains of obscene civilizations that worshipped creatures out of another dimension. Not far from my new house, there is a town called Whately, and when I first passed the sign for the Whately Inn, I received a slight chill from childhood. In Lovecraft, the Whatelys are worshippers of the so-called Old Ones, always getting into trouble for mating with fish creatures or harboring accursed books.

Three hundred years after the massacre, on a relatively warm winter morning in New England, I paid a visit to the burying ground that lies like a hushed secret behind the school. On that day, it was deserted, an ice-patched corner beneath pine trees, centuries-old stones of slate at a tilt, overlooking practice fields, and in the distance, the line of the Deerfield River. I had a personal connection to the place; my parents had almost sent me to Deerfield Academy, and one of my closest friends had gone. But I had no family or friends in western Massachusetts. Moreover, I had landed about as far from the country's evangelical hub as possible, in a bucolic home of liberal sentiment and gay and lesbian lifestyle. But the region has older, deeper memories.

It turns out that western Massachusetts is also one of the cradles of American Protestant faith, arguably its real birthplace, the Puritan homeland, where Jonathan Edwards, the author of the best-known sermon in the country's history, "Sinners in the Hands of an Angry God," led his church in Northampton for two decades, from 1727 to 1749, where many of the descendants of Cotton and Increase Mather settled and preached, where the divine mission to spread the gospel to the rest of the country, and the rest of the world, got its start in small colleges and schools like Deerfield, Amherst, and Williams.

For American evangelicals, it is no overstatement to say that western Massachusetts constitutes a kind of holy space. Three hundred years ago, this land beneath my feet didn't belong to the United States, which wouldn't exist for another seventy-five years. It sat at the outer rim of the British colony of New England, on the frontier with New France, and experienced all the upheaval and instability of a war zone. It was a bitter and difficult place for Christians. But it was also God's land, and when the Mohawks and the French Catholics attacked, their incursion had a divine significance. For the Protestant settlers, the pope was the Antichrist, and his warriors came with a cosmic intent—to wipe out or convert the enemy. They killed men, women, and children and took dozens of captives away with them to Canada.

IN 1706, AFTER his return from captivity, the Reverend John Williams wrote an account of the experience, a bestseller of its time, called *The Redeemed Captive Returning to Zion*. He is identified on the cover of the book as "Minister of the Gospel in Deerfield," and the tale is steeped in scripture. Its implications are explicitly Christian. "The enemy came in like a flood upon us," Williams wrote. "They came to my house in the beginning of the onset, and by their violent endeavors to break open doors and windows, with axes and hatchets, awaked me out of sleep." Williams fought back, but was overcome. "I reached up . . . my hands for my pistol, uttering a short petition to God, for everlasting mercies for me and mine, on account of the merits of our glorified Redeemer; expecting a present passage through the valley of the shadow of death." He recited verses from the book of Isaiah and readied to fire his gun. "Taking down my pistol, I cocked it, and put it to the breast of the first Indian that came up; but my pistol missing fire, I was seized by three Indians, who disarmed me and bound me naked." Two of his children were murdered in the attack. He and his wife and the rest of his children were taken as prisoners to Canada.

The journey became a hell of its own. "I sat pitying those who were behind, and entreated my master to let me go down and help my wife," Williams writes, "but he refused and would not let me stir from him. I asked each of the prisoners (as they passed by me) after, and heard that, passing through the river, she fell down and was plunged over head and ears in the water; after which she traveled not far, for at the foot of that mountain, the cruel and bloodthirsty savage who took her slew her with his hatchet at one stroke, the tidings of which were very awful."

His consolation came from scripture: Job 1:21, "Naked came I out of my mother's womb, and naked shall I return thither; the Lord gave, and the Lord hath taken away; blessed be the name of the Lord."

I've been educated to believe that an unbridgeable gulf lies between myself and people of other historical eras, that I can only hear the voices of the past through profound distortion, all of my attempts at intimacy across the dimension of time in vain. But I wonder how true that is for me and John Williams. He knew Jesus Christ to be the son of God. He saw himself redeemed through that saving knowledge. To believe meant salvation in eternity. Not to believe meant hell. These had been roughly my beliefs. Where was the unbridgeable gulf? Where the distortion? In the burying ground, I wondered if it existed only in the minds of secular historians.

No matter the differences in technology and industry, the changes in fashion and education that have occurred between 1704 and my day, I tell myself that I could appear as a visitor from the future before the startled eyes of John Williams and we would understand each other in the most basic way. Our English would be different, but our faith would be roughly the same. I could offer him solace from that same book of Job and could talk to him of the promise that lies on the other side of the terror of the world. The gospel doesn't change through time, not in its essence; that is the conceit. "That's the great thing about God," says my cousin Michele. "We humans change all the time, but he never does." It is the unshakeable belief of tens of millions of American Christians.

The name of Jesus was everywhere in the Deerfield graveyard, in inscription after inscription, in name after biblical name: "Here lies the remains of Moses Stebbins, Jun., who died Dec. 14th, 1800, in the 39th Year of His Age. And when the last trumpet sounds, arise, come forth ye dead, the call shall be to all them who sleep in dusty bed." By the time of this man's death, a few years after the American Revolution, and seven decades after the raid on Deerfield, 75 percent of those who declared themselves free of the British yoke classified themselves as members of the Puritan faith. Had their belief evolved in any significant way from the era of John Williams?

Benjamin Franklin and Thomas Jefferson did not believe, in any orthodox sense, but George Washington, John Adams, and John Quincy Adams had some form of belief, if we're to accept their letters on face value; James

Madison and John Jay did, as well as lesser-known signers. Roughly half of the first fifty-six members of Congress held seminary degrees. Four were pastors. A dozen others had denominational ministries of one kind or another. Many believed that the future of the country depended on their belief. Their great legacy to the rest of us, the American Constitution, is steeped in Jesus and his forebears, the ancient Hebrews, with hundreds of references and precedents embedded in the laws of the land. On a gravestone in the Deerfield burying ground are these words, "Our fathers trusted in thee, they trusted and thou didst deliver them."

A FEW YEARS ago, in central Texas, my cousins Scott and Michele got into a fight with a Catholic school over homosexuality. Michele and Scott maintained that the school was too accepting of this behavior. The fight turned into a pitched battle with the diocese, and eventually, their children were expelled from the school. In the course of this fight, which resulted in their departure from the Catholic Church and a new start as evangelical Christians, Scott and Michele found a set of friends and allies who would change their lives. One of them was Steve Partlow, a representative of the organization Focus on the Family, and an expert at finding people disgruntled with the culture and arming them with weapons for the fight; another was a man named David Barton, who offered moral support and a new perspective on American history.

Barton was one of their neighbors in the small town of Aledo, a few miles southwest of Fort Worth. His wife belonged to Michele's Bible study and encouraged and supported Michele during the months of the struggle. Barton himself did even more. He introduced my cousins to their own country, opening the door to a version of American history that Scott and Michele had never heard before, never seen with their own eyes or touched with their own hands. As he has done for countless others around the country, Barton produced documents: letters, first editions of books, early Bibles. He made clear that homosexuality was the least of the aberrations in this country. The entire nation, Scott and Michele learned from Barton, had been carried into a captivity every bit as stark as that of John Williams, and men like David Barton had set out to redeem it.

Barton would never put it that way, but it's the essence of what he does. It's his mission. He excavates history and uses it to make law and influence politics and change the country. His view is long, and he is particularly concerned about educating the young. "I've always got to be training the next generation," he told me. "I think one thing we've really screwed up on is that we're very poor on the intellectual side. We've got a whole lot of guys who want to go and be teachers, but we ought to have guys who want to go and be professors and teach the teachers. There's a very biblical side to economics, for instance. From my viewpoint as a Christian and what the Bible addresses, economics has got to be dealt with as well. And the military's policy's got to be dealt with. Everything, every aspect of life. Media, entertainment, architecture. I want to see kids go into all those areas with an understanding of what they're supposed to do."

In Aledo, home to his organization Wall Builders, he has a collection of more than 70,000 documents of the founders of the country; among the items, one of the twenty-six surviving Bibles of the American Revolution, the first Bibles ever printed in the United States, by special order of Congress. Through much of the late 1980s and 1990s, he traveled around the country, amassing the collection, paying $5 here, $10 there, for the forsaken letters and libraries of the founding generation, in particular the Christians among them. The collection amounts to an argument. In 1987, Barton has written, he received a commission from God to do two things: go to the library and find the date when prayer was prohibited in schools; and get a record of national SAT scores since that time. God had set him a task—to prove that the American way of life had declined since the prohibition of prayer.

At the very least, he found, test scores had declined. To one kind of mind, the decline could be explained by changes in demographics; by the population explosion; by a new wave of immigrants in 1965; by the integration into American public schools of African American children who had been denied decent educations and who couldn't compete initially with the scores of their white counterparts; and by the failure of schools to keep up with these changes. For Barton, some of these facts might be more or less true, but the bigger picture was clear. Once prayer stopped in schools, once that conversation ended, the country's mind began to die.

That fact-finding mission grew into a much larger quest. He would set out to find the truth about the state of the nation since its beginnings. Slowly, with purpose, he gathered the founders' documents—their letters, diaries, various writings. It's never been about mere esoterica. He puts the documents to use. He uses every opportunity to restore continuity between the American Christian past and what he sees as its broken present. He travels around the country, lecturing to law school students, judges, attorneys, and pastors, speaking on radio stations and cable TV, hosting conferences and advising politicians, reminding everyone who will listen about what he sees as the country's true heritage. He has argued religious freedom cases before the Supreme Court, before lower federal and state courts. He has written legislation at the state and federal level. He served a term as vice-chairman of the Texas Republican Party, ending in 2006; and in the 2004 election, he told me, the Republican National Committee paid him to stump for President Bush in the battleground states.

Barton's work is political, but in the broadest sense of the word. He is out to transform the polity. He publishes a line of books, cassettes, and DVDs, reprinting forgotten works like *A Primer of Ethics* from 1890, *The Pioneer Mothers of America* from 1912, and *Biographical Sketches of the Signers of the Declaration of American Independence* from 1848, as well as publishing his own works on everything from the original intent of the framers of the constitution to a spiritual heritage tour of the U.S. Capitol.

Barton doesn't believe that church and state should ever have been separated, not in our current sense. He believes that concept of a "wall of separation" arises from an incorrect reading of the Constitution, an interpretation based on a letter written by Thomas Jefferson to Baptists in Danbury, Connecticut, in 1803, and that it has served to drive out religious practices that formed the basis of American national character and culture for most of its early history. And he believes that the nation courts its own annihilation by turning its back on those practices, and on the faith that its founders understood to be the source of national strength. Most of the establishment law profession disagrees vehemently with both his interpretation of the letter to the Danbury Baptists and his views on the Constitution, but he seems to enjoy that fact.

On a visit to see my cousins in Aledo, I stopped by Barton's office—and museum—to pay a visit. Given the scope of the man's efforts and the seriousness of his connections, I was surprised by the modesty of the setting. The building could have housed a group dental practice. There are no signs, except for words painted on a glass door at the entrance. The Wall Builders home office sits at the back of a new housing development, at the end of a street that peters off into dirt, on the edge of an empty upsweep of Texas land.

Barton is an unassuming man in appearance. On the day we met, he wore faded blue jeans with frayed hems, black cowboy boots, and a knit shirt with a vague Southwestern pattern. His hair was salt-and-pepper, his features plain and soft. We shook hands. He has an easy drawl and an infectious way of talking about what he loves, a quick-moving stream of enthusiasm, as I heard when he opened a glass case and insisted that I take hold of a musket dating back to the American Revolution.

"Have a grab," he said, as he talked rapturously about what he saw as the remarkable attention to detail in Mel Gibson's movie *The Patriot*.

"So there at the beginning, when Gibson's kid is taken by the British, and he and his two sons go free, he turns his gun into a club and swings it, but this literally is the gun that was used by Americans at that point in time."

He asked me to raise the gun, as if I were firing it. The weight struck me as untenable for battle, like trying to hoist a wet flag. I tried to do an authoritative stance. I held it to my shoulder and sighted down the barrel. I could tell that the old gun gave Barton a real thrill, and I didn't want to seem as if I didn't appreciate its pleasures. He showed me a canteen used by Revolutionary soldiers, again demonstrated its weight, and explained to me that the average height of American soldiers during that era was five foot one. "Little bitty runts, five foot one, hauling this stuff forty to fifty miles a day. It's just unbelievable to me."

Our conversation turned from the Mel Gibson movie and guns to military chaplains in the American Revolution and the religious beliefs of the founders. In Barton's talk, all roads lead from the past to the present, and our conversation was no different. He showed me his sole copy of the Bible of the Revolution, with its inscription by Congress. There were 20,000 printed in 1782, and hundreds of them went into the rucksacks of revolutionary soldiers; still more went to schools for education.

"I've got one," Barton told me, back in the voice of the enthusiast collector, "the Library of Congress has one. We got that from a guy in Philadelphia who had it, and he was kinda like, my kids don't appreciate it, but somebody needs to, and it's a really cool Bible 'cause it's got a big Congressional endorsement in front and it says in the records of Congress it was printed for use of schools, so you get this philosophy of the founding fathers."

This was the point of everything in the collection, and he made it a dozen times before we were done: America was a country of faith, no matter what the courts and the politicians have said. When our conversation finally got to the courts and their rulings on religious freedom, Barton's enthusiast side gave way to that of the experienced political street fighter. He spoke with the relaxed confidence of a man who has seen time and again that he's right, has seen his opponents in argument melt away, has the proof for his own arguments like a loaded gun in his back pocket, which he had pulled time and again, always with the same result.

I asked him what kind of response he got from people in his trips around the country, and he told me with barely restrained glee about his lectures on separation of church and state.

"You know, it's really funny. When I go into classes like that, I take boxes of these old documents, and so when I come to this issue, I just let the kids or the judges or the attorneys read it themselves out of the original documents. I've seen these guys—congressmen, too, we did this training for congressmen—and I've seen 'em get cussin' mad, but," his voice lowered to a whisper for emphasis, "never at me. They go, Why wasn't I taught this? This isn't what I heard in law school. And so they get really ticked, but it has never been at me. And so I would say 90 percent of the people who see this stuff do a radical reversal on their opinions."

Barton's argument about separation of church and state, one that he shares with a large number of conservative Christian lawyers and activists, is basically that there was never supposed to be any such notion, not in the sense that American courts have defined it for half a century. Barton turns to the documents to back up his points. In his 1802 letter to the Danbury Baptists,

Thomas Jefferson used the phrase "separation of church and state" in an attempt to reassure wary Baptists that there would be no attempt by government to regulate or define a national faith prejudicial to their own, Barton says. He never had any notion that religion itself, or religious expression of any kind, would be banned from government. On the contrary, shortly after he wrote the letter, Barton always relates, Jefferson joined a Baptist friend for a church service held in the halls of the U.S. Capitol. His friend preached the sermon. This proves, Barton insists, that Jefferson could never have had a problem with the mixture of faith and government. When I pointed out that neither the Declaration of Independence nor the Constitution made any reference to Christianity, he answered that the founders had no need to mention a condition as pervasive as oxygen. No argument shakes him.

People do fight back. Barton told me about a law professor at the University of Iowa. In a debate, the professor conceded that the founding fathers would not have bought into modern ideas of religious expression, but he didn't believe that contemporary Americans should be bound by views of people who had died two hundred years before. "I said, now wait a minute, let me get this straight, are you saying that you think policies today should reflect what people today want rather than what they wanted two hundred years ago? He said, that's right. I said, I'm glad to hear you say that. Seventy-seven percent of the nation want the Ten Commandments up today. Eighty-one percent of the nation want prayer in schools. I went through all these numbers. And I said, so if you're right, then we've still got the same expressions. He said, yeah, but you can't forget that constitutional separation of church and state, and I said, so now we're back to history, I thought you said you didn't want to use history."

The polls bear out Barton's assertions, though nonreligious Americans approve in far lower numbers. Barton told me he believes in a living constitution, and that the majority of the population should continue to amend it at will. What he can't abide are judges and law professors who, he believes, want to change the document over the expressed views of the majority—and he believes that's what's going on. "I said, what your position is, is you disagree with the 77 percent or the 81 percent, and you want the courts to enforce your position over what the people want."

For Barton, the nation began as Christian. The documents back him up, as do the graveyards, the churches, and the Constitution. In the twentieth century, through a concerted effort by intellectual elites in the law, politics, and culture, the nation abandoned its faith, and Christians became a vilified minority. In his view, if we care at all about our history, and we should, we must acknowledge the country's roots in religion, and if we acknowledge those roots, we must ask ourselves whether we truly want to sever them. Barton's bet is that we don't. His bet is that, consciously, we never will. The United States of America is Christian, or else it is no longer itself, no longer the United States. In his eyes, Barton believes as those first Americans did. The inscription on the grave in the Deerfield burying ground lays down the creed. "Our fathers trusted in thee, they trusted and thou didst deliver them."

## chapter 3

# Lilies

*L*ong before I loved Jesus, I worshipped John Wayne. And long before I had any notion of heaven, I walked in the garden in southern Oklahoma. The fields and farms in that part of the country mark the beginning of my understanding of God and America.

Barton speaks a lot about the American nation, as in "One Nation Under God," but I have never had much of a relationship with that idea. He loves Washington, D.C., with all its history and monumental significance; I have always experienced an antipathy for the city, based on a gut aversion to government and its institutions. More than that, the nation's capital is the place furthest removed from my sense of what it means to be a citizen of this country, because, for me, the idea of the nation doesn't suggest anything holy, but rather brings to mind nothing more than the ideology of nationalism.

There is the nation, a nervous idea held in 300 million minds at once in about as many different ways, and there is the country, the thing itself, the land and its people at any given moment, and this I have always loved, especially my piece of it, a territory that stretches from southern Colorado to southern Oklahoma, and everything in between. I'm a Texan, born and reared. Before my eighteenth birthday, I only saw a handful of states beyond the Texas border, most of them contiguous to the state. I crossed the Mississippi River exactly once before going to college, on a birthday trip to Vicksburg, Mississippi, which lies right on the eastern bank. To the south, on one occasion, I crossed the international border into Mexico to visit Juarez for a reunion of my father's side of the family. But for most of my childhood, the heart of my America lay between the various forks of the Canadian River running through the southern half of Oklahoma, home to my mother's side of the family.

My immediate forebears, on both sides, come from the small cities and towns of the Midwest, the South, and the Southwest, places like Bartlesville, Oklahoma, where my mom was born; Harrison, Arkansas, where my father spent much of his childhood; Clovis, New Mexico; Odessa, Texas; and Checotah, Oklahoma. Of these places, I came to know Checotah best. My parents met in west Texas in the early 1940s, when they were children, and my father always told my brother, my sister, and me that he intended to marry my mother the moment he laid eyes on her, one of those amazing tales of lifelong romance. But by the time they were adults and living in Dallas, my mother's parents had moved to Checotah, where their parents had lived, and every year, once or twice, we would make the three-hour drive north, a trip that remains as vivid in my mind as if it happened yesterday. On our way, we passed a series of magical landmarks: Sherman, Texas, birthplace of Dwight D. Eisenhower, whose white clapboard house could be seen right below the highway as we entered the town; the interlacing steel joists of a bridge across the Red River, which runs low and sandy and truly red; a ridge of roadside basalt in Oklahoma that Dad called the hogback, because it resembled the long and bristly back of a wild pig; and finally, sinister and exciting, the barbed-wired fence and lookout towers of the federal penitentiary at McAlester always followed a few miles later by a work crew of prisoners cleaning trash off the roadside.

ONE OF MY earliest memories comes from the country around Checotah when I was four years old, and it involved a Methodist church.

"You were all dressed up for church," my great-aunt Fay told me. "Your mama brought you out to the car so I could take you with me. But I started backing out of the driveway, and you started crying and saying, 'I want to stay with Mama.' So I stopped, and you run into the house as fast as you could. Before I got started out again, here you came again. So I just stopped and let you in the car and went on." As she told the story, Aunt Fay gave me a look of great dismay, a recollection of panic undiminished by the passage of years. "Well, your mama didn't know you'd got back into the car with me. They just thought you were out in the yard. They started calling you, and you weren't to be found. And your poor little mama almost lost it." As I heard all through my childhood, my mother thought that I had somehow drowned in the pond across the road from the house. She thought that she'd lost me, though I was perfectly safe. "They looked and looked, and finally your grandfather got the idea that you might have come with me. And there I was, in that little Methodist church, holding your brother in my lap, and you right beside me. But when we got home, your mother took you and she explained very clearly that you were never to run off without telling her."

IN OKLAHOMA, I find the roots of what became my faith. Later, as a teenager, the great promise of Christianity found its clearest expression in a few lines from the book of Matthew, chapter 6, verses 28–29, which I memorized at the age of sixteen and carried around in my head and hip pocket: "Consider the lilies of the field, how they grow; they toil not, neither do they spin. And yet I say unto you, That even Solomon in all his glory was not arrayed like one of these."

At sixteen, I took the verse to be God's direct appeal to my memory. In his unending wisdom, he knew that I had first encountered the secret beauty of existence in a five-hundred-acre stretch of bottom land on the shores of Lake Eufala, a few miles west of Checotah, Oklahoma, in the dying town of Pierce. There weren't any lilies that I remember, but summer fields full of watermelon and yellow squash, red clay roads hedged with wild blackberry, apricot, and grape, meandering muddy streams where you could find four kinds of poisonous snake—copperheads, cottonmouths, rattlers. What I'm talking about is something other than physical beauty. I don't know if there is a word for that first childhood encounter with the natural world, when every sense comes awake and every horizon burns with wonder. At that age, nothing gets lost. Clouds at sunset hold immense ideas, and one can hear them with an untranslated clarity. The darkness beneath an old elm tree trembles with spirits. The cry of birds at dusk beyond the light of the farmhouse comes from the dead who are murmuring not very far away in the cemetery where your own distant relatives lie buried. Nothing at all separated my imagination as a child from the wildness of the world itself, and so I came to believe, in Oklahoma, that God was the world, and the world was God. And this experience feels like the first pure source of my faith, the launching pad for so many things that I can hardly name.

In their bestselling inspirational book, *The Sacred Romance: Drawing Closer to the Heart of God*, Brent Curtis and John Eldredge write about that first childhood experience of God as the defining one, the first act in a drama that will come to dominate the rest of a believer's life. The book has been a phenomenon, spawning a kind of romance movement within contemporary evangelicalism, generating a mini-industry in workbooks, videos, conferences, and lifestyle counseling. Don McWhinney gave it to me when I asked him for a list of books that had helped him in his faith, and it struck a chord with me as I set out to understand my earliest kindling of religiosity. In *The Sacred Romance*, Eldredge and Curtis describe the human relationship with God as a wild affair between a beloved and a constantly wooing lover who calls from the moment we are able to hear and never ceases the effort—until we answer. When we're very young, the authors tell us, we hear the lover's call most clearly, and it is often linked to one particular place or time in life. For Eldredge, it was a place even less remarkable than rural Oklahoma: "My own earliest memories of the Romance come from 120 acres of New Jersey farmland, bordered by a stream to the southeast and a low and broad hillside to the northwest. . . . I first remember the Romance calling to me when I was a boy of six or seven just past dusk on a summer evening, when the hotter and dustier work of the farm had given way to another song. . . . Something warm and alive and poignantly haunting would call to me from the mysterious borders of the farm that was my world." I read these words, and I thought of Oklahoma.

AUNT FAY HAS a sister-in-law, Esther, and in the last years of her life, Aunt Esther wrote me three letters. In the first, she thanked me for bringing my son to meet her and her husband, my Uncle Dick, in Checotah and exhorted me gently to love the Lord. She wrote in the spidery but meticulous script that filled the pages of her Bible, which she had covered in thousands of penciled commentaries over the course of decades. Her second letter came in the form of a card from the Thomas Kinkade collection, a reproduction of a painting entitled *Blossom Bridge*. By that time, Uncle Dick had passed away. The letter was steeped in melancholy. "The flowers you hung to the porch stayed until the cold weather finished it," she wrote me. And she concluded with a postscript: "I'm a lost and lonely person now that my loving pardner of seventy-one years is waiting for me in a better place. Bye-Bye."

The third and final letter came on a small Hallmark card featuring a photograph of a teacup containing pink primroses. I'd written Aunt Esther to say I would be coming to Checotah for another visit, this time alone, and she insisted that I stay in her house. She lived in a nursing home four blocks away. So it was arranged. I would come in June, as soon as I left my job at *60 Minutes*.

IN CHECOTAH, AS a child, I found an entire hidden past, a place where my life seemed to connect to the grandeur of the American West and all its mythology, through my older relatives who were connected through their own childhoods to pioneers and Civil War veterans, to Creeks who had come from Georgia on the Trail of Tears, to U.S. marshals who had known famous outlaws like Cole Younger and Belle Starr, and who had hunted men for the famous hanging judge, Judge Parker of Fort Smith, Arkansas. We'd see my grandparents and our great-aunts and uncles, and hear our favorite stories, how our great-grandfather on my mother's side helped to put down the last Indian uprising in the United States, in what our relatives called the Crazy Snake War, hearing in the same breath that his son, my grandfather, had married a woman, my grandmother, who was half Creek. It was for me as if the entire town belonged to our saga by virtue of family history, every corner of the town related to some person or incident in the lives of our elders. My grandparents were personal friends with a former chief of the Creek Nation, an amazing man named Dode McIntosh, who, at ninety, told us with shining eyes that he could do a hundred push-ups and proceeded to prove it. In the old graveyard down the street from my grandparents, many friends of the family lay buried. Out in the countryside lay the remains of Indian graveyards, and my grandparents, aunts, and uncles, knew their hidden locations. They knew every inch of the relatively empty land to the west of Checotah, in my imagination a last stretch of the great American wilderness, haunted by mountain lions and the ghosts of dead Creek children, the mystical heart of my experience of the United States, and the center of my own identity as a human being, an American, and a Christian.

We'd sit down to feasts of fried chicken, and the children would listen to the grown-ups talk about the past, about friends and incidents from the days of my mother's early years or before, tales of murdered oilmen and buried treasure, of the time that my great-grandmother went to visit Harry Truman in Missouri and talked with him for an hour; how her son, my grandfather, lied about his age to fight in World War I; and how another son, my Uncle Dick, landed on Utah Beach in World War II. We would pray before meals, but no one talked much about God or Jesus. We rarely went to church, though my grandparents were Presbyterians of long standing in the community, my aunts and uncles lifelong Methodists.

By the time of my visit, in June of 2005, my grandparents had long since passed away, but my grandfather's brother and sister, Uncle Bill and Aunt Fay, and his sister-in-law, Aunt Esther, were still alive. I had kept in touch sporadically over the years with my relatives. Once, right before Uncle Dick died, I had taken my son Joe to meet them. By that time, I was almost forty. I had gone out into the world, lived overseas, married, and had a son, and yet here they were, these ancient, beloved people, who had all known me since I was an infant.

Aunt Esther had turned ninety-two, Uncle Bill and Aunt Fay were in their eighties, the last living witnesses of a long-faded era in my family history. I wanted to talk to them about the religious faith on my mother's side. I drove north out of Dallas to Checotah on Highway 75, the old road from my childhood. In Sherman, I passed Eisenhower's birthplace. I crossed the Red River, out of Texas and into Oklahoma, low and crimson with clay. I saw the hogback, the guard towers of the penitentiary in the McAlester, the work crew of inmates in orange jumpsuits.

Somewhere along this stretch, my cousin Judith called me on the cell phone. Aunt Esther had gone into the hospital in Muskogee. The day before, she had begun to shake uncontrollably with a high fever. No one knew what was wrong.

Two days later, I was a pallbearer at her funeral.

IN A SMALL service in the chapel of the Smith Funeral Home in Checotah, we said good-bye to my aunt. My Texas cousins in their dark suits and boots arrived, my mother and my aunts from Dallas, Austin, and San Antonio. The inscription inside the funeral program read, "Lord, when my soul takes flight, may it rise swiftly to live forever in your love and care." The senior pastor was away for two weeks in Indiana, but a junior minister filled his shoes. He spoke softly of resurrection to the assembled friends and family. "Dying, Christ destroyed our death. Rising, he restored our life. Christ will come again in glory. As with baptism, Esther put on Christ, so with Christ may Esther be clothed with glory."

We sang one of her favorite hymns, "He Walks with Me (in the Garden)," and we buried her.

## chapter 4

# The Country

*H*ow many other believers passed away that day? When David Barton talks about the nation and its faith, he is talking about an abstraction, an ideal of a city on a hill, but my aunt had lived in the reality of a country that would seem to be among the most religious on earth, in which as many as 84 percent of the citizenry, according to some polls, claim to be Christian.

But talking about the reality of faith is like talking about the reality of sex or politics. All three are a morass of extremely personal and highly subjective opinion. People lie about all three to pollsters. The natural gap between what people say about themselves and what they really do is called the "halo effect." When taking the halo effect into account, that number of 84 percent dissolves quickly, and most pollsters give it little or no credence. In reality, according to most data, about half of the country has some genuine connection to genuine Christian religious experience, but no one can really agree on the details about that half.

The most wide-ranging study on American faith came out in autumn 2006. The Baylor Religion Survey, "American Piety in the Twenty-first Century," as it's officially known, contacted 1,721 Americans and asked them each 350 questions. In that poll, half of the respondents called themselves "Bible-believing" Christians. Another quarter identified themselves as members of mainline denominations, and yet another used the term "born-again." The most striking aspect of the survey, however, had to do with God's identity in these various groupings. The study found that Americans worshipped four different versions of God—Authoritarian, Benevolent, Critical, or Distant. African American and white evangelical Protestants favored the Authoritarian, who has a "high level of involvement in daily life and world affairs." He also punishes those who don't believe. Catholics were more likely to believe in the Benevolent, who "is mainly a positive force in the world, still active in daily life but not condemning of individuals." Mainline Protestants and some African American Protestants went for the Critical, who "stays mostly out of world affairs, providing a critique of them from afar." And most Jewish respondents and those unaffiliated with any particular faith favored the Distant, who "is not active in the world and not especially angry."

A much more focused study comes annually from southern California. Every year in January, the Barna Group in Ventura, California, conducts a poll about the spiritual state of the nation, charting the progress of particular beliefs through the populace. The survey has a large sample, about a thousand people, selected at random from around the country, chosen across race and class lines, and Barna uses the information to create an annual map of the faith for the benefit of pastors and other church leaders. Without buying the efficacy of every single statistic, it is possible to use this map as a rough guideline to the actual state of evangelical Christian worship in the country. Certainly, many Christians do. To their consternation, Barna comes to a similar conclusion every year. The high number of self-professed Christians is an illusion that masks a massive indifference nationwide to the actual tenets of the faith, as he sees them.

According to his numbers, in 2006, only 32 percent of Americans, a third of the country, had what he would call an "active faith," as defined by three activities performed in conjunction—reading from the Bible on one's own, that is, not at church; attending a church service that was neither a funeral nor a wedding; and praying to God. For Barna's purposes, all of these activities had to have been performed within the space of the same week. Barna also found that, in 2005, less than 50 percent of the country attended a religious service of any kind, apart from funerals and weddings, a finding backed up by Gallup, which routinely puts the figure of active evangelical believers at 40 percent, or about 132 million people. But another prominent researcher, Dave Olson, who has focused his attentions on the success of more recently established churches, cuts the number way down, to about 17.7 percent of the population, or 52 million people. No one says that any one study is definitive, because no one knows for sure what the respondents actually believe.

Barna found that men were even less likely than women to go to church on a regular basis, by a differential of 10 percent; white men, in particular. Blacks and Hispanics were much more likely to attend church on a regular basis, and African Americans are statistically the most religious people in the country.

But if we're talking about trying to find real believers, people whose worship reflects more than habit or social norms, someone like my Aunt Esther perhaps, church attendance itself becomes a misleading indicator. One's self-identification as a Christian is even less helpful. Lillie McWhinney once told me that her church was full of nonbelievers, as did a pastor in Baton Rouge, who estimated the number in his church to be as high as 20 percent. Barna makes an even more astounding claim. "From an evangelistic standpoint, the nonbelievers sitting in the pews represent one of the largest missionary fields in the world," he writes, "more than 40 million adults—and they are literally sitting next to believers in a house of worship every week."

Barna doesn't believe that the vast majority of Americans who claim to be Christian have any earthly idea what that means. He does know what it means, however, and he can quantify that reality. According to him, there are five different "faith segments" in this country: atheists and agnostics make a tenth of the total population. Members of non-Christian faiths—Jews, Muslims, Hindus, Buddhists—an even smaller percentage, somewhere around 6 percent. The rest of the country adheres theoretically to Christianity, though it's a fantastically murky designation, and Barna has taken great pains to parse out the meaning of that term, especially when it comes to his own segment of the population. He names three large subgroups within the general rubric of Christianity—"notional Christians," whose affiliation to the faith has its basis in tradition or ethnic identity and is tied more closely to Catholicism and mainline denominations; "non-evangelical born-again Christians, or NEBACs," whose belief has a basis in some kind of personal experience of conversion; and "evangelicals." Rather than try to more closely identify the characteristics of the first two categories, by far the majority of the people in this country, it makes more sense to work backward from Barna's definition of evangelicals, who, in his belief, if I read it correctly, are the only real Christians in America.

Evangelicals, to qualify for that name in the poll, must agree to nine points of doctrine, and these are nonnegotiable.

First, they must have made a personal commitment to Jesus Christ that governs a significant part of their life. In other words, they don't just accept Jesus and go on about their business. They incorporate this truth into their behavior and decisions.

Second, they believe that after they die, they will go to heaven because they have confessed their sins and have accepted Christ as their savior. This is crucially important. For a typical evangelical, heaven can never be a reward for good deeds or self-sacrifice. Those things are sideshows to the main event, which is belief. Only through right belief, never through right action, can heaven be attained. Humans can never be good enough for God to merit salvation on their own.

Third, they "strongly" agree that the Bible is totally accurate in all the principles it teaches. This is another way of talking about biblical inerrancy, the idea that the book itself is perfect in its execution. This belief instantly commits the believer to a series of other beliefs that aren't mentioned in Barna's definition. For instance, if one accepts that the Bible is "totally accurate," then one will more likely have problems with the teaching of evolution, and will also tend to believe that the world will come to an end according to prophetic passages in the Bible. If the book doesn't have to be accurate in the sense that we understand that word, for instance, Darwin's version of origins becomes much less problematic because it doesn't challenge anything central to the salvation message. On the other hand, if the Bible must be accepted as "totally accurate," Darwin becomes a major problem, as do a whole range of sciences.

Fourth, evangelicals believe they have a responsibility to testify to others of their own redemption. Once saved, they have to talk about it. For these believers, as I have pointed out, the act of witness is the central activity of their belief. I would call it the defining activity.

Fifth, seemingly redundant, they agree that religious faith is very important in their life. This is a slightly different way of affirming that all kinds of important decisions will be made on the basis of faith rather than, say, economics or pragmatism. The answer to this question would be a good indicator of the person's political persuasion.

Sixth, and crucially, they believe that the devil, or Satan, is a living being and not just a symbol of evil. This belief separates them from huge numbers of people in the mainline denominations, for instance, who view Satan in all kinds of ways—as metaphor, as suffering, as death, as an outright embarrassment—but almost never as a real person.

Seventh, a reiteration of a key conviction, they don't believe that a person can go to heaven simply by being good or doing good works.

Eighth, they believe that Jesus was completely sinless while on earth. Decades of historical research allied to the secular imagination have steadily reduced Jesus to the status of a very fascinating man. The belief in his lack of sin rejects any such characterization and sends a signal that all historical research will be viewed through this lens. Jesus was God. Jesus didn't marry, no matter the evidence. Jesus wasn't conceived through the sexual union of a man and woman.

Finally, evangelicals believe, in the words of the Barna poll, that "God is the all-powerful, all-knowing, perfect creator of the universe who rules the world today."

Notice that all but one of these criteria involve an emphasis on right belief rather than right action. The beliefs may imply action, but actions are not definitive. The lone exception is the requirement to spread the word. We certainly don't find the conviction that one must do acts of kindness or charity; that one must participate physically in a worship service or read the Bible. On the contrary, active demonstrations of faith are downgraded forcefully—in two separate polling questions, we read that evangelicals do not believe that good works and charity lead in any way, shape, or form to salvation. The importance of this conviction in evangelical identity can't be overstated. Unlike members of the Catholic or mainline denominations, the nature and quality of Christian belief, the precise contents of that belief, are the decisive measures of the reality of the life.

By these criteria, then, Barna says, "evangelicals . . . constitute less than one out of every ten adults, one out of every five born-again adults, and just one out of every nine Americans who consider themselves to be Christian." The number comes to about 7 percent of the total population of this country, something like 20 million out of 300 million souls.

BUT HOW DOES that translate into the demographic reality of a place like Checotah, Oklahoma? Many Oklahomans consider themselves Southerners and therefore reliable citizens of the Bible Belt. Oklahoma is the home of Oral Roberts University, one of the best known evangelical colleges in the country. Senior members of its congressional delegation, Senators Tom Coburn and James Inhofe, are among the most assertive Christians in American government. A state policy on marriage and divorce was devised for the government by evangelicals, and a federal judge recently ruled that the Ten Commandments outside a courthouse in Stigler, Oklahoma, should not be removed. If any state in the country can claim a pious population, surely it's this one.

Checotah itself has twenty-five churches and is a classic conservative small town, according to Mayor J. Hayes, a community of ranchers, farmers, and retired military. It's also hometown to a star of the country's most popular TV show, *American Idol*, 2005 winner Carrie Underwood, who has since gone on to record the chart-topping gospel tune "Jesus, Take the Wheel." Arriving a few weeks after Underwood's victory, I passed signs all over town: "Congratulations, Carrie Underwood," on the red, white, and blue banner near the Wal-Mart, and "Carrie, Hurry Home," posted on the Checotah High School. Briefly, my corner of the country had become the pop culture symbol for heartland America.

Without going door-to-door, it's hard to determine the content of people's faith in any given town or county. But if we take Barna's evangelical category and measure it against church affiliation statistics in Checotah, it's easy to imagine the size of the discrepancy between his version of Christianity and everything else.

In the year 2000, in McIntosh County, Oklahoma, where Checotah is located, there were 9,756 people with religious affiliations out of a total population of 19,456, according to census records collected by the Association of Religion Data Archives. So about half of the county population claimed to be connected to one church or another, implying, for the sake of argument, at least one trip to church a year. Of those who claimed a religious affiliation, a tiny handful, in this case 8 members of the Bahai sect, did not have a Christian one. A mere 75 people claimed to be Catholics. Another thousand and change belonged to the mainline denominations: United Methodists, Presbyterian Church (U.S.A.), Disciples of Christ, and Episcopalians. Everyone else belonged to the evangelical Protestant category, and more than half of those, 5,591 in all, were members of the Southern Baptist Convention. In Checotah itself, which is the second largest town in the county, after Eufala, the county seat, I counted more Baptist churches than any other denomination, including the First Baptist Church, right across the street from my grandparents' old house, with a sign out front that read, "Forbidden Fruits Create Many Jams."

According to the data, in the ten years between 1990 and 2000, the total population with a religious affiliation stayed virtually the same, at 9,756, even though the population as a whole grew by 16 percent, from roughly 16,000 to 19,000; that means the number of people with any religious affiliation at all in McIntosh County fell by about 6 percent. It's a common observation among all researchers in this field, including Barna, that church growth is not keeping up with population growth. The numbers would also seem to track with the national trend asserted by Barna and other researchers that far fewer people are believing Christians than the 84 percent typically polled. And if Barna is right about that, he may also have a more accurate view on the numbers of true believers among the churchgoing evangelical Protestants. Applying Barna's math crudely to Oklahoma, only one out of every nine of the self-professed Christians in McIntosh County qualifies as his kind of Christian. Out of 9,756 adherents, that leaves 1,084 people, a mere fifth of those who claim to be members of the Southern Baptist Convention.

I asked a local about those numbers. Rev. Larry Haggard has been at

West Side Free Will Baptist Church in Checotah for five years. He says that his flock is more conservative than most Baptist denominations. I asked him about the findings of the Barna research, and he told me that the math made sense to him. "In any church, you're going to have a certain number of people who regularly attend, who are among the most active members, who have never known Christ," he told me. "They missed first base, and now they're on third, but they'll be out when they get home. On that final day, they'll be out at home."

THIS IS A limited picture of a very complicated reality. It's next to impossible to know how the raw numbers really translate in this particular population. Even my cursory investigation does suggest, however, the ramifications of the Barna approach, what it might mean to millions of people around the country who happily consider themselves to have continued in the faith of their ancestors.

In the case of my mother's family, after talking to my Uncle Bill and Aunt Fay, I have a better sense of my own religious heritage, and it's a pretty mixed bag if one is trying to adapt it to Barna. Uncle Bill is my grandfather's youngest brother. To hear him talk is to go back in time to the era before automobiles became common, before Oklahoma had decent roads, to the years just one or two decades removed from the lawlessness of the frontier. One evening, at Uncle Bill's farm out in Pierce, I heard a story about my great-grandfather's fateful first encounter with organized religion.

His father, my great-great-grandfather, died penniless in 1875, a Southerner who lost everything in the Civil War. Before he passed away, he made arrangements for his four sons to be taken into the homes of four Methodist ministers. My great-grandfather, Lee, went to the home of a preacher in Hackett City, Arkansas, where he lived until he was twelve or thirteen, and the following incident occurred. Lee was supposed to feed the chickens, Uncle Bill told me, "but a neighbor's goose got into the feeding area, and he threw a rock at the goose, and hit it in the head. That addled the goose, and it went to flopping and kicking. The preacher saw him do it, and because the goose belonged to a neighbor, he told my daddy to pick up the goose and take it and put it under an apple tree in the wheat field, where the neighbor would find it." Along the way, my great-grandfather got mad at the goose, Uncle Bill said, and he wrung its neck, killing it and throwing it into the woods. When he got back to the farm, the preacher asked him if he'd done what he'd been asked, and my great-grandfather lied. "He [the preacher] was going to give my daddy a whipping," Uncle Bill continued, "because he told a lie."

My great-grandfather pulled a knife. That was the end of the relationship—with the preacher and with Jesus.

But Uncle Bill told me that his wife, my great-grandmother, whom we called Granny Bee, read the Bible every day of her life. She was born in 1879 and died in 1980 at the age of one hundred, and toward the end, her children had to hold the Bible up and turn the pages for her. Her youngest son, Uncle Bill, wasn't religious in any orthodox sense. He'd made walnut wood coffins for himself and his wife, my Aunt Lucille, who had wanted a church service when she died. He gave her one, burying her in Pierce Cemetery, just down the road. But he didn't want a service for himself.

"I just want to be taken to the graveyard," he told me. "I don't want to be embalmed. I want to be buried within twenty-four hours." He added, "I've seen so many funerals where a preacher gets up and talks about what a fine fellow this was that passed away and didn't even know his name till after the man had died." Maybe he was thinking of my grandmother's funeral, when the pastor had mispronounced his sister-in-law's last name. He continued, "There's one thing I don't believe, and that is, if you don't believe in this or that church, you're going to hell. I don't think the church is going to save you at all. I think you're going to have to save yourself. That's my belief."

"How'd you come by that belief?" I asked him.

"Just naturally," he said.

AFTER SPEAKING WITH Uncle Bill, I went to Pierce Cemetery, the first place where the mystery of death captured my imagination. When I was a kid, we'd drive west on I-40 from Checotah to Pierce, a trip of ten miles that seemed to take us back half a century in time. My mother would always show us where the Creek had buried their dead, though by that time, most of the burial site was submerged in Lake Eufala. We'd exit I-40 on a concrete road and turn left beneath the interstate onto an asphalt road running into the heart of the country. Just there, off to the right, you could see the tops of the headstones of the white man's graveyard, rising above the grass.

Decades later, not much had changed. I turned off the same asphalt road onto the dirt. It was a June afternoon, and no one else was around. I pulled the car onto a patch of spear grass. The cicadas buzzed in early summer waves. A relatively new storm fence surrounded the graveyard. I unlatched the gate and entered the grounds. A sign on the gate asked for donations. Unpaid volunteers cared for the place. In the middle of the cemetery rose a pole without a flag. I saw a bench for sitting and a stone tablet inscribed with the words: "Dedicated to All Veterans Who Served Our Country to Preserve Our Freedom That Our Flag May Forever Wave." At the bottom of the inscription ran a reference to the great eternal promise: John 3:16. There was no scripture, but I knew the lines by heart, like every born-again. "For God so loved the world, that he gave his only begotten Son, that whosoever believeth in him should not perish, but have everlasting life." I found Aunt Lucille's grave, and I saw the bare earth where Uncle Bill would be buried. Eighteen-wheelers boomed on the highway above. For a moment, the memory of childhood wonder abated, and I sensed the way that this graveyard, this countryside, and these people connected me to two enormous historic forces that made the foundations of the world into which I'd been born—and by definition, the world of the Christian faith in the century of my birth. Without these two forces, it was impossible for me to understand the nature of modern American evangelicalism. In the Pierce graveyard, they were not abstractions. They were personal.

The first was economic and technological transformation. My people grew up in a country that had been wild nature two hundred years before, inhabited by natives who were driven completely out of the region. There had been neither roads nor cities nor churches in what later became known as the Oklahoma territory. But more important than that, before the 1840s, there hadn't even existed such a thing as a railroad. There had been no standardized time. There had been neither refrigeration nor large markets for selling wheat or livestock. By the time my great-great-grandfather died in 1875, Chicago was emerging as the central market for all of midwestern commerce, changing the landscape and people profoundly, and those changes brought the industrial revolution and everything that it implied: a revolution in the relationship between humans and land, between humans and the seasons, between humans and God. In this little world, the growth in population, the coming of churches, and the improvement of roads had also meant the consolidation of education. Aunt Fay and Uncle Bill had started school in one-room schoolhouses, like the pioneers of a century before. By the 1930s, the one-room schoolhouses had closed, and the students gathered under one roof where they received a standardized education. Pierce might seem timeless, as if it had existed in one form forever, but this was an illusion, the clearest evidence of which could be heard like a loud wind from the bench in the cemetery, the rushing of computerized trucks on an interstate built in the 1960s and 1970s on top of a native cemetery where there had been neither crosses nor headstones, only rocks and mussel shells. There was horrible magic in that fact, the sorcery of change and destruction.

The other great force revealed in the graveyard—through the veterans memorial—was violence. I had been born into the second half of the most violent century known to the human race. In my century, human beings intentionally murdered 187 million of their own species. The killing could be said to have begun in earnest in 1912 with the Armenian massacres in Turkey, 1.5 million dead, the first mass slaughter of the century to be seen later as genocide, a word coined in 1948 to describe the emerging horrors. World War I, in which both of my grandfathers fought, claimed more than 8 million lives. My uncle Dick fought in World War II, in which 50 million people died. There were veterans in the cemetery whose friends and brothers could be counted among the dead.

OKLAHOMA, AND THE stories and experiences of my family there, hold so many mysteries for me. Aunt Esther, who loved God all her life, died a most horrible death. She fell in her room in the nursing home and lay there for an hour before anyone found her. When she fell, the cut became infected with streptococcus, which killed her quickly.

By all indications, at the age of ninety-two, my aunt suffered terribly. And she was alone, unless, as a real believer would jump to add, you believe in God, which she did, in which case he was right beside her every step of the way. But, as I asked my cousin Scott, sitting with him in his home in Aledo, Texas, a few days later, how was it possible to believe in a god who would visit such horrific destruction on one who had adored him all her life? How could such a thing happen? My cousin, a devout evangelical Christian, replied, with an honest sense of his own loss, "I don't know, John. I've asked myself the same thing. In the end, there are certain things we simply can't understand."

## chapter 5

# *Heaven*

*I*n the Christian life, along with the insoluble mysteries, one receives from time to time intimations of a future glory, dimly perceived but unmistakable.

At the end of my time in Pierce, one of these intimations came to me, an old reflex come briefly back to life. I drove down one of the winding, unnamed dust roads to see the place where Uncle Dick and Aunt Esther had lived, and had a shock. Every trace of their dwelling had vanished. The house had been torn down long ago, but I had hoped to find at least a foundation. Instead, I found Rhema Ranch, a Christian recreation center belonging to a charismatic church in Broken Arrow, Oklahoma, now covering 600 acres of bottomland on the shores of Lake Eufala. More than 100 acres of that land had once belonged to my mother's family, but it had been sold years before, and Rhema had bought it in turn. The new church, without any negative intent, had set about destroying my past, breaking down the invisible wall that had kept Pierce remote from the world. By buying so much real estate, Rhema had broken the spell of the place.

Where once there had been a forest right at the edge of the road, a lawn now stretched. The trees had been cleared and a six-foot-high fence of stone pillars and metal wires had been erected to keep out unwanted visitors. That land had once been open to hunters and wanderers. Now it belonged to a mini-Christian empire based in Broken Arrow, sixty miles away, with 8,000 members in its congregation, according to the website; a ministerial training center with 23,000 graduates and fourteen campuses worldwide; plus television and radio broadcasts and a magazine mailed to 250,000 subscribers. "Rhema is all about one thing," the website says. "Our purpose is to help usher in the last great move of God's spirit and the Second Coming of Christ."

In the name of Jesus, and his heaven, they had cleared my childhood wilderness. The land lay in wait.

After a few minutes, standing by myself in the road, something else occurred to me. I hesitate to call it a vision, but it came to me with a powerful intensity. Rhema Ranch could be seen as a sign and a wonder. It might have an almost prophetic meaning. The land had once been sacred to me in private. Now it was sacred for all. There was a literally transcendent message here, engraved in the Canadian River bottom country. As my cousin Michele had said, we change. God doesn't.

The ground had not stood still in two hundred years. Once, there had been only the natives. Then the settlers had come. They had made roads, churches, cemeteries, and one-room schoolhouses. Their children had brought telephone lines and country stores and post offices. Eventually, the interstate had plowed right through everything, completely altering the landscape for yet another generation. Now the country stores had gone, and the post offices closed, and the old churches were almost empty. Human existence, the very nature of the land on which we live, is mutable. But in all that time, as my cousins believed, God had not changed. There were neither roads nor graveyards upon his face. His call to me in childhood, his wild cry across the fields of Pierce in another time, could no more be silenced by the latest alteration in the landscape than the moon could be changed by the touch of human feet. The land changes, but God endures, and in the appearance of this facility in my own personal Garden of Eden, if I believed, I could see a reiteration of that promise. Instead of loss and sorrow for the banishing of my past, I could feel an ultimate joy. If I believed, my sadness and bafflement at the ravaging of Oklahoma would be as nothing.

†

ONE NIGHT, IN Nashville, I had a live experience of heaven, an intimation of coming glory in the form of music.

I had come to Tennessee to take part in Gospel Music Week, the annual gathering of the Christian music industry, and a friend of mine named Joanne insisted that I spend Sunday night at the McCain Guitar Pull. In one sense, it was a promotional event, designed to feature the roster of clients represented by the McCain & Company public relations firm. Gospel Music Week is steeped in spirit, but it's all about commerce in the end, the buying, selling, and marketing of a multibillion-dollar industry.

The guitar pull took place in a nondescript suite of the downtown Marriott. It started at about six, around the same time that a violent storm system descended on central Tennessee. In the next few hours, twenty-seven people would die in tornadoes to the west of the city. Winds reached 200 miles an hour. Out the window of the suite, directly in my line of vision, I saw two flags on a pole on the summit of a downtown skyscraper, the Tennessee and American flags, both of them boiling soundlessly in the wind.

I sat on the floor, legs stretched in front of me, arms splayed behind. Around me sat singer-songwriters, guitar designers, record producers, session musicians on mandolin, banjo, and guitar, winners of Grammy and Gospel Music awards. Across the room sat Phil Keaggy, one of the most famous guitarists in the United States. Beside him sat Muriel Anderson, the first woman ever to win the National Fingerstyle Guitar Championship, her instrument looking magical and strange across the room, her own modification, a thing called a harp guitar. Lynn McCain, the founder of the publicity firm, introduced the musicians, one by one. Then she introduced her pastor, and he stood.

"There really is an amazing image I want to share with you," he began, soft-voiced and tentative. Holding a Bible, he referenced the last chapter of the last book, Revelation 22. "What the Lord gives us is the completion of our story. It's kind of amazing to realize, the Bible begins and ends with two chapters in which sin is no longer present. In Genesis 1 and 2, God created the world in which we get a picture of what it was like before sin and death permeated all things. The last two chapters again show us what it's going to be like when sin and death are completely eradicated by the completion of the work of Jesus."

He had a short beard; he looked like someone who had once played music himself. From Revelation 21 and 22, he described the state of the new Jerusalem after the end of the world we know. He told us that these passages from the prophet John drew upon Old Testament scripture from the book of Isaiah, chapter 60, another vision of the new world to come. Then he said something that I had never heard before from a Christian. "The great cultural artifacts throughout history are envisioned as carrying over from this life to the next. I don't know how much time you've spent thinking about the continuity between this life and the life to come, but the continuity is great. Our God is not going to annihilate culture and story. He's going to redeem it."

A few of the musicians had started to tune their guitars. Strings plucked, an impromptu orchestra percolated. The pastor continued his description. "Let's think of music, for instance. What is it going to be like in our eternity where all cultural musical forms are going to be represented, not simply as individual entities, but the grand diversity coming together in one enormous symphony?" I stared at the carpet as he spoke. "What is it going to be like for every string instrument represented in the history of music to show up in that new city? What is it going to sound like?"

He reached for an example from the music industry. "The gospel does several things. One of the things it does is it frees us from a sense of competition. The new Jerusalem won't be a battle of the bands. I had a great musical moment in 1970. Within a seven-day period, I saw the original intact band Chicago and then, seven days later, I saw Blood, Sweat & Tears. Watching Chicago, the members of the band were very much side-by-side, putting forth a wall of sound that was impressive, but when I saw Blood, Sweat & Tears seven days later, I saw amazing jazz musicians literally stopping and looking at each other and enjoying the improvisation with one another. They weren't just showing up and playing the same music for another night and another gig."

Someone in the audience murmured "Mmm" in agreement. "These incredible jazz musicians—a sax player would play something, upright bass player—and the rest of the band would stop and simply say 'Awesome. You're good at what you do.' Does it not thrill your heart to know that that will be our eternity in every sphere of life?"

Then, in the middle of a Tennessee storm, the pastor turned the hotel suite into a vision of paradise. "That's what the gospel does. The gospel takes us and gladdens us to be a part of something so much bigger than who we are. So may the next hour and fifteen, twenty, thirty minutes simply be for us the foretaste of the end of our story. Let's enjoy one another. Let's enjoy the sound of tuned guitars and tuned hearts, complementing one another, getting us ready for an eternity of celebrating perfect hearts and perfect art, forever. Amen."

In a thick southern accent, Lynn McCain cried out, "All right!" And the great Phil Keaggy began to pluck out the first chords of a song.

THE PASTOR'S WORDS laid the groundwork, but the moment of glory came an hour later, when I experienced once again the truth of those verses from Matthew 6: "Consider the lilies of the field, how they grow; they toil not, neither do they spin. And yet I say unto you, That even Solomon in all his glory was not arrayed like one of these."

Intentionally, in this miniature sermon about the music of God for a roomful of musicians, the pastor had turned a Marriott hotel suite into a church. It happens all the time in Christianity. "Wherever two or more of you are gathered in my name," the gospels tell us, "I am there also." There were more than two hundred of us jammed into that suite, a respectable congregation for a church summoned out of nothing. But I don't want to suggest that I felt a member in good standing there; far from it. During that sermon, I listened as an outsider allowed into a closed world. I didn't consider myself a future citizen in that new Jerusalem. The streets of that city had been bought many times over by the blood of nonbelievers. This was one of my thoughts, as I stared at the carpet and listened. I thought of all those others who would have to burn in perdition for that city to have its eternity. And, to be honest, when the pastor talked about seeing Chicago and Blood, Sweat & Tears within the same seven-day period, he was painting a vision of my own personal hell. If I thought that anything in heaven would sound like either Chicago or Blood, Sweat & Tears, I would willingly serve Satan for the rest of my days.

Despite these alienating thoughts, his words had their effect, indirectly, because they summoned up a vision of the gospel as pleasure. And here is what I most wish to convey here. I want to suggest that what I felt in this room was a seldom-mentioned and yet indispensable part of the Christian life. It is something that most non-Christians may never have grasped: at times, it can be the most delirious of pleasures to believe, to sit within a circle of existence that extends back to the beginning of time and forward to the end of time while never leaving the most intimate circle of human contact. When Jesus tells his disciples about the lilies, he is telling them something about the way they are to live; how they are to live differently than others, how they are to relate to existence as if immortality and peace had already been provided to them; that the grace and beauty of the natural-born lily already belonged to them. This is not a message of superiority over others, in my reading. It is a statement of a reality that even the disciples had a hard time comprehending. We are born beautiful and we die beautiful, and nothing in this world can ever change it.

"Thank you for today," Phil Keaggy sang in a delicate voice. "I am grateful, for today is all I have." A husband-and-wife team of singer-songwriters went next, a pair who had made a fortune running their own label and designing their own instruments, doing a song called "Slow Down," sort of a lifestyle tune, male and female voices harmonizing. The room applauded. On mandolin, an amiable, bearded session musician plucked his way through a heartbreakingly lovely rendition of "Over the Rainbow." At that moment, a deeper strain of feeling entered the room. You could feel it in the heavier silence of the listeners.

The circle came back to Phil Keaggy, who said, in a quiet voice, "This is an old Beatles tune," and that's when it happened. He began to play and sing, "Here Comes the Sun," and everyone else joined on the instant. How can I explain what I felt at that moment? I tried to sing too, but something came over me, and tears filled my eyes. I was ashamed and kept my face aimed at the floor. The emotions in my chest came close to rapture, an overwhelming joy at the sound of all those voices lifted in one of the essential secular songs of modern times. What was it? Did I secretly rejoice in the fact that, all Good News aside, there was nothing closer to God on earth than a terrific pop tune? Was it a bizarre schadenfreude, a release of tension by someone who, until that moment, had felt an outsider? Or was it just the opposite? At that moment, with the opening bars of "Here Comes the Sun," I was one of them, because I knew the song and could join the symphony with my voice, had I been able.

I felt then, and still do, that it was the latter, and more than that, I experienced something inside of myself, a movement that I can only describe in the form of a very old cliché, as a temporary union between the opposed pieces of my divided soul, between the secular man and the believing child, and further, between the secular country and the religious country, a ridiculous swelling of hope that everything in this torn life and nation would be redeemed, that every sorry horror of the human animal would one day be recast in joy in a universe created by love rather than by indifferent physical force.

It did not occur to me till later that many of the people in the room might have given voice to the words with a different spelling, "Here Comes the Son," a reference to Jesus rather than the star that shines indisputably on us all. If I'd had this thought in the moment, it would have ruined everything, but I didn't, and so the tune in the suite remains for me a singular example of revelation in my life, a moment of transcendence created out of nothing more than guitar string, human vocal cords, and four walls, an abject lesson in why millions of people had embraced so fully and deeply what I had rejected.

## chapter 6

# The Man Himself

*L**et** me be clear about this: I hadn't rejected a religion. At the most basic level, I had rejected a man, a human male of the species *homo sapiens*, born 2 million years or so after the first sign of the family branch appeared in Africa, Jesus by name. Evangelical Christians place enormous emphasis on having a "personal" relationship with this human being, this Him, always capitalized, and it's critical to understand what they mean when they say that. Either he walks and talks, or he means nothing at all.

In other words, he's as real as you or me. He's not a painting; he's not an idea or an ideal. He's a guy who shows up on the radar. But how exactly does this happen? What does it feel like?

Once a week, in the months between June and August, thousands of high school kids descend on a valley in the Collegiate Range of the Rocky Mountains, the nesting place of a summer camp known as Frontier Ranch, run by the veteran Christian youth organization Young Life. Every week, while camp is in session, its director, John Sharp, sends an e-mail to his financial sponsors, detailing the ways that money and prayers have been used in the effort to introduce kids to Jesus. In mid-June 2005, he sent the following report under the heading "Notes I Took During the Week As We Observed

How God Was Pursuing His Lost Sheep." The report amounted to a list of encounters between mortal teenagers and the man himself.

Sharp wrote of one rebellious teenager, Jack, who "came in looking and acting like Ozzie Osbourne, trench coat, dark clothing and black make-up, and left looking and acting like a character in Carrie Underwood's (*American Idol*) band. It was as substantial as 'transformation' gets. He was pursued at every intersection, by his leaders, their cabin of guys, our whole team knew him by name. He started the week at the back of the Kachina (club room) and slowly moved forward at every meeting. His demeanor changed from bleak and dark (night 1) to sitting almost on stage (night 7) singing Carrie Underwood's 'Jesus, Take the Wheel' at the top of his lungs. He stood up along with 116 others to say, 'My name is Jack and this week, I gave my life to Christ.'"

BUT WHO EXACTLY is he talking about? In my experience, it's among the hardest questions in Christendom to answer.

My college roommate and old friend Craig Detweiler met Jesus just like those teenagers in Colorado, at another bucolic Young Life camp, on a lake in North Carolina called Windy Gap, and he says it was love at first sight. "It was such a high," he told me. "I was like, look at the sky, it's so blue. Look at the grass, it's so green. I love Jesus, he loves me."

Nowadays, Craig works as a professor at Fuller Seminary in Pasadena, California, and he tells me, "that dude is a living reality." He starts every day with a prayer to a specific person: "Lord, what have you got for me today?"

TWO DAYS AFTER Aunt Esther's funeral, I drove back south to Texas to see Don and Lillie McWhinney for the first time in two and a half years. We were going to have dinner and talk. In the waning days of my *60 Minutes* job, I'd contacted Don and told him about my project, and he had been kind enough to open the doors wide to me. Not only would he and Lillie consent to meet with me for dinner, he would share his network of contacts. In a subsequent e-mail, he gave me some sense of what to expect.

"John, what are you willing to share with me regarding your journey as an evangelical Christian?" he inquired. "Do you have the freedom, at this point, to tell me what happened? You told Lillie and me during our initial visit that you became disillusioned with Christianity in the past because of the way the Christians and Muslims were fighting during the Bosnian conflict. Do I have that right?"

He went on, revealing in a few sentences the contours of a life that I hadn't remotely expected: "What would you like to know about my Christian journey—about the time I poured five gallons of gasoline under the garage door of a grocery store and set it on fire—or about the time I was kicked out of college for cheating? Do you wish to know the end game of these situations and what I did, restitution, recovery, and getting on with my Christian life. All of this in my years of rebellion (there is much more) before I met Lillie. And would you believe at the time I was a Christian? How is this possible? A Christian pours gasoline under the door of a grocery store and sets it on fire? Where does this fit in?"

Don closed the e-mail with this remarkable last paragraph: "What about my son that is mentally ill (schizophrenia and manic depression) at forty-one years of age? How do Lillie and I deal with this and God, and life, and the pain and tears this has brought to our lives, to our other sons and our extended family? Where do we find answers that give us the ability to carry on with life and have happiness and joy in our marriage? How do we deal with a son that was on his way to medical school and then, after six years of medical research, began to hear voices, and have a messiah complex, and prepares to end his life with a gun. Since then, he has made six serious attempts to end his life. Where does all this fit in to our Christian lives and marriage? What have we learned and what do we say to others who come to us with the same pain? Is this something you would like to talk about?"

It was.

WHEN I STARTED my research, I made a list of questions, at the top of which was an easy one, or so I thought. What is personal about the personal relationship with Jesus Christ? In other words, what is the nature of the encounter between people like the McWhinneys and a historically recorded human being who died on a cross under the Roman Empire two thousand years before they were born. Over the course of a year, I asked this question everywhere I went, and before long, I realized that it was far from easy to understand the question, much less give an answer. On the contrary, the answer invariably caused the greatest difficulty of all, perhaps because the "personal" aspect of the relationship between God and human beings is the deepest mystery of the faith. Even if God does exist, how and why would he want to relate "personally" to the inferior beings that are his wayward creations?

When I asked Don the question, for instance, he told me that he'd never personally "heard" Jesus speak, if that's what I meant. He'd never had an actual experience of the physical presence of Christ. But he knew from scripture that the relationship existed, and he'd seen the efficaciousness of that relationship throughout his life. Many times, his prayers had been answered. Other times, they hadn't. In my experience, he was the norm, but there were plenty of exceptions, particularly if one omits Jesus and replaces that name with God. According to scripture, Jesus himself said, "no man cometh unto the Father, but by me," and for Christians, it's a clear understanding. All relationships with God are mediated by the person of Jesus, by that man who became divine. I spoke to a professional actor who told me that he'd always had the gift of talking to God and hearing from God. I spoke with a woman who was sexually abused by her father and stepfather, who recalls, in the depths of despair, visitations from an angel sent by God who would stand at the foot of her bed. I heard countless times of the closeness of God, of a thing or a person or an event being "anointed," meaning that it conveyed the feeling of having been intended by God, blessed by him personally, a term that has passed into Christian popular usage so that judges on a gospel version of *American Idol* can tell a contestant, "That just felt so anointed."

It would be hard to limit the ways that God, and therefore Jesus, interact with Christians. When I believed, I actually spoke to Jesus, addressing him as "Lord," and I heard the answers. I don't mean to say that I heard his voice, as Don McWhinney said, but I felt a kind of oceanic comfort and solace that was very specific, as if an insistent warm wind whispered in my ears. My pastors and youth leaders told me that God wasn't a gumball machine, so I shouldn't trouble him with requests for petty and immediate satisfactions. I should pray to God for the largest things, for wisdom, for healing, for comfort, for judgment.

So I did, for the most part. Once, I can remember praying for a girl to call, and she obliged. That was a rarity. Mostly, I prayed that God's will be done in all matters, and I told him that I trusted his will, but that I wanted him to give me greater faith to believe, to know that his judgment was sound. That verse from Matthew, "Consider the lilies," always reminded me that God had made me to be perfect, that I didn't have nearly as many needs as I thought. My conversation with Jesus often consisted in this verse, running through my mind, filling me with joy, if I felt down, if I'd been rejected, if I'd made a fool of myself on the football field, which was a frequent occurrence. I didn't ask to catch the ball on a seven-yard pass during practice—that would have been the gumball machine God—but I pleaded for calm in my soul, not to be afraid of getting hit, not to "hear footsteps," as the coaches put it. If I prayed not to hear footsteps, meaning the footsteps of someone who was about to tackle me, then I wasn't asking for personal glory or attention. I was asking for freedom from fear. And I said all these things to Jesus, who kept close. I heard his footsteps, or so I told myself. Sometimes, in beautiful places—in the Colorado Rockies, or early in the morning before football practice in a Dallas August, when the air was fresh, before the heat descended—I would just say hello. And there would come the feel of a response.

I MET THE McWhinneys at their home in Corinth, Texas, north of Dallas. They lived down an asphalt road past a pioneer cemetery, old and new headstones beneath the shadows of live oaks and mesquite, yet another grove of the dead on my road. The first inhabitant of the cemetery, I later learned, was a member of a party of settlers in a wagon train. A young girl died of an unknown disease and was buried in the shadow of mesquite trees beneath a metal cross that still stands. The McWhinneys and their pug JJ met me at the door. We went to a Cajun restaurant just off the interstate and exchanged life stories.

They wanted to know the specifics of how I lost my faith, so I told them. It's safe to say that the story of how I lost my faith opened far more doors than my *60 Minutes* credentials or anything else in my background. It was the necessary prelude to every serious conversation and very much like the requisite first offer in a bartered exchange. You reveal your soul, I'll reveal mine. In most cases, before I started to ask questions, I told people where I came from, what I wanted, and how my faith stood. I didn't want anyone to think that I came to these conversations as a believer. I didn't want anyone to feel that they had been misled, so I never failed to clarify my position. Usually, until that moment, people assumed that I was a believer, and when I said that I wasn't, that I'd lost my faith, it puzzled them, and they wanted to know immediately what I meant by that word "lost." Was it possible to "lose" one's faith in Jesus? To be lost to him?

IN MAY OF 1993, at the age of thirty, a few months after being hired by *U.S. News & World Report* to run their Berlin bureau, I was sent to the former Yugoslavia to relieve a colleague who had been covering the Bosnian civil war from Belgrade. He had been there for six weeks and needed a break, so I rotated into his spot for a prolonged stay. Before leaving, he told me that I should check out an underreported story in the southern part of the Serbian state, a region known as the Sanjak of Novi Pazar. Evidently, according to human rights sources, a group of Muslims had been driven out of their villages in Montenegro and herded into a ghetto in the city of Priboj, which sat right on the Bosnian border. Our sources believed that these people, already expelled from their villages, but off the radar of the international community because they weren't technically Bosnians, were prime candidates for further ethnic cleansing, meaning concentration camps or worse. My colleague asked me to go to Priboj and check out the story. He gave me the name of an interpreter and the address of a rental car agency and left Belgrade for the Hungarian border, and home.

I found the interpreter, a woman named Jasmina. In addition to her interpreting duties, she worked part-time for human rights organizations who were compiling lists of the dead and dislocated. She was something of an expert on affairs in the region of Novi Pazar. We rented the car, and the two of us drove south to Priboj. When we arrived in the long valley that ends in the provincial city, we stopped at a ruined farmhouse on a hill and saw the barrels of large-caliber guns rising from a line of trees on the opposite side. Once in the town, we found a desolate, scary warren of streets patrolled by paramilitary groups with Kalashnikovs and names like the White Eagles, white crosses painted on the chests and backs of their uniforms.

After asking around, we found a de facto Muslim ghetto. Behind a mundane storefront, inside a room on a quiet side street, sat a gathering of old men and woman. Jasmina asked if we could have a seat and ask them some questions, and a white-haired older gentleman indicated that we should. They offered us tea. Jasmina sat to my left and interpreted his words. I asked him how he came to be there. He pointed to his wife, seated behind him with her back to the wall, and told me their story.

Six months before, Serbian paramilitaries had entered their village in the mountains of Montenegro, a remote hamlet containing a few dozen people and situated not far from the place where the borders of Montenegro, Bosnia, and Serbia come together. The paramilitaries told everyone in town that the government of Yugoslavia had determined that spies and weapons were reaching the Bosnian Muslims through such villages, and everyone would have to leave. The village would be burned. When the old man's neighbor protested, he was executed on the spot. The invaders torched every house, giving the inhabitants just enough time to grab a few possessions. They drove the villagers out of their home and across the border into Serbia, and the old man and his wife had ended up in Priboj. To my ears, it was a textbook case of ethnic cleansing.

But there was more. The old man could still smile because he had one enormous consolation. His sons worked in a local factory that lay in Serbia, separated from the Montenegrin village by a thin strip of Bosnian territory. Every day, a bus picked them up in Montenegro, carried them across that strip of Bosnia and into Serbia, and every day, it brought them back. Except that one evening, a month or so before the paramilitaries showed up, the boys didn't make it home. They had been taken off the bus by heavily armed Serbs and hauled away. After making discreet inquiries, the old man had learned that his sons were safe, working in a labor camp in northern Bosnia, and as soon as the conflict ended, the family would be reunited, and they would immigrate to Australia, where they had family.

At that moment, Jasmina leaned against me and whispered in my ear, "I happen to know that this man's sons are dead."

It is hard to explain what happened to me then. Most Balkan reporters saw much worse than I had or would. Many of them stumbled across mass graves or saw executions. Unlike reporters who spent the war in Sarajevo, I never saw a child killed by a sniper, or human beings ripped apart by a mortar fired into a market. Some of those reporters may have been more hardened by what they saw, or by their work in previous war zones, but I had never been close to such a conflict before, and what I heard that afternoon in Priboj stunned me.

At that moment, I hadn't been a Bible-believing Christian for many years. I didn't believe in my salvation by grace through the sacrifice of Jesus Christ. I didn't believe that Christ had risen from the dead. I didn't believe that Jews were the chosen people. Later in this tale, I'll explain why. But in Priboj, I still held on to my experience of God. He existed, in my mind. He hadn't abandoned the universe or me. He was waiting, or I was waiting. There might be a sign of hope here and there. There might be moments when I might even ask, What are you trying to tell me, God? I'm listening. I hadn't been able to walk away from the immense reality of that relationship. But the ground beneath must have been much shakier than I knew, because when I heard what Jasmina said, the entire structure of my faith collapsed.

It wasn't the identities of the probable murderers. Serbs are Orthodox Christians by confession, the key marker of their identity, along with patterns of settlement. I had seen the men in Priboj painted with white crosses. But I didn't believe that their ethnic symbols amounted to a connection with real Christianity. I never saw the Bosnian conflict as a primarily religious war, and I didn't lose my faith because some nominal Christians turned out to be butchers. No, it was something else that astonished and terrified me. It was the very fact of what had just occurred. I had walked into that town a complete stranger. Within a few hours, I had met this man and heard his story. In a short time, I would leave and never see him again. And yet, in that fleeting moment, I had learned the most important single fact of whatever remained to his existence. An American, an outsider, as fleeting in his presence as an afterthought, I knew that his one hope in the world was obliterated. I knew that a day would come, sooner or later, when someone like Jasmina would tell him what she had just told me, unless he died first, which would no doubt have been less painful. I couldn't breathe a word. I couldn't be the one to break the news to him that his sons were dead. So I nodded at him and smiled and wished him luck and left.

But I was a changed man. From that moment on, it has never been possible for me to believe in any notion of a supreme God that could preside over such a sorrowful madness. I have never been able to believe in a plan that could account for that man's sufferings, and my knowledge of them, the obscenity of that small constellation of human misery. What final plan could ever make it worthwhile? And by extension, what plan could ever remotely justify the 250,000 who died in that horrible war? The 800,000 Rwandans murdered just a year later in Africa, many of them small children hacked to death by machete? The 6 million Jews murdered earlier in the century? And these are just the more spectacular horrors.

It was hard for me to tell this story to Don and Lillie. I had never told my parents or anyone in my family. Most of my closest friends have never heard it. It sits like a dark weight at the bottom of my mind, my little piece of the horrific twentieth century; the proof of the nonexistence of God seems the least of its implications. When I told the McWhinneys, my emotions overwhelmed me.

IN TURN, THEY told me the details of their sadness. I had come at the end of a terrible week. Their eldest son, forty-one-year-old Tedd, was a diagnosed schizophrenic, as Don had indicated in his letter. For the previous two weeks, Tedd had gone missing and was presumed to be living in a homeless shelter in Dallas. Shortly before his disappearance, he had showed up around midnight, drunk and banging on the front door and yelling obscenities, and Don had called the police. The police had come and taken Tedd to jail. It had been a ghastly decision to have to make, Don told me, but he'd had no choice. After his release, Tedd had vanished, and Don and Lillie had come to the end of their efforts. They'd agreed to have Tedd committed, a bitter choice, and one that they had put off for years.

It had been a long road with their son. Though he'd been a quirky kid, he had never been mentally ill as a child. His problems began when he was a promising graduate student in medical school, doing AIDS research, when his parents could already see the contours of a future success. The disease had destroyed their son. He had tried to kill himself many times—downing a bottle of Drano, taking pills, slitting his wrists. He had tried to bury himself alive and drown himself. "He is too unruly and violent for most buildings," Don told me. "The best we can now hope for is a room with a roof and air-conditioning."

Don then asked me a tough question. "How is my sorrow different than the sorrow you experienced in Bosnia? And yet I still believe. My faith has been strengthened. Why not yours?"

His faith had been strengthened. I couldn't see how. Like the death of Aunt Esther, which I kept to myself, the life of Tedd McWhinney struck me as a profound challenge to the reality of that man Jesus, and no vindication whatsoever. I didn't say that. Beyond what I had already said, I didn't feel that I had good reason, in light of their recent struggles, to be more nega-tive. But I could have told him that one big difference was obvious to me. Don and Lillie had suffered far more than I had. Compared to their travails with Tedd, my experience in Bosnia was no more than an intellectual whim. I would never have compared the two. But he had, and I could only tell him that my experience had led me to one irrevocable conclusion, his to another.

We parted ways in good spirits, feeling a mutual bond. It was a Friday night. We made plans for Sunday. I would go to the 10:30 service at Denton Bible Church with them. Afterward, we would go with their friends to a local breakfast place, a weekly tradition. It was the quiet beginning of a fellowship.

## chapter 7

# The Fundamentals

*O*nce more, I come back to the reality of Jesus. Who is he, this walking corpse? Don and Lillie believed that my return to their lives was no mere coincidence. Jesus had brought us together for a purpose. He attended our meeting that night at the Cajun restaurant, and five hours later, while we slept, he walked with their homeless son Tedd.

I asked Bob Davidson, a thirty-one-year-old Young Life leader who comes from Arkansas but lives in Chicago. Bob has been with the Young Life organization for ten years, and his work consists, officially, in bringing teenagers to Jesus. I met Bob in Colorado Springs at a class on faith and the movies taught by my friend Craig. He had sort of a Mick Jagger vibe. His brown hair covered his ears, and he wore clothes that would have put a teenager at ease, a T-shirt and jeans. He was good-looking, and his eyes had a sleepy quality with a cool, skeptical gaze that projected unassuming confidence, a self-effacing authority that struck me as crucial to his work. High school kids would pay attention to him. He also struck me as honest.

So I asked Bob to explain to me what was personal, in his view, about a personal relationship with Jesus. "For the first time, in the last year and a half," he told me, "I've been asking myself that same question.

"One of the things about the Christian world that eventually becomes frustrating," he told me, "is that things are copied and copied and copied and copied, or stated and stated and stated, to the point where we're not even quite sure what we're saying, and the words lose some of the gut out of them."

He said that he preferred to address the question of Jesus in the most basic terms of experience. "Okay, so for me, in my mind, a relationship is a dual deal. It's a two-way street. It's not a just-me situation. It's not a just-someone-else situation. There's something else going on there."

Already the subject began to feel elusive, as if it could only be approached in the broadest abstractions. Bob tried to narrow it. "From a practical standpoint," he continued, "I look at, What is the question that seems to drive me? And the question that seems to drive me is the question that gets to how I experience anything that I engage in, and it usually has something to do with some form of me experiencing love. I'm showing up to the world, saying, more than anything, I want to engage in experiences where I receive love, not only receiving in the sense of information for the mind, but something that transcends the mind—allows me to feel love, to be loved." He measured out these words very slowly, deliberating over each one. "At the same time, it goes the other way around. I'm showing up in the world looking for places where I can love, so that I can engage in love, get me out of myself."

He talked about the natural world, and how much easier it was for him to commune with God when he encountered the incredible beauty of the Rocky Mountains, where he had just finished his summer as a Young Life counselor at Frontier Ranch. "That's kind of where I feel an experience occurs, it's some form of transcendent experience that is hard for me to get my mind around. The only thing I know for certain," he told me, "is that *something* is occurring."

But, I asked him, what about all of those people who have transcendent encounters with the natural world, or moments of perceived divinity, as when a child is born in their presence, and yet don't profess any personal experience with Jesus Christ? Lots of people claimed to have seen the face of God in the beauty of the natural world. But, I said, it was another thing entirely to talk about that encounter in the context of Jesus. In other words, what did Christians get out of the experience of divinity in the mountains, or anywhere, that non-Christians could not? What did Jesus himself bring to the game?

"I'll tell you," he said. "Here's how I really answer the question, because it was posed to me about a year ago by a kid, a Young Life kid. He asked me, 'How do you know God is real? Today?' I thought I knew what he was asking," Bob said, "and I just tried to clarify. I went, 'How do I know God exists, you mean?' 'No,' he said, 'I believe God exists. I want to know, you know, what the hell he has to do with your life.' And it was the first time I had ever answered the question, or even tried to have the conversation, outside of the context of scripture. I told him a story. I said, 'You know, if I'm really being honest, this is how I answer the question.' And I told the story of probably the lowest point in my life. It was my freshman year in college, and I had broken up with my girlfriend, who is now my wife. We'd broken up, and we weren't dating, and hadn't been dating for some time, but I saw her dating somebody else, and it was really difficult for me, really hard for me, and to a point, not of crazy depression, but levels of depression that I hadn't personally experienced before. I felt like I really pushed my relationship to Christ to an extreme level, saying, 'I don't even know what to do. I don't know what this thing is. I don't understand prayer. It's never made sense to me.'"

Then a few months later, Bob told me, he saw a couple on the steps of the college cafeteria, and he was overcome. "In my mind, I'm saying, 'This is it, God. I'm going to pray this one last time. Help me.'"

Here, Bob paused, knowing that he was about to venture into territory that freaked some people out.

"I'm really hesitant to tell this story," he said, "and yet, instantly, as I said in my mind, 'God, you must help me,' this girl puts her hand on the back of my head and says, 'I know this might sound weird, and I don't know you, but God just asked me to pray for you.' It was very tangible. It was very bizarre. My heart kind of dropped. I don't know how to describe it except to say that I walked back to my room, and I told my roommate that I didn't even know how to make sense of it."

He let the story sink into the silence, then he said, "I felt like it was the first time that I tasted the reality of the resurrection. It was the first time that I actually believed that Christ didn't die two thousand years ago."

BOB DAVIDSON WOULDN'T care to be called an evangelical. He told me that he even has a problem with the word "Christian." "I'm not even sure what that means anymore," he said.

I asked him about the Barna Report, estimating that 40 million unbelievers were sitting in the pews of churches. Had these people experienced the reality of the resurrection in the way that Bob had? He knew of the report, but he took issue with Barna's definition of a Christian.

"There seems to be an idea that Christianity has something to do with getting into heaven," he said. "It's a prevention from hell and a ticket into heaven. You get this mysterious bar code that gets you in, or something to that effect. And I feel like folks who engage in the life of Christianity with that mind-set miss the heart of who Christ is and what I think a real faith looks like."

THOUGH BOB CAN'T abide definitions, his words perfectly articulated the dividing line between modern fundamentalism and evangelicalism. It's not a new division. This particular kind of encounter between a more doctrinaire version of the faith and a more inclusive one goes back at least a hundred years and can be traced ultimately to the revolutionary challenge of the Enlightenment, when the new arts of rational inquiry suddenly cast Christianity in the role of an irrational throwback to ages of ignorance and barbarism.

In Europe of the eighteenth century, that battle occurred largely between an appalled Catholic Church, which saw its land expropriated, its worldly prerogatives stripped away, its dogma mocked, its priests imprisoned or murdered, and a rising middle class that set greater store by industry, science, and reason. Two hundred years ago, many Protestants welcomed those changes as a blow against their archenemy, the pope; Luther was seen as a founding father of the transformation. Science offered no insult. Newton professed a belief in Jesus, as did most of his contemporaries. In the early years of the eighteenth century, in western Massachusetts, Jonathan Edwards made it his business to know the latest in scientific discovery and considered himself something of an amateur naturalist. His short essay on the spider is a classic example of the harmony between the pursuit of rational truth and the acknowledgment of God's larger reality.

Science advanced its claims. Reason undermined one doctrine after another. By the latter half of the nineteenth century, the nominal Christian Charles Darwin had published *The Origin of Species*, and neither Protestants nor Catholics could ignore the implications. The Vatican introduced the notion of papal infallibility to protect its claims to universal truth. For Protestants, it wasn't so easy. They had never believed in the infallibility of humans or their institutions. Only God held that honor. But if God did not exist, as Marx claimed, or if he had died, as Nietzsche balefully suggested? Then what?

That moment saw the birth of what we now call Christian fundamentalism, a term that is fast becoming a linguistic relic. When secular people and even some Christians talk about evangelicals, they often use the term fundamentalist, as if the terms were interchangeable. But few Christians will now identify themselves as fundamentalist. Particularly after the September 11 attacks, when the use of the term "Islamic fundamentalism" came into vogue, the word became impossibly loaded from a public relations standpoint. But even before 9/11, Christians who had once identified themselves as fundamentalist referred more frequently to themselves as evangelicals, and the latter word has now become so widespread that it is almost universal. Its universality probably signals its coming demise, as the word "evangelical" has come to be identified slowly but surely with exactly the same things that brought "fundamentalism" into disrepute.

It's an ironic twist, because the term "evangelical" has its roots in a reaction against the Christian fundamentalist movement of the nineteenth century. In fact, evangelicalism, as originally construed, might be called the Bob Davidson version of the faith, wary of dogma, focused on experience, accepting of the gospel as the inspired and living word of God. Inerrancy was problematic, placing the text itself above God. Fundamentalism was the opposite of evangelicalism, an adherence to the rules, the proverbial "ticket to heaven," as Bob put it to me. The movement took its name from a series of twelve volumes, called *The Fundamentals*, published in 1909 by a man named Lyman Stewart, cofounder and president of Union Oil, the first oil company to drill west of the Mississippi River. Stewart was an arch capitalist and a devout Christian unnerved by the advance of modernism on his faith. Other Christians, liberal Christians, might entertain the ideas of Marx, Nietzsche, and Darwin, but Stewart, under the stewardship of D. L. Moody, chose to react in the spirit of the nineteenth-century Vatican: he financed the Protestant version of papal infallibility. In 1908, he provided the money to found the Bible Institute of Los Angeles, also known as Biola University, and a year later, he financed *The Fundamentals* as a kind of roadmap for the new institution. As my college roommate Craig Detweiler tells his Biola mass communications students, "So where is the birthplace of Christian fundamentalism? Not Texas. Not Georgia. Not Tennessee. It's Los Angeles. And more specifically, Biola University. You're sitting on it."

*The Fundamentals* defended scripture as the inspired and unassailable word of God. The volumes, written by various prominent theologians of the day, railed against a critical liberalism that questioned the validity of biblical claims, the historicity of biblical events, and even the character and person of Jesus. Mainline denominations embraced these challenges as the means to survive and thrive in the modern age. *The Fundamentals* demanded a return to strict belief.

So does George Barna, using scientific measuring sticks rather than dogma to bring about the same effect. He shuns the word "fundamental," calling his believers evangelicals, a word that arose in theological opposition to Stewart's *Fundamentals* in circles centered around Fuller Theological Seminary. Fuller was founded in 1947 in Pasadena, just a few miles up the coast from La Mirada, home of Biola, and it was meant explicitly as an alternative to Biola and everything that it stood for. To this day, among the most rigorous traditionalists, Fuller has a reputation as a hotbed of radical sentiment. These early evangelicals rejected the defensive posture of fundamentalism and instead emphasized the mission to spread the gospel, to evangelize, from the Latin *evangelium*, bringing the good news to the people. Billy Graham is the best-known figure in this movement.

Bob Davidson is an heir. Jesus, rather than the Bible, is his polestar. And his opponents in Young Life, like George Barna, are the children of Lyman Stewart, even if they no longer see themselves as fundamentalists. Today, all of them are called evangelicals. Twenty years from now, no one will use that word, but the division will remain, I believe, far sharper, far deeper, than it is now.

## chapter 8

# Man of Shadows

$O$n September 27, 1967, when I was four years old, a twin-engine Aero Commander carrying seven passengers crashed into Mockingbird Lane, a few blocks from my house. The plane slid off the street and into the side of Bradfield Elementary School, bursting into flames. It was late afternoon, and the children had already been dismissed, though some kids were playing YMCA football in the fields. Everyone aboard the plane, mostly air force personnel, perished. I wasn't in school yet, but the crash, like the incident at the Methodist church in Oklahoma, which had happened only a few months before, constitutes another one of my earliest memories. I can recall driving down Mockingbird in our family station wagon and seeing the firefighters in black uniforms and broad-brimmed hats moving amid burnt and twisted curls of metal.

The crash occurred in a place called the Park Cities, where I grew up, a northern suburb of Dallas. Known to most Texans as Highland Park, my hometown occupies five square miles of land, containing a modest population of 30,000, but its reputation far exceeds its geographical and demographic boundaries. Texans have an image of Highland Park that corresponds to a corner of reality. The grand old homes on Turtle Creek seem to float on islands of paradise, where rich, beautiful women glide like dreams across tennis courts and football serves as chivalry, dogma, and big business. George W. and Laura Bush socialized there in the 1980s and 1990s, before he became governor of Texas, and their home church, Highland Park United Methodist, sits on the edge of the city limits, next to the campus of Southern Methodist University, which tops the short list to build his presidential library. Vice President Dick Cheney lived in Highland Park for four years until he received word that he'd been added to the ticket.

The Park Cities have been called "island cities," because the two small municipalities of Highland Park and University Park were incorporated in 1945 to stave off development by the city of Dallas. They have their own municipal government, their own water and sewage system, their own police and fire departments. Outsiders have a name for the islands: the Bubble. Forty years ago, when I was a child, the world inside that bubble seemed to exist apart from the events of the time, outside all mortal time, in fact, and I've often felt that I spent the 1970s in an era closer to the spirit of Eisenhower, all white, mostly Protestant, deeply conservative.

The Park Cities seemed to have stopped the clock, preserving a way of life that was disappearing elsewhere. I attended cotillion when I was young and can recall the little girls in their white gloves, the bowl of pink icy punch, the music of the Kingston Trio in the hushed halls of the Dallas Country Club. The actress Dorothy Malone, of *Peyton Place* fame, would come to those gatherings in dark sunglasses and watch the dancing of a daughter or niece. In the 1960s, flower children were uncommon, but they massed on the borders, just south of the neighborhood. One of my only memories of the 1960s consists in an image of wild, bright, hairy human beings swimming naked in the dark city water of Turtle Creek, not far from the statue of Robert E. Lee, and my father informing me that they were hippies. The year 1968, with its riots and assassinations, seemed to pass our town like a distant thunderstorm.

Here I went to Sunday school. Here I first read the Bible. Here I became an Eagle Scout and played five years of Texas football—badly. Here I was saved.

The serenity was an illusion, of course, superbly maintained by a population that fought hard to remain unscathed by upheaval and change. My mother and father moved to Dallas in 1965, two years after the assassination of John F. Kennedy, and that event remained very much in the air, though rarely mentioned, especially in the Park Cities where the president had never been much loved. When I was little, walking on our street, I found hypodermic needles in the grass, and one of my babysitters smoked marijuana with her friends and got caught. Later, when I was in third grade and the Vietnam War was in full swing, I got in trouble for instigating a pretend war in the classroom of a teacher who had a son of draft age. And when I was a little older than that, a girl was kidnapped off the street near our middle school and a panic hit the community. Everyone kept their eyes out for a particular kind of car. The police found the girl in the nick of time, tied up in a room in north Dallas, a small homemade coffin underneath her bed. And finally, much later, as if to underscore the total reckless unmanageability of life, Highland Park produced John Hinckley, the man who shot Ronald Reagan, among my neighborhood's most beloved saints.

DENTON, TEXAS, WHERE Don and Lillie McWhinney live, lies about thirty-five miles north of Highland Park. Their church, Denton Bible Church, has around 4,500 members, technically fitting the definition of a megachurch, according to the Hartford Institute for Religious Studies, which has extensively studied the phenomenon. According to Hartford, a megachurch must have at least 2,000 members in attendance per week to qualify for the title, and 10 percent of American houses of worship belong in this category, most of them in the South and the West. People at Denton Bible dislike the term; the church's nationally known senior pastor, Tommy Nelson, dismisses it. To him, the word "megachurch" means something showy and empty, where Sunday morning services tend to be light on scripture and the music favors the popular culture and overshadows the message.

Nelson isn't just the chief administrator at Denton Bible. He embodies its innermost principles and has instilled in members like Don and Lillie a sense that the work of Christian disciples should be rigorously bound to scripture. He wouldn't care for the term "fundamentalist," knowing its connotations, but he is completely fundamental in his theology. The shape of the faith must be determined by the word of God, and his sermons are among the meatiest that I've ever heard, dense with Bible verses, thick with exegesis, bulging with anecdote and vivid expostulation. Nelson has been with Denton Bible for more than three decades, since 1977, despite various offers, most recently to pastor the U.S. Military Academy at West Point. He turned down the opportunity for two reasons, he said: one, because he would have had to shepherd cadets of non-Christian faiths in good conscience; and two, because his work at Denton Bible continues to satisfy. At DBC, as it is called, he teaches twenty times a week. He has a media ministry that broadcasts his sermons around the world, and he has written at least a dozen books on a variety of subjects. He has developed a yearlong program for young men, his "Young Guns," he calls them, a deep immersion in scripture, evangelism, and what is called "discipleship," a term that signifies the teaching and nurturing skills that one brings to the spreading of the news that Jesus Christ is the son of God.

That program began in 1990 with four men in their early twenties living in his home, according to his rules, unencumbered by marriage or children, with no commitment to anything or anyone but God. "Steroids for the committed guy," he has called the 500-hour course of study, which now has thirty participants per year. The Young Guns go on to become missionaries, Christian community leaders of various kinds, or pastors in their own right. Don McWhinney introduced me to two of them, John Brown and Mike Scheer, the former a slender, bookish, ex-Buddhist intellectual from a ranching family in Levelland, Texas, the latter an ex-baseball player from Louisville, Kentucky. Tommy Nelson has made room for both kinds of men in his church. He himself is a former college baseball star who passed up a chance to play with the Cincinnati Reds, and his son John made the majors with a spot on the St. Louis Cardinals. At the same time, Nelson quotes Nietzsche and Marx in conversation, loves to read and write poetry, and considers himself a natural-born introvert. He's a man's man, in just about every way, but he's also an intellectual, and he's created a church that is very much focused on the thinking man's experience of an inerrant, evangelical faith.

ON THAT SUNDAY morning, Tommy would be giving the sermon, and I was eager to hear him. At dawn, I drove to the McWhinneys, and Don met me at the door in slacks and a short-sleeve shirt. Lillie was dressed in a kelly green blouse, a pale green sweater, and a long skirt. They gave me a Bible in a brown leather cover, notes scribbled in its margins, a supple object, almost alive in my hands. They had their own Bibles. Don drove, and Lillie sat in the backseat. At first, she and I spoke about her work running the home office of the DBC missionary operation. She told me about a time when some of her missionaries had been killed, and Rick Warren, author of *The Purpose-Driven Life*, had called her office out of the blue and offered to help the children of the deceased.

"Thanks to him, all those kids will have college educations," she told me.

Don interrupted. "John, let me change the subject for a few moments."

It was an oddly formal interjection, though much in keeping with his style of address.

"Our son Tedd has been killed."

I'm sure that the blood rushed from my face. I could hardly speak.

We had been chatting about nothing at all. Their demeanor had been subdued, but it was Sunday, a reflective time. Don had kept unusually silent, but he was at the wheel. Their faces had given nothing away of tragedy, or maybe I hadn't known them long enough to know. I was horrified and mortified at once to be in that car, taking up the time of two people whom I barely knew and who had just been plunged into one of the worst moments of their lives.

Don continued. "He was apparently walking along westbound near LBJ Freeway. We don't know what time it happened."

I stammered incoherent condolences.

"That's all right," Don reassured me. "We thought about having somebody come by this morning and take you to church . . ."

I tried to tell him that it would have been perfectly fine to do so, but he gently cut me off. "The best way for you to help us with our grief is you just stick with us. We've had our pain, we've had our tears, and there will be more to come." He didn't linger on that subject. "All we know is that he was hit, it was hit-and-run. The police are investigating."

Don told me that they'd called their other two sons—John, a writer in London, and Jimmy, a missionary in Shanghai—and the boys were making plans to fly home. They'd called their pastor and let him know. Tommy Nelson had offered to come by, but they had declined his offer. They'd called old friends from Baton Rouge to Birmingham, and those friends were driving to Denton for the memorial service, the date and time of which hadn't yet been set. Don had called in to his job at Marketplace Ministries, where he served as a chaplain to businesses in the Dallas area, and made arrangements to be out of the office.

Seamlessly, he changed the subject from logistical matters to larger, deeper visions. "The joy for us, John, is that he's over the finish line. The battle is over."

Don's words had their usual broadcaster's cadence, but tinged with a deeper gravity.

"If we want to know where he is today, all we have to do is go to Revelation 21, and we read about a city that's fifteen hundred miles wide, and long and high. The ground floor alone is 225 million square miles." He paused in emotion. "It's a city surrounded by walls that are 200 feet thick, made of pure jasper."

Tears in her eyes, Lillie said, "Don's daddy had that whole chapter memorized."

Don turned again to the subject of his son Tedd. "If he could come back now," he said, "he wouldn't want to, and I don't think we would want him back in the way that he had to live, because he was just absolutely miserable, pushing people away from him. The interesting thing, however, is that he was walking west toward home." Don's voice broke. "He was our prodigal."

BY THE TIME we pulled into the parking lot, Lillie and Don had recovered somewhat. We sat in the car for a moment. I held Lillie's hand and put another hand on Don's shoulder, and he said, "As Christians, we have hope. The Bible says we can have sorrow, and pain, and tears through the night, but joy comes in the morning. It says in Psalm 116," another chapter that his father had memorized, "precious in the sight of the Lord is the death of his precious ones. The death of his saints." I got the feeling that Don was, in fact, explaining something to himself. "So God is more grieved over the combined grief that we have in this car because of the curse of sin in the world. He didn't want it to be this way, but he gave us freedom. He gave Adam and Eve freedom, and they made bad choices, and when they did, it affected all of their children. One of these days," he concluded, "the venue will change, we believe, but we're not here to set dates. We're not here to make a big deal out of that today. But just, our hope is looking forward to the future."

Lillie wiped her eyes and prepared herself to face people. We had come late so that most members would be inside the sanctuary, and they planned to leave early to avoid a scene. As we got out of the car, Don said something that made me laugh and took me aback at the same time.

"We thought we'd get you in the car before we told you," he said in an effort at humor.

"We didn't want you running away from us," Lillie added.

"I would never have done that," I said.

"We didn't want you to say, Oh no, we can't do this," Don laughed. We were all laughing. "We didn't want to leave you any options."

"THAT'S SO CREEPY," said my old friend Jim when I mentioned this exchange. Jim is a self-described stone-cold atheist who also claims to be a small-town Calvinist at heart. What he means is that his basic belief system would never admit to the existence of a god or God, but that his moral universe borrows heavily from the mores of the religious people who settled the small towns and cities of Michigan, where he's from. Renounce Jesus and worship Satan, fine; but tell a lie or act the hypocrite, and you can go to hell.

In Jim's opinion, the McWhinneys clearly used their son's death to evangelize me, and the mere thought struck him as repellent. It confirmed every suspicion he'd ever had about these people. They talked about the love of Jesus but practiced a loveless Machiavellianism when it came to recruitment, their behavior an echo of the whole, cruel Christian story of a god not just willing but eager to murder his own children in order to extend his power and prestige. For Jim, using your own child's death to evangelize was worse than a moral breach: it indicated an entirely warped being. People who would do such a thing, their behavior suggested, had never loved their child in the first place.

I thought about it then and many times since, and I think that Jim may have been right about their intentions. But is his condemnation just? I wonder. It probably wouldn't occur to Don and Lillie that it would be wrong to turn their son's passing into an opportunity to help someone else into the kingdom of heaven. It would be a reflex impulse, as much as anything else. But it is also a central commandment of their belief system. In a part of our *60 Minutes* interview that never aired, one of the authors of the Left Behind series, Jerry Jenkins, compared the injunction to spread the gospel to knowing that a neighbor had terminal cancer. If he knew and cared about the neighbor, Jenkins said, how could he not tell him that he had cancer? If he refrained, wouldn't he, Jenkins, be the immoral one? The McWhinneys would agree with Jenkins on this point. Nonbelievers do have a cancer—it's called sin— and they must be told. God holds believers responsible. From their point of view, it would be "creepy," at the very least, not to use any means necessary to convey that message.

But I don't think evangelism was the only motive. Far more important was their sense that God had sent me as a solace, and they would not refuse the gift. To put it more plainly, they needed a son in that hour of grief and I fit the bill. At one point, almost inadvertently, Lillie even called me "her son." Tedd was forty-one when he died. I was forty-two. I was a Texan. I had come back into their lives literally hours before their real son died, bearing flowers, telling them my stories. Their other two sons wouldn't arrive for another day or so. It was an emotional transference, no doubt in my mind, and the evangelism followed upon it in dutiful habit, not the other way around.

WE ENTERED THE sanctuary of the church, a large place that sticks in my memory as a vessel of shadows. Nothing stood out architecturally. My eye wasn't drawn to stained glass or dazzled by a sound system. There was a nondescript quality that must have been intentional, an anti-megachurch vibe. Organ music and strings softly played. Someone handed me a program containing the latest news about the congregation, a list that might be found in any independent Bible church in the country on a summer morning in the United States. Vacation Bible school would begin in July. At DBC, a small notice informed, there would be no passing of the plate; wooden Giving

Boxes at two separate entrances allowed people to make their gifts discreetly. Female "prayer warriors" were needed. "If you would like to participate in a PRAYER CHAIN, fill out the information below and drop in the Giving Box and you will be contacted with details." Another bulletin requested prayer for mission trips to Uganda, Romania, and Kenya.

The service began with an important symbolic emphasis on tradition, the congregation rising for a hymn that I had recalled from Sunday morning services at Highland Park Presbyterian, "Joyful, Joyful, We Adore Thee," set to the strains of Beethoven's "Ode to Joy" in the Ninth Symphony, words by Henry Van Dyke. It was a moment that I have always feared, whenever in church. I cannot carry a tune, but I feel that it is impolite not to try. That hymn was followed by a contemporary tune that had all the heft of Muzak.

Tommy Nelson stepped forward in a long maroon robe. This was my first glimpse of him, and even then, from far away, he was a shockingly large figure, well over six feet, with a glaze of hair on an oval block of skull. He was totemic, as if carved from northern wood. He would speak for most of the next hour, and what he would say would shock me in more ways than one, but I should have known, right from the start, what to expect.

He began in his resonant, superbly modulated voice with the book of Acts, chapter 14, in which the apostles Paul and Barnabas do miracles and are mistaken by the crowds for deities. Paul and Barnabas try to tell the crowds that they're not gods themselves. Their miracles reflect the one true God who, the pastor intoned, does not leave himself in the world without witness.

He finished with this initial reading and made a brief announcement. "Don and Lillie McWhinney lost their firstborn son yesterday," he said. "A lot of grief over the last ten or fifteen years has come to an end, and so our hearts go out to the McWhinneys."

He asked everyone to bow their heads, and he began to pray. "Father in heaven, as we move into the teaching of your word this morning, our hearts go out to Don and Lillie, for the loss of this first son." During prayer, I always close my eyes and bow my head as a sign of deference to the prevailing spirit, but it's also habit. If someone is praying, and I keep my head up, and my eyes open, I feel as if my forehead has become a target. "Only you know the great struggles that went on inside of Tedd, and yet from an early age, he had no doubts where his salvation lay." Tommy's voice took on a tone of timeless sorrow, as if McWhinney ghosts had entered the room, one by one, as if he reached to them with his voice, back to the Civil War and beyond. "His salvation lay in the faith of his *grandfathers*, his *grandmothers*, his *father*, his *mother*, his *brothers*."

The use of those elemental words summoned a presence that lingered before vanishing. Tommy prayed on. "This morning, would you draw our eyes to the beauty of thy word, the excellence of Christ, to the condition of man, that we are guilty, whether we sit in the presence of stained glass and hear a gospel presented and renounce it, or whether we renounce the god of creation and substitute deities in his place."

He prayed for more specific needs. "For our country, that very quickly, Lord, you would establish peace there in Iraq, that our men and our women might return to us. Give grace to our president and all who surround him." And finally, he addressed an appeal to people like me. "I pray if there is one here this morning, Father, who does not have that assurance of what to rest in outside of himself after death, on the person of Christ, who came to fulfill your promised word, I pray for his heart to be illumined."

We arrived at the heart of the morning, the sermon.

## chapter 9

# Words

*I* *cannot* think of a more incendiary, less merciful subject than that which Tommy Nelson preached that morning. I had come into the sanctuary with two stricken, grieving parents and expected words of compassion. What we received, to my ears, was cruel and complete, the definition in full of the gulf in sensibility that divides Christians, one from another, and the country. For that reason, I repeat it here at great length. The sermon had body, like a miniature globe of the world as seen by millions of Americans in thousands of churches, detailed by a master orator, drawn as large as the world in scope, as deep and wide and old as the universe. I heard the words, of course, with different ears than my companions. For Don and Lillie, the sermon must have resounded with solace and truth and hope. Everything that I loathed gave them, if only briefly, the promise that they must have sought. I had forged a bond with Don and Lillie, and I wanted to be there for them, hold their hands, sit beside them, and do whatever small thing I could to make these hours less difficult. But the bond could only go so far.

Tommy asked the flock at Denton Bible to open to the book of Romans. "We have looked at a number of problem issues over the last few weeks," he commenced, "and this is one you hear quite often. What about the fellow that has never heard the gospel? What about the heathen in Africa, the heathen in Borneo, the heathen in Australia, in the outback, the *heathen* in Coppell, Texas?"

That got a laugh. Coppell, Texas, evoked, at best, the exoticism of a McDonald's. Tommy has a gift for dropping grenades of wit into the fire and brimstone, but the wit never quite undercuts the sense of rebuke. When he says "heathen," he means it, but he's also aware of the word's humorous possibilities. He rarely used his hands or even his body, like other preachers I saw. The movement lay in the sound. "Does God save on the curve?" he asked an attentive congregation. "I mean, if you never hear, can you be saved on the curve, if you've merely been a good guy—and we call that responding to the light that you have—will he impute that to you as righteousness?"

TOMMY PROCEEDED TO sketch out the ills of the entire American civilization, as he saw it, and the whole thing seemed directed right at me. Early on, my heart began to pound with anger, guilt, and fear, just as it had done at that first lunch with Don and Lillie.

"The Bible is not silent on this," he told us. "It's very clear. Like a lot of times, it's not the answer that we always want. That's why we need the revelation of God, to free us from our own intuitions."

In my mind, I began to debate with him. I categorically rejected this last notion. What is wrong per se with intuition? Don't soldiers in war rely on intuition to survive? Don't women use their intuition to avoid dangerous men and find the right ones? Don't children use their intuition to identify predatory adults? Old books are more likely to get us killed than our instincts, I argued back, more likely to become manuals for evil than our own natural intuition. I knew what he would say. I suppose that I've been arguing in my head with someone like him for most of my life. And I could hear him argue back faintly, that's a mighty optimistic assessment of where our intuition leads.

He asked us to turn to Romans, chapter 1. "The first thing the Bible says on this issue is that all men have a knowledge of God, that there is not a man anywhere on planet Earth that does not have before him and in him a knowledge of the infinite, personal God."

Most of the time, Tommy didn't so much as nod at the modern attempt to speak in gender-blind terms. He used "man" and "men" for everyone. The wrath of God is poured out on men.

He said: "Romans, chapter 1, Paul is speaking, and in verse 18, he says the wrath of God is revealed, and that's in the present tense. He doesn't say the wrath of God *will* someday be revealed. He says it is presently being poured out on the cultures of the earth who suppress the truth in unrighteousness." He applied a layman's exegesis. "The word 'suppress' means to hold something down. It means that you refuse to admit something. It means it's like a beach ball underneath the water that wants to pop up to the top, but you keep the natural tendency from taking place." He returned to Paul. "These men, he says, suppress truth in unrighteousness. It's not that they do unrighteousness out of ignorance. They do unrighteousness in light of what they *know* is there."

All people instinctively know and see the truth of God in nature, he told us, but they reject the knowledge. Instead, they worship false idols. And that's vile.

"They exchange the glory of the incorruptible God for an image in the form of corruptible man," he said, and the words sounded dry and dirty in his mouth, as if he wanted to spit them out, "in the form of birds, four-footed animals, and now in the form of crawling creatures, the *snake*," and at the utterance of that noun, snake, his voice dropped what seemed an octave or two, and it was a chilling, horrible sound, as if a bolt of repugnance had gone through him, as if he would kill the creature right there with his own hands if he could, "and in verse 24, you've got the word 'reprobation.' God now acts in judgment."

The term "reprobation" had a haunted, exciting, ancient sound. It signaled the direction of the sermon from afar: Sodom and Gomorrah. Even before that, the mention of the snake hinted that we were entering darker territory, perilous worlds where no light came. I wondered how everyone else in the room processed reprobation. Did the word sound fancy and academic? Or did it sound to others as it did to me? Did these Bible church folks think themselves above reprobation? Or were they mired in it? Did anyone in that room besides me feel a certain thrill at the sound? There had to be sodomites in the room, tucked away. There always were, as I discovered—the sons, fathers, mothers, and daughters of every large congregation in America. How would they hear that word?

"You have made an animal of God," Tommy Nelson charged us, "and animals do not hold you accountable. Animals don't hold you to right and wrong. And so now God says, I give you over, and I will let your culture do anything it wants. That," he told us, "is called reprobation. It's the judgment of God, or in verse 18, it is the wrath of God. The culture doesn't wait until hell to experience wrath. The culture experiences wrath right then, and you see what they do here in verse 26," he wielded the Bible like a shovel, dumping more coal into the flames of his oratory, "God gave them over to degrading passions."

Here he changed his tone a bit; he halted the pace of his own cosmic drama, set in motion by Paul, as if wanting to make sure his audience received the next part of the narrative with a readied mind. "It's interesting," he said, "that in the list of sins, Paul doesn't list homosexuality. Paul lists homosexuality as *the* visible evidence of the wrath of God on a culture."

In other words, homosexuality is either far worse than sin or far, far better; it is, in fact, an attribute of the divine. But Tommy didn't mean that exactly.

He concluded his aside on homosexuality with utmost damnation. "That is when culture has reached the point of virtually no return."

And it occurred to me that he was saying something quite monstrous, and that he himself might not even be aware of the implications of his own line of reasoning. He was suggesting that cultures like National Socialism in Germany in the 1930s, which had persecuted and murdered Christians, or Stalinist communism of the 1930s, which had banished all faith from society, were more just, more favorable in the eyes of God than our own culture; those cultures had, at least, persecuted and murdered homosexuals. They had taken steps to eradicate this "visible evidence of the wrath of God on a culture." As a student of twentieth-century history, how else could I possibly read such a statement? In his magisterial book about the church and the Jews, *Constantine's Sword*, James Carroll makes a strong case that Christianity, from its inception, contained the seeds of the religious crimes committed in its own name, and here it seemed to me I saw the truth of his argument, uttered as its own form of justice in the mouth of a gigantic Texan Protestant. On the other hand, if I could not get past this idea, I thought, if I could not overcome my sense that his statement somehow forgave Nazism and communism, then I would never be able to understand his point of view. I would simply consider him a ruthless barbarian while he would never have seen himself in the company of Nazis and communists and therefore would never in a million years accept my argument. I had misunderstood or misinterpreted or deliberately misconstrued his words in order to deny the validity of his larger point.

But Tommy had moved on to the subject of pit bulls.

"If you take a pit bull and chain him up," he began in a voice brimming with pure physical menace as it grew quiet, "that pit bull will not go beyond that chain. If you take away that chain, there may be just a few moments where that pit bull will act out of memory, and out of an echo of the past, and will only go the length of the chain." It was possible in the shadows of the sanctuary to imagine the slavering brute, eyes black, teeth razor sharp, brain visibly working at the new dispensation. "But then he starts to realize nothing binds him, and he lives out his newfound freedom, and there is *devastation*," Tommy's voice changed again, going low, "and there is *pain*."

Here was the point, for anyone in the audience who had not quite grasped the meaning of the dog. "God doesn't treat those cultures who reject him as innocent sociological phenomena. He doesn't treat them as an evolving religious system." He was referring to terms of anthropology, quieting the intellectual objections that he could probably feel sprouting around him in the moist darkness. "He treats them as a culture that has a revelation of him, and that rejects him."

We moved from the evidence of the natural world to the evidence embodied in the conscience of the species, riding from one subject to another on the back of his voice, which carried us like a stallion carries a woman in the movies. His body, as far as I could tell, hardly moved at all, and yet his voice seemed to have telekinetic possibilities.

He cited C. S. Lewis: "Men may call themselves atheists till someone takes their oranges. Then, all at once, they instinctively, they intuitively say:

that is wrong." Can a Protestant sermon in the United States be complete these days without a word from C. S. Lewis? Every preacher, every scholar, every Young Life leader I met brought up Lewis. He is the closest thing to an intellectual celebrity in modern Christianity, the scorned equal of all those giants of twentieth-century thought, the David to the Goliaths of Marx, Freud, and Nietzsche. Tommy continued: "Men may act like there is no God, but they don't react like there's no God. You've heard me say it before. Men may act atheistic, but they react like seventeenth-century English Puritans. They want to be treated morally, uprightly, judicially."

In my mind, I conceded this point. He was right. We do. And, he said, through our conscience, which is the moral part of our consciousness, we are called to recognize God. Our own minds insist that we call him real and bow before him. "You can find Americans all over the place, within the shadow of church spires, that have no knowledge of the deity, the death, and the justification by faith in Jesus Christ, but they are called to seek the God of mercy. The Australian man in the outback is called to seek him. The Native American in the 1800s in the deserts of the Chiricahua was called to seek a god whom he knew to be a moral and righteous God, but he didn't, and man doesn't. They are all guilty."

In my years of churchgoing, I had never heard such an inflexible line on salvation. It had been out there, I'm sure, but none had spoken it aloud. It was a truly horrific message to my ears, the hard knife of Calvinism. He kept going.

"Men are guilty," he said, "whether they ever hear the gospel or not. They are guilty." And then Tommy made it personal. "They are guilty in Highland Park, and they are guilty in the Congo. They have replaced God in Highland Park, and they have replaced God in the Congo. Both suppress truth."

DON MCWHINNEY INSISTED later that he'd never told Tommy about my Highland Park origins. Tommy knew that I would be in the audience, Don told me, and nothing else. So maybe he just got lucky, I thought, sitting there, isolated in that room, quite possibly the only man from Highland Park in the sanctuary. Or maybe, I honestly thought in the back of my mind, with a sense of shame, God is real and has divinely inspired this piece of the message for my ears only. Or maybe, just maybe, Tommy Nelson had Googled me. Later, when I asked him, he denied it.

"Are you with me so far?" Tommy asked us, reiterating briefly before moving into the final point of his message. "This is what the Bible teaches. All men have an awareness of God, and that awareness of God should cause them to glorify him and seek his mercy, but men don't."

"And that is why," Tommy continued, "we conclude by going to the very end of your Bible to the book of Revelation." The pages fluttered and whispered, and I thought of Don and his heavenly city with walls of jasper, Revelation 21, memorized for all time by him and his father, and for all I knew, his father's father. "Your last point is this—not only *can* God save anyone out of the guilty cultures, God *will*. In Revelation, chapter 7, verse 9, I want you to see who is in the presence of God. Verse 9," and he began to read, "I looked, and behold, a great multitude which no one could count, from every nation and all tribes and peoples and tongues, standing before the throne and before the lamb."

Tedd McWhinney would be there. His parents had told me so in the most explicit terms. The immensity of the consolation came home to me.

Tommy's sermon rose to its moment of great hope and glory after the dark despairs of rejection and reprobation, and it felt a little like those old hymns that had started the service. "So God will populate heaven. Just like the Ark had one of every species, God will populate eternity with one, at least, someone, from every place. You know why? Because they believed in Christ. You know why they believed in Christ? Because they felt their heart pricked at their own sin. You know why they felt their heart pricked at their own sin? You know why they turned from their pagan religion to seek after God? Because God called them. You know why God called them? God chose them. And whom he chooses, he calls, and whom he calls, he justifies, and whom he justifies, he glorifies."

He told us some anecdotes of redemption: about himself, about missionaries in the Pacific, about a pagan from Africa. He let these stories linger a moment in the air. It was almost over, but he wanted to make sure. Had everyone in the room absolutely, completely understood?

"Can God get who God wants? You bet. Can God choose, call, convert anyone he wants to? He shall. What about the man who has never heard? He has heard, and he is guilty. But you know what? *You've* heard now." I felt one last time that he was speaking directly to me. "If you had an excuse before this morning, you don't now."

HE BADE US to stand. He said a brief prayer. We sang one short hymn about the name of Jesus, and the service ended. Most of it had been Tommy Nelson. The McWhinneys didn't say much, filing out ahead of me. We didn't talk about the sermon. We left the cool shadows of the sanctuary of Denton Bible and made our way into the livid sun of a Texas Sunday morning, in which Tedd McWhinney remained absent, but perhaps not so far gone as he had been when we walked in.

book II

*The Truth*

## chapter 10

# The Great Commission

*W*hen a Bible-believing Christian talks about truth, as Tommy Nelson does, he is not talking about a theory or an idea, an ideal or an ideology. He is not speaking about a thing conditioned by culture or crafted ultimately by language or affected by tides and times or rendered different from generation to generation. As Tommy pointed out on another Sunday morning in yet another sermon on the book of Romans, which he likes to call "the freeze-dried" version of the Bible, the very essence of biblical doctrine, when the apostle Paul went to Rome to deliver his message, he did not come as a philosopher or teacher. He delivered the explicit word of God, given to him by God, in the language of God. In other words, Paul possessed nothing more and nothing less than the ultimate fact of existence, raw and undiluted. Neither the Greek language nor first-century Roman culture adulterated that fact's purity or shaped its content. Jesus was the son of God, born of the Virgin Mary. Crucified, dead, and buried, he rose again to redeem all of humanity, first the Jew, then the Gentile. And that message, as Tommy sees it, remains the very same today. The gospel is not conditioned by anything. It does not dissolve in water or burn in fire. It is Truth. It is final. And this is how it is taught from one end of the country to another, every Sunday morning, every Wednesday night, to tens of millions of Americans.

In the early Christian church, in those first centuries after the death of an obscure Jewish leader on a cross, news of Jesus spread across provinces ruled by demigods and goddesses and haunted by spirits of the most local origin, inhabitants of rock, tree, water, and hearth, creatures whose last folkloric traces can still be found in less developed pockets of eastern Europe and the Balkans, vampires, werewolves, witches, and their demoted kin. A cosmic daily fistfight took place among these deities, among which Christ emerged as just another contender, admittedly with a Jewish pedigree, which gave his case a unique flavor in the Roman Empire. Rome allowed the Jews special tolerance in worship, exempting them from the obligation to make ritual sacrifice to the emperor, and therefore to worship him. The cult of Jesus came out of Judaism, and so was identified with it at first, as one more camp in a fractious religious environment, but as time passed, observers grasped that Christians were more problematic than Jews. They demanded special status in the metaphysical sense. As the Jews received preference from Rome, so the Christians claimed to have the preference of heaven.

The apostle Paul is the key figure in this effort, one of the most effective, beloved, and despised figures in human history, a sojourner across the eastern Mediterranean, pounding down doctrine wherever it starts to fray. My King James Bible from high school shows me that I was taught with special emphasis the book of Romans. I can remember hearing adults and fellow students saying that they preferred Romans over every other book. In my Bible, highlighted in yellow magic marker when I was sixteen or seventeen, Romans 6:23 told me, "For the wages of sin is death; but the gift of God is eternal life through Jesus Christ our Lord."

In Romans, Paul exhorts believers to hold fast to the true faith. Distorted accounts of the teachings of Jesus, and there were many from the point of view of the early believers, had to be attacked. Paul himself had been accused of encouraging Christians to sin and had to correct the misinterpretation. Above all, Jesus must not be seen as just another god. He must not be mistaken for Mithras or Cybele or Osiris, objects of the netherworld cults of the era, or interpreted as a particularly gifted and talented man. He must not be confused for a teacher or a philosopher using wildly poetic language. He must be identified as a living human being who had walked the earth in a specific time and place, namely, Roman Judaea, who had come to fulfill a thousand years of Jewish prophecy by offering his life as a perfect sacrifice to God in exchange for the salvation of fallen humanity.

Our first encounter with Paul, and the initial spread of this news through a demon-haunted world, constitutes the central tale in the book of Acts, written by Luke, which begins, in my King James, with these words: "The former treatise have I made, O Theophilus, of all that Jesus began both to do and teach, until the day in which he was taken up." Here we have the real beginnings of Christianity, the launch of the history of the faith, as opposed to the life of the crucified Jew upon which the faith was based. In Acts 1:4–5, after Christ returns from the dead, he orders the apostles to stay in Jerusalem and wait for "the promise of the Father." He tells them, "ye shall be baptized with the Holy Ghost not many days hence."

Those words echoed what Jesus had said earlier to the disciples, in the face of their doubt on a mountain in Galilee. As recounted in Matthew 28:18–20, he utters one of the most important passages in the written history of the human race. "All power is given unto me in heaven and in earth," Jesus said. "Go ye therefore, and teach all nations, baptizing them in the name of the Father, and of the Son, and of the Holy Ghost: Teaching them to observe all things whatsoever I have commanded you: and lo, I am with you always, even unto the end of the world." These words are decisive in terms of their impact on the development of Christianity, and their significance for an American sense of identity can't be overstated. The Pilgrims were following their lead. So were the Puritans. And so were many of those who headed west in wagon trains.

The passage has come to be known among evangelicals as the Great Commission, a kind of creed within the gospel, laying out in capsule form the entire obligation of a believing people, setting the stage for the creation of a church, for the central activity of that church, and for the total purpose of that church through time till the end of time. Neither James Dobson nor Jerry Falwell, neither Tommy Nelson nor Bob Davidson, can be understood without an understanding of the Great Commission. If you've ever asked yourself what it is precisely that a missionary does, the answer is here. A missionary devotes his or her life to following the central command of Christ to his church, repeated for emphasis in the final moment of his earthly divinity. God didn't implant a chip in every human mind at birth. People must be told the truth. Jesus places the responsibility for this effort squarely and completely on the shoulders of the believers.

The early followers of Jesus, blessed by the Holy Spirit, were given the abilities to heal the sick and dying, to perform miracles and predict the future. Armed with these weapons, they took the gospel out of Palestine into the distant reaches of the Roman Empire and beyond, to Africa and the Indian subcontinent. They believed that Christ would return imminently and worked feverishly under that assumption to convert as many people as possible. Slowly, as that first generation died off, it became clear that God might not return for his people anytime soon, and the revelation of Jesus had to be maintained in a single disciplined form.

In his letters, which make the bulk of the New Testament, Paul set that form. Three hundred years after his death by martyrdom in Rome, his writings became the state-sanctioned truth of the later Roman Empire. In a turn that might have been inconceivable to the first apostles, the Roman emperor Constantine saw a sign in the sky above a battlefield north of Rome and embraced the God of the Christians as his own. With one notable exception, the era of persecution had ended. The era of worldly sovereignty had begun. Called together by Constantine in 325 A.D., the leaders of the Christian world assembled in the town of Nicaea and formulated a creed that would survive dispute for most of two millennia, the Nicene Creed, which begins, "I believe in one God, the Father Almighty, maker of heaven and earth, and of all things visible and invisible," a phrase that I have uttered hundreds of times in my life from the time that I was seven or eight.

These words in my mouth: nothing more than the fruit of the Great Commission. The disciples might well have kept Jesus to themselves. His death and even his resurrection might have been their private affair. But Jesus made it clear that they should speak about him, that their central purpose after his death was to spread the word into the reprobate world. He had come. And thanks to the Great Commission, he remains a living reality to millions, rather than a historical footnote to the Roman Empire.

## chapter 11

## The World

*M*ore than a year after the death of Tedd McWhinney, a few months after Tommy Nelson stepped down from the pulpit of Denton Bible Church, crippled by a bout of unexpected and unprecedented depression, I sat in the pews of Tremont Temple Baptist Church in Boston and watched a mustering of the faithful. Tremont has one of the more beautiful sanctuaries that I have ever seen, an art deco masterpiece beneath columns of yellow veined marble and a coffered basilica ceiling, painted pale blue. On a gilt arch above the stage ran the opening line of the Great Commission: "Go ye therefore and teach all nations, baptizing them in the name of the Father, the Son, and the Holy Ghost."

The church, founded by Free Baptists in 1839 and eventually located in a former theater, lies in the heart of historic old Boston, right on the Freedom Trail, across the street from the Granary Burying Ground, where Paul Revere, John Hancock, Samuel Adams, and the victims of the Boston Massacre are buried, and down the street from the King's Chapel Burying Ground, last resting place of Mary Wilton, one of the Mayflower passengers. Between these two burial grounds lie the one hundred and fifty years between the arrival of the Pilgrims at Plymouth Rock and the American Revolution; and between these two milestones lies the period of the First Great Awakening in the 1730s and '40s, a time of fervent religious revival. The location didn't feel coincidental to the occasion.

At a meeting with journalists in September 2006, the president of the United States, George W. Bush, speculated that the country might be undergoing what he called a Third Awakening. At a press conference the following week, when asked about the comment, President Bush replied, "I'd just read a book on Abraham Lincoln, and his presidency was right around the time of what they called the Second Awakening, and I was curious to know whether or not these smart people felt like there was any historical parallels. I also said that I had run for office the first time to change a culture . . . helping to change a culture in which each of us are responsible for the decisions we make in life. In other words, ushering in a responsibility era."

When believers heard those words, they knew that he wasn't talking about responsibility, or only responsibility. He was talking about God. The Awakenings are explicitly religious movements that change American society and culture. The first began in 1739 in my adopted hometown of Northampton, Massachusetts, under the auspices of Jonathan Edwards. According to New England records, churches filled, a new and godly spirit touched human relations, and the effect lasted decades, fueling opposition to both slavery and British rule. Since that time, there have been at least two more awakenings, and from one end of the country to the other, people have told me that we are on the verge of another one.

If that's true, New England will be one of the last places to feel it. In an irony of American history, the birthplace of American Puritan faith has become the last bastion of resistance to its renewal. I had come to Boston to see a program by Focus on the Family, the organization led by Dr. James Dobson, the most influential member of the conservative Christian movement in the United States. The main speaker at the event had a name that sounded like a brand: Del Tackett. He was a former air force officer who had been a vice commander at NORAD at Cheyenne Mountain in Colorado Springs, and later an intelligence official in George H. W. Bush's White House. For the past fifteen years, Tackett had worked as a teacher in the field of Christian worldview studies, founding his own tiny seminary in Colorado Springs and later joining the Focus on the Family Institute, which offers a one-semester curriculum on Christian worldview to college students from around the world. Tackett had come to godless Boston for two nights to talk about something called the Truth Project to a crowd of five hundred Christians from around New England.

The Truth Project is Tackett's brainchild, first conceived during his stint at the White House, when he began to discover the nation's Christian heritage in the buildings and history around him, a past that he found hidden beneath decades of secular culture and government. But his two-day lecture, which he had previously given to crowds of a thousand or more in North Carolina, Illinois, Oregon, and Colorado, is not first and foremost political, except in the broadest sense, in the sense that the fight to save Christianity could be seen as a political struggle between God and his enemies. The Truth Project, he tells his audiences, must be seen as an act of righteous hostility in a campaign of spiritual warfare.

THE ENEMY IN this fight: the world. When secular people use that term, "the world," they mean something abstract and large. It can mean almost anything—from the public eye to a refined state of being, as in "worldliness"; from a subculture, as in "the world of skateboarders," to the global community. The world is value-neutral, a placeholder for other, more specific terms. But in my walk as a believer, it had another meaning. It was an epithet, an imprecation. I am tempted to call it a curse. "The world!" It exists as a term of opprobrium that believers use for everything that tempts them away from God, evoking the very antithesis of holiness, the trap of this corrupted earth in which the devil, the flesh, and the desires of the heart endlessly fester. The world, in this usage, is grounded in many places in scripture, but most pointedly in 1 John 4:6, the basis for Tackett's comments above: "They are of the world; therefore they speak of the world, and the world heareth them. We are of God: he that knoweth God heareth us; he that is not of God heareth not us. Hereby we know the spirit of truth, and the spirit of error."

The "world" encompasses all manner of banal darkness. If you do especially well at sales in your business and take inordinate pride in that fact, you have begun to feel the creep of the world. If you buy an especially flashy car, build an especially big home, enjoy the company of especially beautiful and witty friends, you may be showing signs of having succumbed to the world. None of these things are bad in and of themselves; they become bad if they, as pleasures, replace God. God has created no bad thing, scripture tells Christians, but evil in the human heart, and the wickedness of the fallen angel Satan, have poisoned creation. And poisoned creation is the essence of the world, which has endless means to seduce humankind. If you go see a Hollywood movie instead of attending Wednesday night Bible study, that's the work of the world. If you would rather check out Internet pornography than make love to your wife, that's the world, too, and if you would like to have anal sex with your wife because you saw it on the Internet, that, too, might be understood as the influence of the world. Increasingly, if you call yourself a Christian and yet support gay marriage, a woman's right to choose, and the Darwinian view of the earth's origins, you might be suspected of contamination by the world, because these positions stem from arguments made outside of God's word; they may be persuasive in and of themselves; they might even be true, in the strictest sense, but that's beside the point. Truth with a small *t* is a favored weapon of the enemy.

Del Tackett believes that, in the cosmic war, the world has won, hands down, and most American believers have become unredeemed "captives." He says explicitly that he works to set the captives free, that the Truth Project is a prison break, financed to the tune of $3 million and hatched by the most powerful force in modern conservative Christianity, Focus on the Family, whose founder and leader, James Dobson, has insisted that every single employee of his organization take the course.

Dobson, a child psychologist and radio personality known to millions of his fans as Dr. Dobson, wasn't mentioned much at the Truth Project conference in Boston, but his sense of engagement hung in the air. A few days after the Boston event, his organization cosponsored the Washington Briefing, a self-described "values voters summit," which brought a thousand conservative Christian activists to D.C. to talk about the midterm elections, which were two months away. Participants celebrated legislative victories, including the Broadcast Decency Act of 2005, the Fetus Farming Prohibition Act, the Freedom to Display the American Flag Act, and the Children's

Safety and Violent Crime Act, all of which had been signed into law in the previous six years. But at the heart of this conference, of greater concern, was voter apathy among the Christian base. For all the talk of victory, the well-warranted fear of a coming loss loomed over the proceedings. These legislative victories were merely temporary, a result of a happy alignment of forces in Washington, D.C. But the long-term prospects for a true Christian revival? To hear Tackett and his team tell it, they looked grim.

A FEW MONTHS before the Boston event, I paid a visit to Focus on the Family headquarters in Colorado Springs, a campus of corporate buildings at the northern end of the city, not very far from the U.S. Air Force Academy, at the other end of town from Cheyenne Mountain, where Tackett had served with distinction during the cold war. On an early June afternoon, I had a chat with Gary Alan Taylor, the project manager, and the man who knows most about the logistics of the operation.

In Boston, he was the first to take the stage, setting up the aftermath of the weekend. Everyone in attendance would receive a set of seven DVDs, twelve hours of material that make up the heart and soul of the Truth Project.

When I met him in Colorado Springs, Taylor had been at Focus for five years. Before that, he had been a historian with a specialty in early American history and then an admissions director at a small Christian college. He explained to me that the need for the Truth Project came straight out of the research done by George Barna, identifying a low percentage of so-called Christians who actually believed in the most basic biblical principles, including the divinity of Jesus and the inerrancy of scripture.

"Even born-again believers don't believe this stuff," he told me. We sat at a round table in a room with a video monitor and a DVD player. He said that most Christians have some vague sense of who they're supposed to be, but it's not quite enough to change their lives. "Most of us know what the problem is," he said. "We're fallen. We know what the solution is—accepting Christ as our Lord and Savior and attaining to him, and we know the outcome—God is fulfilling his kingdom. We are part of that story, and so the world around us at least makes some semblance of sense and order."

But that's not enough, he told me. A real biblical worldview would find all of the answers to life's problems in scripture. "It [The Truth Project] is based on the foundation that the scripture is the authoritative word of God. If you don't get that, then this is irrelevant to you. I think that's why it's not necessarily for a nonbeliever, because so much of what the Truth Project is about is relying on scripture, pointing everyone back to scripture, saying, okay, look . . . we do have the actual word of God."

"We've kinda got Sunday morning down," he went on, "but how do I make sense of the rest of my life? What does my Monday morning look like as I engage in my work, as I try to be a good husband or wife, as I try to raise children, as I deal with a difficult neighbor, as I'm just going through this fallen world? As I'm dealing with terrorism? How do I make sense of that? We've bifurcated spirituality and faith with everything else in our lives, and that doesn't make sense."

In the speech, and on the DVD, Tackett discusses every aspect of life. The program has been conceived as a "worldview tour," and one of the central images at the outset of the tour is a compass with four central points—north, south, east, west—and twelve intermediary points. Due north is truth; due east is God; due south is social order; due west is man. When Tackett takes up a subject for the first time, he'll say we're heading southwest, which means in this context a point halfway between the south of social order and the west of man; that is, we're going to talk about the state. Other categories are science, philosophy, ethics, church, community, family, law, arts and media, labor and history. On the DVD, Tackett stands in the middle of a lecture hall built at the Comcast studios in Denver to look like a tradition-bound classroom, à la Harvard, and filled with students of every race and gender.

The end result, says Taylor, if the experiment works, will be transformation of individuals, followed by transformation of communities, followed by national transformation. "Our prayer is that it won't be long before Boston has been taken back for the Lord," Tackett told the crowd.

In Colorado Springs, Taylor mused about the ultimate effects of this effort. "What would it look like if the body of Christ in America truly began to live by a biblical worldview? In all of life?" For one, he told me, the academic field in all areas would become a real battlefield, particularly in the areas of science, philosophy, and ethics. "Why have we, as Christians, abandoned that sphere? Why have we allowed secular philosophers to try to come up with those answers? We have the answers, and we should try to engage them intellectually, academically, and spiritually with that pursuit."

The sciences are of special concern, he says, as a place where God is completely visible—and utterly banished. "Can we know this God? Well, yes, he's revealed himself through creation, and he's revealed himself through the way he's created, which is a very ordered, systematic world and universe. It's not random. It's not chaotic. It's not evolved, in the Darwinian sense. It truly is an intelligent design."

He told me about a moment in the primate section of the Denver Zoo, when he had been reminded of the deep need for Christians to possess arguments and knowledge to back up their beliefs. "The placards were talking to me from an evolutionary standpoint, asking why do we look so much like apes, and answering that we had a common ancestor." He seemed stupefied by the matter-of-factness of the zoo's claim. "That's even more harsh than assumptive language. That's telling me I'm related to apes. But it's also assuming that there's no transcendent imminent God that is active in creating this universe."

He told me that Christians routinely get these signals from the culture and accept them out of habit. But they're also afraid, he says. "Frankly, I think we're terrified. We're scared to engage people because first and foremost we're not educated enough to do so, and then sometimes I think we're afraid at what we might find. What if I find that God isn't real? Or what if evolution is real? What does that mean about my God? But no, if Christ is the ultimate source of truth, and God is the fountainhead of all truth, we should be okay to explore every area of life, and specifically science."

And what about history? When I arrived in Boston, this was very much on my mind, and for a particular reason. That afternoon, before going to registration at the church, I had picked up a local newspaper and made a surprising and yet somehow familiar discovery. My friend Doug Wright's play had been in town since Tuesday, and I hadn't known it. A bit of my personal history had come to Boston ahead of me.

†

BUT I SHOULD go back two and a half decades, to my senior year in high school. In the fall of 1980, about the time that Ronald Reagan became the fortieth president of the United States, I decided to try out for a fall production of George Bernard Shaw's *Pygmalion*. I auditioned and won the part of Alfred P. Doolittle, father of Eliza Doolittle, who is transformed by Professor Henry Higgins from a flower girl in Covent Garden to a fine lady of Mayfair. That production proved fateful for two reasons.

I met my first girlfriend, a blue-eyed Texas blonde named Ellen, who played my daughter, Eliza. I still have photographs of her from that production, charcoal smeared on her cheeks, her hair in a black bonnet, her body draped in the homemade tatters that some hard-working member of the theater department had assembled for the character. Another picture shows me in the costume of Alfred P. Doolittle, shaking hands with Professor Higgins, played by a taller boy in an ascot and smoking jacket, his hair silvered with greasepaint. The actor's name was Doug, and he was the towering genius of our high school in writing, theater, and almost any other thing that had to do with culture, the only teenager I knew who had clearly and completely staked out an identity for himself as an artist. The photograph from *Pygmalion* shows the first meeting between Alfred P. Doolittle and Henry Higgins, and I've often thought, looking at it, that it represents in ludicrous theatrical overstatement the moment when I started to become what I am today, that my introduction to Doug marked the beginning of a destiny.

Through college, Doug and I kept in touch. He went to Yale, and I attended Davidson, but I visited him in New Haven, and we saw each other on holidays back in Dallas. Even though we were in separate places, having radically new experiences, redefining ourselves, we stayed in touch, two Texas boys trying to figure out who we were. Doug stopped acting and focused more on writing plays. I continued to act, but scribbled away at novels and short stories. I can remember one holiday, a Christmas or Thanksgiving, the two of us seated in a Big Boy on Northwest Highway, stuffed into overcoats, complaining about our parents, talking about our work. We'd both begun to fight our way to new identities.

Sophomore year, Doug told me that he was gay. I knew what he meant, but just barely. Kids in high school had called other kids fags and queers. One of my friends had a father who worked as an interior decorator, and grown-ups made veiled jokes about him. A middle school football coach had landed in trouble for giving inappropriate rubdowns to teenage athletes. That was the extent of my information. In Christian circles, no one ever spoke of homosexuality. When Doug told me, the news didn't concern or appall me. I don't know why—given my upbringing, it probably should have. But it was just a fact and didn't seem to alter anything that I knew of him.

As a playwright, Doug began to blossom. Once, I traveled to the Fringe Festival in Edinburgh to see a performance of his one-act play, *The Stonewater Rapture*, about two Christian teenagers in Texas. I had read the play on the page, but watching actors perform the parts in a small room in a hotel in Scotland transformed my sense of possibility. My friend had made a reality, like God, and if he could summon those spirits, then so could I. After college, he would send me his latest play, and I'd send him my latest stab at a novel, or some ragged short stories about the South or Texas. We'd infect each other with our enthusiasms. I introduced him to Nietzsche by sending him a copy of *The Antichrist*. He took me to see a Sam Shepard play on Broadway and opened my eyes to the boundless sense of possibility in the theater. In 1990, around the time that Doug's plays began to appear in Off Broadway productions in New York, I moved to Berlin with my girlfriend, Debra.

Berlin proved to be a turning point. I saw firsthand the drama of history. I started work on my first published novel. I became a husband. In so many ways, the city changed me. In a completely different way, it changed Doug, too. Charlotte von Mahlsdorf entered both of our lives.

I TRY TO imagine Charlotte participating in the Truth Project. I try to see her, with her incredible past, her unshakeable sense of self, her survival skills, seated in one of the small groups, munching on a chocolate chip cookie, watching Del Tackett talk about the nature of God on the DVD, absorbing with her steady gaze and friendly smile his views about the state, man and woman, heaven and hell, and sex. Certainly, from the point of view of the people who conceived the Truth Project, and most of its participants, she must be understood as an abomination. Even at her most heroic, she cannot be excused from the irreducible spiritual reality of her condition. As Tommy Nelson implied in his sermon, even while defying the Nazis and the communists, the arch enemies of Christendom, Charlotte von Mahlsdorf must serve as the unmistakable emblem of God's wrath toward humanity.

But in her own account of herself, God plays no role at all, neither as savior nor scourge. God is a matter of indifference. Sex is everything. Charlotte was born a boy, with the name Lothar Berfelde, in 1928, in a part of eastern Berlin known as Mahlsdorf. At a very young age, Lothar discovered that he liked to dress as a girl. An east Prussian aunt recognized the tendency and introduced him to a book that would become a kind of bible, Magnus Hirschfeld's *Die Transvestiten*, or *The Transvestites*, in which the author makes the argument that all human beings possess to a greater or lesser degree both feminine and masculine traits. Lothar grasped where he stood. During World War II, in his long hair and fur coat, he was almost executed by an SS firing squad. But the most serious danger lived closer to home. His introduction to a sexual identity developed at the same time that his father, Max Berfelde, rose through the ranks of the National Socialist Party, which he had joined in the 1920s, long before Hitler took power. Lothar's father didn't join out of fashion or practicality. He believed in the program. He was also violent. By the time his son was a teenager, he was beating his wife and threatening her with a gun.

Years later, Charlotte would tell the following story to her visitors. In 1944, her mother and siblings moved to the country to avoid the air raids. Father and son stayed in Berlin. One night, they began to fight. His father demanded that Lothar choose sides in the family. He pulled a pistol. Lothar refused, and his father locked him in a room. After a few hours, the boy escaped from the room and found his father asleep on a couch, whereupon he took up a rolling pin and beat the man to death in a fury. For this crime, he was sentenced to four years in juvenile detention. The Russian liberation of the city released him.

The cold war followed, and Lothar found himself on the Communist side of the division of Berlin into east and west. As an East German homosexual, he was deemed a member of a deviant social group and driven underground. Gay nightspots were destroyed, and gay life became clandestine. During these years, Lothar Berfelde became Charlotte von Mahlsdorf, adopting dress characteristic of a modest housewife of the Wilhelminian period of the late nineteenth and early twentieth century, a long black frock and pearls. To make ends meet, Charlotte bought and sold antique furniture that furnished a large rundown villa in East Berlin. There is also evidence, in the form of police files, that in order to survive, she took the path of many East Germans, including numbers of clergy, and cooperated as a spy with the state security operation known as the Stasi.

One afternoon, in 1992, Debra and I went to see her give a tour of the Wilhelminian antiques in her museum. The story of her life, dropped casually between descriptions of old furniture, astonished me, and I mentioned it to Doug in a letter. He came to visit, and we made a special evening appointment for a tour. At the conclusion of the tour, she placed a wax cylinder into a machine called a harmonium, and nineteenth-century orchestral music welled into the German night. I experienced the sudden and direct presence of a banished past, rising up in the way that ghosts are said to do in graveyards. The dying twentieth century seemed to rush out of the folds of her black, floor-length dress. Doug walked out of the villa a changed man.

He had seen transvestites before. He knew that homosexuals had been persecuted and murdered by the Nazis; 10,000 of them, at least, had died in concentration camps. But Charlotte exploded his sense of what it meant to be gay and a victim. She gave him a sense of pride in his identity that went beyond marches and protests and the usual stuff of political activism. She had survived the Nazis and the Communists. Without a bomb, without a gun, with a mixture of compromise and amateur theater, she had defied the two most vicious ideologies of the twentieth century.

More than a decade later, Doug finished the final draft of a play called *I Am My Own Wife*. The work contained more than forty separate characters, each of them performed by one man, the New York stage actor Jefferson Mays, dressed in a costume of black frock and pearls. The central character is Charlotte, and the play recounts Doug's encounter with Charlotte as well as her life story, and in this narrative, I appear by name, as myself. *Wife* had its first run Off Broadway in the late spring of 2003. In the fall, the show opened on Broadway. The following May, it won the Tony Award, and a few months later, it took the Pulitzer Prize. Since then, it has been performed all over the world and was, in 2005, the most frequently performed play in the United States. It came to Boston on the same weekend as the Truth Project.

ON DAY TWO, Del Tackett finished his lecture. Gary Alan Taylor returned to the stage and gave instructions on how to use the DVDs in a small-group setting. He gave tips on how to choose the twelve people in the circle. They shouldn't be a random group. In our packet, we had a sheet with the heading, "Praying for Your Participants," and we were asked to write down the names of family members, friends, neighbors, coworkers, and church members who would be likely candidates.

Taylor strongly urged us to follow the Focus on the Family guidelines. This was an exact science, road-tested first with employees at Focus, and later with small groups in Colorado Springs. The series should be watched twelve times in twelve weeks, one hour per week. He mapped out what should happen before and after the DVD viewing. From 7:00 to 7:15 P.M., the recommended time to start, there should be cookies and coffee. After that should come the DVD. Then he suggested a short break before a thirty-minute group discussion. Each group meeting should be followed by prayer and dialogue with the participants.

Taylor warned us about the potential awkwardness of that first session. "My first time was a catastrophe," he said, and he recounted how his wife and he had invited people whom they didn't know very well. During the cookies-and-coffee welcome, no one said a word. People clung to the walls, exchanging brief words before glancing away or looking down. "I went into the kitchen, where my wife was hiding, and I said, 'Who are these people? We have to get them out of here.'" The DVD came as an act of mercy, allowing everyone to sit in the darkness, but when the lights came back on, the discussion was excruciating. Taylor prodded and cajoled, but no one talked. As the guests filed out the front door, he didn't expect to see any of them again. The following week, when the first knock came at the door, his wife and he were amazed. "They all came back."

†

TAYLOR AND TACKETT present the Truth Project to audiences as a matter of life or death for American Christianity. In the generation of the builders, otherwise known as the greatest generation, the people who survived the Depression and fought Hitler, studies reported that 65 percent of Americans were churchgoers. By the time of the baby boomers, that number had dropped to 35 percent. For their children, it was 16 percent, and the so-called bridger generation, those born after 1984, could be expected to fall in attendance to 4 percent. The faith was dying. Tackett hit the point even harder. According to George Barna, "if you were to invite 100 born-again Christians to a barbecue, 91 of them would not believe even the most basic tenets of the faith." Truth Project participants must return to their communities and fight back. They must begin to wage spiritual warfare.

That was the idea, anyway. After the last day's lecture, I met Tackett, a big, balding man with sad eyes and an exhausted smile. Tackett told me that 94 percent of participants had said in post-conference surveys that they would either "absolutely" or "most likely" teach a small group. "The surveys are taken three or four weeks afterwards," he said, "so any of the post-retreat high is gone, and people are back in their lives. Now the jury is still out on whether they will do what they say, but that's the pragmatic thing that we hope will happen. We are praying that God will allow this message to occur within God's people, multiplied through small groups."

In Seattle, the Truth Project attracted 1,300 people from forty different states and five countries. Gatherings in Colorado and Washington, D.C., had attracted well over 1,000 people each. The question is whether these participants take the message home. I asked one couple from western Massachusetts, a pair of Boston transplants to the town of Longmeadow, if they planned to teach the Truth Project in a small group. The husband, it turned out, was the youth minister at a church and wanted to show it to some of the older kids. In fact, he told me, he was going to bring it up at the big fall youth event in Amherst, Acquire the Fire, the opening shot in the year's evangelism effort. Other participants were less willing to say, one way or another, but there was a positive buzz in the room. Dozens of people lined up to talk with Tackett afterward.

For himself, Tackett says, the goal is to change the lives of the people who participate. "The thing that thrills me the most is to see God do something deep within them, and it's not an emotional thing, though emotion is a by-product. It is a deep transformation. They are not the same."

I mentioned the Barna Report and asked him if those people who didn't have the specified biblical worldview could even be considered Christians. "You know what," he replied. "I can't answer that. I know this. There are a number of believers that I know to be believers in Christ, who have been born again, through God, who have been regenerated, and the spirit of God dwells within them, but they have been so taken captive by the world that it doesn't matter. I know people who have sexual addiction problems, bulimic problems, all kinds of problems that are destroying their lives, and because of that destruction, one might look at them and say, Well, is this a believer? But I know them personally, and I know that's not the case."

He told me that he has been interested for a while in writing the kind of test that might actually capture real belief, but he hasn't managed yet to come up with a formula. Even Barna's test, he says, is inadequate. "That 9 percent is based on only a few questions, but from my standpoint, a biblical worldview is comprehensive. So if 9 percent have a biblical worldview in this one small area, what's the percentage of those who have the full comprehensive worldview? I think it's less than 1 percent, way less than 1 percent, and that's a huge problem. And that's what we're trying to fix."

I DIDN'T MENTION Charlotte von Mahlsdorf to Tackett, but the DVD gives me his thoughts on the subject of homosexuality. In lesson eight of the Truth Project, on sociology, he tells his class that God has created a social order every bit as perfect as the physical order of the universe, as complete and available to our senses as the simple chicken egg. He is a god of order, after all, not disorder. But this ordered part of creation, the human institutions of our world, are where "the real battleground lies," he says, "this is where the struggle occurs, this is where the battle rages. Right here."

He says that God's true social order is under attack by the world. Blind humanity sees its most cherished institutions—the law, the arts, the state, the family—as human, and therefore contingent, and random, and changeable. Not so, says Tackett, and he begins his elucidation of the proper social order by asking a student to read Genesis 2:18. In my King James, this reads, "And the Lord God said, It is not good that the man should be alone; I will make an help meet for him."

At this very moment, not long after the dawn of creation, Tackett says, God creates woman, and with her, the beginnings of the order inherent in the nuclear family, which is not arbitrary in the least, but reflects God's own triune nature. Just as God is three persons in one nature—Father, Son, and Holy Ghost—the family becomes triune in the form of husband, wife, and child. Just as Jesus submitted to the Father again and again, up to and including his decision to die on the cross, and just as the body of the church submits to Christ, so the wife submits to the husband. The world, he says, has corrupted the idea of submission into something bad, but in the relationship between Jesus and the Father, it is wholly good, and so in the relationship between husband and wife, it is good.

"It is not going to be a surprise to us," he says, "that the world, the flesh, and the devil that hates the nature of God also hates this structure as well, and you and I know that this structure is under huge attack today."

To go against that order, then, is to go against God. "And it is not good to go against the nature of God," he tells us.

When Lothar Berfelde was a young man, his mother asked him why he hadn't ever found a young woman to marry. His reply: "Don't you know, Mama? I am my own wife."

It is a statement of survival and identity and individuality all in one. Charlotte is triune in the most secular sense, three in one: husband, wife, self. She is complete.

In the Truth Project, Tackett quotes Ephesians 5:31: "For this cause shall a man leave his father and mother, and shall be joined unto his wife, and they two shall be one flesh. This is a great mystery: but I speak concerning Christ and the church."

In Boston, I could see the two trinities balanced: God and Charlotte. But this was surely the world, corrupting my feeble mind. No matter that she suffered persecution under the same Communist regime that persecuted the followers of Jesus, no matter that she resisted the Nazis in a way that most Christians didn't; she cannot enter heaven. She must die and go down in the dust of human delusion, just as the monsters wanted.

## chapter 12

## *Specklebird*

*A*t Southeast Christian Church, in Louisville, Kentucky, I experienced a drama made by evangelical Christians for a fallen world: a Broadway-sized show halfway between the Truth Project and *I Am My Own Wife*. For more than a decade, Southeast has mounted the second largest passion play in the United States, featuring a cast of 400 and a total participation of 1,500 or so volunteers from every walk of life: bankers, farmers, doctors, lawyers, students, ministers, actors. As of 2006, more than half a million people had seen it.

On a night in early March, I saw it, too. Giant projection screens showed the creation of the world in lava, storm, and wave. A male voice boomed the Old Testament. The ages passed. Herod ordered a slaughter, and Mary sang away her fear. The baby came, the star shone, and female angels descended in waterfalls of hair on harnesses from the roof of the sanctuary, their sopranos shivering the night. John the Baptist sang bass. Eighteen-hundred-pound camels lumbered down the aisle. Jesus laughed and danced. Jesus did wonders. He entered Jerusalem on the back of an ass. Pontius Pilate washed his hands. The crown of thorns came down. The centurions hammered. Jesus was crucified, dead, and buried and rose again on the third day. Nothing seemed to go wrong. I walked out in a state of amazement. In the lobby, the performers gathered in their costumes to sign autographs and talk to the dazed audience.

The night before this performance, I had attended the worship service preceding the show, and it was a revelation, a spectacle in its own right. The play told the story of Jesus. The worship service told the drama of the church itself, an unintentional but powerful depiction of the way that believers make their way through a dark and fallen world.

At last count, there were 340,000 churches in the United States. Southeast is the tenth largest, one of the most prominent of the country's so-called megachurches. In 2006, the Church Report listed Southeast as the sixth most influential in the country. The passion play exemplified much of what made the place special, its wealth and voluntarism, its dynamism and sense of mission; but 2006 would be the last official season of this legendary production. In 2007, there would be a hiatus, and in 2008, the church would launch a brand new Easter show centered on new priorities. Southeast was in the midst of the most profound change in its four-decade history. For the first time since its establishment in a small family home in Louisville, the congregation of 22,000 would be led by a new senior pastor. The departing pastor, the Reverend Bob Russell, would step down officially in June, but his successor, the Reverend Dave Stone, groomed for the role for eighteen years, had already taken over the reins of the operation. The coming hiatus of the play signaled the depth of the changes, an echo of a much greater transformation throughout American Christendom, as the era of vast growth and spectacle inside the church gave way to an era of mission outside. The war against the world, preached in the Truth Project, is a reality in places like Southeast.

One sees very clearly the mission: to leave behind the walls of the sanctuary and take the gospel into the streets. The worship service before each production of the passion play has a martial ring.

A few hours before the show, the actor who played Jesus said to me, "You have to picture it. We're in a large choir room that seats two to three hundred people. We're all singing. Everybody's in their Hebrew garb, and I'm dressed like this," he gestured at his wardrobe of robes and rags, "and someone said this is what heaven will look like, because we're all worshipping God, Jesus is there, the disciples are there, and angels all around."

But what I saw in the choir room before the show didn't look or feel like heaven. It looked like an X-ray of a great American church in the fullness of its glory, with all its ingenuity, piety, vanity, and power on spectacular display. And, rather selfishly, I felt as if the entire effort were aimed, like a scud missile, right at me.

AN HOUR AND a half before the start of that night's performance, I found a seat among the Roman centurions. They could have been mistaken for a college football team, leather breastplates for shoulder pads, sandals for cleats, helmets with plumes instead of face guards. The burnished helms sat in rows beneath the benches, beside the spears, sharp metal points bound to wooden shafts with coiled ropes. Homemade broadswords leaned against the wall. Most of the legion were white and had Kentucky accents. For a Mediterranean look, their faces had been greased with umber. One was black, middle-aged, and hearing-impaired. He signed to a young shepherdess. It wasn't hard to imagine backstage romances. A centurion with a buzz cut flirted with my official Southeast guide, Kylene. Another shook my hand and welcomed me to the show. He had a square jaw, pale blue eyes, and a wave of chestnut hair. He sold real estate for a living.

In the middle of the choir room seating area, the nubile angels gathered, young girls glimmering in ponds of chiffon. In another sector sat middle-aged men in plump gowns, Pharisees, and in another were ranks of dusty shepherds. Last-minute preparations came to a boil. Technicians in headsets and stage crew with props scurried between video screens and scattered folding chairs. Beyond lay the darkened wings of the stage, accessed by two doors leading to the backside of the façade of ancient Jerusalem. Jesus hid, but I saw his people, older men and women in head-dresses and robes, real married couples, drinking soda pop from the bottle and finishing fried chicken off white Styrofoam plates. One particularly striking angel flowed through the crowd like an evening star, golden hair shining behind her. In an hour or so, she would drop in sensual benediction through the roof of the Southeast sanctuary and hang in a dazzle above our heads, her wires invisible. I picked out Mary and found John the Baptist, a burly brown mulch of a man in a wild animal pelt, receiving hair implants.

Kings of the East wandered in robes among taxpayers, and a corpse-faced woman in dark drapery brought notes of Halloween, an androgynous Satan trailing demon children, permutations of the Mel Gibson monsters in *The Passion of the Christ.*

The director, Shane Sooter, stepped forward. He wore a black turtleneck and a baseball cap. His dark hair fell to his shoulders. He was off schedule and anxious. "Ten minutes late," he said. "Lord help us."

The cast got quiet. The director offered a prayer. His voice shifted into supplicating mode. "Father, thank you for the way you protected us and got us through a number of mishaps last night. I thank you that you're greater than any of those mishaps. Thank you for the pressure that you take off us so that we don't have to get everything right. Because our ultimate goal isn't something we're capable of reaching anyway. Only your spirit can touch hearts and move people to salvation."

The cast said amen. The corpse-faced woman, Satan, approached the director from behind with a cup of coffee. He gave a few notes on the previous night's show, then asked the Roman soldiers to stand. The room burst into wild applause.

The night before, during the crucifixion scene, one of the straps on the crossbeam of the crucifix came loose, making it impossible for Christ to keep one of his outstretched arms in place for any length of time. The centurions lowered the cross, unhooked Jesus from the other strap, brought out the emergency replacement crucifix, nailed Christ down a second time, and hoisted again. The new strap held.

The director lifted a trophy. "I would like to present this," he said, and he read the inscription. "Awarded to captain and soldiers of the Cross, for quick thinking on their feet, and in so doing, they double-crossed the Devil."

The centurions left their corner of the choir room and walked down the aisle to accept the award. The captain of the legion raised it like an enemy's head. The director made a last observation about the incident. He said he had been thinking about how many thousands of tickets had been sold for that performance, and how many secular people had been in the audience, how many souls had been at stake when that crucifix started to come down, potentially blowing the entire evening. And yet the centurions prevailed. "I was thinking," he said, "how ticked off Satan must have been."

THE SHOW'S PRODUCER and creator, Dale Mowery, stepped forward. He was an ordained minister and would take the cast the rest of the way to the performance. It was an hour till curtain call and time for worship. He asked an actress to step forward and offer testimony. A woman named Janet, in long robes, told us she wanted to share a story about the night that the people from the homeless mission came to see the show. She'd had an encounter with a young woman.

"I noticed her after the performance, when she walked out of the door," Janet told us. "There were tears in her eyes, and I was just standing there at the door, greeting people. She said, 'You know, I don't know anything about the Bible, but I think I just got a crash course.' She went on her way, but I thought that maybe I should pray for her. I walked up, and I asked her name, and if she minded if I prayed for her, and she cried and cried and cried."

The homeless woman turned out to be a prostitute.

"She's been in prison," Janet told us. "She's at the mission now on a court order, and she has to stay there. She shared with me how she tried to commit suicide three weeks ago, and the doctors told her there was enough cocaine in her body to knock down three football players, but that she only weighed eighty-seven pounds, and the doctors didn't know why she had lived, and I told her, Scotty—her name was Scotty—I know why you lived. You lived because God has a plan for your life."

Janet continued, but she sounded on the verge of tears. The story got worse. "She's had three babies taken away, because they're crack babies, and she's lonesome. She's only been off drugs, well, today is day seven, that was day five. She says the hardest part is that, at night, she has dreams all night about drugs. So a couple of ladies and I went upstairs and prayed for her. I got an idea to make her a quilt and have my friend embroider some scripture all over it, and I thought I would take it down there, and we could say to her, 'Listen, we have prayed over your dreams,' and I thought that would make her feel love and comfort. If any of you ladies want to donate a dollar, I'll do that, and I'll take it down there, and I'll say this is from all your sisters at Southeast that love you."

More applause concussed the room. The producer took center stage again. The noise of a crowd dinned beyond the walls of the choir room; numbers ran between 6,000 and 7,000 per performance.

"Satan hates you," Mowery said. "And he hates this church, and he hates what's going on in this place, and he's going to try everything he can to stop us: if that means a cross breaks, or a dove doesn't fly, or a baby cries, as one did the other night. But I truly feel that when worship takes place, God binds Satan, and those things don't become distractions. I had a lady come up to me last night and say, 'Man, that was awesome, I've never read in the Bible how the cross broke . . .'"

Everyone laughed, but Mowery returned quickly to the awesome seriousness of the undertaking. "Your whole purpose here is to worship God. And I believe that he goes before us when that happens, and Satan is bound in this place, and blind eyes are open, and deaf ears hear, and broken hearts are mended."

He had seated himself at the piano. Now he began to play, and voices lifted in song, arms lifted in praise, bodies began to sway, the deaf signed, and it was a communion of music, with centurions, angels, shepherds at their flocks by night, kings of the East, Pontius Pilate, the disciples, the devil, the demons, Kylene of Indianapolis, Jesus himself, even me, "Give thanks to the Lord, our God and King, his love endures forever, for he is good, he's above all things, his love endures forever. . . ."

After the song swept through us, Dale started a chain of prayer, and others followed him, calling out their concerns, "God, you are the all-powerful healer." "Father God, we praise you tonight," someone else said, "for you are the only one worthy of any praise, not Roman centurions who think fast, not technicians who think quickly and push the right buttons, not singers, not instruments, only you. . . ."

The prayer ended, and the new pastor of Southeast, Dave Stone, walked into our midst, escorting a special guest backstage. "I know you just had prayer time," he told us, "but it's not real common that we have a governor who is a brother in Christ, who has a passion for prayer, and a passion for what you guys are doing. And so tonight, Governor Fletcher and his wife are going to get to see the pageant for the first time, and I'm going to ask your brother to give a word of prayer."

The governor of Kentucky, Ernie Fletcher, stepped forward. He had once been a preacher himself, and a spokeswoman for the church told me that he relied heavily on certain Southeast members for close counsel. That week, he'd had his own woes, a state supreme court hearing arguments about malfeasance in his administration

"As I walked in here," Governor Fletcher said, "it was almost like stepping back two thousand years, seeing all of the soldiers, and all of the rest of you. I know it's a tremendous amount of work, and you volunteered to do this work, and I know down in your heart the real purpose of all this is to focus on what the meaning of the pageant is, and that's about our savior who gave his life that we might be redeemed."

Cast members called out "Amen!"

He offered up his prayer. "Dear Heavenly Father, we thank you for the opportunity to come together. We thank you for this church, this collection of your people, this segment of your kingdom that has had so much influence in this area in their commonwealth. We want to say thank you for the work of all those who have had such an impact to grow your kingdom here. We want to ask for your blessing on each of these that are participating in this pageant." Then the governor of the great state of Kentucky began to pray for *me*. "Father, you know the purpose of this. We trust, as this pageant is conducted tonight, that there are those in the audience whose heart might be touched, that that seed of faith that you plant there might blossom, it might change their lives, not just here in this time, but for all eternity."

The show was about to start. Outside, someone told me, the camels had entered the building. Four hundred souls of Southeast Christian Church prepared to embody the great drama of human history. They would enact the birth, betrayal, denial, crucifixion, and crowning of Christ, and in that effort, they would throw down the living Satan. He would lie bound at their feet, and yet, in his mischief, he could still make the doves panic, the babies cry, and the holy cross itself disintegrate. That was the real drama. It happened every day, every hour, at Southeast, and nothing on Broadway could ever compare.

†

THE CHURCH FALLS at the extreme end of the scale in many ways: in physical size, membership, weekly attendance, and offerings. Southeast can seat 9,000 per service on weekends and sees about 18,000 people on average. The average staff of a megachurch has 22 full-time employees. As a tour guide informed me, Southeast employs 300 full-time, 40 of whom are ordained ministers.

Its size puts it in a rarefied category, almost deserving of its own name: *uber*churches, perhaps. But in most other respects, Southeast stands as a model example, and a good test case for understanding why the heyday of these vast places is coming to an end. Like Southeast, most megachurches were built in the newer suburbs of American cities, where land was cheaper, and population growth has been rapid, places like Mesa, Arizona; Plano, Texas; South Baton Rouge, Louisiana; and the east end of Louisville. Most megachurches, 89 percent, have white pastors. Around 80 percent use electric guitars and drums in their worship services, and almost all use visual projection equipment for display above the stage. What was once an innovation has now become the bare minimum, as everything from baptisms to Bible verses gets shown on screen. Most important, in thinking about Southeast, the majority of these churches, almost half, have no denominational affiliation. They are Bible churches, independent of any higher organizational structure, autonomous in their governance, able to make their own decisions about their future without interference from ecclesiastical authorities beyond their own walls. They are intrinsically and aggressively local, which gives them a lot of appeal in an age when local churches are fighting battles over homosexuality and abortion with their national denominations.

Independent Bible churches, particularly the big ones, are the leading edge in modern Christianity, setting priorities that are then adopted everywhere else, whether in the use of rock music in worship services or the emphasis on service to the poor, the adherence to biblical worldview, or the importance of evangelism. And even when a megachurch has a denominational affiliation, whether Assembly of God or Southern Baptist, the leadership downplays the connection. By dint of numbers, whether measured by membership, growth in membership, real estate, or wealth, Bible churches and their like-minded brethren have replaced the mainline denominations as the voice of authority and change in American Christianity. Rick Warren, the author of *The Purpose-Driven Life* and pastor of one of the most influential churches in the United States, Saddleback, says the evangelical faith of the big local churches has become mainline Christianity. The old mainline of the denominations has become the sideline, he says.

That means, in particular, two things: a focus on a simplified version of the faith, aimed at stripping away the trappings of historical development to get back to New Testament essentials; and the primacy of evangelism. Ninety-five percent of all megachurches stress evangelism. Members are encouraged to do everything possible to spread the word. They are urged to invite friends to services and tell everyone in their lives about their faith. Most megachurches sponsor some large event, like the Southeast pageant, to attract the lost.

A few weeks after my visit to Southeast, at my Aunt Margaret's house in Midland, Texas, I met an oilman who introduced me to a phrase that I'd never heard before. He was born and bred in the Presbyterian Church, but his children preferred a nondenominational megachurch that had sprung up in the nearby city of Odessa. A lot of the older generation in Midland and Odessa were in the same boat. Having been loyal to their denominations, Methodists, Baptists, Presbyterians, and Episcopalians, they saw their kids turning to a more emotionally fulfilling experience that involved more music, less preaching, and none of that distracting talk about doctrinal differences. Denomination had become uncool, boring, distracting. I told the oilman about my experience at Southeast, and he told me about an old Methodist preacher who had a name for such freestanding, freebooting, nondenominational Christian churches. He called them "specklebirds."

The term instantly grabbed me. I asked the oilman what it meant. He didn't know exactly, but he didn't think it was a compliment. The Methodist preacher had long since passed away, and I couldn't find anything on the Internet about "specklebird churches." None of my scholarly Christian friends recognized the term. Country music gave me a clue. I had heard a song all my life called "The Great Speckled Bird," a gospel tune by country singer Roy Acuff. I went to my King James Bible and looked up Jeremiah, chapter

12, verse 9. "Mine heritage is unto me as a speckled bird, the birds round about are against her; come ye, assemble all the beasts of the field, come to devour." This passage is the one and only mention in scripture of this mysterious fowl.

My MacArthur Study Bible, a favorite among fundamentalists, given to me by a young Australian named Rodney, calls Jeremiah 12:9 "God's answer" to the age-old question of why the wicked prosper. God answers with the line about the speckled bird, which, the commentary explains, represents the honored memory of the Jewish bond with Yahweh. Those who adhere to that bond find their heritage under attack, but God will punish those who attack them. Those who betray the specklebird will pay.

I will hazard a guess that the Methodist preacher's "specklebird churches" were those that, decades ago, turned their backs on the liberalism embraced by the mainline denominations. They were the Bible churches who saw themselves in mid-twentieth-century America as beggars crying in the wilderness, who saw their secular enemies prospering on all fronts, their Christian brethren betraying the truth, who cried out to the Lord for answers and vengeance. Their great hope lay in their heritage, the great speckled bird that was their connection to Jesus Christ, to which they clung with tenacity. I don't know if the preacher meant it strictly as an insult. I suspect that the old Methodist meant to express ambivalence about a particular style and sensibility, a highly individualistic approach to the gospel that took direct aim at the denominations, and people like himself, who, in their view, had succumbed to lies and godlessness. But there might have been a touch of admiration, too, in his mind, for a thorny, unpopular view of righteousness so passionately and stubbornly held.

The Roy Acuff song isn't ambivalent; at least, not about the bird: "What a beautiful thought I am thinking, Concerning the Great Speckled Bird, remember her name is recorded, On the pages of God's Holy Word."

I USE THE term, then, with more ambivalence than negativity when I say that Southeast strikes me as a prime example of a specklebird, though no longer embattled in an era of hostility. In Kentucky, Southeast is an institution, not just because it is one of the great local success stories, growing in spectacular leaps and bounds during an era when other churches were shrinking and dying, but because it symbolizes within Christianity a certain kind of success. If I had to find a single word, I would choose discretion. That might seem an odd choice for a place so big that it can be seen from a great distance, and looks like a small airline terminal at night, but I don't mean to apply it to the reputation of the place, which casts a large shadow throughout western Kentucky and southern Indiana. Rather, I mean that the senior pastor, Bob Russell, and his lieutenants have made a stylistic choice in their leadership to avoid placing themselves in the national spotlight. Self-effacement seems to be the management creed.

In the introduction to Russell's book about Southeast, *When God Builds a Church*, Thom Rainer, the dean of the Billy Graham School of Evangelism, writes, "Southeast Christian Church is the story of what God can do when his people are obedient and his leaders are pure." What that means, in the most practical sense, is that Southeast has never advertised much—its services can't be seen nationally—and yet it has flourished. Moreover, it has managed to flourish, to become a powerful regional institution, without either great controversy or aggressive publicity. That's no small feat when you realize that, in the years of its ascendancy, the Jimmy Swaggart empire in Baton Rouge disintegrated in the wake of a national scandal, Jimmy and Tammy Faye Bakker imploded in even more spectacular form, pastors as different as Tim LaHaye and Rick Warren became bestselling authors and celebrities, James Falwell and Pat Robertson became household names, James Dobson rose to prominence as one of the most important figures in the Republican Party, and Ted Haggard went from being one of the most widely seen and heard pastors in a generation to one of its most disgraced. Meanwhile, year to year, quietly and purposefully, Southeast grew 18 percent in ten years under the guidance of one relatively unknown man who kept his job for four decades before retiring in June 2006.

When Bob Russell left, the news made front-page headlines in Louisville, and both the Kentucky House of Representatives and the Senate drafted resolutions in his honor. The Senate resolution reads more like an inspirational biography than an act of government.

WHEREAS, Bob Russell came to his calling much to his own surprise, born in Pennsylvania, nursing the ambition of becoming the coach of his high school basketball team when God spoke to him and turned him towards a life as a "fisher of men" rather than a coach of them; . . . and WHEREAS, Bob Russell demonstrated the power of God, acting through his servant, taking a church that had few members at the start of his tenure, and creating the majestic structure that is Southeast Christian Church today . . .

## chapter 13

# Shepherd

*I arrived* at Southeast at night, and my first impression remains vivid. I didn't see a building. I saw a shimmer of pale reflected light in dark glass, hard to separate from the darkness. I didn't see a cross, didn't see the contour of a dome or steeple. I didn't see words that would identify the palpable shadow of the place. I saw only the shimmer. Mapquest told me it was Southeast.

That night, I stayed at a hotel on the opposite side of the highway. When I called the media coordinator, Debra Childers, she walked me through the last changes in the schedule. She concluded with a kind of warning: "Now I hope you'll understand that we won't be alone together. It's our culture. We won't have lunch together by ourselves or spend any time by ourselves. It's better for us, better for our families, and it's just how we do things around here. I hope you'll understand."

I was taken aback, to say the least. Out of the blue, before I had even laid eyes on her, this woman had implied that the mere fact of our togetherness, by ourselves, might lead to some untoward sexual complication. I wondered if I had somehow sent an unintentional signal during our phone conversations. In our few words, we'd exchanged commonplace pleasantries about family life and our mutual Southern heritage. Had that been perceived as inappropriate flirtation? From the beginning, she'd told me that the church had a "relational" vibe, so I'd tried to see our exchanges as building a relationship—but not in the biblical sense. I told her that I would, of course, comply with her wishes.

I had come to Southeast at a moment of radical transformation in the life of the church. In addition to the final performances of the storied Easter pageant, on top of the ongoing transition from Bob Russell to his successor, Dave Stone, several other dramas unfolded at once. As a result of the transition, the entire management structure of the church had been changed, and a new system of team leadership had just been instituted. Some people were discovering that they no longer had positions of responsibility while others got promotions. At the top of that chart, just as before, sat the name Jesus in a box. Everything below Jesus, however, had changed. Also changed, after decades: the church mission statement. Under Bob, it had been fourfold, "We exist to evangelize the lost, edify the saved, minister to the needs of others, and be a conscience to the community." His successor, Dave Stone, did more than tinker. He turned the mission sentence into the mission phrase and made the entire statement about one big idea. The mission statement now read, "Connecting people to Jesus and to one another." It was less beautiful, I thought, and more vague, but perhaps it better served a less literate, more hurried time.

The main lobby of Southeast runs as long and wide as a football field between the main sanctuary and a suite of offices and chapels and is bisected by a circular information desk. Above the lobby floor are four floors of offices. Off the lobby, on the first floor, sits a small museum about the church, and one night, before the Easter pageant, with twenty other visitors, I listened to an orientation. Our hostess, a woman in a pale green dress, fed us facts and details. When it was finished, in 1998, the building cost $78 million. A full tour of the structure covers a mile and a half of ground. Before the carpets were laid and the walls painted, members came into the building and scrawled Bible verses on every square inch.

She pointed out the most intriguing item in the room, a circular gadget with plastic tubes running out of the top and concentric rings of cups below. It looked like a prop from an early Frankenstein movie, a piece of the laboratory that brings the monster to life. In fact, the machine dispensed communion wine, or rather, grape juice. Someone inquired about the frequency of the Eucharist at services.

"Every Sunday," the guide replied, moving to one side of the room, towards the gadget. "We call this machine our Holy Cow," she said. "It's designed by one of our members, and he has a patent out on it." She gestured at the bottom. "You put the tray under this cup dispenser first, and then you slide it under here and pull the lever. We'll use about forty gallons of juice on a weekend. We do three services, two on Sunday and one on Saturday night, and there's communion at every one."

She ran the numbers for us: three hundred fifty on staff, forty or so ordained ministers, three preaching ministers. She mentioned the pastoral transition from Bob Russell to Dave Stone, and said that it had been planned according to the Joshua principle. As Moses had prepared Joshua to take the Hebrews into the Holy Land, so Bob Russell had prepared Dave Stone to assume leadership of Southeast.

Overall church membership figures had recently been adjusted. "Several months ago, they said it was 24,000," she explained. "But in the fall, we had what we called the 'I'm in' program, meaning 'Are you still in the church?' Because we realized over the years that we hadn't really purged our records." I had heard from someone else in the church that there were people who had moved out of Louisville and even passed away who were still on the rolls. "Everybody who was sitting on the fence was urged to go ahead and make a decision, and the purge was finished, the number was 22,000. We did have 360 people baptized on one weekend during that campaign."

"Good gracious," an elderly listener whispered.

Our guide said that as many as forty people per weekend will walk up the aisle to be baptized. An average weekend, it's closer to twenty.

Every church service offers an altar call, giving people the chance to step forward. And every person who chooses to accept Christ gets paired with what is called a decision counselor. "One on one, man to man, woman to woman," she said. "That decision counselor takes them back into an area and takes them through the whole plan of salvation, no matter if you walked forward and said, I'm a deacon in my church, and I've served in the choir for twenty years, we still would take you to see where you truly are, and the decision counselors use the 'bridge' illustration, which shows Sinful Man on one side of a gap, or a chasm, and Holy God on the other side with no way for Sinful Man to get to Holy God except by the bridge, which is the cross. So we take everybody through that whole plan of salvation and root it biblically and give them an opportunity to say where they are on that. If they don't understand, or just plain don't to accept it at that point, or if they're not ready, then we just channel them into different programs so they can get involved and get an understanding and learn and grow in their knowledge of Jesus Christ."

The "specklebird" question arose. "What denomination are you?"

"We are a nondenominational church," she told us. "We have no structure above the local church. We just try to go back to biblical times and do it the biblical way. People say that we're really just a big Baptist church. We're not, but a lot of times, when Baptist people do come, they'll say that we're biblical, all right, nothing more, nothing less."

At Southeast, commitment meant a full-body immersion in water. One had to be baptized.

"I'll tell you a personal story in that regard," the guide told us. "I grew up in a tradition where you were sprinkled with water, and when I came here, I considered myself a Christian, and I literally went up to Bob Russell and said, 'Are you telling me I'm not a Christian because I haven't been immersed?' He's so good about stuff like that. He said, 'No, I'm not telling you that.' He said, 'Let me tell you a story,' and I knew something funny was coming. He said that this guy wanted to be baptized, and he walked to the top of the baptismal steps, and he fell over dead with a heart attack. 'Is he saved?' Bob asked me. I said, 'Okay, what's the punch line?' Bob said, 'Depends on which way he fell.'"

The room cracked up. She continued her Bob Russell story. "'Look,' he said, 'that's not what we believe. We just try to be as close to what the Bible says as possible. It does say accept Christ. It does say to be immersed.' The Greek word *baptismo* means 'to be immersed,' so Bob says, 'Since that's the way it's written in the Bible, that's what we do, and it's just an act of obedience.' So I said, 'I can do that.'"

"Jesus was baptized, too," someone in the room offered.

"And that's something else Bob said. It is following the example of Christ."

The orientation ended on a mysterious note. Someone asked if the church was available to baptize at any time of the day or night. "I heard a story here one time," our guide said. "Somebody called in the middle of the night, and there are ministers on call at night. For whatever reason, the caller's heart was working on him, and he said he just had to talk to someone, and the minister told him to come on over. And at one o'clock that night, he was baptized."

She left it at that.


I HAVE TO confess an ambivalence about churches in general. I have never liked them. In fact, I kind of hate churches, an attitude which I inherited from my father, who has a similar aversion. To this day, he can't bear to sit in a pew and listen to a preacher.

But until I graduated from college, I went. Church, like football, barbecue, and blond hair, belonged to the landscape of my upbringing. As an infant I was baptized Presbyterian in Odessa, Texas, but my first memories begin when my parents took us to a Methodist church in Dallas. I remember, at age five or six, a pudgy, red-haired bully who beat up a skinny kid named Philip. I stood up for Philip against the bully, and the bully backed down. This happened on the playground after Sunday school. My parents left the Methodists and joined Highland Park Presbyterian, which became their church home till after I graduated.

At the time, HPPC was the largest Presbyterian church in North America, the second largest in the world. Nowadays we would think of it as one of the smaller megachurches, but in the 1970s, Highland Park Presbyterian had a national profile, though nothing like megachurches Willow Creek or Saddleback in our day. Such celebrity is a more recent phenomenon. Around the time my parents joined, though, the church had more than 6,000 members who gave in excess of $1 million a year in tithes, a huge sum in the late 1960s, but yet again a tiny fraction of what such churches can muster in 2006. In one week in November 2004, at Prestonwood Baptist Church, in north Dallas, members gave more than $800,000 in total offerings. Southeast takes in about $400,000 a week.

In 1973, Highland Park Presbyterian stood for power, continuity, and stability. Its neo-Gothic design, limestone walls, and stained glass evoked church tradition within a modest American framework. There were no Mc-Mansions then, though a few members of the congregation lived in what could safely be called mansions. Some of the wealthiest families in the United States belonged to the church, including the Herbert Hunts, who had been in oil, silver, and everything else lucrative in Texas, but they loathed ostentation. To show off their money would have been the height of tackiness. If anything, their church erred on the side of banality, bespeaking a modest but sturdy ambition to influence the community in which it stood, plain to a fault, offering nothing original, excelling in all things familiar. The building sat high on a few acres of cut green grass, a block or so from the fire station and city hall, the same distance from one edge of the Dallas Country Club golf course, half a mile from the high school. Every year, the Fourth of July parade moved slowly past the church, as if to salute its abiding presence.

In 1973, with the arrival of its new pastor, Highland Park Presbyterian achieved a new status. The Reverend Clayton Bell was the son of Nelson Bell, a renowned medical missionary, and his sister Ruth had married Billy Graham. I can still recall shaking Rev. Bell's hand after church and have in my memory a soft voice and kind eyes. My mother spoke with great reverence of Rev. Bell and was honored by the fact that he was our pastor.

I have dozens of fleeting, unremarkable images of Highland Park Presbyterian, azalea bushes that burst into pink fire in the early spring, an unremarkable interior, long halls with polished floors opening onto uninteresting rooms that smelled of sugar-glazed doughnuts and hot coffee, a bookstore that stocked the Narnia books by C. S. Lewis, men in dark blue Brooks Brothers suits, women in heavy makeup, bright tailored dresses, and heels, all of whom seemed to know my parents. There were pretty blonde girls with red ribbons flashing in their curls, talk about the Dallas Cowboys, who played on Sunday afternoons, lots of stacked Bibles with shining gilt edges, old folks taking each other's arms, walking cautiously down the parquet, elders and deacons from the 1940s and the 1950s. I don't think much of Jesus when I think of that church. Highland Park Presbyterian represented something else: a comfortable, worldly, dignified way of life—if that's what you wanted.

When I was in high school and heavily involved in Young Life, I lost interest in HPPC Sunday school and cut classes. The lessons didn't seem relevant enough. None of the cute girls attended. My brother, who never showed much interest in church, would cut Sunday school, too. My father hadn't attended in years. He'd buy a box of doughnuts and stay home and read the Sunday editions of the *Dallas Morning News* and the *Dallas Times Herald*. In our Chevrolet Caprice Classic, a burgundy red four-door, my brother and I would drop my mother at the entrance to the sanctuary, my sister at the nursery school. Then he would hop out of the car and walk quickly around a corner and out of sight, headed for the home of a friend who lived nearby. He knew to reappear at about 11:00 A.M., when church let out. I would drive for an hour, circling the church, windows rolled up, blasting Tom Petty and the Heartbreakers. To this day, when I hear "American Girl" or "Breakdown," two great pop songs about sex and death, I think of that car, those mornings, and the steeple of the church, which made the center of the compass around which I would turn and turn until my brother resurfaced, and my mother exited the sanctuary.

I ENCOUNTERED OTHER churches here and there, but none ever persuaded me. All felt artificial. But then, I never attended a church like Southeast.

In the spirit of the Truth Project, I go back to the book of Ephesians, where the apostle Paul describes in chapter 4 the essence of the ideal church: "One Lord, one faith, one baptism, One God and Father of all, who is above all, and through all, and in you all."

Does such a place exist, where all human ambition, desire, and community can be caught in a single droplet of holy intention? It is one thing to preach the gospel in its purity to a group of strangers for two days, as Del Tackett does at the Truth Project; it's quite another to assemble hundreds, even thousands, on a weekly basis, and turn the assembly into more than a casual gathering of souls. As always, the early church sits as the model. One study claims that the first Christian churches grew by 40 percent a decade. In the Roman Empire, people saw a difference when Christians gathered. Christians didn't keep slaves. They disapproved of gladiatorial combat.

They cared for the sick, the poor, the orphan, and they refused to honor the Roman gods. The behavior spoke and the faith spread.

At the most successful megachurches, it still works the same way.

A LOT OF it has to do with the pastor, and at Southeast, that meant a man who inspired something like hero worship: the Reverend Bob Russell. I had lunch one day with Russell. To my surprise, our meeting felt like a big deal to me. I had always looked askance at churches, but pastors somehow escaped my disdain. They prompted an automatic regard, bordering on awe, yet mixed with boredom. It may have been a simple matter of recognized authority. Adults in my childhood talked about ministers as if they belonged to a remote class of human being, higher morally, perhaps, but also slightly off the subject. Or my regard may have been of a more specific nature, inherited from my parents. In our family, in my memory, we always showed respect for the powers that be. It amounted to a house rule, akin to honoring your mother and father, not hitting girls, and keeping your word. We venerated the absolute ideals of American life. In movies, John Wayne embodied those ideals. In the sphere of government, the president of the United States merited our trust and loyalty.

I'd never known the senior pastors of my early churches. At the time, I didn't care. If anything, I had an aversion. Likewise, I'm sure, they would have had little or no interest in a pimpled teenager with braces, even as a conversion opportunity. A few times, I saw Rev. Bell give sermons in the sanctuary at Highland Park Presbyterian. I can remember sitting in the pew, praying for the sermon to end. He wasn't a terrible orator, but the pew bothered my back. My suit itched. I hated the hymns. Rev. Bell had no personal life that resonated with me, no personality, no hobbies, no favorite films or songs. He was nothing but church.

Years later, his humanity became more apparent. In the 1980s, after the unification of the Presbyterian denomination, Highland Park Presbyterian began to split over the issue of governance. The Presbyterian Church (U.S.A.) tried to exert control over the real estate, and thousands of people left to start a new church, including some of the wealthiest members. Rev. Bell fought the schism, and it probably cost him his life. In the late 1980s, he suffered a heart attack that almost killed him. More than a decade later, at Billy Graham's retreat in North Carolina, he had another one, and it did the job. The collapse of his church destroyed him.

Back in the day, I had no clue about any of this. I knew one pastor at the church, a guy named Murray Gossett who ran the youth ministry. When he visited the cafeteria, he greeted me by my first name. The Young Life representative, Bobby McCreless, was a youth minister, too, and they both shaped my early feeling about pastors. Later, I had friends who went into the ministry, but none of them impressed me as typical of the breed. One, Nick, had been with the U.S. Special Forces in Vietnam and wanted to be a fiction writer. He smoked and drank red wine and loved to talk about Hemingway and Faulkner. The other, Craig, clearly loved Bruce Springsteen and Martin Scorsese more than Jesus. I had never personally met a pastor who filled out the role with both personal appeal and spiritual authority. More than that, I had never had a chance to speak with one, to ask the hard questions, to receive counsel and advice from someone in possession of wisdom, experience, and biblical knowledge. How many people at Southeast Christian Church would have given anything to spend an hour in conversation with their senior pastor, the man who had led the church from a private home to the tenth largest in the country?

Speaking with Bob Russell turned out to be one of the best experiences in my travels, another of those moments when the appeal of the Christian way of life came home to me. Had I been pastored by this man, I came away thinking, I might never have left. A lot of my response had to do with his personal charm.

We ate sandwiches together in his fifth-floor office, and before I could ask my first question, without making it seem like an interrogation, he began to ask quiet, thoughtful questions about my work. He asked me if I'd always wanted to be a television producer. I told him that I had started in print. He asked me if it was strange for a print person to work in television. I told him that it was. He asked me what it had been like to work for Morley Safer at *60 Minutes*. I told him that it had been an education. He listened with great attentiveness and asked sincere follow-ups. I can't describe my relief. I had come to Southeast feeling like an alien. He made me feel welcome. He made me feel like a human being. He opened the door to a conversation that could be both personal and informative. In answer to a question about the difference between TV and print journalism, I told him about my frustration with the medium, in particular the necessity to use pictures, rather than words, to tell stories.

"That's one of the struggles we have in ministry, in preaching," Russell told me. "You find you want to say some things, and you know that they're going to be applicable to certain situations, and people need to hear them, but there's a mind-set out there. I don't think we can keep people's attention with this, so you've got to find some creative way to say the same thing."

That's how my interview with him began. I asked him if he had experienced the shift from words to images personally. It's a shift that has occurred everywhere in American Christianity, as movies, television, and music television replaced novels and newspapers as the main source of entertainment and news. Churches are merely adapting to the country. "I feel like we use a lot more illustrations," he said, "a lot more humor, a lot more visual aids, PowerPoint, a ton of stuff that I don't like. It's not right or wrong. It's just a preference. We have to work so hard to keep people's attention."

He told me that he preferred small venues and small crowds. He liked to teach the Bible to people who had a sincere desire to learn, and he especially liked to work by himself with a video camera, creating tapes for people to see at home. When he left Southeast, he planned to do a series of presentations on different aspects of the Bible.

I asked him if leaving the church after forty years would be hard on him. He paused to consider the question. "I'm really surprised that I'm as calm about it as I am," he said. "I thought when I got to this point I'd be really melancholy about it, and I still may get there. You don't do something forty years at the same place without having a lot of friends and knowing that you're making a big adjustment."

He told me that he was never one of those preachers who received messages from God. This time, though, he was sure. "I can look back over my life," he told me, "and can think God was there, and the Lord helped me. But very few times have I been confident of his message. Very few times have I been really confident that I was doing what God wanted me to do."

He said that it had happened only one other time in recent memory, when he had decided to go on a mission trip to India. His son had a premonition of danger and begged him not to go, but Russell had a strong conviction that God wanted him there. He went, and he had a great trip, but something bad did happen. Russell suffered an attack of deep-vein phlebitis, a serious condition that causes blood clots that can lead to pulmonary embolisms and death. "I wound up in an Indian hospital for a week. By the time I got home, it was one of the deeper experiences of my life, and it was probably good for the church, and good for us all, so I felt like God probably wanted me to go through that."

He told me that he had the same sense of assurance about leaving Southeast. I asked him if he had any insight into the church's success. Was he, Russell, the reason for its growth? He demurred.

"There were about 125 people when I came," he told me, "and I didn't have any vision for a big church. I came from a church of 35 in a little country town. I was skeptical of big churches. My wife, when we started dating, took me to a church of 500 people. It was the largest church I'd ever been in, and I remember going away from there, saying 'It's too big, God can't be in there, people don't know each other, preacher doesn't know everyone.' And so the Lord had a sense of humor to put me here."

IN A BOOKLET commemorating the fortieth anniversary of the founding of the church in 1962, I came across a blurred black-and-white photograph of Bob Russell. It's dated June 12, 1966, and shows the twenty-two-year-old pastor, fresh out of Bible college, preaching his first Sunday at Southeast. The photo has an iconic quality. In the foreground, backs to the camera, sit members of the flock, leaning forward on metal, fold-up chairs. Most of the men have buzz haircuts. In the middle distance, against a backdrop of sun-ribboned bluegrass, stands a young man who might have been cut from wood. The quality of the photo isn't great. His features can't be seen clearly, but his hair is short and dark, his eyes slashes of darkness, his mouth parallel to the eyes, nose bisecting both, bringing a geometric feel to the face. The young man is dressed in a white, short-sleeved shirt and dark pants, nothing else, no coat, no tie, and his stance can only be called preacherly. His lower right arm is bent at the elbow in a right angle to his upper right arm. His left is cocked up, fist against his waist. I can almost hear him quoting Ephesians, chapter 4, verse 1, to the small Kentucky congregation, "I therefore, the prisoner of the Lord, beseech you that ye walk worthy of the vocation wherewith ye are called."

Behind him, in the far distance, morning sun has turned the grass into a river of light. The church had begun four years before this photo was taken, in May 1962, when the General Board of South Louisville Christian Church sent a handful of members to spread the gospel to the rapidly growing east end of Louisville. The early years were modest. The first worship service took place in the auditorium of an elementary school. A few months later, the membership had doubled, from 53 to 105. With seed money from their sending church, members bought a single family home, and that became the first Southeast "church."

In 1963, in that house with a two-car garage, Southeast launched its first organized Bible classes. Four years later, one year after Bob Russell's arrival, in 1967, another milestone: the membership dedicated their first official sanctuary. By that time, the congregation had grown to 550, ten times the size of the original. Growth continued at a relatively modest pace into the mid-1970s; there were 800 by 1975. Three years later, in an effort to expand its numbers, Southeast held what it called Decision Day, during which 50 folks stepped forward to "commit their lives to Christ or Southeast membership," according to the booklet. A few years later, one of these would be hard-living Liz Curtis, a.k.a. "The Motor City Mama," as she was known when she worked as a disc jockey in Detroit. Shortly after moving to Louisville for a new job, she came with friends to Southeast.

"The first Sunday Liz came, I was preaching through the book of Ephesians," Russell writes in his autobiography of Southeast, *When God Builds a Church*. "Paul's emphasis on wives submitting to their husbands in chapter 5 happened to be the text for that day. I talked about husbands being the leaders in their homes. Liz admits she struggled with some of the concepts as a single woman. But then I said that husbands are called to be like Christ—to sacrifice for their wives and even lay down their lives for them. Liz leaned over to her friend and jokingly whispered, 'If I ever met a man who'd die for me, I'd marry him in a minute.' Her friend whispered back, 'Liz, a man has already died for you.'"

A couple of months later, on a Decision Day, she gave her life to Christ. A party girl, she had been living hard, but, as Russell tells it, "the excitement of the people and the inspiration of the people . . . had intrigued her."

She later went on to write bestselling Christian books, including *Bad Girls of the Bible and What We Can Learn from Them.*

Twenty years after the founding of the church, in 1983, about the time that I was headed for a study year abroad in Germany and breaking for good with the faith of my youth, church elders bought 22 acres of land for the purposes of building a 2,400-seat sanctuary. Already, the congregation was demonstrating its wealth as well as its hustle. Members gave "a miracle $1.5 million sacrificial offering" to help build the new sanctuary. In 1986, the sanctuary was finished, and more than 2,000 people walked from the old church to the new, a matter of a few blocks. And that year marked the beginning of the new era, when Southeast and a dozen other churches would explode in numbers, creating a kind of national church movement. If Rick Warren is right, and the local church has replaced both the mainline denominations and the para-church organizations like Young Life as the leading edge of Christianity in this country, these were the years in which that change occurred.

Up to that point, the growth of Southeast had been healthy, but nothing spectacular: 1,500 people in twenty years, 75 per year. Twelve years later, nine times that number would attend Southeast—more than 9,000 people, a leap of 700 per year. By 2006, 9,000 had doubled to 18,000. And by then, miraculous growth had become a problem.

THE HEADACHES HAD been around for at least a decade, ever since 1987, Russell told me. "By that time, the church had reached a thousand members or more," he said, "and I thought that I was in over my head. All of a sudden, I've got a big staff, I've got all these things going on. I wanted to get together with people who knew what they were doing. So I called all of the pastors in the Christian church movement who had congregations of a thousand or more. There were eight of them, and I asked them to come, and let's just talk. I found out they didn't know what they were doing either."

Among the problems, chief among them, and a symbol for everything else that had got out of control, was traffic. Parking had become impossible. Four shuttle buses had to bring people from off-site locations. The 150-member choir and the 22 church elders had to park off campus as well. As long as the lay people had to ride the bus to church, the leadership would, too. A weekly hassle had been turned into an advertisement for the humility of the Southeast elders, but it didn't solve the problem. And neither did the construction of the current sanctuary in 1998. By then, Southeast had become what we now know as a megachurch.

"It's a neutral term for me," Russell said. "I heard Rick Warren say one time that nobody likes big churches except preachers. But you reach a certain size, and that size becomes a detriment. We have a meeting every week with all of the people who became members the previous week. We sit around the table with them and say, 'Tell us about yourself. We want to get to know you.' Half of them say, 'I swore I'd never come to this church because it was too big.' The postmodern mind-set despises bigness. Big government, big corporations, authority. People look at them and say, 'It's just too big. It can't be personal.' So we say, 'Let's not talk about our size. It's obvious to everyone that we're big. Let's try to be as personal as we can and get people into small groups and help them to have a church within a church experience.'"

With a sigh of resignation, he added, "People have all kinds of names for us. Six Flags Over Jesus. Even the God Dome."

I asked him about the Christian attitude toward "the world."

"There are two sides to that coin," he told me. "We're not to love the world or become enamored with it or get involved in it. There's an old illustration that says it's okay for the ship to be in the water, but when the water gets into the ship, you're in trouble. But the other side is this. We're to engage the world. We're to love the people in the world. One of the problems of the church in the past is that we condemn the people of the world rather than saying, hey, these are fallen people who have been wounded like we have, and we're out there to save them. Jesus associated with the world."

He asked me if I remembered the scripture in Matthew where Jesus said, "I will build my church; and the gates of hell shall not prevail against it."

I nodded that I did. I had heard it somewhere. In very clear terms, he proceeded to explain to me the nature of the profound change that had occurred
in Christianity. "For years," he told me, "our concept of that scripture was
that we've got the church, and we've got gates around the church, and Satan's going to pound up against those gates, and he's not going to prevail
against it. But someone pointed out that Jesus isn't talking about the gates
of the church. It's the gates of hell, and the church ought to go right up to
the gates of hell and rescue people from hell. That's why we've got support groups for people with alcohol addictions, for people who have gone
through divorce, for men with sexual addictions. We're here to rescue you
when you've fallen, to say, hey, there's nothing you've done, there's no journey you've taken from God, but what you can turn around and he'll be right
there. He's still reaching out to you."

He had started to work his amazing gifts on me, though he didn't admit
it quite yet. "Here's what I love to see: those people who have been broken
and hurting and searching, and the light comes on for them, and they find
the Lord. It's like having children at Christmas. Have you ever celebrated
Christmas with no kids? It's boring. And you go into some churches today,
and there are no baby Christians. The people in the pews have been Christians so long that they've been through the motions too many times. But
when those new people are coming, they're so excited. Someone's preaching, and they're wiping away tears. You see them hugging the people around
them. It's like children at Christmas. It lifts everybody else up."

I asked him about the attitudes of Christians toward nonbelievers. How
did it feel to be around people who didn't share his faith?

"I always say that some of the worst times in my life spiritually were at
Bible college."

"Why?" I asked.

"Because I saw a phoniness with some. Some of it was my fault. I was
spreading my wings a little bit. But I need the exercise of being around
people in the world. I need them to hold me accountable, because I know
they're watching me."

He gave me an example. He has a Jewish friend, a banker, who has horses
that he races at Churchill Downs, near Louisville. "I go out to the track with

him once or twice a year," Bob told me. "I just laugh and carry on. I don't think it's corrupt of me. I think I'm able to reach some horse trainers and some owners, and so I'm not afraid of the world. I'm trying to engage the world. Now, having said that, I don't think I ought to be out there every day and betting on horses."

"Do you bet at all?" I asked him.

"No," he said, "but I want to." He laughed. "There are some sins of the world that have no appeal to me, and there are others I really battle. That would be one of them. I could get caught up in that, so I don't need to go too often."

We talked about race, sex, and politics. We covered everything that I could think of, but our conversation seemed to be narrowing to a point.

We talked about the issue of gay marriage. He was adamantly opposed to it. Homosexuality was a sin, but he admitted to me that he had probably preached too harshly against homosexuals, calling them sodomites. "An old friend of mine used to say, You can't preach Jesus with a clenched fist."

I came to my last question, the one about the nature of evil. I told him the story of what I had seen in Bosnia, and the room became very quiet.

"How do you grapple with something like that?" I asked him.

He replied, "I'd be an awful shallow person if I pretended to have the answer to that."

I can't tell you why, but in all my travels, out of all the answers to all of the questions, nothing moved me more than this heartfelt response by a great preacher to an impossible question. He went on. "I'm not a Calvinist," he said. "I don't believe that God makes everything that happens to happen. There's a lot of evil that goes on in the world that grieves his heart. I believe that Satan is temporarily the prince of this world, and he delights in murder and lies, and he grieves the heart of God, and that one day, God is going to make all things right. Until that day comes, I don't understand why he waits and why he permits. I don't think he's got his arms folded and is just watching the world unwind. But I believe that he does tolerate evil because, in the end, he's going to make all things right."

"The alternative," he said, "is to believe that the whole thing is a farce. There's no justice in the world, no ultimate meaning, so I have to come to the place where I say, Okay, what am I to believe about Jesus Christ? Did he come back from the grave? If Jesus came back from the grave, that's kind of the bottom-line issue for everything, don't you think? If he came back from the grave, he's got answers that I don't have. What does he say about evil? Don't let your heart be troubled." His voice had grown soft as a whisper. "Do you believe in God? Believe also in me. In my Father's house, there are many mansions. I will go prepare one for you. And one day, it will be made all right. Do I have all the answers?" It was clear to me that the pastor meant himself and was no longer referring to Jesus' words. "No. But I believe Christ does, and I'm going to put my trust in him. The reason I don't have all the answers is because my mind isn't sharp enough to get them, and if I wait till——"

He interrupted himself. "Am I going into areas where you don't want me to go?" he asked. He wanted to know if I wanted him to stop evangelizing me.

"No," I said.

"If I wait till I have all the answers before I have faith," he said, "then there's no faith necessary. So I don't know the answers, but I believe God does, and since Christ came back from the grave, I'm going to put my trust in him. That's the only hope I've got."

"Do you ever doubt?" I asked him.

"Sure." He corrected himself. "I don't doubt much anymore. I did more in the past. I feel like the guy who was asked, How do you know you were saved? He answered—because I was there when it happened!—'Everyone's walk with the Lord is up and down. I was thinking just this morning, I don't know if I've ever felt closer to the Lord than I do right now. I can't always say that. There are hot and cold spells, but I really feel like I'm in a groove right now, so I'm not plagued by much doubt. But I can understand those who do feel doubt.'"

He was drawn back to his central theme, the professed purpose of all those who really believe that the man, Jesus Christ, was the son of God. "There's a measure of faith and a measure of doubt," he told me. "So the great thing is that Jesus said if you have faith as a grain of mustard seed, you'll be able to move mountains, so I'd just encourage you to plant that seed of faith that you do have—" He interrupted himself again. "I'm starting to preach at you."

"I asked," I said. He laughed.

"To come to that place," he continued, "where you say, I don't have an answer to that question of evil, and it really bothers me. And Jesus said, 'In my father's house there are many rooms,' and one of these rooms is going to be the question-and-answer room. When I get up there, I've got some questions I'm going to ask because I sure don't understand them here. But I believe that Jesus Christ came back from the grave, and I am going to put my trust in him." He paused and smiled. "Are you sorry you asked the preacher yet?"

We both laughed now, and it was a laugh of relief.

BEFORE I LEFT him, Bob Russell gestured for me to follow him. He wanted to show me something. He led me through some doors, down a corridor, and into a wide dark room with a domed ceiling. As we entered, a technician walked out. The room was the dome of the sanctuary. Below us, hundreds of feet down, under the floor beneath our feet, stood Bob's stage. Jutting from the ceiling, I saw the base of the fifty-foot cross that rises above the church, and Bob told me that it wasn't just an ornament, but a load-bearing element of the structure, which he loved. He loved the idea of the weight of that metal cross, holding up the sanctuary, directly above the spot where he preached; the burden, the responsibility, appealed greatly to him. I felt privileged to be there, but someone later told me that the outgoing senior pastor of Southeast takes everyone to see that sight. The base of the cross hung right above his pulpit, invisible, but he felt it and wanted others to know it.

Finally, he showed me the spot where the angels sit before they descend on harnesses into the sanctuary. One of them was pregnant, he told me. I could smell the presence of angels in that room. They had been there the night before and would come again in the evening, after the sun had set. I could smell the perfume and sweat of angels. I didn't say anything, but I was sorry when the door closed, and I had to leave those heights.

## chapter 14

## Weather

*I*n Baton Rouge, Louisiana, nine months after Hurricane Katrina, I met another pastor, a guy named Dino Rizzo, whose pale face and dark-ringed eyes suggested a state of deep and total exhaustion. Pastor Dino, as his flock called him, looked a bit like a sleepwalker. And why not? The better part of a year after Katrina ravaged his state, he was still dealing with the aftermath, and a new hurricane season approached, and New Orleans hadn't even fixed its levees yet. Pastor Dino couldn't run or change jobs or be somewhere else. This was his show and these were his people. With his untucked shirt, jeans, and scraggly beard, he didn't at all fit the mold of an earlier generation of Baton Rouge evangelists, the clean-shaven, telegenic Jimmy Swaggart, for instance. He looked like a man who had nightmares of flooded churches and delayed food shipments. I couldn't imagine the burden of his life.

The U.S. Department of Labor counts 350,000 members of the clergy in the United States, among them 4,000 rabbis, 49,000 Catholic priests, and 300,000 Protestant ministers. According to psychologist Andrew Weaver, quoted in a 1995 article in the *Journal of Pastoral Care,* these clergy spend 15 percent of their fifty-hour workweek on counseling members of their congregation, and that doesn't include those times when counseling happens in myriad unofficial forms, from constant administrative meetings and preaching to informal conversations and emergency aid in a hurricane. Pastoring is counseling on a cosmic scale. And it never stops.

In the best of times, pastors must take the urgent phone calls and the midnight visits, they must spend the hours in the company of deep grief and rage, no matter how exhausted or depressed themselves, in the mouth of human despair and delusion, bracing for the inevitable announcements of sudden death, unwanted pregnancy, business collapse, and recurrent addiction. They must deal with every malady and controversy known to the species, up close and personal. Unlike politicians or even doctors or cops, they're not just answerable to their people—their constituency, their citizenry, their civilian charges, their patients. They are also explicitly answerable to God. Dino Rizzo's life has not been his own. He would say that his burdens sound heavier than they are, thanks to the nurturing power of the Holy Spirit. But he carries a heavy load, no matter what he might say. I have to admit that such commitment to serving others, whether for God or man, has never sparked even the slightest interest within me.

LET ME BE as clear as possible about this. Like a lot of Americans, for years, around Christmas, I watched that sentimental war horse of a movie, *It's a Wonderful Life*, in which a man named George Bailey, played by James Stewart, becomes trapped by family obligations and community need in the stifling little town of Bedford Falls. George stays home to help others rather than pursue his own romantic dream of life elsewhere, and even though an angel tries to convince him that he made the right decision, I always felt that the angel had an agenda to conceal the hard truth; to stay behind meant personal catastrophe for George. I always hoped, just once, he would get out of there. No matter how much he meant to the people of Bedford Falls, no matter how deeply he affected their lives, I longed for him to realize that he would have been much happier on the stage of the great world. There, and only there, would he find a destiny that would be both significant to others and fulfilling to himself. Nothing, not even his daughter Zuzu's rose petals, could convince me otherwise.

It isn't that I'm a completely heartless bastard. I have some sense of feeling for my fellow human being. In high school, I became an Eagle Scout, and for my final project, I served as leader for a troop of disabled kids in north Dallas. I didn't undertake the project in a cynical spirit. I truly wanted to help those kids and enjoyed spending time in their service, organizing field trips and excursions. But it was a rare moment of genuine civic virtue in my life. I always had a much greater love for the romance of existence than I ever did for my fellow man.

The fact came home to me with striking clarity a few years ago when I wrote a piece for *U.S. News & World Report* about the adult children of the Kennedy family, the sons and daughters of the political dynasty. To this day, tens of millions of Americans consider the Kennedys and their offspring the first family of the United States, American royalty. In my corner of Dallas, we despised them. My parents and their friends spoke of the Kennedys as crooks and hypocrites who had stolen the election from Richard Nixon in 1960. Until I went to college, I thought that everyone felt this way and almost got in a fistfight over the matter with a theologian's son from Saint Louis. In my family, in my community, we rarely talked about the assassination of John F. Kennedy in 1963, the worst thing ever to happen in Dallas. A hideous embarrassment hung over the fact that a president held in base contempt by most of the city fathers had been murdered in cold blood on their own streets. Dallas was the last place on earth prepared to feel guilt on that score, though Dallasites secretly did, and much later, after I left, spent a lot of money to build an excellent museum commemorating the dark day.

But it came too late for me. When I got the Kennedy assignment, I resisted. I didn't think that the kids merited a story. It was an election year, and a Democratic convention approached, but I didn't consider the Kennedys to be emblematic of the party. No one did. My editor insisted and gave me the summer to meet and interview as many of the children as I could. I tracked down about a dozen of them, from Bobby and Timothy Shriver to Kathleen Kennedy Townsend, then lieutenant governor of Maryland, and Joseph Kennedy Jr., then a congressman from Massachusetts; I met Rory Kennedy in Manhattan and the late Michael Kennedy in Hyannisport and Robert F. Kennedy Jr. at his home in Mount Kisco. The whole thing turned out to be an education in civic commitment. I don't want to imply that I fell in love with the Kennedys or decided that they were saints or anything so extreme, but for the first time, I came into contact with a natural and spontaneous attraction to the public good. It wasn't just an act or a bit of successfully manipulated public relations. The Kennedys I met were the children of ambitious, competitive, world-conquering people who had instilled in their young a romantic and at the same time compulsory sense that a life without civic duty wasn't worth living. They seemed to have as deep a romance with civic duty as I did with individual experience. The family history of sexual excess and political scandal went hand in hand with this legacy of obligation. So Robert F. Kennedy Jr. saves rivers, Rory Kennedy makes documentaries about poverty and war, Timothy Shriver runs the Special Olympics, which his mother Eunice Shriver started, and Anthony Shriver founded Best Buddies, which pairs grown-ups as mentors with disabled kids. Bobby and Mark Shriver have both been in local politics, their sister Maria, a famous journalist, is married to the governor of California, and Senator Ted Kennedy's son Patrick still holds a congressional seat in Rhode Island. And it goes on and on. Some of it is about power, I'm sure. But more than that, I had the feeling that you lost face in that family if you committed your life to a purely private notion of work. Among the Kennedys, a purely private notion of anything smacked of self-indulgence.

Nothing could have been further from my family's sensibility. It wasn't that my parents didn't instill in us compassion and empathy for others. My father did plenty of pro bono work as a lawyer, and my mother gave her time with the Junior League of Dallas, working with disadvantaged girls. We were constantly reminded of the importance of courtesy to others, of treating every human being with respect, no matter what their station in life. But courtesy did not mean commitment. My parents raised us in a community where caring for the less fortunate belonged to the accepted and necessary package of social graces but could not be understood by most as an emphasis for its own sake. Idealism focused on family, friends, sports, business, and faith. Integrity of the personal kind mattered far more than sacrifice for one's neighbor. A man could spend his entire life amassing a private fortune in Highland Park and retain the high regard of his neighbors as long as his handshake and his word remained his bond. If these lost their value, however, he would never overcome the taint. Members of my family and most people in their circle loathed Bill Clinton because he failed the ultimate test of personal integrity—he lied under oath. No matter what else he might achieve in office, he could never overcome that lapse. For the opposite reason, George W. Bush earned respect despite his failings. He might have blundered on any number of policies, but in the view of a lot of people back home, he never demonstrated what they would call "poor character." This isn't a Christian thing. It's a habit of mind that cuts across a number of religious and cultural lines, and it was mine.

In short, civic virtue didn't figure much in my notion of the ideal life, even a highly moral one. Civic virtue in government mattered even less. To me, no glamour whatsoever has ever attached to politics or politicians. In junior high and high school, my one and only contribution to student government came in the form of campaign management. Junior year, I came up with the slogan for the winning candidate for student council president: "Make My Mama Proud." I enjoyed the game of selling someone as a candidate. I didn't give a damn about the issues.

In college, I had even less interest in government or anything related to it. The year after I graduated, I was traveling around post-Fascist Spain with a friend, and I told him that my preferred form of rule would be a monarchy. He was incredulous, but I meant it. In hindsight, it's easy to see one reason for my contempt for democracy. I grew up in an economically prosperous, deeply conservative, socially and culturally sheltered community in which most of my creature comforts and all of my rights were implicitly protected. I was white, straight, and upper-middle-class in a white, straight, upper-middle-class town. What could politics do for me? Who needed government when you had great Mexican food, an excellent football team, the best-looking girls in the state, and Jesus?

I recall another moment, more disturbing. Years after college, when I had become a professional journalist, I went to Washington, D.C., to do some interviews. After my work was done, I went for a stroll on the Mall. I came to a spot just below the U.S. Capitol building and stared up at the creamy classical dome, framed in mid-May by a close, hot, blue sky. I had spent time as a reporter inside the building—as a clerk for the *New York*

*Times*, helping the Hill reporters do their job and stealing away for delicious barbecue in the basement. But I had never had a moment to regard the building itself, to think about its larger meaning. Right then, on that May afternoon, the moment came. It should have been tremendous. It was totally meaningless. I felt nothing at all. I didn't feel pride. I didn't feel excitement. I didn't feel gratitude. I might as well have been staring at a high-rise parking lot. The building itself was more beautiful than that, of course, but nothing about it touched my emotions or thrilled my mind. The absence of feeling shocked me, but it shouldn't have.

I turned ten years old in 1973, the year that the broadcast networks began to show the Watergate hearings on national television. In the afternoons, I would come home and watch without much understanding the unfolding investigation into the misdeeds of the president of the United States. It's my first political memory. For a kid who had grown up in Dallas, Texas, where the murder of another president, this one's opponent, shadowed the local sense of identity, the natural state of government seemed to be bloodshed and collapse. I have never loved a president or even a presidential candidate, never had a JFK, like my aunt and uncle in Ohio, never had a Barry Goldwater or a George Bush, like my parents, or an FDR, like my grandparents in Oklahoma. My heroes were adventurers, athletes, philosophers, revolutionaries, rock musicians, filmmakers, writers, and messiahs: Danton, Nabokov, Nietzsche, T. E. Lawrence, J.R.R. Tolkien, Roger Staubach, Mick Jagger, Bruce Springsteen, Sam Peckinpah, Joseph Conrad, Jesus.

It will probably come as no surprise, though I'm ashamed to admit it, that I didn't participate in a U.S. election until I was thirty years old and married to a much more responsible citizen, my wife, a lover of libraries and a dedicated voter. Until then, I didn't see the point.

My lack of civic virtue found metaphysical justification in the New Testament. Many of today's Christians cite their faith as a reason to go to the polls. I experienced the opposite. I have a vivid high school memory of a series of Wednesday night Bible studies devoted to the New Testament book of James. Our Young Life leader, Bobby McCreless, taught us, a group of sophomores, mostly football players, including some of the stars of the team, I the exception, that faith alone justified us before God. Without faith, good works were as ashes and dust to him that made us. It's a remarkable reading of James 2:21, in which the author seems to be saying the very opposite, that "faith without works" is dead. "But wilt thou know, o vain man, that faith without works is dead? Was not Abraham our father justified by works, when he had offered Isaac his son upon the altar?" Yet our Young Life leader insisted that the traditional reading was a misinterpretation, that belief alone made the difference, that these passages meant to underscore the frailty of good works compared with grace and glory of God. It was all I needed. Belief meant everything. Good deeds meant nothing. This version of Christianity put the highest priority on the deep interior of the soul, and it suited my natural inclinations beautifully. I had no great desire to serve others anyway, and the most influential Christian in my circle vindicated my indifference by underscoring the divine indifference to worthy action.

Later in life, when I pondered what God had called me to do with my faith, I knew the answer. I should be a missionary. I knew this in my guts. But I didn't want to be a missionary to bring clean water and medicine to impoverished Africans, though these efforts might provide a necessary aesthetic frisson to my calling. I wanted to be a missionary to experience the romantic life at its most exotic and extreme. I wanted to risk death in hot climes. I wanted to catch sunrise over the Serengeti, rushing toward the blaze like T. E. Lawrence in the desert in the David Lean movie, which I had watched a million times on cable TV. I wanted to sit beside a beautiful, saved woman in an International Harvester jeep, sunglasses reflecting glory, sleeves of my blue chambray work shirt rolled up, as the natives cheered my dust, as the soundtrack swelled.

One night, my sophomore year in college, my father and I had a fight about my future. He demanded to know what I planned to do with my life.

"I'm either going to be a missionary or a film director!" I shouted.

"For God's sake," he shouted back, "be a director!"

I became neither, and that old conversation was long forgotten by the time I showed up in Baton Rouge, most of a year after Katrina came and went. I had heard a lot about faith in my travels. Now I wanted to see the works, despite what my Young Life leader had told me long ago. I wanted to see what Bible-believing Christians might do to ease the suffering of the world, and more than once, people had told me about a relatively new but quickly growing church in south Baton Rouge, run by the grandson of an Italian immigrant. This was Dino Rizzo.

A FEW DAYS after Katrina, which had arrived on his wife DeLynn's birthday, Dino broke down in tears in the kitchen of his home. He'd never seen anything like that terrible storm, though he'd not been unprepared. In his mind, in his faith, his church had been set up specifically to deal with human suffering. Before the hurricane, his Cooking for Christ team already served meals to thousands, and his congregation had given tens of thousands in aid to tsunami victims in Southeast Asia in a matter of days. But this was another dimension. That had been charity. This was survival. The week before the storm, with Katrina turning from a tropical depression in the Bahamas to a hurricane across Florida, he had known that it might be a bad one. He'd called his network of associated churches in the Pastors Resource Council and begun to strategize. His church had opened its doors to evacuees before. It wasn't a registered shelter, but the next best thing, a place to stop, shower, and make a few phone calls.

Ever since he had accepted Christ as a pot-smoking surfer dude in Myrtle Beach, South Carolina, helped along by a man dragging a cross down the strand, Dino Rizzo had been looking for a way to reach those people who were at the miserable end of existence, whether the drag prostitutes who worked the late-night shift in the beach town or the poor he encountered during missions work in South America. In the early days of his Baton Rouge church, thirteen years before Katrina, as the membership grew from a few people to its first thousand, his congregation named itself Trinity Christian Church, the kind of title one might hear anywhere in the country: solid, unremarkable, theologically impeccable. But seven years into its existence, Dino and his leaders began to feel restless about the direction of the church and wanted a new slogan to reshape the identity. His mother-in-law, a wizard with words, came up with the answer: "A Healing Place for a Hurting World." The phrase conjured exactly what Dino wanted. The words grew in his mind, like God's own whisper, until he began to feel called to change the name of Trinity Christian to Healing Place. It was a big decision for a large and growing church, the kind of thing that could drive people away. At best, it guaranteed some level of controversy. No one loves change, certainly not Christians happily settled into a church home. But the thought kept nagging, and the distance between him and Jesus kept growing, so Dino did it.

"Didn't ask anybody," he told me. "Didn't tell anybody. Just got up and changed the name of the church."

Three weeks later, after an aneurysm hit him on a mission trip in Ecuador, half his body was paralyzed. His people prayed for him, he recovered, and the name became fixed. The Healing Place was well and truly born.

ON AUGUST 29, 2005, at dawn, Katrina made landfall in Buras, Louisiana, a town of 3,000 or so in Plaquemines Parish, 140 miles south of Baton Rouge. To call it a storm, or even a hurricane, seems misleading. Weather and sea came like Satan and all his angels. Buras was buried. Out over the Gulf, Katrina had been a category 5 hurricane with winds of 165 miles per hour and storm surges thirty-five feet high. By the time she reached the shore, she had declined to a category 4, but the technical downgrade smacked of mockery. In Baton Rouge, Dino and his family and some friends gathered at home. Wind smacked down trees, toppling power lines, but the tempest didn't quite summon biblical metaphors. Generators were humming. It looked like the worst might miss Louisiana and hit Mississippi instead.

By 7:30 A.M., the Industrial Canal in New Orleans had breached, though Dino and his people had no news of it, and floodwaters rose in the Upper Ninth Ward, Bywater, and Treme neighborhoods. People had begun to die in their homes, or scuttle to the rooftops, or head for the Superdome. Three hours later, canals had breached in three places and the deluge had commenced. Before the end of the day, 80 percent of New Orleans would be underwater, as deep as ten feet in some places. The banner headline of the New Orleans *Times-Picayune* that Monday morning blared two words: "Ground Zero" in big black letters. By the next morning, the word count had gone down to one: "Catastrophic."

Pastor Dino got news that the levees had breached at about 1:00 P.M. on Monday, and he began to muster pastors in the region, the two hundred or so members of the Pastors Resource Council. Communication was the indispensable first element in a coordinated plan of attack; in local, state, and federal government efforts, communication failed time and again. In the churches, it worked. That Tuesday morning, the doors of Healing Place Church opened, and a massive church relief effort crossing all sectarian lines in the Christian world was under way in southern Louisiana. "I've told people I could die and go to heaven now," Dino told me. "I have seen the church—the body of believers—in their finest hour, working together, laying down ego, logo, agenda, and motive. You didn't hear 'My church is bigger than your church,' 'I don't like the way you sing,' 'That's not the way we do liturgical calendar'—none of that."

For Healing Place, the storm came at an awkward moment. The year before, the church had begun a massive renovation of its fifty-six-acre main campus. The new church annex hadn't been completed yet, and the ground had barely been cleared for its new arena to be modeled on vast glass megachurches in Sydney, Australia, and Dallas, Texas. That arena would have been ideal for housing thousands, but it didn't exist. The annex offered a bit of unfinished office space, nothing more. Real estate is inert, the leadership knew. On its own, it promises nothing. It decides nothing. Readiness was everything. If the Healing Place couldn't justify its name now, then when? The weather had broken into Louisiana like the proverbial thief in the night, and there couldn't be any hesitation. Pastor Dino and his team moved into the annex, which began immediately to serve as a command center for relief throughout the entire region. The pastor went before his flock. For the first time in his ministry, Dino asked that every single mother, father, son, and daughter lend a hand, whether with time or money or prayers. A thousand people stepped forward immediately to offer physical assistance. Tuesday, the evacuees began to show, a wave of people coming off Interstate 10. Baton Rouge received 250,000 human beings in those days, doubling in size overnight. It became the central theater for all rescue-and-relief efforts in Louisiana. With government in New Orleans drawing national scorn, a sense of uttermost responsibility fell on the shoulders of the churches.

In that hour, after a long stretch of sleepless nights, of haggling and scrapping over every cot and water bottle, Dino had his breakdown. "I hit the wall," he told me. "I just sat in my kitchen and boo-hooed, because I thought this was too big. I can't do this. There were so many people calling. A lot of the major ministries in the country were calling, and I didn't want to drop the ball. I didn't want to misrepresent Christ or drop the ball or do something stupid. Or watch as, all of the sudden, the church and our networks of pastors eroded due to ego and pride. I felt like one of my roles was to keep us all on board."

HE WASN'T THE only pastor in Baton Rouge under the gun. Churches throughout the region had to act fast. And, though no one said so explicitly, maybe the pastors of Baton Rouge had something extra to prove. Almost two decades earlier, one of the most famous televangelists in the world and a hometown boy, Jimmy Swaggart, had been caught with a prostitute, and the scandal brought about the near ruin of his ministry. Along with televangelist Jim Bakker, who had his own sexual misadventures, Swaggart had seriously fouled the image of American Christianity and given tens of millions of people an excuse to ridicule Jesus and all those who spoke in that name. In Baton Rouge, Swaggart's downfall became a very personal loss, a civic disaster, in fact, as what had once been the largest business in town, Jimmy Swaggart Ministries, became a ghost town. People who had worked for Swaggart for years had to find new jobs and a new place to worship. He could still be seen around town, dining out with his family, and he still had a ministry, but the damage was done. Big personalities might drive growth and bring wealth, but without accountability, without oversight, they endangered the faith. By the 1990s, televangelists like Swaggart ceased to be the face of innovation and leadership among evangelicals, no matter what the public might think, and in those same years, local churches like Rick Warren's Saddleback in California, Southeast Christian in Louisville, and Willow Creek in Chicago had become the vanguard for a new ethos that enforced much tougher codes of personal conduct—though never foolproof, as the case of Rev. Ted Haggard in Colorado Springs brought home—much harder lines on church finances and a much greater commitment to helping the poor and the vulnerable. Healing Place Church wasn't just an isolated example of one pastor's vision. It was part of a movement, and when Katrina came, that movement came into its own.

Florida Baptist Church, also in Baton Rouge, fed 16,000 people a day for weeks, according to the *Detroit Free Press*. Exciting Istrouma Baptist Church, the opening adjective a part of its proper name, served as a Red Cross shelter, housing 700 evacuees. Bethany World Prayer Center, a megachurch with 10,000 members and the most prominent local successor to Swaggart's ministry, put all of its size and cash into play. On Tuesday, the same day that Healing Place opened for business, Bethany opened its southern campus to Coast Guard workers and others, housing and feeding hundreds who returned every night from rescue work in New Orleans. Its 12,000-square-foot warehouse became a distribution point for fifty-six churches in the area. By the next day, Bethany's northern campus had become the so-called City of Hope, home eventually to 800 misplaced people, who were given much more than a temporary shelter. They had medicine, counseling, eventually job opportunities, and the potential to receive help rebuilding their homes. In some sense, the inhabitants were also given a chance to become masters of their own destinies in the moment of their greatest vulnerability. On the second day of the shelter's existence, the evacuees held a town meeting, and the pastor, the Reverend Larry Stockstill, declared the reign of a new "law of love."

The stress on the Baton Rouge area was profound and unsustainable. The leader of the coordinated effort, Gene Mills, who had worked for years with pastors to lobby in the state capitol on behalf of Christian values, told me that the churches soon reached the breaking point. "Look, we had prayed all of our lives for the churches to be full," Mills told me. "The analogy used in scripture is that the disciples prayed to catch fish. Well, they prayed and their nets broke. Our nets were breaking. We had more fish than we knew what to do with. We had people dying in the sanctuaries, in the pews. We had babies being born in the pews. I'm talking about hundreds of churches around the state. We had bipolar and other schizophrenic needs that were dramatically affected. We had the loss and separation of loved ones who had no place to go but the church. We knew that we couldn't handle it much longer."

One answer was clear. Baton Rouge couldn't be the staging point for everything. Mills and his fellow church leaders cooked up a plan to start distribution centers in nearby states. Supplies would come into those relay stations in Texas, Oklahoma, Arkansas, and Mississippi and wait for directions on where to go. As quickly as possible, in the same spirit, churches started moving people out of Baton Rouge. There simply wasn't room or space to meet all those needs.

Most remarkably, given the public perception of race tensions surrounding the Katrina episode, most of these church efforts took place seamlessly across racial lines and barriers. Dino told me that Healing Place saw a mix of every ethnic type in the Gulf region and didn't give a damn about it. "We had whites, blacks, Hispanics, Vietnamese, good old Cajun. You had everything here on the property, so we stayed out of all that. . . . We just tried to say, hey, let's help people. This is our state. We'll let everybody else sort out that other stuff. We've got to cook some rice. That was our mentality."

Another reflection of that mentality: Dino and his people rejected all talk by out-of-state believers that New Orleans' sinful ways had somehow brought on the catastrophe. When I asked him about those sorts of opinions, the pastor dismissed them with moral contempt. "That's not a statement you heard much from people in Louisiana," he said. "These were real people. They were moms and dads. They were grandparents, special-needs children. They were our uncles, our cousins, our friends who we work with, play ball with. So we would hear things like that, but we were so in the trenches that we just said, 'Quit talking and help! Quit casting your thoughts on us and load up a truck with water. Can you come down here and sort out a mom who is illiterate but who is having to fill out thirty pages of paper to get food stamps. Can you go to the airport and clean up senior citizens?' When you're working, and you're getting a few hours of sleep a night, and you're looking at a staff that's getting even less, you're totally immersed. . . . There were days when I had no idea what was going on. I just knew that we needed to get clothes to people. I knew that I needed to call thirty pastors and let them know what was happening. I'm getting calls, and people are telling me, 'We're in Mandeville, and we've got six hundred people in our parking lot,' or 'We're in Saint Bernard, and we've got fifteen hundred people in our warehouse, and we've run out of food.'"

There was literally no time for Judgment, with a capital J, and I would argue that this was a watershed moment in the history of American Christianity, when the old-style hellfire and damnation politics of the Moral Majority era finally gave way to a radically new dispensation, deeply uncomfortable, even embarrassed by such statements. By Friday, September 5, 200 pastors in the area were gathering to give their blessing to PRC Compassion, a new faith-based relief organization under Gene Mills's leadership. The following Monday, President Bush and the first lady showed up at Bethany World Prayer Center's City of Hope, where relief efforts made a mockery of the federal government response. The president and first lady, accompanied by the Louisiana governor, the Baton Rouge mayor, and the Reverend T. D. Jakes of Dallas, stayed for an hour and a half, speaking with evacuees. Almost a year later, the White House issued a report, "Lessons Learned from Katrina," and singled out the failure of the U.S. government to adequately partner with the churches in the relief effort.

Along with other nonprofits, the White House paper said, "Faith-based organizations also provided extraordinary services." It chided the U.S. government, saying, "Unfortunately, the Nation did not always make effective use of these contributions because we had not effectively planned for integrating them into the overall response effort."

Whatever critics of the cooperation between church and state may feel, and no matter what happens in the politics in coming years, the Katrina moment very quietly announced a shift in the perception of Christianity within the body of Christendom. Plenty of people outside the faith might still identify Christianity with the style and scandal of the Jimmy Swaggarts; Ted Haggard's fall certainly reinforced those feelings. But nothing spoke more eloquently to believers, and to nonbelievers who were paying attention, than the success of a population of believing volunteers measured against the massive and near-total collapse of secular government efforts. The storm laid bare an unmistakable truth. More and more Christians have decided that the only way to reconquer America is through service. The faith no longer travels by the word. It moves by the deed.

DEBBIE WARD KNEW it long before Katrina. Ward is the team leader for service ministry at Southeast Christian and was the point person at the church on hurricane relief. She'd worked for twenty-two years in the corporate world, first as a CPA with Arthur Andersen, later in a succession of high-profile banking jobs, and service had been part of her portfolio. She's one of those women who demolishes stereotypes about the evangelical female, a tall woman with short blond hair, and a very direct and businesslike manner. The Bible may tell women to submit, but it's hard to see how Debbie Ward might accommodate: she's more likely to be giving the orders. Service hadn't always been her passion. Ward grew up in a small farming town, and community service never figured much in her education or upbringing. But when she moved from Arthur Andersen into banking, her boss insisted that she sit on the board of the local United Way.

She saw up close what United Way did for people, and that job led to more responsibility, and service eventually became a hallmark of her corporate leadership. She had already been a member at Southeast for years when Bob Russell told her that the church wanted to put a much greater emphasis on community service and asked her if she wanted to run the show. By that time, burned out after a series of bank mergers and acquisitions, Ward had left the corporate world. She didn't particularly want to work at her church—it was almost too personal, too important, to be considered a workplace—but at the same time, she realized that the moment had come, and the ideal opportunity, to put her beliefs about service to the test. She became the official Southeast gadfly.

"I think it's great what we do internationally," she told me, "but I thought that we needed to be doing more locally. I'm the kind of person who would keep saying, 'I don't understand why we go to Poland and do basketball games, but we don't do basketball camps in Portland. I was the one who would say, 'It's too easy for our people to get on a plane and fly to another country and serve and come home, and they can sleep at night. I wish they would go down to our local Christian mission and serve, because I don't think they could go back home and go to sleep necessarily as easily as they can when it's so far away.'"

When Katrina blasted out of the Gulf, Bob Russell turned to her again, one week after the storm. The church had done storm relief before. When tornados hit Indiana, the members had been asked to bring mops, brooms, and Clorox, and they'd delivered. But it had been a complicated and messy situation, and getting the stuff to Indiana had taken far too long. This time around, Ward got corporate fast; she wanted to be precise and strategic in her approach. She didn't want to waste a dime and insisted on finding a bona fide partner. The quarterly food drive became a Katrina offering, and the congregation came through with truckloads of goods.

"I didn't just want to jump in the car and drive," Ward recalled, "so I started looking on the Internet and talking to churches."

She eventually found PRC Compassion, the Gene Mills operation, and, among other institutions, Healing Place Church, with which Southeast formed a loose partnership. At one point, a member of Southeast affiliated with the Texas Roadhouse food chain delivered tens of thousands of bottles of Willie Nelson water to the HPC annex in Baton Rouge.

But there were bigger, more long-term issues. In the weeks after the storm, Ward went down to Louisiana and Mississippi, seeking the right partner. She found just the right fit in Mississippi, a guy with a tent and a hamburger grill in Pass Christian. But in Louisiana, she had a more difficult time. "It just wasn't connecting," she said. "I guess the passion that I felt, I couldn't find the equivalent. I felt like—and I don't want this to sound arrogant—some of the folks saw me and thought, this is a big church with big bucks, and let's get a piece of that."

Around that time, she got word from Louisville that should have made her day, but it only made her more anxious. "I was in Mississippi or Louisiana when they called to tell me that they'd collected $695,000 that weekend, and I said, you know, that's good news and bad news. The good news is that we've got $695,000 for Katrina victims. That's also the bad news. It emphasized for me that we had to do this right. We had to find the right partners."

And she added, "It's easy to write checks. That's the easiest thing in the world."

A church in Texas finally helped her find the match, a small church in Algiers, Louisiana, run by a pastor who had built a program for single moms. He would rent low-income housing to the mothers and grandmothers, then invest the proceeds in a summer camp for kids in Mississippi. Katrina had damaged most of the homes, so Southeast moved into a partnership, not just to provide relief money but to rebuild the entire community. Ward saw in the Algiers pastor a living example of what she thought Southeast, and all churches, could be but weren't.

"He gets it," she said of the pastor. "It's not about entitlement. It's not about any of that. It's about helping them get through this. It's about helping their children see things differently. It's about the whole thing. He helps with employment. He helps with GED classes. And when he walks around, they come out of their houses. They all know him. It's not just about his church service on Sunday mornings. He's part of that community. He's a part of the heart and breath of that community."

That's what Southeast wants to be in Louisville. And it's not just a matter of being kind to others. It's about the most urgent business of the church.

A few months after I paid a visit to Ward, Southeast volunteers raised the frames of thirty new homes to be erected in Louisiana. Volunteers showed up by the hundreds to do the job. "It's an opportunity to invite my neighbor to come work with me, because it's a nonthreatening environment," Ward explained, "because we're going to help people. It's not like saying, hey, come to church with me. We have a lot of members who wouldn't be comfortable asking their neighbors to come to church, but they're more than willing to ask them to come and serve. And as folks see Christians serving in the community—" she stopped herself and inserted a new thought. "We only do that because Christ commands—I mean, we do it because we're passionate about it, we do it because we get so much out of it—but we do it because Christ commanded it. He set the example, and that's what we're supposed to do, and so that's what we'll do."

It was a rare, awkward moment in our conversation, and I got the feeling that Debbie Ward didn't feel comfortable having to say those words. After all, she started doing community service in the corporate world, long before she did it explicitly as evangelism, and she had implied earlier in our conversation that she did it out of the joy of doing for others, service for the sake of service. In our chat, she had backed herself into a sentence that sounded bad in her own ears, that invoked the reasons why millions of Americans have problems with faith-based relief. She had implied that the church did its work not out of compassion, but in order to win souls for Jesus. I have no doubt that Debbie Ward believes that to be true, but she was too much a corporate animal, too aware of the negative image, not to feel the sour taste of that sentiment in her mouth.

ON DECEMBER 1, 2001, the *New York Times* ran a front-page story with photographs about churches around the country giving money to small businesses in the vicinity of the destroyed World Trade Center buildings. The piece began with this sentence: "The preacher from Kentucky went store to store on the edge of Ground Zero, an understanding look in his eye and money in his pockets."

That preacher was Dave Stone, Bob Russell's successor at Southeast. I hadn't remembered the story, though I had been living in New York at the time. When I asked him about the church's response to 9/11, the first thing he mentioned was the article. "It's one of the greatest memories of my life," he told me. "But it's also a little awkward, because the *Times* went around with me, and a photographer, so it turned into a front-page story, and the awkwardness is that my memories of that day are from the face-to-face interaction with people in New York. But for people around here, and my buddies around the country, the memory was the article. People said, 'You went around and handed out money from your church, and boy, the *New York Times* article was great.' But the moment for me was just getting to see these people who were not expecting anything. We would just be having a casual conversation with them, and then I said I'd like to give you something in the name of Jesus, to show you that Christ loves you, and for you to know there's a church back in Kentucky that's praying for you. They didn't have a clue what this church was like. They just knew it was some Christian people in Kentucky, and that's all they needed to know."

Like Ward's awkward moment in our conversation, this was a revealing moment. Stone was proud of what he'd done, and he obviously welcomed the newspaper coverage—it would have been possible to turn the reporter and photographer away—but he also knew the downside. The coverage itself would raise the profile of the church, but it would also remind him of the worldly, self-serving benefit to him and to Southeast of handing out checks at Ground Zero. There was an element of P. T. Barnum there, and he knew it whenever a pastor from another church congratulated him on that great article in the *Times*.

It's a real dilemma. In a media-driven age, how do you get out the word about Jesus, and the word about your church, without appearing to be burnishing your own image for purely worldly reasons, or worse, lining your own pockets? The enemy is always waiting to pounce, and even your allies can make you look bad. Shortly after Katrina, *The Nation* ran a piece on Pat Robertson's relief effort, Operation Blessing, noting that it had been "prominently featured on FEMA's list of charitable groups accepting donations for hurricane relief," this despite the fact that Robertson had been in all kinds of trouble, calling for the assassination of Venezuelan president Hugo Chavez and calling the Supreme Court a greater threat to the United States than Al Qaeda. *The Nation* implied that Robertson had cut some kind of sweetheart deal with the White House, offering to defend it against Katrina criticism in exchange for making the relief list. Meanwhile, more prominent secular relief organizations hadn't been chosen.

None of this would matter if Bible-believing Christians hadn't decided to take a much more active role in the affairs of their communities, and their country, if the bunker mentality of earlier decades had not given way to a new spirit of evangelistic activism and engagement. Before leaving Southeast, I had a chat with Stone about the changing character of his institution. Stone had a certain sturdy, unaffected quality that reminded me of Bob Russell, but otherwise he struck me as a different kind of man. For all his demeanor of rustic charm, Russell had a formal air. Even in slacks and golf shirt, he seemed to be wearing a tie. Stone had more in common with Pastor Dino. I can't remember if his shirt was untucked, but he himself had an untucked quality, slightly unkempt, a bit frazzled from a thousand responsibilities. Stone had hair on his face; Russell came from a generation that didn't much care for facial hair and didn't much wear it. Both men could both be funny, but Russell seemed to lean more toward jokes and anecdotes while Stone's talk had more of the observational wit in the Seinfeld mold. More than that, though, my conversation with Russell had an intimate quality, as if we were talking from the heart, as if he could afford the time and personal space to be curious. The talk with Stone was all business; he was the new leader of the church, being interviewed by a writer from outside. His answers needed to be cogent. My questions tended to be tougher.

It was March 2006. Since the previous September, Southeast teams had been traveling down south to help the relief effort, one team per weekend, 700 volunteers or so in all. I had seen one of the teams pull up in a minivan in front of the church, passenger door rolling back, travelers tumbling into the mild morning sun, voices still buzzing from their adventure.

It was all part of the Southeast effort to become what Stone called "an externally focused church." The term is the title of a book cowritten by his best friend, another pastor, Rick Rusaw, who had been a senior minister at Lifebridge Christian Church in Colorado. In the book, Rusaw asks one of the most basic questions any person can put to a pastor: "If your church vanished, would your community weep?"

If not, Rusaw writes, your church has failed. Stone hasn't just taken the message to heart. He's made it the basis of a local revolution. Under Russell, Southeast focused more on spreading the gospel, gaining converted members, and deepening the faith of those believers. It was what Rusaw and his coauthor, Eric Swanson, have called an internally focused church. "These churches are good at preaching and teaching, worship and serving the needs of those *inside* the church," they write. "When people come to these churches, they will hear biblical truth and the message of salvation, and they will see people coming to know the Lord." An externally focused church, on the other hand, focuses its energies outwardly, and it proves the efficacy of the gospel through actions more than words. Less talk, more touch, is the point, though the talk is indispensable. "These churches are effective at proclaiming good news and showing love to their communities. . . . They don't believe you have to compromise truth to show grace. Jesus, after all, was full of both grace and truth."

Rusaw and Swanson make a basic argument. It's not enough to just believe in Jesus anymore and probably never was. In the postmodern age, everyone has a belief. What nonbelievers want to see is a belief backed by deeds. Good deeds actually benefit other people, regardless of their beliefs, and in so doing, they "validate the Good News."

That's the main reason why Dave Stone took a $500,000 collection from his church and went to New York after 9/11. That's why Debbie Ward moved earth and more earth to model heaven in Louisiana and Mississippi.

Stone says it's not just about winning over nonbelievers. Within the church itself, younger people want to feel that their faith issues into action. "Our younger generation wants their life to count for something," he told me. "They want their lives to matter. Size and bigness don't impress that culture like it does the people in their thirties, forties, and fifties."

The most popular new trend is the house church, which meets in someone's home once a week, like a regular church, but which favors longer services, according to a Barna survey, and allows members to be more involved in the service, speaking prayers and reading aloud from Bibles while at the same time allowing people to share personal experiences and get to know each other. Most large churches, meanwhile, want to become multi-site campuses. To that end, Stone wants to see the numbers of people who attend Southeast at the main campus drop from 19,000 to around 15,000. The rest will go to new branch campuses of 750 or so, churches that bear the Southeast brand but are closer to home and can more adequately serve their communities. With less focus on size and growth, he wants to see service transform people into better believers.

"I'm thinking of a guy in our church," he recalled, "one of the most successful home builders in the state. He went to Romania on a mission trip, and it changed his life. Next thing I know, I see a sign outside one of his homes, and all of the profits and proceeds go to that orphanage, where he spent just one week of his life. But it totally changed him. So now, he goes out there once a year, and he's become a huge fundraiser for them, but more important than that, he's a different man. And anyone who knew him ten years ago would say the same thing."

Stone had had his own recent experience of transformation. For Thanksgiving, he'd taken his family down to the Gulf Coast to serve meals and help distribute clothes in a parking lot. There were tears in his eyes as he talked about the experience. "To see my daughter, who is a junior in high school and has taken Spanish classes, interpret for me with a gentleman who spoke Spanish, to see the friendship she formed with him, and to see her writing Spanish in a Bible and giving it to him, and marking certain verses for him— not only is that a life-changing experience for a seventeen-year-old kid, for her dad, it puts a lump in his throat just talking about it."

BACK IN BATON ROUGE, Pastor Dino got through the dark night of his soul. Fear of disaster had overcome him when he had a minute to breathe. Until that night in his kitchen, he'd been too caught up in the relief effort to think much about the consequences of failure. In that moment, he saw and was terrified.

But, he told me later in an e-mail, God calmed the waters. "I felt him lift the burden off my shoulders and I believe that he simply told me to serve the *one*. The one person who is hurting, the one who needs help, the one single mother, the one child, the one husband. After that, even though the work did not slow down, all was well, and God gets all the glory."

AT HEALING PLACE, the junior ministers have a motto: "It's not the title. It's the towel." By title, they mean their job description, which should never become their obsession. By towel, they mean the cloth that Jesus used to dry the feet of his disciples. In the book of John, chapter 13, Christ wraps himself in a towel, kneels before the feet of his men, washing and drying their feet. The disciple Peter resists, saying, "Thou shalt never wash my feet." Jesus insists.

In the year 2005, Healing Place Church had a total income of $12 million, $7.2 million of that in tithes from members. The church gave $1 million in disaster relief, mostly for Katrina and the Asian tsunami, almost $2 million to missions. The other $9 million went to maintain the church and membership and construct its new buildings and grounds, which will be open to all comers. Despite everything, despite storm, death, and despair, it had been a year of blessings. The ministers had taken up the towel. The members had demonstrated obedience, courage, and generosity. The church never had to take a dime of federal faith-based money. And then something most extraordinary happened. It was reported in the annual church bulletin. On New Year's Eve, 2005, at a Saturday night church service, God himself spoke to the people of Healing Place, telling them that he would hold back the enemy. He would prepare a table for them in the wilderness.

## chapter 15

## *Nineveh*

*B*y her own account, God led Niki McDonnall into death and disaster in the high desert of northern Iraq. On March 15, 2004, a year and a half before Hurricane Katrina, the god of Niki's fathers, the god of the Old and New Testaments, the god of my youth, led her to a traffic-choked street near the university campus in Mosul. And when she arrived, at a place to which she had been traveling all her life, ever since she was in ninth grade when she first read about the harvest and the laborers in Matthew, her god allowed six men to surround the truck in which she sat and open fire with automatic weapons, five AK-47s and probably an Uzi, though no one could say for sure. She didn't see the men. She didn't want to. She closed her eyes when the carnage began.

As she tells the story in her harrowing autobiography, *Facing Terror*, Niki experienced the violence in a state of dislocation. "It was like living in a nightmare, everything in slow motion," she remembers in an opening chapter. "Only the throbbing, pounding explosive noises persisted, and the metallic scent of gunpowder and blood filled my senses." Niki sat in the backseat, in the extended cab of the truck. The woman to her right, veteran missionary Jean Elliott, died instantly. The woman to her left, Karen Watson, another veteran, died slowly. In the front seat, her husband seemed to be all right, but the fifth passenger, Larry Elliott, slumped in his place. He had been killed, too.

A few days before the second anniversary of the attack, I asked Niki if she and her team had been too quick to cross the line out of Kurdish northern Iraq into more dangerous territory, and she became heated. "We didn't just go running in," she shot back. "We had been there for several months in the Northern Zone. But the thing about that zone, it had been infiltrated with all kinds of relief and development. Those people weren't the ones in need. The people in need were unfortunately south of there, and they were being neglected. And so here we were," she said, with her dark eyes and blond hair, a soft-target survivor of the war in Iraq. "It was what we came to do, and we sat on it for a while. We went to the military, and they showed us not to go into certain areas. They knew where we were that day, and they said, go ahead, and so we weren't just blowing and going because we were twenty-six-year-old fools. We definitely had mentors who told us we just needed to be sure, but they would never tell us not to go, because they understood that we weren't going to follow men's advice. We were going to follow what God said."

In the introduction to her book, McDonnall writes about Nineveh, the Assyrian city memorialized in the Old Testament story of Jonah; it sits beside the Iraqi city of Mosul, where she was attacked. On the day of the attack, the missionaries breathed the same air that touched the ancient city. In the Old Testament book of Jonah 1:2, God says to the prophet: "Arise, go to Nineveh, that great city and cry against it, for their wickedness is come before me." But Jonah despised Nineveh, and he fled on a boat to Tarshish. God raised the sea against him and sent a giant fish to swallow Jonah and teach him that the will of God could not be thwarted, and Jonah brought the message to Nineveh and preached it in the streets. The people listened, and the Lord spared them—for a while.

That morning in March 2004, the McDonnalls and their associates had received the usual warnings from the U.S. military. The area around Mosul had a nasty reputation as a locus of insurgency. But that winter, Iraq had seen a lull in violence; so much so that the military had rotated troops out. The missionaries got the go-ahead and crossed the Kurdish checkpoint out of the secure zone. They drove through the Mesopotamian desert to a refugee camp inside an old, abandoned factory, where they met several members of the camp. In accordance with Arabic and Islamic custom, the women spoke to the women, the men to the men. Everyone drank tea. The people told the missionaries they needed clean water, and the Americans agreed to help. It was late afternoon by the time the missionaries headed back toward the Kurdish sector.

There was some discussion about which of two roads to take, a way that bypassed Mosul or one that led through the center of town. For a fleeting instant, Niki favored the road that would have taken them around the city. "Yeah, I had one of those moments where I was, like, we should have turned right instead of going straight, you know? But I didn't know that going straight was going to lead to danger. I just thought going right was a faster way out of town. Hindsight's twenty-twenty. Maybe we should have turned right. But that doesn't mean anything." In our conversation, she didn't go so far as to call her feeling about the other road a premonition. It hadn't been that strong. But as we talked, it became clear that she had wrestled many long hours with that decision—and others. "There were situations where that gut feeling says don't go down that road," she told me. "But that wasn't the case here. I just thought the other road would be faster. We weren't thinking anything other than we need to get home. So you can sit there, when you're in that situation, and say what about this and what about that, but there's a point where you just have to put it in God's hands and understand he is a sovereign God, and if you're doing what he wants you to do, then that's where you need to be. It's all about following and being obedient."

After the attack, David McDonnall stayed alive long enough to save her life. He was hit, but it didn't show, and he convinced a group of extremely reluctant Iraqi men to overcome their cultural and religious scruples, to "defile" themselves, as Niki put it, with the blood of a strange Western woman. Under his guidance, the men got the shattered woman out of the backseat of the car and into a nearby taxi. One of the men turned out to be an off-duty Iraqi cop. He helped them both to a hospital, where Iraqi doctors notified the U.S. military. Troops came quickly, one of them a believer named Chad who set aside his weapon and knelt at the foot of Niki's bed and prayed for her. A chopper came and medevaced her and her husband to a U.S. military hospital.

The doctors had to work fast. She had been shot twenty-two times. Her right hand had been blown to pieces. Her left leg had been shattered. When she fainted on the operating table, David was still alive. Eight days later, when she awoke in a hospital in Dallas, he was gone.

ACCORDING TO THE World Christian Database, used by organizations across the country to analyze trends and possibilities in global evangelism, there are roughly 4,000 mission organizations in the world, sending out 419,500 people in the service of the gospel. Every single day, if the data is to be believed—and it's a tough call—74,000 people worldwide "come to faith in Christ," 3,083 new believers per hour per day. "Since you started reading this chapter," claim the authors of *2020 Vision*, a popular book on missions, "you have about 100 new brothers and sisters in Christ!"

If nothing else, the stats can be read as evidence of a staggering effort by the world's 2 billion Christians in pursuit of the other 4 billion people on the planet: 3,500 new churches every week around the globe, added to the 3.45 million churches already in existence, planted at a cost of a breathtaking $15 billion a year, $13 billion alone in lands that are already Christian, another 2 billion aimed at the more difficult regions, where evangelization is either outlawed or restricted by politics, geography, religion, or culture. In sheer financial terms, global evangelization outranks the $13 billion organic food and online gaming industries in size, and looms quite a bit larger than the $12 billion porn industry. To give some idea of the magnitude, the federal government spent about the same amount, $15 billion, to bail out the airline industry after the 9/11 attacks.

The so-called unevangelized world consists of twenty-six closed countries, including much of the Muslim world, plus a handful of others, among them Cambodia, Laos, and Bhutan, one of the toughest nuts of all to crack. In these countries, the ban on the spread of Christianity means that evangelization must take place in secret or not at all. Nevertheless, $250 million a year goes to the effort to break open these areas. Iraq, under Saddam, fit into this closed category. After the American invasion in 2003, however, it became part of a second category, that part of the non-Christian world where some form of evangelism can exist openly. Another $1.7 million goes to work in these middle-ground countries, supporting 103,000 foreign missionaries and a certain amount of Christian literature and radio. But the Christian world, where the fight for believers can be far more disheartening than in the theoretical pagan lands, costs the most money and consumes the most evangelism.

It might seem a paradox, but only on the surface. The "Christian" world includes countries that have either become thoroughly secularized, like most of western Europe and the United States, or have been long under the sway of Catholicism, like Mexico, Peru, Poland, Brazil, and the Philippines. The latter countries have shown themselves increasingly open to evangelical Protestants, especially Pentecostals, who bring a mix of emotional fervor and an almost primeval sense of mystery to the faith, as well as a message of equality under God, that have great appeal in places where Catholicism has failed to address economic disparity and class inequality. But the Christian world also includes the United States, where plenty of people profess a nominal or indifferent faith. This is what George Barna means when he calls the local church in the United States one of the greatest mission fields in the world. In the post-Christian era, to be a "Christian" country is to have a certain cultural designation. It has little or nothing to do with actual belief.

But what is all of this effort really about? Why in the world would men and women spend their entire lives—risk their lives—in the service of telling other people how to think? Believers will answer, first and foremost, the mission is not about telling other people how to think. It's about telling them the Truth.

That's how the International Mission Board of the Southern Baptist Convention sees it. The IMB, as it is known, is one of the most venerable institutions in the effort of worldwide evangelization. As of September 2006, it had a staff of more than 5,000 missionaries in the field. In 2005, 800 people from every walk of life took up the work. In that same year, the IMB counted 459,725 baptisms, the official seal on a conversion; 108,713 churches, of which more than 17,000 started in 2005; and an overseas church membership of 7.3 million people. The total budget for 2006 came to $282.5 million, all of it donated by Southern Baptist churches, which support the IMB as the mission arm of their denomination. The IMB had sent David and Niki McDonnall to Iraq. When I looked at a color-coded map of the global effort to spread the gospel, I thought of the IMB and what its head, Jerry Rankin, had told me about how to read it—how he reads the kind of information that proceeds from such a map, which shows those places where evangelization has succeeded and where it has failed.

"It's very important in determining our strategies and our priorities," Rankin told me. "Even being as large a mission-sending agency as we are, we've always got limited personnel. We can only deploy them one place or another. You never have enough to do all that you want to do."

So how does one decide where to put those limited resources? "I think it has to go back to an understanding that nonevangelicals usually don't have," Rankin tried to explain. As a veteran of decades in the field, in Indonesia and India, Rankin had had ready answers for my initial questions, telling me about experiences in the field that made sense to him, but would sound utterly unconvincing to an outsider with no clue about the nature and objective of missionary experience—that, for instance, the most emblematic part of the work was the moment when a native of some other faith or culture accepted the truth of Jesus. But what was the nature of that acceptance? What exactly did the missionary want? In truth, I myself had never understood.

"We are not trying to proselytize people and get them to change their religion," he insisted. "That's of no benefit whatsoever. A person can choose one religion or another religion, even a Christian religion. The only thing that makes a difference is that personal relationship with Jesus Christ, and that's our message—a saving message, an eternal hope that can only be found in Jesus Christ. But you can't coerce a person to accept that, to believe that. You don't use humanitarian relief and get them to genuinely embrace a faith in Christ. It's of no use if they just choose to be of the Christian re- ligion rather than a Buddhist or a Hindu, apart from that personal faith in Christ. Our objective is simply to make the message accessible and available. Whether or not a person responds is due to the work of God and the power of the Holy Spirit convicting them of sin and bringing them to faith."

This hardly made sense. If the missionaries weren't able themselves to convince people to accept their God, then what was the job about?

"What I'm getting at," he told me, "is that we can't convert anyone. We can't change anyone's religion. It doesn't do any benefit to do so. We can't start any churches. That's the work of God's spirit. But God's spirit works through our witness and our testimony. Therefore, the objective of our missionary effort is simply to gain access and make that message known to all people, and so we really give a high priority to places where there's no church, no scripture, no Christians, where people don't have access to Christian witness, where they don't have an alternative. We give our priority to the unreached people groups because that's our Great Commission mandate from Jesus—to make disciples of all peoples, but how can they become disciples and followers of Christ if they never heard of him? In the end, our mission strategy is really to plant the gospel, to provide that witness among all peoples."

THREE WEEKS AFTER Hurricane Katrina, I flew to Arizona to meet with the American coordinator of a very different kind of mission organization, one of the most secretive in the world: Frontiers. Unlike the International Mission Board, with its mandate to go everywhere, Frontiers people ministered exclusively to Muslims. Unlike the IMB, they didn't much care for the word "missionary," and, in fact, had problems with a lot of the trappings and language associated with their work. I met Robert Blincoe, the Frontiers coordinator, at a Starbucks in Mesa, Arizona, a booming exurb of Phoenix. He showed up in a button-down shirt, open at the collar, looking a little frazzled, holding a worn copy of a book in his hand, a work by Dietrich Bonhoeffer, a German theologian murdered by the Nazis. Titled *Living Together*, the book had heavily influenced Blincoe's thinking on how to do the work of reaching out to Muslims, which he had performed for years in the Kurdish portions of Iraq. In general, Blincoe talked a lot about Bonhoeffer and Saint Francis of Assisi and other monastics, and less about Jesus.

At the time of our meeting, Frontiers had 715 workers in forty-five countries, gathered in 134 community teams of between seven and fifteen people, typically, though there were fifty-eight people in Iraq alone, including Blincoe's daughter. He had interceded on her behalf with the *mukhtar*, or chieftain, in her neighborhood, asking in a personal letter that he take the young woman under his wing as if she were his own. Blincoe cited this request as an example of one way to reach out through the local culture to establish connection. That act, reaching across cultures, had been much on his mind lately.

"As church people, we use words that are so dripping with presumption," he told me. "We use words like 'proselytizing' or 'conversion' or 'missionary.' We have to be careful, not in order to be deceptive, but careful because we want Jesus to come through in a way that gives us a chance."

The week before my visit, Blincoe had closed the local office for three days and hosted a conference on this very issue. In the effort to improve contacts in the Muslim world, he had begun to examine a term that, on the surface, didn't seem to have much to do with mission work: "peacemaking." When he talked about his people, he often referred to them as peacemakers, as in the Sermon on the Mount, when Jesus says, "Blessed are the peacemakers, for they shall be called children of God."

Blincoe told me that Frontiers existed in a state of constant self-improvement and constant change. Its structure was unique, he told me. Unlike the IMB, there was no official leader. Each community team had its own autonomy, but each member of the team must be answerable to every other member, and the teams and their leaders were mutually accountable to each other as well. Every two years, the team leaders would meet to discuss strategy, but no one would dare to impose their view on everyone else. There was no home office, precious little training, no real support system. In terms of money, Frontiers people had to find their own sponsors and do most of their own preparation. In the field, they relied on "the Lord's provision," which meant thinking and working fast on one's feet, taking what came along. Language skills were a priority but not a requirement. Blincoe's main job was to find recruits willing to undertake such demanding work on such small means. I asked him what kind of person would make his ideal candidate.

"We're looking for people who want a cause larger than their own lives," he told me. He referred to these recruits not as missionaries but as "social entrepreneurs" and "change agents." "We're looking for people who are unstoppable, who are willing to bear a lot of pain. They're going to have to work through a lot of failure, but they don't wait for other people. They go first. That's another thing. We attract a lot of leader types who are rough. They probably don't get along well with others, even in church. They're not the kind of people who should be in church."

There was an obvious paradox: unsocial types who had a problem forming community back home sent to a Muslim country to start communities. "We take people who are unsure of themselves," Blincoe told me. "They're not the shining lights. They didn't graduate most likely, or succeed in school. But they're willing and available, and they can plod."

It was an odd verb, and an odd concept, in the context of the utmost extremity and challenge of the work—a team of loosely structured, antisocial "plodders" talking Jesus very quietly to Muslims in the land of jihad. But in the end, it may have been safer than the highly visible work done by the Southern Baptists in Iraq.

TWO YEARS AFTER the attack in Mosul, close to the second anniversary, I met Niki McDonnall at a Starbucks about an hour west of Dallas. She was living by then in Garland, where she had grown up, and had surrounded herself with family and friends. She had a new ministry, traveling around the United States and Europe, telling her story to Christians. She walked into the coffee shop in a green T-shirt tucked into blue jeans, looking every bit like the grown-up version of the girls in my high school—a big blond Texas woman with dark, sad eyes. She was attractive and down-to-earth and honest. She had a country twang and said "kind of thing" to refer to almost everything, as if a version of her theology had crept into the struts of her language, so that all experiences and people existed as comparisons to another reality. During our conversation, she showed an occasional self-consciousness about her hand, which consisted of a thumb and a pinky and nothing in between. Other than that, I would never have guessed, had I not known, what she had endured.

Missionaries wander in the wilderness. That's the definition of the job, or it was my definition when I was young and wanted to be one. They wander in the wilderness and find lost souls. Missionaries live the drama of the faith to its utmost. Or seemed to, I thought. They couldn't afford to rest or relax or take anything for granted. They had joined the Delta Force of Christianity: the best, the hardest, the toughest. I think of that long-ago conversation with my father and my defiant challenge to him: I'm either going to be a filmmaker or a missionary. But I had no clue about the reality of that life. McDonnall opened my eyes to the nature of the sacrifice.

She told me she received her calling on a given day, at a given hour, in the ninth grade. She grew up in a Christian home and church, but missions didn't figure much in her upbringing. One day, her youth minister gave her a pamphlet containing scripture, including, in particular, selections from the book of Matthew. Niki landed on those verses, or did they land on her? She felt the immediate will of God.

The verses were found in Matthew 9:36–38 and followed an account of Jesus wandering the regions around Galilee, healing the sick and casting out devils. When Christ sees how many people remain to be healed, he says to his disciples, "The harvest truly is plenteous, but the laborers are few; Pray ye therefore the Lord of the harvest that he will send forth laborers."

"That just blew me away," Niki told me. "It was one of those moments when I knew exactly what the Lord was telling me, and it freaked me out, because I had never had such a big God moment."

She had been called there and then to be a laborer in the harvest of humankind. No mistaking it, she told me. She had been at home when it happened, flipping through the booklet given her by the youth minister. "It was just something to help encourage us to have a Quiet Time," a term meaning a few minutes out of the day devoted to scripture, thought, and prayer. "I was just trying to do that, here and there, like five or ten minutes kinda thing, and that particular day, God had something else on his mind. I struggled over it for a while, for a long while."

I asked her why she had struggled, if it had been so clear.

"I didn't know what to do with it."

But she prayed, and as time went by, other signs pointed the way. "Everything from that moment, be it scripture, be it friends talking, or going to church—God was trying to point to that one thing that I was trying to ignore. Finally, I went to a church camp, and there was a counselor there who had just returned from serving in Africa for two years, and it was his passion, in the end, that really spoke to me, and I knew that I couldn't run anymore, that this was a God thing, and I had to admit it."

I never in my faith had such clarity, or else I refused it.

MY JOURNALS, KEPT in high school, tell the story of my response. In those pages, bursting with the emotion and melodrama of a hormonally unbalanced teenager, I can't find the moment where I came to believe that Jesus Christ was the son of God. It didn't happen in ninth grade, when McDonnall found her calling.

It must have happened sophomore year at a Young Life function. Over the next two years, thoughts of God consumed me. By senior year, I'd become obsessed with his plans for my future, and in the last months of high school, signs of a revelation began to appear. On Sunday, March 1, 1981, I had an encounter with a woman named Myrna. This page in my journal comes after a seemingly frivolous entry, a list of favorite movies, beginning with *True Grit*. My family watched it every year around Thanksgiving, when it played on network TV. Number two on the list is the musical *My Fair Lady*, which may seem an odd choice but ranked because I had performed the previous fall in that play *Pygmalion*, where I had met my girlfriend, Ellen, and my friend, Doug. But, at that particular moment, number three on the favorite-movies list mattered most. It transcended the personal and touched on my larger destiny—David Lean's *Lawrence of Arabia*, which had been playing nonstop on the new pay cable channel HBO. More than any other movie of that time, *Lawrence* influenced my thinking about my future.

In one of my favorite scenes, the diplomat Dryden, played by Claude Rains, manages to get Lawrence, played by Peter O'Toole, sent on his first trip to Arabia. Lawrence talks about the immense adventure that lies before him, but Dryden warns him. "Lawrence, only two kinds of things get fun in the desert, Bedouins and gods, and you're neither. Take it from me, for ordinary men, it's a burning, fiery furnace." Rolling up his sleeves to do a match trick, Lawrence replies, "No, Dryden, this is going to be fun." Then he snuffs out the match, and the movie cuts to the Arabian desert as the sun starts to appear like God's eye over the lip of the earth, and Maurice Jarre's lush, orientalist score prickles, then booms out of the silence. I felt that I was a Lawrence, one who would find pleasure in extremity, in places that other people might avoid at all cost. I had a destiny.

By March 1, 1981, I had been watching the movie over and over and made it somehow the framework for my own cosmic drama. What would I be? Where would I go? What did God intend? A Sunday school teacher pointed the way. I wrote in my journal, "Myrna Little, a Bible study teacher who I admire very much, said something to me today that took me aback, but deep down I felt a sense of relief. She said, out of the blue, 'The Lord's got his finger in you, John. I can sense it.' I don't know whether to rejoice or be scared as hell, but there are explosions going on inside me daily: realizations, new thoughts, widening perspectives. Things I never dreamt of are happening inside me. Nobody can grasp what I feel either. . . . Except Myrna Little. I don't know where I'm going."

This is the first and last appearance of Myrna Little in my journals. I have no idea what became of her. But her intervention may come closest to my Niki McDonnall moment, when I felt that someone or something from beyond had prodded me into focus. God had spoken to me through this lady. What did I do with the information?

I struggled. A month later, I knew that I'd been accepted to a few liberal arts colleges, but this information brought no immediate clarity to the larger matters. On April 16, I was struggling with the question of Truth. "God himself is the only absolute, the only complete truth, and he is undefinable, and therefore a creature of constantly shifting possibilities." I referenced C. S. Lewis, whose book *Mere Christianity* had made a great impact on me. "As C. S. Lewis once explained, to truly exist, to become aware of the absolute truth of God, is to depart from the plastic shell and begin winning the age-old battle for yourself."

Days and weeks passed, and I seemed to make some progress in the battle. On May 15, 1981, I addressed the question of freedom and dispensed with the topic quickly, ending after one page with the words, in caps, in pencil: "Next week, we discuss: The Nature of Reality," each of the last four words underlined, followed by: "God and Christ solve most all of the philosophical questions, though it would take an incredibly wise person to not only understand the answers but use them." And then comes the postscript to remind me that Arabian magic is still in the air: "Mom and Dad brought back from England a rock that lay on T. E. Lawrence's lawn. It's small enough to hold, and I called it the Courage Stone, because it comes from the oldest, most mystical, most enchanting country in the world—England."

So much confusion and provincialism mingled with so much desire and hope. A few days later, a kid in my high school and his father died in a car accident. Mortality made its arguments. "They're in a world far from strife, pettiness, envy, and hate, and though it's saddening for us, they are on a piece of ground that we cannot possibly imagine. In a way, I envy them. They are with Lawrence (maybe, I hope he's there), with C. S. Lewis . . . among a cast of zillions. Because of things like this, I really have to crack down and think about my own life. Where are my priorities now? Is my future planned in accordance with God?"

Summer came, high school was over, and I decided that I made myself sick, because I had done nothing for God in the previous year. My girlfriend was away on Chesapeake Bay: "All I can think about is Ellen." And then comes this aside, on June 21: "Oh, and I've made a big decision (only time will tell just how big). I'm going to be a director . . . I'm going to be a *Christian* movie director." At this point in my life, at the age of eighteen, I knew nothing about the film industry. It was a fantasy out of movie magazines. Moreover, I'd hated the one or two strictly Christian films I'd seen, but my ambition felt revolutionary and Jesus-filled. Myrna Little's provocation had started to bear fruit. God had stuck his finger into me and said, "You will be a movie director."

By August, most of my high school friends had left for college, and I'd begun to see through the sham heroics of my Lawrence phase. "Until three months ago, I was still slaying dragons, still waging wars on every front, as a misunderstood hero, a 'Lawrence of Arabia' disguised as a skinny high school senior. My imagination and dreams sustained me through a hundred new hurts, and God was there to soothe each wound with his constant glimmering touch of hope."

I looked at these entries as a forty-three-year-old, noting their mercurial and meandering quality, and I realized that I never even remotely had the sense of calling that Niki McDonnall possessed. I never had that precision, that clarity, that purpose unfolding in a clear path. Did I not read enough scripture? Did I not pray enough? And yet my thoughts returned constantly to God. I had seen him. I had known him. I wanted to follow.

"The point is that, though I've had a wonderful childhood, it's time to go. It is time to say good-bye to the wonder that Marvel Comics used to bring, and good-bye to the mystic moment of sunset, when you can almost believe in hobbits, wizards, and elves. It is also time to give up my fantasies of life as a search for the one girl or as a background for my adventures. . . . I will hold close to Christ, because, of the many magic fountains I drank from as a kid, this was the only true enchantment, and I will never forget that life is too short to be wasted on meaningless pursuits."

I was constantly trying to look at my life with vast detachment. College immediately brought doubt, but I squelched it. On October 26, two months into my first semester at Davidson College, on a rainy Monday after classes, I wrote: "I have questioned my Christianity. I cannot lie. It has been a rough course, but the truth is the truth. I cannot deny the existence of God the Father Almighty and his Son. They have been too much a part of my life. In hours of peril, grief, and fear, he was here. He is here, and always will be. I cannot hope to have any other life, though inside I feel a part of me struggling."

McDonnall told me that, in college, at Texas A&M, she entertained other ways to serve God. She considered going into business and devoting herself to rural development in third-world countries. While she doubted her path, she never seems to have doubted the reality of Jesus, which I find amazing. That kind of faith must be one precondition for those called to the life of a missionary, especially in Muslim countries.

On December 16, I came as close as I ever would in my journals to saying that I wanted to serve God in that way. "The ace card, for me, is Jesus Christ. If he wants me out on the 'frontiers of experience,' working on projects where my mind and my soul are challenged each and every day, then I am willing. I don't know what use I would be out on the border, but it's where I belong. I detest myself really."

In March, not long after my nineteenth birthday, I was writing about politics in El Salvador, something that had never interested me in the slightest, in the written record, anyway. By the end of April, Brezhnev was dying in the USSR, Britain was threatening to invade the Falklands, and a girl named Nancy had entered the picture. I wrote, "I have been thinking more about God, without all the ostentatious claptrap so typical of me, and I have come closer to him. Don't know what he's got planned for me, but it ought to be good. (And, I hope, fun.)"

In May, I wrote, "I have sexual hang-ups. Is that not obvious? I'm nineteen years old, and I still talk about girls in an extremely childish sense. . . . Do you have to ask whether I'm a virgin or not? Of course not. . . . My view of girls is—I'm in big trouble, because I don't even know where to begin. Is this an important Christian understanding? I don't know. This is something that runs through all I've written. It is part of the reason for depression, and maybe all of it. I can't cope with sex, or the opposite sex. What the hell is wrong with me?"

The game is up. In the battle for myself, as C. S. Lewis would have it, the missionary ideal had already sunk beneath the waves.

That summer, I did an internship at a small north Dallas film company called Brimstone. Plenty of Christians would take that name seriously, as a cue that I was under the spell of darker forces, but one couldn't have found more ineffectual devils. There were two of them, an aspiring director named Charlie Brim and a cinematographer of industrial films named Karl Stone, hence Brimstone, and they made commercials and small film projects, like a pilot for a syndicated series called *Wanderlust*, starring Ernest Hemingway's son, Jack. At the premiere of the pilot, I wore a beret and served strawberries and champagne to prospective investors in future episodes, while Sandy, the six-foot-five blond producer, whispered to me, "John, don't you ever doubt that Karl Stone is a genius."

In the autumn of that year, October 11, thoughts of sex had returned with a vengeance. "I am making a vow before God and myself right now. I have not kept vows before. I haven't given a damn. But this time, I'm doing it, because it means more than anything—to my well-being, past, present, and future. I have put myself on the railroad tracks and just laid there for nineteen years of my life. The end! I vow that Nancy will be mine by June 1, 1983. There is no other course, no other outcome. She's mine by summer."

It didn't work out. Destiny eluded me on every front.

November, end of term, still thinking about being a filmmaker, I had decided that artists were all a bunch of frauds. "The world of the artist hates Christ . . . it is the most earthly of professions. It vaults mankind and his delusions to awesome heights. An artist in this world does not see the world in which Christ operated."

This had become the central dilemma—to be an artist or to follow Jesus. In January of 1983, one of the most fateful years in my life, I wrote, "If I pursue film or writing without a sure knowledge of God's acquiescence in the matter, does it mean I'm turning away from him and following my own course? Am I saving my life only to lose it in spiritual terms? How will I know if I'm a truly committed Christian, sealed so tightly in the body of Christ that I can't be wrenched out? On the other hand, do the emotions and empathy that I have which enable me to act and write with significantly more maturity and understanding than my peers have to be dropped to maintain my faith? Does God want me to use this burden or cast it off?"

Reading these words, it's impossible not to think of my sophomore roommate, Craig Detweiler. The year before, at a Young Life camp in Windy Gap, North Carolina, Craig had accepted Christ as his personal savior. Because I was a Christian, too, we had roomed together on a hall with a bunch of other Christian guys. Craig slept in a bed on a loft. I slept on the floor beneath. That year, we were both leaders of small-group Bible studies in an organization called Davidson Christian Fellowship. In addition, Craig had become much more active in a leadership role in DCF, while I had focused with growing intensity on acting in the college theater and on writing poems and short stories. One night, while we tried to focus on homework, Craig stuck his head over the side of the loft and declared, "God doesn't like artists because they ask too many questions."

Something ended then. From that moment on, there was no chance that I would do what Niki McDonnall did. I would not try to convince other human beings to believe that Jesus Christ was the son of God. I would not labor in the harvest. I would ask questions instead.

On February 13, 1983, I wrote: "I wish I could express the mystery I'm beginning to feel around me. It's the rush of angel wings and the howl of wind just above my sight, and I can only feel them and not write about them. Friends are going their ways. . . . What questions a single man raises to his God are for that man, and none other."

My Jonah moment never came. I didn't go to Nineveh. Fifteen years later, a girl from Garland, Texas, just down the road from my town, made a very different decision. God didn't need a big fish. She obeyed. She went to Iraq.

WITHIN MINUTES OF the attack on the McDonnalls and their fellow team members, at International Mission Board headquarters back in Richmond, IMB head Jerry Rankin and his people got the news. On his cell phone, from Mosul, David McDonnall had called regional headquarters in Amman, and Amman had relayed the information.

The year before, the IMB had reached out to the McDonnalls, who were attending seminary in Fort Worth, and asked the recently married couple to go to Iraq. They needed people who knew the culture, spoke the language, and could establish contacts quickly. The McDonnalls had the skill sets. Both young people had the necessary conviction and commitment. Personnel had done an extensive psychological, spiritual, and professional profile. Niki had gone to Israel under the auspices of the IMB Journeyman program and proven herself there. Her husband had braved all kinds of danger and demonstrated responsibility and leadership. Once the call came, they'd both prayed in separate rooms and consulted scripture, and both received a positive response from God. Prayer prompted a sense of affirmation and scripture ratified it.

No one underestimated the challenge that lay ahead of them. "Even then, we realized the danger," Rankin told me. "We knew that it could happen to anyone, anywhere. . . . They realized that. They were well trained in security issues and protection and safety, but you're just vulnerable in that situation, and the significant thing is their willingness to be vulnerable for the sake of ministering to people."

Rankin himself had been a missionary in the Muslim world, and he had experienced moments of danger, but he told me that the world had changed dramatically since his day—not so much for missionaries, but for Americans. In the 160-year history of the IMB, out of 18,000 field staff serving overseas, 44 had died a violent death. Rankin didn't count accidents. He meant hijacking, armed robbery, terrorist bombs. Forty-four in the entire history of the operation, but eight in the last four years, he told me. In 2003, three were murdered in an attack by terrorists on a Baptist hospital in Yemen. A few months later, a bomb killed another in a Philippines airport. The Yemen attack had been intentional, the Philippines had been random. The attack on the McDonnalls had been somewhere in between. The assailants had wanted to kill white-skinned Westerners. No evidence has emerged that they intended to slaughter Christians or that they even knew the identities of their victims.

"They were just Americans who happened to be there when terrorists were shooting foreigners," Rankin said. "We call them martyrs, but they're really not Christian martyrs who die because of the witness of their faith. They were just Americans in a hostile, volatile world."

EIGHT DAYS AFTER she was attacked, Niki McDonnall woke in the hospital in Dallas. She wanted to die. She wanted to be "home," she told me, with her husband and friends. She wanted to know why. Counselors took great pains to talk her through it.

"I had two roads," she told me. "I had a road that I could walk real easily down bitterness and hate and that kind of thing. Or I had that narrow road that is very hard to find, and very narrow, and only comes by taking Christ in. I had some dark days, some very dark times, but I just knew that the only way that I was going to get through this was by leaning on God. I could not turn my back, though that would have been easy."

I asked her if she wondered why God had led her down that road. Was she angry at him?

"There was some time of anger. There was some time of bewilderment, because of all that I had learned since I was a child about God being love, and God being sovereign. To me, when I mixed those things together, and I saw what had happened in my life, I just wasn't grasping, and I wasn't seeing how these things could be true in the full form that I'd been taught. . . . To me, I was, like, maybe I misread something. So people who really understand scripture would talk to me about it, and I would verbalize: Okay, was I a bad wife? Was that why my husband was taken?

"And they would answer back, okay, so you're saying that because you were a bad wife, maybe you weren't doing what all you were supposed to do in that role or what not, for whatever reason, so God came down and took David and everybody else and left you, because you were a bad wife, to punish you for that. So, from what you know of scripture, they would ask me, does that back up? You know? And I would be, like, well no, God doesn't punish in that way."

But there had to be something, an explanation. "What I have come to understand in all of this is that we live in a fallen, fallen world, and God was very much sovereign on that day, just as he is today, and was the day before, and for whatever reason, when he allowed that to happen in his sovereignty, it wasn't his first pick for things to happen. But I know that my God is a redeeming God, and he will redeem that day. And you know, I'm probably not going to find out until I look into Christ's eyes, and he's not going to have to say anything. At that point, it'll be all understood."

Before I left, we spoke about her health. She had finished the last of the major operations, she thought. She could walk and work well. One day, if God called, she might contemplate going back to Iraq to serve. But the call would have to be strong, and she would have to overcome her fear. She still had nightmares. Every day, at least once, she relived it; a turn of the steering wheel, a flash of sunshine, these could bring the moment back. In the present, the shrapnel kept coming. Pieces of metal would erupt from her skin. A few months before, one had emerged around her ear. The attack would come out of her skin for the rest of her life.

FOR THE SAKE of argument, let's say there are only two ways to understand the lives of these two people: Niki McDonnall and John Marks.

In her version of the story, she sacrifices her life on earth for glory in eternity, and in death, she receives her reward. She is reunited with her husband and brought into the heavenly City. Meanwhile, I lead a healthy, relatively happy, self-centered, and stable existence on earth, but when I die, I drop into a torment that lasts for all time, separated from all that I ever loved, conscious of my wickedness. I didn't accept Jesus Christ as my personal savior, and torment in perpetuity is my punishment. Needless to say, I refuse to accept this interpretation. In my version of the story, she is a young woman under the spell of a complete delusion, who believed in a God that did not exist, prayed to that God for wisdom and received the command to go to a place where she and her message would be despised, where men under their own delusion would wreck her body with twenty-two shots of lead, killing her husband in the bargain. That loss will never be redeemed. He is gone. Her sacrifice means nothing, less than nothing; it was a gesture based on a lie. Her life amounts to a living hell, and only death ends her torment. She would have to reject my version just as strenuously.

These two interpretations are incompatible. They are mutually opposed translations of the same original text and can never be squared. Their two hells cannot coexist. If one is true, the other must be false. Or both are false, and the truth of existence lies elsewhere. Theoretically, we are free to choose. But I suspect that Niki McDonnall will stick by her story. The question is whether I stick by mine.

## chapter 16

## Sweet D

*L*ong before I met Niki, I knew another missionary: Craig, my roommate at Davidson College. After we graduated, Craig went to Japan to preach the word. I once asked him why, and he told me that he wanted to let the Japanese people know that Jesus loves them. He spent two years in Tokyo, speaking English and spreading the gospel. He founded a small church that still exists today. A small number of people converted on his watch, and he explained to me that it was a big deal; to become a Christian in Japan meant social opprobrium. Not long ago, he paid a return visit and met one of his converts. She had become a nurse to lepers.

While in Japan, Craig didn't learn the language. The Japanese all wanted to learn English, so he didn't need the skill. He hadn't been an Asian studies major in college and had possessed no profound understanding of the culture before he embarked on the mission, as he freely admitted. Yet he came to believe that Japanese religious beliefs lacked substance. For him, Buddhism and Shintoism were nothing but hollow shells. Jesus stood a chance to revolutionize not merely individuals, but an entire country. I once asked him if he really believed that he had the right to judge an entire nation and its spiritual life without the benefit of language skills or any deep knowledge of the culture. He told me that he didn't know. He went to see for himself if he could. When I first brought up the subject, I had asked him if he really believed that Jesus loved the Japanese people, and he said, "I still believe Jesus loves Japan." And just as Christ had broken down and lifted up Craig in his life, Craig believed Christ could do the same for that nation. At the end of his two-year mission, this belief remained unshaken. But its outer form had changed forever.

Japan altered Craig. At twenty-two, he went abroad to do battle with the world, and the world became real. He grasped the destiny implied in his passport and birth certificate. He was an American. The boundaries of his own national identity became visible. For the first time in his life, he registered international borders and began to wonder what they meant for his message. In the mid-1980s, as Reagan's aggressive foreign policy against the Soviet Union sharpened tensions around the world, Craig began to read foreign newspapers, stories of American military and financial power, begging the question: Could he possibly separate Jesus from America? Was that within his power? Or did his nationality get in the way every time? He wrote me a letter from Tokyo: "I'm here as a friendship evangelist, sharing my faith with folks I've legitimately learned to know and love. Unfortunately, most Japanese are fascinated by American pastimes, so I'm always being invited to play tennis, go bowling, or watch an American movie. Not exactly cultural plunges!"

When I received this letter, I was living on a houseboat in the Indian city of Srinagar, the capital of the Muslim state of Kashmir, doing my utmost to melt into the background, to observe as well as I could the ways of a completely different society. I had become the opposite of the missionary. I was a sponge, aching to be influenced.

The experience of being an alien on someone else's turf struck deep chords in both of us. I saw a flock of sheep slaughtered before my eyes at a Kashmiri wedding feast and turned into dinner in a matter of hours. I saw dead prostitutes on the streets of Calcutta and bodies of Brahmins burned to ashes on the banks of the Ganges in Varanasi. I wrote to Craig about these visceral experiences, and he wrote me back about his own. He had discovered sushi, for one. "Other surprises have included the mass acceptance of pornography, prostitution and suicide," he wrote. "I saw a body being photographed by police sprawled out on train tracks near my apartment. In the darkness of midnight, the flashbulb illumination of the body seared an indelible image in my mind." That image has always haunted me, too. It's not just the body. It's the presence of a devout young American at the late hour, absorbing the shock of such a sight. In the most immediate sense, his response to the depravity may seem predictable. "I feel especially called by God to love these desperate Japanese people. Japanese Buddhism exists as a profitable superstition preserved by the rich priests for tourists and old people. The young people profess faith only in themselves. I'm confident I've got something better to offer in Jesus Christ."

Those lines came at the end of his first letter from Tokyo, written in November 1985, six months after graduation, two months after his arrival. A year and a half later, in January 1987, he was looking homeward and wrote me about his perceptions of himself and the mission. He had paid a visit to Thailand with some college friends of ours. "It was my first chance to relate my Japan experience to someone from home," he wrote. "Guarding myself against parading my mission like a new party dress, I shared my past year quite naturally. It was a relief. I fear becoming like those you warned me about who define themselves by the number of countries conquered."

But he didn't stop there. By this time, I had returned from India and gone back to Texas, where I had started to work a string of day jobs, from bookstore clerk to waiter in a bar that served underage kids. I was struggling with what my future without Jesus would hold. I had begun to grapple one last time with the question of whether to stay for good in Texas, where I'd grown up, or leave for good. I haven't seen my letter to him, but it seems that I had written a very gloomy section about the awfulness of life and the uselessness of the New Testament, and Craig chastised me. "I don't see the New Testament as a major, anti-intellectual leap of faith. I live in the sensual world, but I also can't ignore the spiritual world. To deny the New Testament, to ignore Christ, and dwell only on the senses is too limiting. For me, I desire a complete life—physical and spiritual. I must confess a real fear of encroaching bitterness upon you, John. You've got too much God-given vibrance within you to sink into doom and gloom. The world definitely sucks, but that doesn't necessarily imply life must also. Lighten up, mate."

This was one more round in a conversation that had begun during our year as roommates. He likes to say, "My first year in the faith was your last." It isn't quite true. I continued to believe for a few more years, but sophomore year, Jesus began to lose ground, and my conversations with Craig became a kind of battleground. They still are.

WHEN WE MET, as eighteen-year-olds in the halls of a dorm at Davidson College, we didn't bond over love of Jesus. We bonded over love of movies and music. Neither of us could shut up. He loved Scorsese, I loved Spielberg. He loved the Clash, I loved Tom Petty. We both loved Bruce Springsteen. As a crazed punk football player in Charlotte, North Carolina, Craig had seen *Raging Bull* in high school and fallen in love with the wildness of American cinema. Verses from the gospel of John ended the movie: "All I know is this. Once I was blind, now I can see." Back in Dallas, as a nerdy high school newspaper editor and aspiring novelist and actor, I had been steeped since early childhood in Marvel Comics, Hammer horror films, *Planet of the Apes* movies, and the soundtracks of my favorite film westerns. We came at pop culture from different angles, but we both understood our salvation through that medium.

Unlike a lot of teen Christians, we despised "Christian" music and movies. I couldn't abide, for instance, the anodyne sound of the Nashville Jesus freak Amy Grant. Movies were worse. In high school, I had been subjected to a special Christian-kids-only afternoon showing of a laughably awful movie called *Joni*, about a paraplegic woman whose love of Jesus gets her through life. The worst episode of the gothic daytime soap opera *Dark Shadows*, a show featuring visibly shaky sets, hilariously bad acting, and plots far more unbelievable than the Resurrection, outshone *Joni* at every level. Having to watch that movie felt like insult and punishment at once, and I experienced guilt for hating Joni so much—not the movie, but the person herself, whose life had been so stupidly and sloppily represented by well-meaning but clueless filmmakers that one had no choice but to despise her.

Craig felt the same way about movies and music. Christian pop culture could go to hell. Our sophomore year, Bruce Springsteen released his *Nebraska* album, and that marked a watershed in our friendship and our lives.

We skipped school on the day of its release and drove into Charlotte, a few miles south on Interstate 77. We bought the red-and-black square with the ashen gray dust bowl image on the cover, took it back to our dorm room, lowered it onto the turntable, lowered the shades, turned out the lights, and let the music of utmost American despair rise into our minds. Talk about a prophet. We might as well have been listening to Jeremiah or Jonah or one of those other Old Testament madmen. Bruce had far more authority than any pastor who had ever preached the gospel. He sang right into our ears and made us care about the great, insane misery of being American without money or prospects. He stunned our conscience and aroused our deepest emotions of alienation. He made us feel that the world of blue-collar loss and devastation belonged to us personally. In my case, no verse in the Bible ever connected me so viscerally to the suffering of other human beings. As much as Ernest Hemingway, whose stories I had read in high school, Bruce Springsteen altered my conception of what authors might and might not do in the English language. He was chief among those who released me from the spell of Tolkien.

Craig came from a background a bit closer to Springsteen. His father had sold used cars, which has the ring of something right off one of the albums. Craig had been one of those ruthless guys who looked for redemption underneath the hood of a car or in the arms of a cheerleader. By the time he accepted Jesus during his freshman year in college, sex, drink, and rock and roll had ruled his life for quite some time. They hadn't ruled mine. I lived inside a dream of holy mortification bordering on sexual ecstasy. I didn't lose my virginity or take a swig of alcohol until after I stopped believing in Jesus.

It's always been hard for me to believe that Craig was a bastard in high school. When I met him, I immediately responded to his generous, happy temperament. Someone on our hall called him "Sweet D," for Detweiler, and I've used that name ever since, because it seems fitting. I may no longer share his faith, but I've always basked a little in the warm glow of his personality.

We roomed together for one year, and after that year, our friendship began to wane, as he went deeper into the faith and I moved out. When Craig says that his first year in the faith was my last, he draws a conclusion that makes him a little queasy. He's had the horrible thought that only so much room existed in God's kingdom, and for him to enter, I had to be pushed out. "One in, one out," as he puts it. "Only so much room in the kingdom." After that year, I don't think I ever witnessed again. My junior year, in a German university town, I started to drink beer and wine. My senior year, I slept with a woman. The year after graduation, while Craig embarked on his mission to Japan, I prostrated myself before Allah on the night of Mohammed's birthday in Kashmir, circumambulated the stupa in the village of Bodh Gaya where the Buddha found enlightenment under the bodhi tree in the company of thousands of ohming Buddhists, and said a mantra with prayer beads that I might win the heart and body of a rock singer back in Los Angeles.

In our midtwenties, Craig and I lost touch. In his last letter to me, dated May 17, 1988, he wrote on Young Life letterhead. He'd got a job in the organization, which I'd come to despise, and started an urban youth ministry with African American kids in downtown Charlotte. His own trials with faith had begun, but we never talked about it. He didn't invite me to his wedding. I didn't invite him to mine. When his sister died in a car wreck, I called him, but the conversation was terse. I had no contact with Craig at all until years later when we were in our midthirties, both married with children. By that time, he was a different man.

YEARS LATER, I shocked Craig when I told him about his statement, "God doesn't like artists because they ask too many questions." He told me that he'd spent most of his adult life trying to convince "young Christian artists to ask serious questions if they wanted to create great art." He had another surprise for me, too. He told me that, in our sophomore year, watching me write short stories and act in plays, he'd discovered his own hidden ambition. God be damned, he wanted to be an artist, too.

In the years after Japan, he became disillusioned with Christianity. Matthew Shepard's murder in 1998, when he was in his midthirties, became a turning point. The circus of hellfire and damnation at the funeral repulsed him. His faith had always been rooted in a sense of positive showmanship. He'd wanted to convince everybody of the truth, even to the point of being ridiculed when he stood like a boxer in the middle of campus and challenged

all comers to take on his arguments in favor of eternal life. His feelings about
God's attitude toward artists aside, he'd never placed a particular emphasis on punishment of nonbelievers, and, as far as I remember, had never
made a big issue of homosexuality, even when a love affair between two
guys bloomed in a room on our Christian-themed hall. Years later, after the
Shepard murder, he wrote a small essay in his church circular, saying, "If
Christians did this . . . you can call me queer, you can call me a fag. But
please, don't call me a Christian."

He lost connection with his fellow believers and began to entertain
thoughts of moving west to Hollywood to pursue another kind of vision.
He had married an Italian American from Chicago, Caroline Cicero, and she
had little or no interest in staying down South. Craig got into the University
of Southern California film school, and he started to write screenplays. He
started meeting other believers who were sick and tired of the public face of
their faith: the ridiculous televangelists, the sexual scandals, the demoniza-
tion of abortion doctors and homosexuals, and the same, lame faith-based
approach to cinema that had characterized Christian movies since the days
of *Joni*.

On a trip to Los Angeles in the late 1990s, I looked him up and discovered, to my surprise, a movie business professional struggling with his faith.
We met at a Starbucks in Brentwood and talked about movies and music with
our old enthusiasm. We talked briefly about faith, but Craig's old exuberance
had given way to a hard realism. He still believed. He hadn't given up. But
it was a fight. He described his church as "your last stop on the way out, or
your first stop on the way in."

It turned out to be a way station before he returned to the fold with an
altered consciousness. When I sold this book, my first phone call went to
Sweet D, who at the time chaired the mass communications department at
the Bible Institute of Los Angeles, a conservative Christian bastion. I asked
him if I could come out to Los Angeles and bend his ear for a couple of days
about Christianity. By that time, in 2004, *The Passion of the Christ* had made a
splash, and the professional vista for my friend had changed utterly and completely. Craig considered my request in light of his own dawning realizations
about the possibilities for Christian renewal in the popular culture. That Jan-

uary, after receiving my request, he took his Biola students to the Sundance Film Festival. When he returned, he told me to come on out—as long as he could film the whole thing for a documentary. In Park City, inspired by the surge in documentary work in competition, he'd had an inspiration. He'd film our conversation and turn it into a movie. He had the financial backing of a pair of evangelical millionaires in Idaho, and the film equipment could be borrowed from the Bible Institute of Los Angeles.

Craig has remained a missionary, but his work bears almost no resemblance to that of the International Mission Board of the Southern Baptist Convention, which probably wouldn't approve. Craig has been called to Hollywood, to the great fountainhead of American popular culture, to the movies. In the end, Japan led him back to his own country and to the machine that shapes the culture. Forget politics, forget academics, forget the church. For Craig, the action is the audience.

If the Truth Project represents the leading edge of conservative Christian activism in the United States, Craig and his circle of friends in Hollywood constitute the opposite force, vanguard members of a movement that has been called, among other things, the Emerging Church. Craig has written two screenplays that have been made into movies, one about a dog who inherits the British royal crown, a Disney-style entertainment called *The Duke*; the other a Christian-themed picture set in the world of extreme sports, called *Extreme Days*, made with auto industry money from Michigan. But these professional credits don't begin to describe the real nature of his work.

With a group of other Christian outsiders who showed up at about the same time as he did, he ended up fomenting a revolution in thinking among Tinsel Town believers—pushing for a radical departure in the ways that Christians see Hollywood and fighting every bit as hard to alter the negative perception of Christians by Hollywood insiders. His effort began several years before the box office successes of *The Passion of the Christ* and *The Lion, the Witch, and the Wardrobe*, but he and his allies have been able to capitalize on those victories. Nowadays, lots of Christians really do see Hollywood as a field of endeavor rather than as the enemy, and Hollywood industry people are more likely to open their doors to Christian projects—mostly because of the money made by Mel Gibson and Narnia, but also because people like Sweet D labored long and hard to grease the hinges.

Some of his allies have become major players in the business. Once a year, Craig goes on a retreat with three old pals—Ralph Winter, executive producer of the X-Men movies; Jonathan Bock, head of Grace Hill Media, the top publicity operation for studios seeking to reach evangelicals; and Scott Derricksen, director of the box office horror hit *The Exorcism of Emily Rose* and one of Craig's former students. Craig hasn't had the same kind of box office success, but his eminence can be measured in other ways.

In the last few years, he has launched and run several different film festivals and conferences, promoting Christian themes in the broadest sense. The movies tend to have hopeful messages, even when dark. He is also a theologian and teacher. His book, *A Matrix of Meanings,* coauthored with Barry Taylor, another key figure in the Emerging Church movement, has become the standard textbook in the film studies departments of Christian colleges around the country, and he travels constantly, talking about the movies that he loves, why he loves them, and why other believers should, too. He's taught Bible studies at the White House; the executive branch provides the service to Christian staffers. Craig showed up for his study of theology and film on the first anniversary of the invasion of Iraq.

I've seen him speak to his students at Biola, a gathering of the children of missionaries, pastors, and seminarians, after a showing of the Paul Thomas Anderson flick *Magnolia,* exhorting kids to abandon their inherited preconceptions about movies for a moment and see how a film containing obscenity, nudity, drug use, and violence might be more God-filled than the mediocre NBC miniseries *Revelation,* a prepackaged "Christian" entertainment made specifically for them by a cynical industry. I've seen him stand before a standing-room-only hall of Christian educators wondering just how to present a movie like *Magnolia* to their own students in communities and among divinity school faculties much more restrictive than his. I've seen him awkward but determined in Manhattan, addressing a group of Christian film festival organizers who hadn't done a very good job of attracting people to the event, giving his spiel about the new era of postmodernism in film and society and what it meant as an opportunity, how audiences who had loved

*American Beauty*, *The Matrix*, and *Donnie Darko* were ready for dark and beautiful visions of hope and transcendence.

But the key moment came in Park City, Utah. I wasn't there, but I received the full report afterward. At the 2006 Sundance Film Festival, after a showing of a film called *Forgiving the Franklins*, Sweet D stood in front of a skeptical crowd and sincerely and emotionally apologized to the gay director of the film for any slights that he might have suffered at the hands of Christians. The movie, a black comedy, told the story of a homophobic evangelical family and their closeted gay son; in the plot, the Franklins almost die but are given one chance to go back and redeem themselves, in the process turning into sexual addicts who are then totally rejected by their Christian friends and neighbors. Sweet D watched the movie in growing mortification. Once more, the sins of his community were being shoved in his face, and he couldn't stand it. More and more, followers of Jesus had come to be seen as haters and despisers.

The filmmaker expressed genuine surprise. People in the room gave a standing ovation. Craig saw an entire ministry unfolding before his eyes. *Forgiving the Franklins* was despised by the few critics who saw it and never received distribution, but Sweet D had seized his opportunity.

## chapter 17

# Shofar

*C**raig* still can't stand Christian contemporary music and wouldn't be caught dead at a Christian music festival, but I went one midsummer weekend to an event called Kingdom Bound in western New York. It wasn't like any other music festival I'd ever attended. On a humid July night, Herb Thurn and his wife took the stage of a Six Flags bandshell and lifted a pair of Yemenite sheep horns to their lips. I sat half a football field away, in a sea of families waiting to hear the biggest acts in the gospel music business: MercyMe, Casting Crowns, Rebecca St. James, the Newsboys.

Earlier that evening, Herb Thurn had given me a ride from my hotel to the Six Flags Park at Darien Lake, where the nineteenth annual Kingdom Bound festival was about to begin. When we parked, he showed me a collection of bizarrely antiquated instruments in the back of his van, one purchased in Ukraine, others bought via mail order from Israel. They were shofars.

"The sound is just so anointed," he told me.

I had seen one or two shofars before, at Washington Hebrew Synagogue in D.C., where kids had blown them at a Rosh Hashanah service, a tradition of the Jewish New Year. Until Kingdom Bound, I had associated them only with Judaism, but Herb told me that more and more Christian churches and ministries used shofars to usher God's presence into services and events, a biblically sanctioned use of the horn. Herb had obtained his first shofar on a mission trip to Ukraine, a gift from an Israeli who had used it in performance. The instrument's power stunned Herb, and he told the pastor of his church that a certainty had come over him. God wanted Herb to blow the shofar in weekly services at home. The pastor instantly agreed, Herb blew, and the sound transformed the congregation. God came into that place. Countless times since, at unpredictable moments in the service, Herb will feel the tug on his mind and heart, and he'll raise the Yemenite horn again. The shofar releases something.

"I know it ain't just me," Herb told me.

Others have taken up the practice, too. At conferences organized by Eagle Wing Ministries, Herb told me, everyone in the room will have a shofar, thirty or so people, and when they blow, an unimaginable force fills the room. Herb blew his shofar on the National Day of Prayer in the streets of Buffalo, and he blew it at a musical event in Florida, which inspired the idea of opening Kingdom Bound with his horn. "It opens heaven's gates above the event," he told me, and I felt a chill of excitement at that notion, what it might mean in the moment of occurrence. "We went to Florida on vacation and went to this church. I took along my Bible, my tambourine, and my shofar. And when I saw the music they were playing, sixty or seventy people just singing along, I felt God say, 'Go get the shofar.' I blew the shofar, and the worship went on for another forty-five minutes. The pastor fell down on his knees. It was just one of those anointed times."

Every now and then, he told me, at his church or another, the worship band will ask him to mike the shofar, and he'll actually play it as an instrument. But when Herb took the stage that night, he had no intention of playing with one of the bands. He and his wife wanted to rip open the sky. They wanted God himself to come down. Herb's favorite shofar is about thirty-six inches round and fairly smooth to the touch. The rougher a shofar, he told me, the higher its pitch. I didn't have any idea what to expect. When the couple took the stage, I couldn't even see the horns. For all I knew, in a venue that seats 25,000, the shofars might not even make an impression.

I have been going to concerts since I was sixteen years old. My first, in the age of the big arena shows, was Electric Light Orchestra in Fort Worth, the Out of the Blue tour, a huge glowing spaceship on the stage. I saw Journey, too, and the Pat Travers Band; Earth, Wind & Fire at Southern Methodist University and Tom Petty in front of a Confederate flag in Charlotte; I've seen R.E.M., the English Beat, the Bangles, Elvis Costello; the Pogues above an ice-skating rink in Berlin, Sade in a bullfighting ring in Madrid. I've seen Bruce Springsteen three or four times at different stages of his career, Ralph Stanley and Ramblin' Jack Elliot at the Iron Horse in Northampton, Lucinda Williams, Merle Haggard, and Steve Earle in a tiny, now defunct bar called Tramps in downtown Manhattan, Los Lobos at the Longhorn Ballroom in downtown Dallas, and maybe the best show of my life, the Los Angeles punk band X, playing like a gun pointed at their heads, on an icy cold January night in western Massachusetts. Most of these were unforgettable shows. But I have never seen anything in my life like that moment when Herb Thurn blew the shofar.

He and his wife blew three times, and there could be no mistaking what they meant. In that instant, I tell you, the gates of heaven opened above us. The coming thunderstorm reared back. The dusk broke in wonder. Every heart in that venue stilled. I know now what dispensationalist Christians must feel when they imagine the Rapture. It is a quickening of the inside of the body, a sense of being inside a womb of tremendous power.

As the sound of the horns dwindled, a rock band launched into a praise song. I could feel the heavens close again. God departed, and we were back among the land of the living.

FULL DISCLOSURE: I despise Christian music, now and forever. Its defenders will say that it has changed since my day, when Amy Grant played on the eight tracks and cassette decks of the mild-mannered folks who espoused Jesus in my high school, the music of "the milkshake people," as one of my friends used to call them. Milkshake people didn't listen to Bruce Springsteen or Tom Petty or Led Zeppelin or Queen. They loved Christopher Cross, Dan Fogelberg, and Steely Dan.

And Amy Grant made those guys sound like the meanest punks in New York City. I disliked her because she was such a star, one of the first Christian pop stars to have a name beyond the churches, and because so many times, well-meaning school friends played that music and suggested that I needed to look there for my entertainment, there where God resided. When I think back, few things were as important to me in high school as pop music. To this day, I respond to it with helpless emotion. I can remember sitting in homeroom my sophomore year and dreaming that, in the middle of announcements, the opening chords of the Rolling Stones' "It's Only Rock and Roll" would come booming out of the walls, exerting hormonal force, tearing apart meaning and sense.

I was a kid who didn't lose his virginity until junior year in college. I didn't drink or do drugs. But I loved to hang out with the guys and girls who did, in part, because they loved the right music—the sounds of wild romance. Through sophomore and junior year, I had a crush on a girl named Julie. She always had other boyfriends, so my feelings went unrequited, but we would go in a big group of underaged drinkers to see a band called Vince Vance and the Valiants at a bar called Whiskey River. Once, before that show, while we sat at a long table with juniors and seniors, the tape deck blared Bruce Springsteen's live version of "Devil with the Blue Dress" from the *No Nukes* album. I had never heard it before, and I wanted to stand up and point at the speaker and say, "Jesus Christ!" I felt myself quickened. If there was a god, it had to be there, in that sound, in that urgency, in the company of Julie and the other wild kids at that table.

So when Christians played Amy Grant, it made them worse than fools in my eyes. It made them purveyors of a fraud. Jesus couldn't possibly love that music. To this day, Amy Grant is a favorite on the gospel circuit, but she's also a dinosaur. The music of Christianity has been transformed since my day into the financial and cultural cornerstone of the new Christianity. Not only is it hip and cool for Christian teens to listen to bands like Switchfoot and Relient K, secular kids buy the records, too, unthinkable back when I was in high school. And baby boomer grown-ups hear some of the songs in their worship services and can sing them by heart. Pop music has moved from the periphery of Christian experience in the United States to the very center, so much so that modern evangelicalism can't be understood without its drums and electric guitars.

According to the Recording Industry Association of America, the Christian music industry currently constitutes about 6 percent of the $12 billion music business. The latest sales figures show a 3 percent bump in sales from 2005 for the whole of 2006, which means it's not a boom period. Just as in every other corner of the business, Christians are trying to figure out how to stay on top of the technological revolution.

Every year, millions of Americans descend on Christian music festivals. The largest of them, Cornerstone, draws hundreds of thousands to see the biggest names in the business. I chose one of the smaller, more manageable venues. Kingdom Bound drew 60,000 people in 2005, and bills itself as the family-friendliest of the bunch.

Before the festival, I spoke with its founder, Fred Caserta, who has since died. Caserta was an agent and manager for musicians in New York City. As he told it, he was also a drinker, gambler, and dope fiend until he converted to Christianity. Back in the day, a couple of his bands made the charts, but nothing huge ever happened. Such refugees from the entertainment industry are common, and they often have spectacular tales of debauchery and wretchedness to accompany the story of their transformation. Caserta didn't go into details. He had an accident and injured his hip. Laid up for weeks, he steeped himself in the Bible and started to grasp the deeper implications of his new belief. He realized that the business wouldn't help him walk right with Jesus, so he shifted gears and applied his skills to Christian artists. He told me the Kingdom Bound festival had emerged naturally out of his contacts in the music world. After he got out of the secular side of the business, he did a half-hour radio show devoted to the new sound coming out of Christian pop music. A fan of the show approached him about staging a Christian music day, and after a search for the right venue, Caserta and his partners landed on an amusement park at Darien Lake.

At the end of the conversation, he asked me about the state of my faith. When I told him that I'd lapsed, he exhorted me to shape up. In the midst of the evangelical pitch, I could hear the ragged old rock promoter. "If you're going to work on an endeavor like this," he urged me, "you've got to get right with God. You've got to get your heart right with God."

I told him that I would try.

Over the phone, he asked me if he could pray for me, and I gave him permission. He prayed that I would come back. "Lead and guide his direction, Lord." After the prayer, he continued to press me for a decision.

"If you want to recommit yourself right now, let's do it."

I told him that it would be dishonest. I hadn't decided to recommit yet.

He wouldn't relent. "If you walked out of your office right now and got hit by a car, would you go to heaven?"

"No," I answered.

"Well, why not change that?"

"I told you. It wouldn't be honest."

"But it's a free ticket," he retorted. "Like insurance."

I refused a final time, and he left it at that.

OVER A COUPLE of days at Kingdom Bound, I heard many an exhortation—not all of them had to do with belief. Some had to do with the realities of Christian show biz. I attended a seminar on how to make it in the Christian music industry, a session that turned out to be a bit of a boot camp, with a veteran promoter telling a crowd of eager musicians to think real hard before inconveniencing themselves and others by trying to be the next MercyMe. In between power chords blasting from across an artificial pond, the promoter explained to a crowd of about a hundred people that the game had changed in the last twenty years. When he started, it had been relatively easy to get signed by a Christian label. There wasn't much money in the business, and the talent didn't have to rise to the standards of the secular industry. Nowadays, forget about it. If you think you're great, he told them, but you've been performing for a couple of years and no one likes your demo, has signed you to a label, or even offered to represent you, it may be time to apologize to your spouse, get a day job, and use your musical talents in your church choir. Amateur hour in Christian music is over, he told them. If you're not a major talent, it may not even pay to try.

"Do you have an extraordinary talent?" he asked them. "It's pretty obvious when someone is amazing—Mariah Carey or Céline Dion—that talent has to be there. You have to know that the bar goes up every year, higher and higher. Ninety percent of the bands that get passed on would have had a label twenty years ago. Ninety percent who have their video turned down would have passed the test twenty years ago. The competition is over the moon."

"God can use you, no matter what," the promoter told them, "but is that good enough? I hear music all the time that is extraordinary, but if it's not the music that the kids in the vending tent are buying, you can't get that signed." I could feel the deflation as he talked. He wasn't merely giving them the hard facts of the business. He was telling the vast majority of the hopefuls, maybe every one of them, that they were never going to make it. He cited SoundScan, a record sales measuring device, as the ultimate authority. "Two things are working today—rock music, bands like Switchfoot—and worship music—and everything that falls in between, according to Sound-Scan, the kids are not really interested in."

WITHIN ALL THE music, within every product and recording at Kingdom Bound, the same message repeats. Jesus Christ is Lord. In the park, I met a Canadian youth pastor from Ontario. He'd been bringing kids to the fest for years. This year, he had sixty-two in his group. He told me that he considered the Christian music festivals to be the exact counterparts of the tent revivals of two hundred years before, and the kids found God in them. Back home, his church had generated two rock bands already. He himself had started a radio station to showcase the new music, but he wasn't calling it Christian radio, because that would turn people off. In the meantime, he was writing a book about tattoos and the stories they told. Christian tattoos were the next big thing in pop culture, he told me.

This guy seemed so at home with himself and his musical scene, not at all self-conscious. I could not have been more lost. I didn't recognize the name of a single act. I hadn't bothered to listen to any of the music beforehand because I knew that it would be a huge bummer and a chore. Inevitably, I paid for my ignorance.

Backstage, in the area cordoned off for talent, I waited patiently for an interview with Jason Upton, a bluesy worship leader from Wisconsin. He had a reputation for forging a direct line to God onstage, and I felt that he might shed some light on the faith aspect of the music, which so often sounded to my ears like second-generation rip-offs of alt rock. I stood in a crowd of musicians in a parking lot beside trailers and a mess tent. It must have been 90 degrees or so, and I had dressed in a white oxford cloth shirt and jeans. I perspired heavily, waiting to speak to Jason Upton, who was occupied with a fellow musician.

I noticed a guy next to me, also standing in the heat, hands in his pockets, and he gave me a glance. He had a head of peroxide blond curls tumbling down to his waist, a look that went right back to the cover of the *Frampton Comes Alive!* album from my era. I realized that he was, basically, Peter Frampton with Maurice Gibb's face, big eyes and a narrow chin and teeth canted ever so slightly forward. He regarded me with an air of suspicion and pity. I wore a press badge around my neck, but I had the sudden thought that he might be security of one kind or another. In a thick Australian accent, he spoke several sentences that I didn't understand.

In an effort to be forthcoming, I replied, "I'm writing a book on American Christianity." I tried to explain my premise to a face grown instantly bored. I was still waiting to chat with Jason Upton. I told him so. He didn't seem to know the name.

I asked him what he did for a living.

"A bit of this, a bit of that," he replied. "Where you from?" he asked me. I told him that I was from New York. He was from Nashville, the national capital of the gospel music industry, and, despite the Aussie accent and Frampton locks, he obviously plied that trade. I inquired whether he was a musician.

"I'm a Newsboy," he blurted. He looked at me with mild disgust. I could almost read his mind. I was one of those outsiders from the secular world disrespecting him again, even though the Newsboys had sold however many million records, even though I was covering a Christian rock festival. I must still think it was cool, still consider it okay, not to recognize a Newsboy, and this in spite of the fact that I had set out to write a book about American Christianity.

I knew the name, of course. It was in the program. Everyone knew the Newsboys. They were a headlining act. They were stars in their world. Unfortunately, in my world, they had less standing than the least talented contestant on *American Idol*. I hadn't bothered to listen to any of their music. I couldn't even lie that I had liked his last record—or even *heard* his last record—without sounding like a complete fraud. I turned to find Jason Upton, but he had gone into the trailer to escape the heat. My shirt had become soaked. The Newsboy watched me with growing contempt. The pen in my shirt pocket had leaked all over the front of my shirt.

"Holy shit!" I cried out and then remembered where I was. I fled the parking lot and the hostile stare of the offended Christian rock star. I never did get his name.

JOANNE BROKAW RESCUED me from my place in the abyss. I met Joanne at the press tent, and she immediately helped me out. She was personable and shared a lot about herself right off the bat, a quality that she exhibits around everyone, I later saw, not just musically challenged hacks.

I asked her if we could sit somewhere and chat about Kingdom Bound, and right away, she told me that she had come to this year's festival under a cloud of sadness. Joanne came from Rochester, and she had been attending Kingdom Bound for eight years, bringing kids. She'd come with kids this year, too, but in February, one of her favorites from years before had died in a freak accident, a twenty-one-year-old named John. A van had backed him into a wall and crushed him to death. Her eyes turned red as she spoke. He had loved the band Skillet, and when she had watched Skillet play this time, tears had come into her eyes.

A few months later, when we met in Nashville for Gospel Music Week, everyone at the creative end of the business seemed to know Joanne. She wrote for several Christian music magazines and profiled some of the bigger stars. She pressed a lot of different music on me, full of conviction that her favorites weren't sellouts to the money machine. To be good, for her, the bands had to have a great sound and an authentic faith, a true faith. It couldn't just be about the music business.

She had issues with the Christian music scene. She had become disgusted with the fluff in the industry. She disliked the way that more and more products came logo'd with a fish or a cross. She called it "Jesus junk."

She told me she'd been struggling with "bubble Christianity, where we all just hide ourselves, where we don't associate with gay people or people who have had an abortion." It seemed to me that the music scene offered her a way out of that cul-de-sac. For Joanne, it meant connection to the world beyond her local church, a connection she already sought among friends and neighbors in her community.

Before we went to Gospel Music Week, she schooled me in the scene. Artists in the genre have to ask themselves a basic question. Unlike secular musicians, it's not so much about selling out their art for money, or only their art. It's also about selling out their god for the money. The integrity of their art resides in the integrity of their commitment to faith. Joanne has no problem with a band that sells records because it happens to be good. And she ultimately has no problem with a band that calls itself Christian. What she can't abide are those bands who make music that can hardly be distinguished from the secular side and yet use the Christian label to move records. As long as a band has that label, it can be deemed "good." Without that label, it's deemed "bad," regardless of its value as music or inspiration. Like any canny industry, gospel music makes use of the distinction. If people will pay money to be reassured that a record is evangelism—and they will, even though that record might not contain a single mention of Jesus—gospel music might as well go along.

"The Christian music industry is a business," Joanne concluded. "That's the bottom line."

I SAW IT for myself in Nashville during Gospel Music Week 2006—the yearly convention bringing together the various strands of what is known as CCM, or Christian contemporary music. The radio programmers gathered to talk about numbers and give each other awards. The actor and comedian Judge Reinhold, a born-again Christian, hosted the show, bringing his trademark druggy humor to a drug-free environment. Afterward, at a series of roundtable discussions sponsored by Focus on the Family, radio programmers chatted and networked about various aspects of the business—how to reach women; how to market to churches without being offensive; how to build Christian contemporary music overseas. Hundreds of artists did their showcases and submitted to what must have been thousands of interviews in

hotel suites where their labels hosted them. I tried to meet industry super-
stars MercyMe, but they put me off. At a meet-and-greet for fans and the
press, I did manage to get an autograph from *American Idol* finalist George
Huff, who signed a poster for my seven-year-old, and I shook the hand of
seventeen-year-old Krystal Meyers, one of the hotter new rock acts, sort of
Avril Lavigne with a meaner eye and a punk Jesus bent. I told her about my
book and gave her my card.

"Rad," she said, but I never heard from her people.

MY LAST MORNING at Gospel Music Week, I did score a breakfast with a
legend, the guitarist Phil Keaggy, who had played "Here Comes the Sun" so
beautifully in the hotel room. Keaggy had started playing guitar at the age
of ten, despite losing half a finger at the age of four. At nineteen, in Ohio, he
formed a band called Glass Harp, which was discovered by legendary rock
producer Lewis Merenstein. The band signed a three-record deal at Decca
records. The proverbial dream came true. Merenstein had produced Van
Morrison's *Moondance* album, among many others, and he recorded the first
Glass Harp album at Jimi Hendrix's Electric Ladyland Studios in the Village.
But in 1970, Keaggy's mother died in a car wreck, and he followed his sister
in becoming a born-again Christian. When I met him, he had been recording
albums ever since 1968. At fifty-five, that made him one of the great survivors in contemporary music, Christian or otherwise.

He came from a different place than a lot of the younger gospel musicians. He told me that he had grown up listening to Elvis, Fats Domino,
Johnny Ray, the Everly Brothers, and the Beach Boys, just like everyone else
of his generation. When the Beatles came along, he got into their sound, and
though he patterned his voice after Paul McCartney, he was really a George
Harrison man.

Harrison wrote "Here Comes the Sun," and the song had been in Keaggy's repertoire for years. "To me, the song is neither strongly evangelical,
nor is it anti-God. It's just art. It's good art. It's good music. We Christian
artists, we write from our personal experience, and yet a song like 'Here
Comes the Sun' pulls and draws everyone in, no matter what their personal
experience happens to be. . . . We all have a winter in our lives, and we all feel

the cold and the chill, and we all respond to the smiles of faces, and I think that song just brings out light and illumination."

We talked about the Christian music scene, and he told me that CCM artists tended to sing to the choir, and he expressed some regret about choices made when he was a young man. He specifically mentioned the decision to leave Glass Harp, which might have been his ticket to a major secular career. "I left that group partly because of the pressure of Christians, saying you can't do that and be that," meaning a born-again believer in a progressive rock band. "I kind of acquiesced to that pressure a little bit and ended up going on my own, and maybe it was because I was so young and still trying to develop as a human being that I couldn't handle it."

He looked at the career of a band like U2 and saw that it might not have been necessary to break so cleanly with the mainstream rock industry. "They are believers, and yet they love this world. They love the people in this world, and they reach out and care for issues like poverty. To me, those are real exemplary artists who really know how to navigate the tightrope."

Keaggy doesn't see any real advantage to staying in CCM. "I can't even listen to Christian radio most of the time," he told me, "because it all sounds the same to me." To him, CCM is business, just as crafty as the mainstream kind, with all of the usual headaches for artists. He'd been stung more than once. CCM execs had told him that his songs were not commercial enough. One label had allowed him to get out of his contract, but only after he signed away one of his albums. Scripture didn't guide those transactions any more than they guided the business dealings in mainstream music. Keaggy had recently taught a clinic to musicians in Nashville, mostly believers, and given them a sincere piece of advice.

"I said, 'If somebody wants you to sign your music to their label or offer you a great deal that you can't pass up, ask them this: Are you a believer? Are you a follower in Christ? Are you a Christian? If they say yes, don't sign it.'"

It was sobering news to his audience. "It was very quiet. Very quiet. But I did that, you see. I lost years and years of my publishing. No one looked after me."

To him, the smartest people in the business these days are the independent operators who have their own websites, do their own distribution, and sell their own music. He might have been talking about Jason Upton, the bluesy young worship leader at Kingdom Bound.

A FEW WEEKS after the festival, I spoke with Upton over the phone. He hadn't been easy to reach. He's not a prima donna or a jerk, but when he's not touring churches and worship centers on the road, which he does constantly, he enjoys his downtime with family and doesn't care to do much press. Upton had a career in CCM at one point. He signed to a label and took his stab at the business. But it didn't turn out well, and he turned to his father-in-law, who helped him start an online business for selling records. Upton's records sold in the tens of thousands, and he made a living.

"I would never describe myself as a prophet," he said, "or even as a worship leader. I've always been a musician and songwriter. The great passion of my life is songwriting."

At Kingdom Bound, people had told me that he received his messages from God and put them to music. Sitting at his piano, he uttered God's own phrases. But Upton told me that the messages came from quotidian things, like watching his child grow. It didn't have such a mystical quality. Born out of wedlock, Upton was adopted at three months old through a Lutheran social service agency. Later, when he was a grown man, he discovered that his father had been a full-blood Sioux who had been orphaned at the age of thirteen. So one of his themes is being fatherless, and one of his songs is called "Father of the Fatherless." It has a sort of earthy feel, and so does Upton, with his raspy voice and long hair. His music moved me because I could hear real sadness in it. I didn't love it—it was too emotionally overstated for me—but I got it and wanted to hear more. Also, the music didn't sound like anything else. Upton told me that he'd been slotted in the worship music category, meaning songs directed right at God, but worship venues didn't like him that much because the audiences found it hard to sing along. Upton didn't deliver the message by rote in verses easily followed. He sat on the piano bench and sounded as if he were in conversation with a being too immense, too frightening to be approached with mere guitars. I would say that Upton more than submitted himself in concert; he abased himself. And a believer in abasement doesn't raise hands. He bows his head. Watching him, I felt the heaviness of the relationship with God, and it struck me as much more than a pitch or a pep squad cheer. The performance had a quality of deep concentration and foreboding, as if the conversation with God might well end in lightning or a knife fight. But that's my opinion. Upton never put it that way.

Adoption has become one of his major themes. He doesn't know much about his mother, but as time passes, he's become more interested in her. She did leave one request at social services: her child should be raised by a spirit-filled family. And he was. His foster parents raised him as a Christian. He showed musical talent at an early age, but in adulthood, he didn't know what he should do with his talent. He had dreamed for a while of record contracts. But in the end, he told me, God advised him to "be still," and when he said that, I realized one great difference between the Christian contemporary sound and Upton. The former went for noise. He cultivated silence.

"In Europe, I do better than in America," he told me. "People are okay with just listening. So when I minister, the atmosphere is more restful and peaceful. You're here, and you're in my living room. We're going to experience the presence of God together. I have a difficult time getting that atmosphere in a setting like Kingdom Bound."

Before a show, he told me that he always prays over his band members. "I pray that it doesn't matter what people think of us. Let's just have a restful atmosphere of not striving, and let's just play the people our songs. If I can do what I do in my own prayer room back home, with my band, then I've succeeded."

Over the last year, I've had a stack of Upton CDs sitting beside me. Every now and then, I play one on my laptop, but it's hard to take in a room by yourself. It gets me down. Unlike secular blues, which always makes me happy, his music gives me the blues.

ON A COLD night in January, I went to an amazing show in Northampton. In our early twenties, before we knew each other, my wife and I both loved a Los Angeles punk band called X. Debra had actually seen them in concert. Exene Cervenka, John Doe, D. J. Bonebrake, and Billy Zoom represented everything that was cool and tough and alive about punk America in the early years of Ronald Reagan. They seemed dangerous—as dangerous as a rock band can be. Before the show in Northampton, we were both apprehensive. What if it turned out to be a nostalgia act? The band members had to be in their late forties and fifties. Billy Zoom, the lead guitar, hadn't played with the band for years, but had joined up for this tour. Right away, we saw that Exene had gained weight, John Doe had gone gray. And Billy Zoom—he just stood there like a pagan idol, smiling wanly at the audience, as if it cost him no effort, leaning back, his fingers moving at high speed through the brief solos, occasionally taking pictures of the audience with a small camera. Debra and I both felt awe for these people who hadn't been commercially viable in years, whose moment in the light had passed two decades back, and yet who managed somehow to believe enough in their music and themselves to deliver a show of terrible power. It was the greatest rock concert I have ever seen in my life.

I walked out of there thinking to myself, That music is why I'm a pagan. It's a love of life, mean but vital, a sound that imitates the circulation of the blood in the frozen night, ferocious, unapologetic, godless to the core, completely divine. It was the shofar in punk.

The next day, my wife showed me an online interview with Billy Zoom. I had a shock. He was a born-again Christian and had been since back in the day, even before the band X formed in Los Angeles. I'm not a musician. I can't sing a note, can't play a note. But my favorite songs have shaped how I see the world in ways that even my favorite books have failed to do. When I heard "Jumpin' Jack Flash" for the first time, I also discovered sex, though I didn't know it at the time. When I heard "Thunder Road," it was the start of manhood, all its glory and compromise. When I heard Sam Cooke sing "Another Saturday Night" or Hank Williams do "I'm So Lonesome I Could Cry," I heard the voice of death. Music has given wing to so much, rage, sorrow, and joy in my life. So when I held Christian music of the late 1970s in contempt, more was at stake than my taste. And when I hear Christian contemporary music now and feel alienated, that, too, has a greater repercussion than one might think. By the same token, when I discover that one of my favorite musicians in one of my all-time favorite bands, whose sense of integrity, artistry, and cool have never been in question, when someone like that quietly tells an online blogger that he's a believer, it makes the deepest kind of impression. He means it, I think to myself. He truly believes, and it hasn't made him any less of an artist. And a voice in my head inquires whether it was really coincidence that took me to the show that night, and had my wife find the article the next day? And I ask myself, if Billy Zoom can be saved, why can't I?

Somewhere, Don and Lillie McWhinney were smiling. They knew how such things worked. The Lord had his finger in me.

book III

*The Life*

## chapter 18

# *Wretch*

*A*t a conference of Christian bloggers, the first ever GodBlog convention, held in La Mirada, California, in 2005 I heard my first strictly evangelical joke. Lady walks into a movie theater and sees a free seat next to another woman.

"Is that seat saved?" she asks.

"No," the other woman replies, "but it's under heavy conviction."

Unless you are under sixteen and taking a confirmation class, you probably won't be laughing, but it's a joke that offers up a key bit of Protestant theology. To be "under heavy conviction" means to be in a state of dread, sorrow, and shame at your own human condition. It means to be aware of the cage of your own sin. That word, sin, doesn't indicate merely a single bad deed or even the penchant for bad behavior. Conviction is neither a matter of conscience, which everyone possesses naturally, nor a prick of the moral imagination, also a perfectly natural state, nor a kind of knowledge. Conviction of sin is supernatural and happens when the third and most mysterious branch of the Christian Trinity, the Holy Spirit, descends on a person. To a Christian under conviction, sin has presence. It smells like the corpse of a rat that's died in the walls. God sets up a kind of trap within the human soul, allowing a man or woman to perceive his or her own fallen state, and once the initial recognition occurs, conviction begins, and one will do almost anything to get that smell out of the house. Salvation alone fumigates.

Why did I accept Jesus Christ as my personal savior? I grew up in a house where family, funny stories, and food mattered a lot more than Jesus. My brother Tolbert, my sister Molly, and I grew up among the most tantalizing smells: chicken, catfish, and chitterlings sizzling in deep fryers full of Crisco; biscuits, cherry pies, apricot-fried pies; thick steaks on the grill, gifts from our west Texas relatives, who were ranchers. On Sunday nights, we went out for the best Tex-Mex in the country at our local restaurant, and whenever we could, we went for the barbecue: slabs of slow-roasted brisket, ribs, and pork sausage. Food was an ecstatic joy for us all and still is. We love to eat a huge meal and talk about how good it is as we plan the next one. We also love to tell stories about each other and laugh, and the combination of meal and memory makes the experience a natural high. I don't mean to suggest that my family had no religious impulse at all. As I've said, my mother went to church every Sunday and has continued to educate herself in her beliefs. I would call my father a spiritual man, but his sense of the divine is deeply individual, and he keeps it mostly to himself. In my footsteps, my sister became a born-again Christian. She still believes, but no longer in the evangelical vein. My brother is more like my father, with a quiet conviction that only rarely surfaces. Having said that, if we were all forced to choose between God and a standing rib roast, our prospects for heavenly redemption would be dim.

My parents raised me to be honest, decent, and loyal, but by the time I was sixteen, I had developed another side to my personality. I had become a bastard, or maybe I always had been. Awareness of that fact marked the beginning of my conversion. My parents didn't have much to do with my nastiness. They raised me with more tolerance and kindness than anything else, making me feel about as normal as a kid with bifocals, braces, and a headgear can. I got the belt and even a switch from a big bush when I misbehaved, but that didn't make me cruel. My mom tells the story about how I welcomed my little brother home from the hospital. When she left the room, I stuck pins in him. I came into this world with a jealous and vicious streak. A little later, when we shared bunk beds, I told my brother that he had a bad brain. No one had to tell him that I could be a bastard. Years later, when I read the memoirs of Saint Augustine, and I got to the part where he steals the fruit from the orchard and recognizes his own evil, I grasped my own condition.

By the time I reached high school, I had become a kind of psychological bully myself. I didn't beat people up. I found other ways to humiliate.

With the help of an even meaner accomplice, a blonde tennis player who drove a blue convertible Mustang, I bought sacks of bean and cheese chalupas from Taco Bueno. On weekends, she and I drove around Dallas in her car and hurled them at people, particularly the men and women who stood at bus stops at night waiting for home, mostly black, mostly working-class, unlike us. Another time, in high school, I came across a meeting of the war games club, five or six geeky boys gathering in the homeroom of a history professor. I returned the following week with an army of junior varsity football players, and we filled the room, passing several motions and kicking out four of the six original members.

Slowly, I became aware that I despised myself. I began to talk to those kids who talked a lot about Jesus. I don't remember who asked me to the Monday night Young Life meeting at Northwest Bible Church, but I went. I was sick of myself. I wanted to change. Bible-believing Christians will recognize this moment. I had come into the very tractor beam of God.

My parents were wary. They had grown up in mainline denominations in west Texas and had never much cared for Baptists, who didn't smoke, drink, or dance and made everyone else feel bad about it. When they moved to Dallas, they had encountered born-again believers right away. They were invited to a dinner party by some neighbors across the street. During the meal, one of the other guests turned to them and asked if they'd been saved. Such occasions, and there were others, confirmed their low opinion of Holy Rollers. My conversion eventually made them furious. When I came home from Wednesday night Bible study, clutching my Bible and telling my mother and father that they were going to hell, it was as if I'd come home addicted to drugs or professing communism or vegetarianism. Nothing could have been worse. My father sagely predicted, "You just wait. It starts with this, and it'll end with him not believing in God at all."

I have looked and looked in my old journals and can't find a record of my actual conversion, so the date and time, which many born-agains remember till their dying day, will remain forever mysterious. One year, I was a fairly average, church-raised teenage boy with a talent for cruel mischief; the next, I was a child of Jesus, raised up in the light.

EVERY CHRISTIAN, EVEN those born in the faith, has a conversion story, and if these stories were gathered in a book, the way the early Romantics gathered the folktales of the peoples of Europe, they would make a kind of American national epic. So many of them are rich in incident and humanity, so many sink to the depths of fear or humiliation or depravity before rising through seeming coincidence, hardship, tragedy, and love to a victorious end. No other stories in the life of the faith have such drama as conversion tales. Before you change, no matter what else happens, you are dead forever. After you change, no matter what else occurs, you live forever. The leap across that divide, as it's described in each life, echoes the entire cosmic drama of death, hell, and resurrection. Don McWhinney tells a good conversion story.

Three months after Don and Lillie lost their son, I returned to Dallas and spent two days with Don as he drove around the Dallas–Fort Worth area as a chaplain to local businesses for a company called Marketplace Ministries and as a hospice worker, paying visits to the sick and dying. One day, we did chaplain work; another, we did hospice. Both jobs entail a lot of time behind the wheel, and the ability to walk into the offices and businesses of near strangers and feel at home enough to ask personal questions.

On our first visit in the chaplain mode, Don walked from suite to suite in a bank. He was impressively meticulous in this work. If people were there, he stuck his head in the door and said a quick hello. One or two people called him Padre, an obvious term of endearment. He asked how they were doing, recalled the name of a wife or a child, and left a strip of paper with a thought for the day, something inspirational rather than religious. Don had a working philosophy, what he called the Five Bs: "Be brief, baby, be brief." If people wanted to talk, their body language indicated it. If not, the same held true. He never spent more than a minute or two in any one room, and if someone had a phone call, he left the thought for the day and moved on. He'd figured out the best places to leave the thought for the day in an empty office. Never on the console, where it would seem an intrusion. Better would be the arm of a chair, best of all the keyboard of the computer. Companies that hire the services of Marketplace Ministries don't want intrusion and certainly don't want evangelism. Don knew the limits well. If a Muslim wanted to speak to an imam, or a Jew to a rabbi, he had a Rolodex and would make the referral. Most people, if they wanted anything, just needed a little assistance. Don had helped a father when his son got beat up in a bar fight, a woman whose electricity had been turned off, and others with money or addiction concerns. Some people wanted to talk about their children, like the eighty-year-old African American filing clerk at the bank, a Baptist and civil rights veteran whose father had worked a section farm off one of the railroads. One of her daughters had been abused and raped by a family member and Don had helped to connect the family with a child advocacy group.

The hospice work seemed more taxing. There was less distance and more need. In Nevada, Texas, about an hour north of Dallas, we drove through fields with small corrals, bare humps of land swelling and settling in waves. We passed a donkey switching its tail and stopped at the end of a white-pebbled drive leading to a one-story ranch house. Don chatted with a woman named Lois, who was hooked up to a respirator. Her husband, Horace, crumpled in blue jeans, was in his late eighties. He sat in a chair beside his wife, and Don tried to engage him—it was too hard for Lois to talk. Horace had been a truck driver, he told us, and he'd been driving since 1928, when the roads were two lanes and the speed limit topped at 35 miles an hour, before Eisenhower built the interstates. The rhythm of his wife's breath, coming hard and slow and with groans of pain, punctuated every word he said. He'd hauled steel and block ice, anything people wanted. He'd seen the Okies headed west. He'd seen violence in the union strikes. He'd fought at the Battle of the Bulge, but didn't want to talk about it. He started to cry, and Don changed the subject quickly.

We visited three or four more people that day, and Don handled each of them with tenderness and genuine interest. We visited a woman named Marcy, overweight and housebound in an apartment complex where the management repeatedly failed to fix the air-conditioning, though we were in Texas, in 90-degree-plus heat. The complex had 120 units and a single Dumpster. When it got hot, the trash reeked. Marcy was a 300-pound stationary woman with a collection of Coca-Cola paraphernalia and no money. She had innumerable health problems related to her heart and weight and wouldn't live much longer. While we chatted, the phone rang.

"Oh no," Marcy groaned into the receiver, and she began to get red in the face. One of her sisters had just that moment been in a car wreck, and Marcy had no way to help, no transportation. Don made a call or two to find a driver to take her to her sister. Tears ran down Marcy's face.

"The devil has just been fighting this family," she said, wiping her eyes. On the couch where we sat, I saw a teddy bear and a big leather-bound Bible. She made clear that she wanted the Lord to take her home.

It was hard to believe that Don McWhinney had ever been anything but a decent Christian man, but as we sat in a barbecue joint in north Dallas, he told me his story.

AT THE AGE of ten, in the presence of his parents, in a Church of the Nazarene in Kansas City, Kansas, Don was baptized into the fold. By the time he got to high school, you wouldn't have known it.

"John, I got into high school, and I really bottomed out. I drank heavily. I figured out how to write hot checks. I got myself dressed up in a suit and a tie, and I got me a checkbook and a fancy pen, and I got a bunch of phony IDs. I even had a name—Donald Moore—to match the DM on my high school ring. I stopped one time at a department store to write a check for cash, and they said we'll have to call the bank. And I thought, Don, don't panic. They called the bank, and sure enough, there was a D Moore, a Donald Moore, who had an account there and apparently had sufficient funds to cover the check. So they came back and gave me twenty bucks. I thought, well, that gives me confidence. So the next time someone showed hesitancy, I said, 'Well, call the bank.'"

Don looked sharp in a suit, and the con worked for a time. But, eventually, the law caught up. He'd gone into a Sears to write a check, and the teller told him that she'd have to call the bank. "She was gone an inordinate amount of time," Don told me. "And I thought, something's up, and about that time, a detective from the Kansas City police force took me by the right arm, and there was another one there with him. And we went into a room, and they said, How long you been doing this, son, and who you been doing this with, and I told them my story, and they didn't believe me. They said, 'That deal is far too complicated for you to be doing it by yourself.' But if you can believe it, they called my dad and released me to the custody of my father. My dad and I went all over town picking up hot checks."

He stopped writing the checks, but he didn't tell the police about another crime he'd committed. "It was about that same time that I poured five gallons of gasoline under a supermarket door and set it on fire."

I asked him why he'd done it.

"Kicks," he said. "Meanness. No big thing. Wasn't mad. Just wanted to do it."

The crime went unsolved. No one suspected Don, but his faith plagued him for years, until college. "I knew that, if ever I was going to get right with the Lord, and have the fellowship with him that I knew that he wanted from me, I was going to have to go back some way and make that right. From a theological perspective, I had not lost my relationship with God, because that relationship is once and for all, it's sealed. But I was in sin, living in sin, and doing things that were displeasing to my Lord Jesus Christ and my parents, and I knew that if I ever got myself straightened out spiritually, I was going to have to go back and make restitution. And, man, I had a war in myself with that issue. I finally came to the point where life is not worth living as I'm living it. I was in college. And I remember getting right with the Lord, asking him to forgive me for my sin, what I had done. I called my dad and told him what I had done. And the tears could be heard over the phone, and he said, 'Don, this is what we've been praying for.'"

That summer, he went to Kansas City with his father and a pastor. They went to the insurance company that had held the policy on the supermarket. "What happened there is typical of what happens for us at the cross. We come to the cross guilty, full of burdens of sin and the hassles of life, and there I was in front of that insurance company. It's as though the chief financial officer of that company had said, 'That debt has already been paid, we have no desire for that young man and his dad to pay any money on this debt.' To me, that's what happens for us at the cross. We come to God guilty, deserving of punishment. Jesus stands there as the chief financial officer, who says, 'Put your trust in me, I'll take care of that debt, you're free to go.' He paid the penalty for our sin."

There were a few more heartaches to come. His freshman year in college at Southern Nazarene University in Oklahoma City, he and his pals spent more time in the bars than they did in class, and Don got kicked out of school. But he went back on probation the following year and finally began to get his life together. His senior year, he met Lillie, a freshman, and told her everything about his wild life. Her elder brothers had been his drinking partners, and they didn't want him in the family. They advised her to dump him. But she saw that he'd changed, and in 1960, the two were married. I met them right before they celebrated their forty-fifth wedding anniversary.

Don had gone on to work for AT&T and Xerox. Bored with the office supply business, he founded his own oil and gas company, and when that went belly up, he got a job as a consultant for W. R. Grace. Through those years, he told me, his faith matured. Over ribs and Diet Dr Pepper, he explained to me his view of the Christian life. He reminded me that, after the *60 Minutes* interview, he'd sent a letter to Morley Safer to better explain his views on who gets saved and who doesn't.

"And I said, what I believe is not important. What I believe is irrelevant. What I believe *is* relevant are the claims of Christ. He said, 'I am the way, the truth, and the life. No one comes to the Father, except through me.'"

That verse had been a touchstone of my faith, too, when I believed.

In his avuncular, homespun manner, articulating every word as if it figured in a speech before a board of directors, he said, "What I strive to do is flesh out my Christian life on a daily basis in my walk. Do I sin? Yes. John, as you and I sit here, talking, we're breathing physically, exhaling carbon dioxide, breathing in fresh air. Same thing we're to do in the Christian life, we are to breath spiritually, exhaling the things in my life that should not be there: sin, evil thoughts, lust, pride, anger, saying things that are said impulsively. And I am to breathe in the fresh things that God has for me: his life, his word, forgiveness. To me, the Christian life is very much like the physical life. I am breathing physically, and I continue to breathe spiritually."

chapter 19

## *Daddy*

*A*t a small church near Plymouth, Massachusetts, in a joyful, almost cherubic voice, a white-haired man in patched cargo pants told a Saturday morning crowd of grown-ups that God was daddy, the Abba Father. "Heaven is full of five-year-olds," he assured us. What a terrible notion, I thought.

The man's name was Brennan Manning, and I had first heard of him at the reception after Tedd McWhinney's memorial service. One of Don and Lillie's oldest friends, a doctor named Earle from Alabama, had driven several hours to get to Texas in time for the funeral. At the reception, over plates of barbecue and potato salad, Earle asked me about my book project, and when I explained, he insisted that I had to get a book by Brennan Manning. On a scrap of paper, he scribbled down the title, *The Ragamuffin Gospel*, but he told me that I had to hear Manning's voice to get the full effect.

A few months later, I found out Manning was coming to Kingston, Massachusetts. On the Saturday morning of his visit, about fifty people attended. The church was small and right off the highway, the bare-walled sanctuary dominated by a single wooden cross hanging over the altar. I saw a pair of kettle drums and a triangle dangling from a bar. My heart filled with foreboding. A musician began to tune a guitar, doodling a "Deliverance" riff.

Female vocalists took the stage. Arms lifted, hands reached, and voices rose in song, the same song, set to the exact same tune, it seemed to me, that I had heard in countless settings from western New York to Louisville, Kentucky, from Nashville, Tennessee, to Los Angeles, California.

Thirty exhausting minutes later, the pastor took the stage. He turned to the guest speaker. "How you doing, Brennan?"

"Feeling frisky," Brennan Manning replied. The audience chuckled, and the talk of God the Father began with an old Yiddish joke told by the speaker in a mock Yiddish accent. He'd heard the joke from a messianic Jew in Flatbush. It was a joke about three Jewish fathers, each of whose sons has become a Christian. One by one, the men admit the shameful secret of their child's conversion, starting their revelation with the words, "Let me tell you a very funny thing." So all three go to their rabbi and reveal the awful secret, and the rabbi says, "Let me tell you a very funny thing," revealing that his son, too, is a Christian. On behalf of himself and the three men, the rabbi then turns to Yahweh, praying for wisdom to deal with the problem of the four Jewish sons who have all become Christians. There's a long silence, and then God replies, "Let me tell you a very funny thing. . . ."

Immediately after telling this joke, perhaps sensing some discomfort in the room, or as a standard measure before crowds hearing the joke, Manning uttered a disclaimer, reminding us that "any form of anti-Semitism is Christian spit in the face of our Jewish savior."

But it wasn't just about the joke. Manning's topic that day, and most days, is the revolutionary leap in the understanding of God from the Hebrew worship of Yahweh to the message of Jesus Christ. He started with the book of Luke, chapter 11, verse 2, where the disciples ask Christ how they're supposed to pray, and Jesus answers with the Lord's prayer, "When you pray, say, Our Father . . ."

Manning insisted on the profundity of the notion. "Isaiah, greatest of the prophets, begins his ministry by seeing Yahweh seated on a high and lofty throne," he said, "surrounded by a choir of angels, chanting holy, holy, holy, but Isaiah never heard what the apostles heard that day. For Ezekiel, Micah, Zephaniah, Jeremiah, Amos, Hosea, Joel, every Israelite, Yahweh was the holy, strong, immortal one, a personal, stable, faithful, relating being," unlike the Canaanite gods. In line with his earlier disclaimer, Manning wanted to reassure us that he meant in no way to disrespect the Jewish Lord. "Israel knew a stable god who was like the rock of Gibraltar in the wind of changing events. To the average Jew, God had a face." And yet, he told us, "No Jew ever dared to pray in the sense that Jesus taught: 'Our Father.' This is the revolutionary revelation of Jesus Christ."

Pagan philosophers like Plato and Aristotle had brought reason into the divine equation, calling God "the uncaused cause" and "the immovable mover." Prophets of Israel had discovered a divine being who was warmer and more personal. But, Manning asserted, "Only Jesus revealed to the astonished Jewish community that God is truly the Father, that if you took the love of all the best mothers and fathers who lived in the course of human history—think about that for a moment, if you took all the goodness, kindness, patience, fidelity, wisdom, tenderness, strength, and love and united all those qualities in a single person, that person would only be a faint shadow of the love and the mercy in our God, the Father, addressed to you and to me this moment."

He turned to Romans 8:15, where the apostle Paul writes, "For you have not received the spirit of bondage again to fear; you have received the spirit of adoption, whereby we cry, Abba, Father." Manning interpreted: "Literally, meaning, in English, Daddy, Papa, my own dear father." And then he brought the message home. "American child psychologists tell us that when the average American baby begins to speak between the ages of fourteen and eighteen months, regardless of the sex of the child, whether it's a boy or a girl, the first word normally spoken at that age level is dada, dada, dada. Daddy. A little Jewish child, speaking Aramaic in first century Palestine, the time of the historical Jesus, would, at the same age level, begin to say, abba, abba, abba."

The way he said it, the infantile repetition from the mouth of a grown man, repulsed me. But later, reading his book *The Ragamuffin Gospel*, I would have a better understanding of his intent. Manning writes in that book: "When Jesus tells us to become like little children, He is inviting us to forget what lies behind. . . . Whatever we have done in the past, be it good or evil, great or small, is irrelevant to our stance before God today." And later, he writes, to follow Jesus means "the willingness to accept oneself as being of little account and to be regarded as unimportant. The little child who is the image of the kingdom is a symbol of those who have the lowest places in society, the poor and the oppressed, the beggars, the prostitutes and tax collectors—the people whom Jesus often called the little ones or the least."

In this context, it all sounds more like a metaphor, but on the day of the talk, I felt that this notion of an ideally infantilized humanity wasn't even remotely an abstraction to Manning. In his ragamuffin cargo pants, with their crazy-quilt patches, he conveyed a visual message that his words fully amplified. "What Jesus Christ is saying to his people is that the God in whose presence Moses had removed his shoes because he was standing on holy ground, the God from whose fingertips this universe fell, the God beside whose beauty the Grand Canyon is only a shadow, the God beside whose power the nuclear bomb is nothing—Jesus says we may dare to address this infinite, transcendent, almighty God in baby talk. With the same intimacy, familiarity, and unshaken trust as a sixteen-month-old baby sitting on its father's lap, going dada, dada, dada."

THIS IS ONE man's very particular, even peculiar, interpretation of scripture, but his focus on childhood, the centrality of childhood to his vision, echoes throughout American Christendom and may account for some of Manning's popularity. In part, the emphasis is a function of the baby boomer fixation on childhood and child-rearing. It is also a logical step in an evolution that has been underway for two hundred years in Western culture, as children have gone from being disposable objects who may be left to die in the open to the treasure at the heart of civilization, the most precious object of an adult's life. As the stock of the child has grown, so modern theology has reappraised the meaning of childhood in scripture, making central what has always seemed to be metaphorical, that is, that human beings are children of God. At the same time, the priority given to actual children has become ever more intense. The growing sense among Christians that coming generations will be utterly lost to the faith has turned a focus on youth into an obsession. It's no longer a matter of exposing children to the gospel at an early age. Children must be steeped from infancy.

A woman named Palma Smiley has made a life's work of the effort. A

Bible study teacher since the age of seventeen, as her website informs us, a graduate of something called the Better Baby Institute for the Achievement of Human Potential, and an educator of long standing in Lubbock, Texas, Palma Smiley has developed a program for submerging infants and toddlers in the faith at the earliest possible age. Her curriculum for babies is a series of four programs, each of them thirteen weeks long: in all a year's worth of Christian indoctrination. The lesson plans exist in the form of a ninety-six-page booklet that contains a hard script, so that no one need improvise. The first lesson handles the subject of "Creation"; the second "Family"; the third is called "God Made Me"; and the fourth is "Baby Jesus," a Christmas lesson. The themes amount to a framework for a larger initiative, the attempt to connect the babies to their families' Bibles. In every lesson, four or five times, the instructor will pass around a Bible and tell the children—show the children, really, who can be anywhere from six months to a year in the first phase of learning—to "pat the Bible." The program has been called "Pat the Bible," in fact, and I'm told that this is the true thrust of the program—to get babies to understand that the Bible is God's word. For many graduates of the program, the word "Bible" is among the first vocabulary words.

One Sunday morning, at Southeast Christian, I saw Palma Smiley's program in practice. A spokesperson for the church, Debra Childers, gave me a tour of the high-security, fully staffed, impressively detailed child-care facilities before the midmorning service. We went first to the nerve center of the operation, called "Oz," where parents check in at a computerized station and workers in green smocks guide the traffic. Southeast has developed its own software, called Fellowship One, to process their massive demand, in excess of 5,000 kids a weekend. The children receive stickers on their backs and the parents receive a receipt, printed out, bearing a number that changes every week. Only the person with that specific receipt can pick up the child whose number is on the receipt.

At an appointed hour, when every stickered child has entered his or her appointed room, and every receipt has been issued, the green-smocked workers at Oz will authorize the closing and locking of all doors until the Sunday morning service has ended. In that time, no unauthorized personnel will enter the spaces where the children learn their Bible lessons.

With Debra Childers, I was allowed to walk along a corridor, looking through glass at the infants. We stopped at a room where a "Pat the Bible" lesson had begun. A female teacher in a smock sat at a table with ten one-year-olds, placed around the oval surface in chairs that attached to the table's rim. We couldn't hear the teacher's words to the babies, but a Southeast child-care staffer accompanied us and provided commentary. She told me that the program emphasizes repetition, and that it's "perfectly okay for babies to come here thirteen weeks in a row and learn the same thing." My sample script for the baby curriculum, a section on creation called "Thank You, God, for Everything," provided the road map. The script read:

> *This is the Bible*
> *Bible words say "God made everything."*
> *He made everything pretty just for me.*
> *He made the clouds, flowers and trees.*
> *He made the sun and moon and stars.*
> *He made the fish, birds and animals.*
> *He made people just like me.*

In the script are instructions to the teacher. "Hold big Bible in your hands, so babies can see and touch it. Turn pages slowly. Teach babies to pat Bible gently. Insert pictures of things God made."

That morning, the teacher did the lesson on "Family." After the Bible went around, and each baby gave it a pat, a wavering, not entirely controlled pat, as when a child in a high chair indicates a desire for more food, the teacher passed around a kind of dollhouse and doll members of the family. The babies tended to stick the dolls in their mouths, so all toys were washed with a nontoxic disinfectant before each lesson. In addition to Bibles and the props, the teacher has lots of Kleenex and crackers. A wind-up duck waddled across the table, an illustration of the duck family. There were also rooster families.

I asked my guide if babies could really gain anything mentally from these exercises. "It's the first introduction to the Bible as God's word," she told me. "They will come out of this program knowing the Bible, having an

enrolling hundreds of thousands of children freed from work by new child labor laws. Colleges and universities followed the same trajectory, with most institutions of higher learning turning increasingly secular with the rise of Enlightenment philosophies of reason and science. Evangelical missionaries to the New World founded Harvard, Yale, and Princeton and turned them into world-class institutions for turning out ministers, lawyers, judges, doctors, and other learned men. By the end of the last century, their roots in faith had become a formality, the last lingering traces often enough resulting in discrimination against Catholics and Jews.

My alma mater, Davidson, was founded by the Concord Presbytery in 1837. Sixty-four students, all male, attended that first year. Among their subjects of study: Evidences of Christianity. When I got there in 1981, the school had recently gone co-ed, but its Presbyterian roots could still be vaguely discerned. I took a lot more Protestant theology than my friends at other schools. Christian kids could feel right at home. Gay kids hid in the theater department or fraternities, well closeted, for the most part. There were very few Jewish kids and no Muslims or Hindus that I can remember. A counter-culture existed, mushrooming in hidden corners. The institution itself had by-laws requiring fealty to the Presbyterian tradition, including a stipulation that only people whose home churches professed the Protestant faith could serve on the board of trustees. By the time I returned for my twentieth reunion in 2005, a lot had changed, in particular those by-laws. The board of trustees had voted 31 to 5 to allow 20 percent of the board to be non-Christian. The decision came at a cost. One of Davidson's wealthiest, most powerful trustees, John Belk, a pillar of society in Charlotte, North Carolina, and the man for whom my freshman dorm had been named, resigned from the board in protest. Another wealthy trustee followed his example.

In general, at the reunion, people were buzzing about Christianity. Most Davidson students of my era came from the American South, and we had all been exposed to evangelical religion at one time or another. A lot of people in my class would classify themselves as liberal evangelicals, for whom social justice and the virtues of compassion and mercy mattered far more than questions of scriptural inerrancy, prophecy, or evangelism to the unreached peoples. The college chaplain, Rob Spach, who had been a friend back during college years, staunchly defended the trustee vote, writing, "For Christians in the Reformed Tradition, God's truth is revealed fully but not exclusively in Jesus. As human beings, our understanding of God's truth is always imperfect and partial because we are limited by historical and cultural circumstances."

This sort of talk would have been anathema at Southeast Christian Church. But at my reunion, a lot of my Christian friends were up in arms about the Southeast version of their faith. One old friend, Todd, who had lived on my hall freshman year, had become a successful businessman in the Charlotte area. We started talking about the subject of the book, and he became irate. He had sent his daughter to a Christian school in the area, and the experience had turned out to be a nightmare. Todd considered himself a Christian, he believed in God, but faith-based education had offended him far worse than anything in the secular world. I spoke with several other parents whose children had been involved as well, and the story, with a few varying details, went as follows.

Todd had been looking for a new school for his thirteen-year-old daughter, who wasn't happy in the Charlotte public school system. He found a local Christian academy with high academic standards and a reasonable price tag, and he enrolled his daughter. At first, she loved it. People were friendly. There hadn't been much pressure to get involved with the religious stuff, and it had seemed a very good compromise. The daughters of other parents had the same experience. Until the incident in question, the school seemed an ideal solution to a problem.

Over spring break, a group of male and female students met at one of the girls' homes, where they played a game of spin the bottle. This happened either in the front yard of the house or at a nearby park, depending on which version I was told. In the game, kids revealed secrets and kissed. The boys kissed girls and urged the girls to kiss girls. No one removed any clothes. The kisses were "pecks" on the lips, according to the parents. At the time, no one seemed to think much about it, but someone in the circle, or a parent who observed the behavior, reported it to the school. The following week, on a Tuesday, parents of several of the girls received cell phone calls from the school requesting their presence at a disciplinary meeting the following morning. That same day, in school, six girls were called into the principal's office and asked, one by one, about the game of spin the bottle. One, at least, was asked if the kisses were "deep kisses." When the parents arrived the next day to talk about it, the principal informed them that there would be no discussion. The academy had a zero tolerance policy on sexual behavior. School policy explicitly stated that the school "retained the right to refuse enrollment to or to expel any student who engages in sexual immorality, including but not limited to any student who professes to be homosexual/bisexual or is a practicing homosexual/bisexual as well as any student who condones, supports or otherwise promotes such practices (Leviticus 20:13; Romans 1:27)."

When some parents objected that the girls had been singled out when the boys had not, that the boys were just as guilty of kissing as the girls, that they had, in fact, *instigated* the girls' behavior, the principal informed them that the boys had not indulged in behavior explicitly proscribed by the school. One look at the school's website revealed photographs of girls in low-cut dresses at a school dance, cleavage amply displayed, making clear that overt displays of sexuality were not the issue. In the immediate wake of these conversations, the principal got on the school's public address system and called each of the girls' names and asked them to come to the main office for early dismissal. Some of the kids were in tears, as were the mothers. In the meeting before the dismissal, one incensed mother, an Episcopalian married to a Catholic, began to quote verses from the Bible, accusing the academy of pursuing an unnecessarily harsh policy. One father called the principal a hypocrite, and the men almost came to blows.

In the event, the school expelled all six girls. That Episcopalian mother still can't understand it. She had been a good person all her life, she told me. Her daughter hadn't done anything sexual. She had been out in public, not trying to hide. She was only in sixth grade. She was a child, playing a harmless game with friends. The boys had done the same thing and hadn't been expelled. Her daughter had been traumatized by the experience. This woman couldn't understand the situation. She didn't know what any of this had to do with Jesus Christ.

ROUGHLY 4 MILLION American kids attend religious schools in the United States, and most of those are Christian. A majority are Catholic.

The American Association of Christian Schools, the most powerful lobbying body for the sector, represents mostly the Protestant faith, and it lists more than a thousand schools as its members, representing 170,000 students in forty-seven states.

As of 2003, another 1.1 million kids were homeschooled, according to the National Center for Education Statistics. Thirty percent of parents of these students gave religious instruction as the reason for schooling at home. Given these stats, it's probably safe to conclude that at least half a million American children, give or take, receive their primary school education in an atmosphere comparable to the one at the Christian academy in Charlotte. But even within that small world, a tiny fraction of the almost 50 million public school students in the United States, there exists a growing divide about how to educate, how far to go with biblical principles, on the one hand, how much to adapt to mainstream standards on the other.

That appalled Episcopalian mother hadn't merely collided with a single school. She had run afoul of an entire movement, which might be called, for the lack of a better term, "kingdom education," borrowed from the title of an influential book by an educator named Glen Schultz. The book argues the case for a version of Christian schooling that would shift the focus of a faith-based education away from an outcomes-based philosophy resulting in acceptances to major mainstream colleges and universities—away from worldly success, in other words, and toward a deeper emphasis on converting children to a true born-again faith as a prelude to a life devoted to Christ.

"The end result of all education is worldview," Schultz is reported to have told an audience at New Orleans Baptist Theological Seminary. He invoked the Barna surveys, telling the audience that only 7 to 8 percent of today's Christians profess what might be called a biblical worldview. It's the same argument used by Focus on the Family to sell its Truth Project vision, except in this case the students are children rather than misinformed adults, and the stakes would appear to be much higher. "That worldview is either man-centered or God-centered. We tell our kids to love the Lord, get good grades, and do well in school. Many schools teach things like evolution, directly refuting our biblical worldview, yet we tell them to get good grades, and therefore they end up believing these philosophies."

Schultz has won major converts, including increasing numbers of members in the Southern Baptist Convention. In 2004, the head of the SBC, Jack Graham, urged members to think more seriously about "establishing kingdom schools." Florida's SBC held an education summit that same year at which the topic was front and center.

I received a copy of the book at Southeast Christian Church, which has loose ties to the Christian Academy of Louisville. The academy, founded by Southeast members, claims to be the largest Christian school system in the country, with more than 3,000 students on its Kentucky and Indiana campuses. Schultz's book provides the intellectual framework within which the system operates. Schultz believes that a school must work in tandem with a student's home and church to be effective at the task of winning kids to the faith and keeping them in it. Teachers should have had a born-again experience of Christ and should model behavior reflecting the experience. In the introduction to the book, Schultz offers a striking comparison. "We should be wise to study how the Jewish community has maintained its culture regardless of its geographical location or size of its membership. The reality is that every individual in the community has the same goal for every Jewish baby. That goal is to instill within that child the Jewish faith."

As with so much else in the faith right now, the answers for Schultz lie in Genesis. He writes that God's original, Edenic relationship with humans must be the basis for the proper kingdom education: "Adam had a direct personal relationship with God, his Creator. When Adam needed to learn something, he could go to God, and God would teach him about anything in the created world."

In this statement alone, one understands why the school in Charlotte could not possibly countenance even the most tenuous show of homosexual behavior. If one believes, as many of these educators do, that the model must be the Garden of Eden, then looking the other way while girls kiss girls would be like ignoring the sound of a snake hissing untruth in the trees.

Modern secular education is seen as relativist, tolerant, and subjective. It is postmodern, in a word, which means that any number of texts may be used to put forward any number of agendas. In that system, the main thing, the hoped-for outcome, is a student who can pursue whatever goals he or she may desire. The goal itself is almost irrelevant, in other words; achieving it is everything. For Christians, however, the opposite is true. Having the right goal is everything. Maintaining focus on that goal is the point of education. In a disconcerting paragraph, Schultz cites the efforts of the twentieth century totalitarians to inculcate "worldview" with something like approval.

"Throughout the course of human history, individuals and governments have used education to shape the worldview of their societies," he writes. "In Germany, Hitler taught the German children a philosophy of life based on the beliefs of Nazism. The former Soviet Union instilled a communist worldview into children's minds through a heavily regimented educational program."

He goes on to quote Charles Colson on Fidel Castro's attempts to keep the revolution alive in Cuba. Colson, in the citation, says that if Castro "fails to teach Cuba's children the communist worldview, the revolution will eventually die out." Schultz follows with this sentence: "Christian parents, church leaders and educators must understand how important worldview development is in the education of their children."

The anxiety in these passages explains why the girls in Charlotte had to be expelled from their school. In certain Christian circles, the possibility of the extinction seems real. Education is the Siegfried Line.

I PAID A visit to the Christian Academy of Louisville and met with its new superintendent, David Patterson. While I sat in the main office, waiting to see him, a tall woman in a red dress walked into the room. One of the administrative assistants asked her offhandedly what she'd been teaching.

"Manners," she replied.

"What's your curriculum?" the assistant asked.

The woman in the red dress raised a large book in a zippered leather case, the Bible.

"What does the Bible say about chewing with your mouth open?" the assistant further inquired, a little cheekily, I thought.

"Nothing as such," the teacher answered. "It's more general."

As far as I could tell, the assistant didn't quite get the big picture yet: nothing worth knowing exists outside of the Bible; or better yet, the Bible encompasses everything that could be taught or known. I asked the school superintendent David Patterson to single out the key difference between a kingdom school and other kinds of educational institutions. "Every subject is biblically integrated," he told me. "History, science, math, language. Every subject that we teach, kindergarten through twelfth."

In math, that means order. God is a god of order and has established logical rules that can be seen and understood through formulas that are both proof of his existence and guides to the Christ-like life. In science, that means discovering the many ways that God can be seen in the natural world. It also means offering students a wide array of views on the creation story in Genesis. Outside of Christendom, what causes a stir is the mere mention of intelligent design. Within a kingdom school, the disputes run the gamut, from Young Earth theories—the earth was created 10,000 years ago and the fossil record has been jumbled by Noah's flood, making the earth look older than it is—to Old Earth theories, which stick closer to the time line accepted by most geologists. Students get a taste of all. Evolution is taught as falsehood.

Each class, every day, teachers begin with a prayer. Each morning starts with the national anthem and three pledges: kids pledge allegiance to the flag of the United States, to a Christian flag ("I pledge allegiance to the Christian flag and to the Savior for whose kingdom it stands, one brotherhood uniting all Christians in service and love"), and to the Bible ("I pledge allegiance to the Bible, God's Holy Word, a lamp unto my feet, a light unto my path. Its words will I hide in my heart that I might not sin against God").

In the end, it's hard to tell how well the system works, so Patterson and other school officials have begun work on measurements of success. A firm called Assess Yourself has been hired to do a spiritual audit of faculty, students, family members, and all others who fall within the orbit of the school. "It's an online study," Patterson told me. "It just asks various questions and gives some situations. 'What should be the biblical perspective?' 'How should I handle this?' We'll have grades 7 through 12 take it, hopefully to get some measure of where we are as a school—and trying to bring out those things like gratitude, thankfulness, prayer life, how much we are putting God's word in our heart, how much we are serving our community, spiritual disciplines like fasting."

To find the answers, Assess Yourself offers a test called the Christian Character Index, which asks thirty-five questions and urges the respondent to spend at least twenty seconds on each question. The test allows five possible answers to thirty-five statements, ranging from "I enjoy helping others" and "I seek God's will through prayer" to "I celebrate life" and "I love God with all my heart." A brochure for the company claims that more than 30,000 Christians worldwide have completed the online surveys.

That information will give academies like Louisville a chance to turn out students who will not lose their faith when they encounter the secular culture, and who may even be strong enough in their beliefs to change the culture. When Patterson got involved in Christian education twenty years ago, the institutions existed mostly as a means to protect and defend populations of children in a secular wilderness. Race played a role, too. White flight from urban areas and their public school systems accounted for a lot of the growth. But flight is no longer an option. Christians can't flee the culture in the same way that they might escape a decayed city. They have to fight. They have to change the culture or be changed.

"What we're trying to do," Patterson said, "is not just tell kids *what* to think, but *how* to think. How to reason. How to get real knowledge. And the Hebrew word for knowledge means 'to change.' So real knowledge makes us different."

IN LA MIRADA, California, after a morning chapel at the Bible Institute of Los Angeles, also known as Biola University, I met a product of this kind of schooling. His name was Dirk, and he had something on his mind. At the invitation of Craig Detweiler, I spoke about myself at a compulsory morning chapel. In that talk, which lasted a few minutes, I said that I had lost my faith; I used those exact words. They prompted Dirk to come forward and speak to me.

Backpack over his shoulder, blond, blue-eyed, and slender, Dirk told me that he was confused. He'd heard of people who didn't believe. He'd heard of people who refused to believe. He'd even heard of people who said they believed but really didn't. He'd never in his life heard someone say that they had "lost" their faith. He didn't know how that was possible.

Everything he'd been taught suggested that once a person had faith, it couldn't be lost.

Dirk had gone to a Christian school in the Central Valley, in the Modesto area. His family, of Dutch and Frisian stock, farmed 90 acres of almonds and walnuts, but, unlike his brother, he'd never wanted to be a farmer. He'd always loved computers and movies. He loved the way the dinosaurs moved in *Jurassic Park* and wanted to be a part of the world that made it happen. He started by making videos for class and became the de facto "film guy." His first work, in grade 7 or 8, dealt with the battle of Bunker Hill. Lego characters acted out the parts. His mom reluctantly allowed him to use the camera, and he caught the moviemaking bug.

He wanted to get into the movie business, but had concerns. His faith told him that a lot of his classmates, despite being Christian, had the wrong reasons for wanting to make movies. One group was making a horror movie and planned to include a decapitation. He disapproved. He didn't like the way that so many in his class yearned to make it big in the industry. He was more interested in making small films about his faith, ones that glorified God in straightforward ways. He'd written an online post in a class folder, laying out his aspirations for Biola filmmakers, what he aspired to and expected of others in a faith-based approach to films. "I wrote this post," he told me. "and I got a post back from this one guy who had a totally different aspiration. He approached it as an attack and said, 'How dare you say I'm not doing the God-glorifying thing?'"

Dirk seemed truly aggrieved by the charge that he was being intolerant, but other people were more encouraging, and he had a mind to start a club or an association with like-minded artists. In Craig's mass communications class, he usually acted as a gadfly, dissing movies that other people praised and raising questions about appropriateness. He couldn't abide some of the trash that others liked. Most kids in Sweet D's class had either seen the new Robert Rodriguez film *Sin City* or wanted to. One kid had ordered a complete set of four posters featuring the most prominent characters, including one of a lasso-swinging Jessica Alba in a halter top. That wasn't Dirk's scene.

He asked me again and again what I meant by "lost." I tried to explain what I meant. I had "lost" my faith, in that I had wanted to keep it, but couldn't sustain it. The world laid out by the Bible, the reality of it, just seemed to nullify with the years, taking one blow after another till I could no longer hold on. I had seen human cruelty that sank my ability to buy the idea of a sovereign ruler of the universe. The faith didn't help me to understand; it closed off avenues for knowledge.

Dirk shook his head. He still didn't get it. He maintained his incredulity. No one had ever taught him that it was possible to "lose" the love of God. He told me that my words had hit him like a "sledgehammer blow." Was it possible that I only *thought* I'd lost my faith, but, in fact, God was drawing me near, drawing me back? I told him that, if it were true, I hadn't sensed it. He urged me to keep seeking; to pray and keep looking. We parted ways in mutual confusion. I didn't really understand his bafflement. One could lose anything, surely, including a faith. But then, I hadn't gone to a Christian school in the 1990s. I had gone to public school in the 1970s, exposed to everything that the wolfish world had in store. Perhaps it had been inevitable that I would fall out of the kingdom.

I have no idea what happened to Dirk. I've thought since that he could be a real test case for kingdom education, a guy that pure of heart, that dedicated to the belief of his youth, and yet ambitious, going out into the business of movies, which swallowed people whole. If Dirk's faith could hold in Hollywood, despite shaken foundations, the kingdom might stand. I had my doubts.

## chapter 20

# Young Life

*A*s a kid, I had been nothing like Dirk. I hadn't even remotely had a kingdom education. I'd been a lot more like a girl named AJ, another student in Sweet D's film class at Biola. Like me, AJ was a public school kid. Like me, she came from Dallas, Texas. I'd met AJ, short for Andrea Johnson, one morning in film class. She showed up early and had a chat with Sweet D. He wanted to know if AJ had seen anything she'd liked at the movies, and she replied that she didn't have time. She worked nights at a nearby bar and bowling alley called Lucky Strike. I sat a few desks over, and right then, as soon as she opened her mouth, I could tell that she had a lot more experience of the world than most other students I'd met. She had the voice of a woman who'd served a lot of drinks to a lot of men, answering a lot of stupid questions. Craig knew that the waitresses in the bar wore knee-high boots and miniskirts. He asked her if she was worried that one of her professors at Biola would come to the bar and see her working there.

"They should be worried, not me," she replied. "They're the ones drinking." She told him that she was a working girl, trying to make a living. She didn't have time for the pieties. That was AJ's vibe, right from the start.

In class that day, Sweet D chose as his text a copy of *Daily Variety*. Both the pope and the Robert Rodriguez movie *Sin City* graced the cover. Sweet D walked the class through the film industry bible as if guiding them through an exegesis of the second book of Peter. A terrible film, *Sahara*, had opened at number one the previous weekend, making $18 million. Sweet D pointed out that the figure looked impressive until you understood that it had probably cost six or seven times as much to make and market. *Sin City* was on everyone's mind—in more ways than one. Sweet D hadn't liked the movie much. He considered it pretty empty and pointless, but he knew that his students were excited. He asked how many kids in his class had seen it, and about half raised their hands.

"When you bought your ticket, what were you thinking about?" he asked them.

"Jessica Alba," someone said.

"The look of it."

"Clive Owen."

Dirk was in the class. He hadn't raised his hand. He'd put on his glasses. The class discussion turned from the subject of Catholicism, prompted by the image of the pope in *Daily Variety*, to talk of how the Christian message had fared in Hollywood. Dirk made the point that the faith had a legitimately appealing side, but somehow it rarely appeared in movies. "It's not being related in good, real-world situations," he told the class.

Another kid criticized Christians. "We need to stop preaching and start listening," the student said, "so that we can start preaching in a language that people can understand. We don't know what's going on, but we talk like we do."

Craig asked how many of his students had read the novel *The Da Vinci Code*. No one raised a hand. He gave a chuckle of disbelief.

"How many of you should read the novel?" he asked them. Everyone guiltily raised a hand.

"Hey," Sweet D concluded in a wry and reproachful voice, "if you don't want to be part of the cultural conversation, and talk with people who are already talking about religion and God, don't read it. Up to you."

AJ hadn't said much. She was a quiet type. Or maybe she was just tired from working those late hours. In general, she didn't tend to come on strong.

She felt cheesy just walking up to people giving a witness about Jesus. It wasn't her style. At the Lucky Strike, her colleagues knew that she attended a Christian college. No one gave her a hard time, and she didn't push testimony. Every now and then, someone would ask her questions, and she didn't mind answering. Meanwhile, she made good money. Bartenders there could rack up $800 tabs in a night. She also told me that the job had helped her to grow up. She wasn't so afraid about being out in the world, and that helped her mentally prepare for her career. AJ wanted to be a talent manager in Hollywood.

She got fed up with Biola at times. "People at Biola frustrate me," she told me, "because they can't even talk to people who don't believe in Christ. I've felt like a nonbeliever at times in my life. I can relate. They're no different than we are."

She didn't like to be judged because she was a Christian, and she didn't care to judge others who weren't Christian. From a professional standpoint, in the talent management business, the latter would be a self-destructive mind-set. She'd done a stint as an intern at one agency, and she'd run the gamut of jobs, working in the mailroom, printing up demo reels, dubbing videos, sending out FedExes—unglamorous work, to say the least. Before she took that job, she told me, she'd been more of a typical Texas girl. She wanted to get married and have babies. She never really expected to finish college. After coming to California, everything had changed, so fast that she'd been a little nervous that she would be tempted into situations for which she wasn't fully prepared.

One incident, in particular, had unsettled her. When she worked at the talent management company, AJ had made friends with an office assistant. One night, she'd gone over to the woman's house. When she'd asked to borrow a shirt, she discovered drug paraphernalia in the closet. "I was freaked out at first," she told me. "I wondered if everybody who could be a friend was going to be like this. Do I go out with her again?"

In the end, she saw the friend one more time, and that was it. But her decision to stay in Hollywood remained firm.

I RELATED TO AJ for obvious reasons. I had been a public high school kid who didn't drink, didn't smoke, didn't have sex, but who liked to hang out with people who did all of those things. In school, my teachers never mentioned Jesus. They never prayed before the lesson, and I didn't say the pledge of allegiance to God and the Bible. In my high school, Jesus came silently, moving like a rumor among the high school kids who professed the faith and passed notes bearing scripture or talked in the hallways about how great Bible study had been the night before. A friend of mine who played first-string varsity football recently reminded me that in prayers before the Friday night games, the coach and players would pray for victory, "if it be your will, Lord."

Those rumors spread by way of an organization called Young Life. In my life, as in many others, Young Life proved to be the gateway drug to the born-again experience.

For sixty-five years, Young Life has been performing one task, as its founder Jim Rayburn intended. The organization plants "seeds of faith" among high school kids by meeting them at their own level. Unlike pastors at churches, Young Life staffers adapt themselves to the ways of their chosen tribe. "You enter that world like a missionary," Denny Rydberg, Young Life's fifth president, told me. "You learn the language, you learn their customs, you learn how they dress. You listen to their music. You understand that if you can get into a kid's bedroom, you see their bulletin board, you've got them."

This experience happens all over the country, every day of the year. According to Young Life, in the 2002–2003 school year, there were 2,500 ministries, with more than 80,000 kids actively participating. Almost half of those kids got involved with Campaigners, the Young Life ministry for teenagers who want to deepen their faith. At my high school, the Young Life leader, Bobby McCreless, made it his business to get at least 10 percent of the school to Monday night meetings, more than a hundred kids. If he got any less than 10 percent, he told me, "I didn't believe I was doing my job." Young Life leaders do not have much office space to call their own. Their offices are the nation's secular public and private high schools, and they do their work in the cafeterias, at football and basketball practice, at theater rehearsal, in cafés, restaurants, and other hangouts where high school kids gather. Some schools refuse to allow the organization on campus. Some come up with a compromise.

My school gave Young Life full access. Bobby McCreless told me that he'd never had as much cooperation from a school district as he had at Highland Park, and I experienced the fruit of that collaboration. He came to the cafeteria during lunch hour and roamed the tables, trying to be present and unobtrusive at the same time. There was another adult who did the same thing, Murray Gossett, the youth minister at Highland Park Presbyterian. He became friendly with my sister Molly and had a great influence on her teenage years, but my spiritual godfather was Bobby. Both guys had played basketball in high school and were tall, but Murray had the imposing quality of a bona fide grown-up. He had a mustache. Bobby, on the other hand, wore a blue Dallas Cowboys windbreaker and a baseball cap, sometimes turned backward. Unlike Murray, who never seemed to cross the distance between child and adult, Bobby chose to be more like a pal, one of the guys. He was balding and could never be mistaken for sixteen, but he talked to the football players with an air of complicity, as if he were an assistant coach. I think that he referred to lots of people by their last names, like sixteen-year-old boys do.

In any case, I was not his target audience. I didn't play football well but had two or three close friends who were stars of the team, and that gave me a certain entrée. Back in those days, Young Life had an implicit policy called the "key-kids concept," whereby a Young Life minister in a new high school would focus a certain amount of energy on kids well liked and admired by other kids in order to attract the larger crowds. At my school, that meant athletes and cheerleaders and their entourage. Bobby McCreless and his wife did their job well. They got enough of those "key kids" to come to Monday night meetings; small fry like myself couldn't resist the inexorable pull. I must have gone to my first Young Life meeting sophomore year. In the same time frame, my friend Murphy, a star football player who had moved to Highland Park from Mount Pleasant, Texas, also got more involved in Young Life. That girl named Julie lured us in equal measure.

Murphy and I became regular participants in the Monday night meetings, though our friend Buzz, a star of the varsity football team, passed. Bobby told Murphy and me that the salvation of Buzz lay on our shoulders. If our friend perished in a car wreck before he accepted Christ as his savior, we would be held accountable on Judgment Day. He spoke these words in a near whisper, and they went right through me.

YEARS LATER, I found Bobby in Fort Collins, Colorado. He had aged considerably, but he still wore a cap. The remaining hair on his head had turned white, and he had a two-toned mustache, half white, half gray. He was fifty-four, and it had been two decades at least since I had laid eyes on him. He had his own business, an organic pesticide operation with warehouses in Texas and a salesforce around the country; the week before we met, a disgruntled employee had set fire to one of those warehouses, and Bobby had had to go down to Texas to sort out the matter. In general, it was a successful business. One of his East Coast salesmen had been a star football player and Young Life leader at Highland Park, someone I had known. Such relationships are common in Young Life, Craig Detweiler told me. He told me that leaders often remained close with men they'd met as students in high school for the rest of their lives, and in some cases, those former students would support them in old age. In Charlotte, he told me, one former Young Life leader had been the best-connected man in town.

I had had the opposite experience. Once I left my high school, I neither wanted nor expected to see Bobby McCreless ever again. I hadn't yet left my faith behind, but by the time I left Highland Park, he had impressed me as a bad advertisement for Christianity. Young Life had come to seem like a club for rich white kids, not a harbinger of a serious gospel. Through the years, Bobby and Young Life had become symbols for me of the failure of Christ's church to make the case. Face to face with him again, I felt the old aversion, but I also realized that I might have been unfair. I had never really known this man who had exerted such an influence on my life. When he knew me, I was a teenager with no clue what it meant to be a grown-up. When I rejected him with such vehemence, I rejected his affiliation more than anything else. As an adult, with children of my own, I wanted to understand what had motivated him to spend so much time among teenagers, a choice, I felt, that I would never in a million years have made.

Bobby told me. He grew up in Fort Worth, Texas, the baby boy of the family. Unlike his two older sisters, who were straight A students in high school, Bobby struggled to make grades. Neither of his parents had received more than a semester of college education, so the pressure to succeed academically weighed on him. He found his release on the basketball court, where he flourished, but he'd had a mean temper and a foul mouth. He'd been a drinker, too. In 1968, at a Young Life camp in Colorado, the now defunct Star Ranch, all that changed. He accepted Christ as his savior. "It changed my life altogether," he told me. "Before that, I'd been kicked out of four or five games because of my foul mouth. After that, a couple of referees remarked, McCreless, what happened to you? You're a different guy altogether."

He went to Texas Catholic University, where he met his wife, Alicia, who eventually worked with the girls in my high school and became as familiar to them as Bobby was to us. After college, he attended Dallas Theological Seminary, which had also educated Tommy Nelson of Denton Bible Church. Dallas is one of the two seats of dispensationalist thinking in the United States, a theological center for thinking on the Rapture and other end-time prophecies. By the time I met him, Bobby had been steeped in the book of Revelation, and his views on the subject became one of my first problems with Jesus. I couldn't easily connect my personal savior, to whom I was linked by an oceanic sense of familiarity and love, to this vision of world death and destruction instigated by God the Father. When I met Bobby, I asked him if he recalled teaching the subject to us one summer, and he did, though he didn't remember the exact lesson plan. I told him that those teachings had provoked one of my first strong reactions against the gospel, and he blamed his teaching ability. But his skills hadn't been the problem, I assured him. The book of Revelation had been the issue.

Before graduating from seminary, Bobby became a staff member at Young Life, and he got his first job at the two toniest private schools in Dallas, Hockaday for girls and Saint Mark's for boys.

After the private schools, Highland Park felt like a cakewalk, and unlike a lot of Young Life leaders, Bobby told me he'd never had a problem walking into a high school cafeteria and approaching people he didn't know, a good thing, because a lot was at stake. He'd been told from the start that his mission at Highland Park had important financial ramifications. Young Life had let him know in no uncertain terms that his penetration of that particular neighborhood would help the organization as a whole. "Quite frankly," he admitted, "the real motivation for some of the people to want HP to do well with Young Life was because they realized the fundraising capacity would be greater in Highland Park, and that would benefit other Young Life organizations, in places like Duncanville, Mesquite, and Garland, that couldn't raise the funds."

Bobby ended up staying for nine years, and his life became consumed by the job. "In order to do really good work," he explained, "you need to be gone about four nights a week, maybe five, everything from Friday night football games and basketball games to Monday night Young Life meetings, and Campaigners for the kids who want to go deeper." Campaigner kids had already accepted Christ as their personal savior and were ready to become more able disciples, to learn more about the scripture and help the adults in their work to attract other kids.

As his three children grew, the job became untenable for Bobby and his wife, and he eventually had to leave, but in Highland Park, he told me, he had the best time of his life. Everyone knew him. The school opened its doors. The coaches welcomed him at practice, and he would take his son to meet the giant ball players who were true stars at Highland Park, and this was during a golden age for that team when legendary athletes like the McIlhenny brothers, Lot and Lance, played ball.

When I asked him how he decided which table to approach in the cafeteria, he told me that he came to lunch twice a week, and his goal had been to meet at least one new kid every time he visited.

"It was the type of deal, when I would walk into a lunch room, I wouldn't necessarily zero in on a particular table. Sometimes, I would literally eat lunch there, so sometimes I'd be eating with people I knew, and I might ask the question, who's that person over there, and find out their name, and as I was taking my tray or walking by, I'd say, 'Hey so-and-so,' and that person would go, 'How do you know my name?'"

This was in the era right before the advent of MTV, before youth culture changed dramatically, long before the age of cell phones, text messages, and iPods. There were fewer distractions. The cafeteria campaign paid off.

Every autumn, Bobby drew crowds. To this day, he measures the success of a program by its numbers. After moving to Colorado, his own kids got involved with Young Life, but their leaders were content to have twenty or so kids out of a high school with 2,500 students. "And I was going, 'Twenty? Don't you want to have maybe a little more of an emphasis on trying to reach out to a lot more people?'"

I asked Bobby about the key-kids concept, and he said he'd known about it. He hadn't necessarily focused on the popular kids, but at the same time, he told me, he placed a real emphasis on football. He attended theater rehearsal on occasion, but never stayed for long. Football and basketball practice, on the other hand, were indispensable. As a former basketball player himself, he was asked by coaches to get on the court and lend a hand. And here's what I remembered. Bobby may not have explicitly gone after key kids, but the upshot had been the same. Athletes were royalty in my school, and Bobby catered to them. But then, for a time, so did I.

WHEN I ACCEPTED Christ as my personal savior, I began to hang out with a different crowd. I didn't jilt my old friends exactly, and I still played poker with the reprobates on Friday nights in the off season, but more and more, I gravitated toward the Young Life hard core. On the other hand, as a rule, I didn't witness much. I took the Andrea Johnson approach. I lived my life, and if people wanted to ask, I told them what motivated me. This relatively quiet approach to the faith allowed me to have friendships with all kinds of people, including Doug, who would have found active evangelization obnoxious, to say the least. But my silence hid a true engagement. I carried Bible verses in my back pocket for my own spiritual sustenance. I practiced a quiet time in the morning, rising at 6:00 A.M. or so to read the Bible. In my mind, I talked a lot to God. Years later, my sister Molly caught the same bug. She went through a period of speaking in tongues with two girlfriends, one of them a cheerleader with a very religious mother. The girls sat in a closed circle for hours, working themselves into a state of divine communion until one of them began to babble in the language of God. My sister's born-again experience happened at the same time that I began to get disillusioned, and I can remember telling her in my car that I no longer believed in Jesus. She cried.

For her, our church was the center of the social aspect of her faith. For me, in high school, Young Life provided the network. At Wednesday night Bible Study, Bobby advised us how to behave when we were alone with girls in our cars. We would confess our struggles with the flesh. It was a privileged circle. Most of the guys were extremely popular. I felt out of my league but honored to be there. I was perhaps inordinately distressed by visions of horror and disaster. Our sophomore year, George Romero's *Dawn of the Dead* came out. Before I saw the movie, I saw the ad, and the ad gave me nightmares. When I saw the movie, the images of zombies devouring human beings resembled my dreams somehow, and I thought that I'd been sent a vision of hell. I dragged my friend Murphy to the movie theater, and after a scene in which an undead husband bites off the shoulder of his wife, he left the cinema in disgust. I stayed, receiving the vision. The Jesus of the football players tended to be the glowing and healthy longhair who had a smile for everyone and a great story. My Jesus had more in common with the zombies in Romero. I felt ripe for some great destiny in a terrible landscape, and I think I told Bobby McCreless so, and he looked at me with some concern, as if I might be taking the whole thing too seriously.

My mom and dad certainly thought so. To this day, they tend to blame Bobby for my feelings about faith. They think he pushed too hard with the born-again message. When I later told Bobby about my parents' feelings, he responded in a nervous voice, "Oh really? Are they still alive?"

One summer, I went to a Young Life camp called Camp Castaway near the Canadian border. On the bus, while everyone else flirted, gossiped, slept, or prayed, I read Stephen King's *The Stand* and found God's wrath in every page. Julie and Murphy were both on that bus—by that time, I think, they had started to date—and I'm sure that we talked about something or other, but what I recall most vividly: the rolling away of American miles outside the bus window while the pages of a fictional apocalypse, plague and fire and monsters, fluttered between my fingers.

Young Life summer camp is an integral part of the experience, and it is often a life-changing one. In 2006, there were twenty-three properties scattered around the country. Each features its own landscape for purposes of evangelism. The camps sit in the high mountain valleys of California, on lakes in Minnesota and North Carolina, along either coast of North America. At Camp Castaway, I recall parasailing as a major activity. At Frontier, one of the earliest camps, where I paid a visit right before meeting Bobby McCreless, a grueling climb up a 9,000-foot peak centers the experience.

The landscape may differ from place to place, but the cycle of evangelism has remained the same for decades. Kids arrive and have fun for the first couple of days. Lodged in cabins around a central space, they play sports, rock-climb, swim, and socialize in a setting completely removed from high school. Once a day, usually in the afternoon or evening, everyone gathers as a group at club. There are familiar pop songs and skits. At Frontier, on the slopes of the Collegiate Range in southern Colorado, everyone sang the ultimate frat-boy sex rave and beer commercial staple, "What I Like About You," which doubled in meaning as an allusion to Jesus: "What I like about you, you keep me warm at night!" Staff musicians played the theme from *Fresh Prince of Bel Air*, and everyone in the room seemed to know the words. I saw a blonde girl with a tambourine onstage, and she looked almost exactly like Julie from my own experience twenty years earlier. That was a Monday night, and in the Young Life cycle of witness, Monday nights at camp mark the turn toward more serious reflection. At Frontier, a staffer named Taco stood in front of the crowd and talked about the point of life. What did kids care about? Playing basketball? Having a cool car? Getting that girl? Was it enough?

After the group talk, the effort got more intimate and intensified. The crowd broke up into cabin groups, and Young Life leaders discussed the message. The next day, the course got even tougher. Taco told some home truth—God offered grace because the alternative was disease, darkness, and death. Not believing meant damnation. What would they choose? Cabin time afterward involved pressing the kids into an understanding of this message, its urgency and severity. That night, at Frontier, a carnival atmosphere would prevail, an effort to counterprogram the grimness of the morning message with lighter fare, and at the same time deliver the same thought in a happier format. On the "Night That Never Ends," as it was dubbed, there were shows and games and other events all over the camp, and each spectacle referred back to Taco's point. Kids could be under no illusion. They needed to make a decision. The next day, they shouldered backpacks and scaled a literal mountain, analogous to life, its travails and challenges. That lesson would be unmistakable. In extremity, in a gorgeous mountain country where every cloud registered the presence of a greater authority and power, who could possibly deny the reality of God? Who could say they didn't need him? By the last day of camp, a Friday, it would be time for the "say-so," where kids who had accepted Christ were encouraged to get up and "say so." That week, dozens did. At Camp Castaway, we had done the same. Not much had changed since my day.

ON A COLD day in February, I drove an hour and a half east from Northampton to Wrentham, Massachusetts, where my old friend Julie had lived with her husband for twenty years. They had four children. He developed real estate, she owned and rode and sold horses and worked as a successful toy and furniture designer. I hadn't seen her in more than two decades, not since our freshman or sophomore year in college. She had gone to Vanderbilt, and after a couple of years, we'd lost touch. When she opened the door, I could hardly believe it. She looked so much the same. One of her daughters was home sick from school, so rather than go out for lunch, we sat in her kitchen, drank coffee, and talked about the old days. Bobby and Alicia McCreless had exerted an equally powerful influence on her life. Her father and Bobby had become close friends over the years and were still in touch. That's how I found my old Young Life leader.

"My parents were very religious," Julie told me. "We were First Baptist Church all the way." First Baptist, for years, was one of the largest churches in the country. "We started there with W. A. Criswell, and every Sunday, I would go to the front of the church, and I would accept Jesus. I would be bawling, and I would go down to the front of the church, and Dad would be, 'You're going down again?' And he'd be, like, all right, 'Go on down.'" She was laughing as she told me the story.

As it turned out, Julie and I had been a lot alike in high school, but hadn't known it. She had always had an artistic bent but hadn't found an outlet till she went to college. She'd considered herself an outsider, and when the time came, she married a guy from Massachusetts and moved far north. She told me that she had her doubts, but at the end of the day, she believed that God was real.

I asked her what Young Life had meant to her, and she told me that it had been about camaraderie. "You got to talk about yourself, and people thought you were funny and liked you for who you were. That's a thing in college that I desperately missed, and up here, there is nobody. Everybody is Catholic. The positive thing about Young Life was that you had fellowship, you connected."

Finally, we came to the subject of Bobby McCreless. Julie hadn't known him well. Bobby's wife, Alicia, had been much more influential in her life, but not exactly a role model. As a Young Life leader, Julie said, Alicia had given a group of teenage girls a forum to talk about themselves and be accepted for who they were.

Bobby had told me that a lot of the kids who went through Young Life at Highland Park remembered a Young Life camp called Beyond Malibu more than anything else. Julie certainly did. When I first asked her about McCreless, she said, "You know I went on that trip?"

She recalled Beyond Malibu with a shudder. "We got there, and they didn't know where the boat was. It turned out to be a tugboat. We slept in the rain on wood benches for eight hours, so by the time we started our hike, everyone was borderline sick. It was weird. We started our hike, and it was a logging road, and then it was boulder fields, and then it was snow above the tree line. It was really intense. I just felt like Bobby was going off half-cocked all the time. We would have meetings where he was so scared that it was not at all spiritual. Fear. Such fear. They taught us how to stop and slide in case of an avalanche. It was hard core. We got above the tree line, and there was a blizzard for three days. We didn't know where we were. We stayed in our tents for three days."

In Bobby's version, he was in full control all the time. He had wanted his teenagers to undergo an extreme test, and they had. Julie and Bobby both remembered that one of the girls wanted to radio her father to helicopter her out. Bobby refused. Bobby maintained that the Beyond Malibu experience taught self-reliance and reliance on God at the same time. It had made a lifelong impression on Julie, and I couldn't help wondering whether it had also contributed to the longevity of Julie's faith. I hadn't gone on Beyond Malibu, and my faith had faded. She had, and hers lingered on. Did his wilderness survival game have anything to do with it?

"If you ask me if I know for sure if I'm going to heaven, I don't know. I question everything all the time. I tell my dad, if you don't question it, you're either a liar or you're an idiot. I question everything all the time. That's how I think. Do I want to know the truth? Yeah. Part of a strong faith, and what God wants you to do is continually search, because that makes us stronger."

I asked her if her Massachusetts friends knew about her faith.

"They do. I'm not as vocal, because I don't want to appear judgmental or self-righteous. The woman across the street is a complete pagan. She works for the theater and does rituals in her backyard. I love her, she's one of my best friends, and we have amazing dialogues about why I believe what I believe and why she does not, and all of her points are very strong. She believes in helping people. She helps a lot more people than probably the pastor at the Park Cities Baptist Church. She's down in the trenches."

The last I saw of Julie, she had combed and saddled her horse and was headed out into the pastures for a ride. I would never have imagined my old friend in such an incredible life. She had made good in the world, and she'd maintained her faith. She told me, toward the end of our conversation, that if she was ever in an airplane and it started to go down, she would never hit the ground. Before the plane hit the ground, God would take her soul. "I really and truly believe that," she told me.

## chapter 21

# *Girlfriend*

*T*wo great forces, at least, pull at the loyalties of every human being. Memory pulls us back, to our childhood, our roots, our homeland, our God. Desire flings us forward, to our future, our mate, our children, and, sometimes, to our death. I don't believe that all of life can be reduced to a formula, but by the same token, I'm certain that every human being lives on some kind of line between these two poles and finds a balance, or doesn't, at one end or the other of a spectrum.

As I read Genesis, the account of the expulsion of Adam and Eve from the Garden of Eden, Eve uses desire to get Adam to eat the apple, to defy the Creator. She is naked and blazingly sexual, juice dripping down her lips. He is her slave, and he eats the fruit, because it implies the promise of her body, some secret that he hasn't yet discovered, which she possesses and God does not. In Genesis 3:7 we read, "And the eyes of them both were opened, and they knew that they were naked." In other words, God showed them first what had caused their own downfall—their bodies—the source of a future that did not require him. That is the knowledge that could not be shared.

I suspect that the same knowledge lies at the heart of the Christian problem with sex in today's America. When believers fight gay marriage, when they insist on abstinence, and even when they oppose abortion, they are acknowledging a deep truth about themselves. Their real alienation from their fellow Americans, from the mainstream of the country, begins with physical desire. The contraception pill introduced the nightmare in 1961. Before the Pill, Bible-believing Christians might have felt slighted and marginalized. They might have felt beleaguered by science and modernity. A few might have sensed in the emancipation of women a foretaste of doom. But after the Pill, suspicion became dread. A much larger calamity became visible on the horizon, the unthinkable, as the children of the faith began to wander away from God, led by unleashed desire toward a future without him. Gay sexuality, pornography, fornication, and abortion had been sins for most Americans until the 1960s. Afterward, they became norms. For Christians, from that time on, the possibility of extinction by sex became more than real. It became imminent. Seduced by desire, their children could wander away into marriages, meanings, and lifestyles that could seem as fulfilling as life with Jesus.

Even mature believers might not be able to withstand the onslaught. A few statistics, cited on an evangelical website called Blazing Grace, give some idea of the magnitude. According to one survey, 50 percent of all Christian men and 20 percent of all Christian women say they are addicted to pornography. Sixty percent of the women who responded to the survey "admitted to having significant struggles with lust." Forty percent admitted to "sexual sin" in the previous year. On five Christian campuses, almost half the students said they currently used porn. Well over half had checked out a sexually explicit site at school. That's the flock, but the shepherds, too, have fallen. In one study, in *Christianity Today*, 33 percent of clergy said they had seen a sexually explicit website. Half of those had visited such a site more than once. In another survey, out of 81 pastors, most had seen porn and almost half had made repeat visits to sites. And finally, a confidential survey of evangelical pastors finds that 64 percent of these leaders are struggling with sexual addiction or compulsion.

I once had a close friend named Nick, a Baptist pastor from the Midwest, and he told me that, if just once, someone in his church could have come to him with a problem unrelated to sex, he would have fallen to his knees and praised the Lord. At the time, it seemed an exaggeration, but I'm not so sure anymore.

As frightening as the porn numbers tend to be, the stats on actual sexual behavior have more far-reaching implications. They reflect a dimensional shift, from the era of the 1950s, when marriage still cloaked most sexual matters and Bible believers saw themselves in line with the mainstream of American habit, through the 1960s and 1970s, when sex became public and political and Christians found themselves isolated and embattled, through the last two decades, when sex became a business, a sport, and a pastime for an entire nation and its children, and no one, in any subculture, could resist its allure.

In a comprehensive study of sex conducted between March 2002 and March 2003 by the Centers for Disease Control, more than 12,000 men and women between the ages of 15 and 44 were asked a series of questions about their most basic inclinations. No particular religion was identified. The study showed, among other things, that practices once considered decadent or immoral, acts of sodomy to be precise, such as oral sex in the form of cunnilingus and fellatio and even anal sex, have become mainstream for lots of American heterosexuals. Fully 90 percent of men and 88 percent of women in the relevant age group have had oral sex with a partner of the other sex, overwhelming numbers that have brought about a revolution in the erotic tastes of Christians, who for years were expected to frown on anything that fell under the rubric of sodomy. Now, most pastors, counselors, and Christian sex therapists make clear that the Bible has absolutely nothing to say, in the context of marriage, against contact between a person's mouth and his or her partner's genitals. In fact, in the fight to save heterosexual marriage, the right to practice oral sex has to be understood as an indispensable weapon.

Anal sex is now the firewall. The CDC survey reports that 40 percent of men and 35 percent of women in this country have had anal sex with an opposite-sex partner, well over a third of the population. When state courts ruled on sodomy laws in several closely watched cases around the country, and sodomy laws were repealed, most Christians weren't thinking about fellatio or cunnilingus. Sodomy meant anal sex, which meant homosexuality. It's more than a taboo—it's an act of subversion. In its compendium on family health, nutrition, and fitness, Focus on the Family recommends a guide called *The Gift of Sex*. In this guide, the authors, Doctors Clifford and Joyce Penner, endorse oral sex as being approved by God in a book of the Bible, the Song of Solomon. They devote three pages of a 350-page book to the subject. At the end of that section, the reader finds a short paragraph under the subheading "Anal Sex," where the authors devote seven terse sentences to the subject, beginning with, "Anal sex, the penis entering the woman's anus, is dangerous," and ending with, "We do not recommend anal sex." Even the more adventurous Christian sex manuals see it as the far edge of acceptable behavior. But the health risks mask a deeper aversion. Anal sex, for many believers, amounts to sleeping with the enemy. Its relation to homosexuality, its complete divorce from any procreative possibility, make the act a near sacrilege. At best, it is a form of sinful and selfish rebellion. At worst, anal sex is the vehicle by which homosexuals will destroy the traditional family as laid down in the act of creation in Genesis.

The CDC report indicates that 6 percent of American men between the ages of 25 and 44 have had oral or anal sex with another man. In the same age group, 11 percent of women have had some kind of sexual experience with another woman. These numbers serve as yet another reminder of the transformation of the country. When my old friend Doug was born in the early 1960s, homosexuality was still seen as a disease, a view that accords with how many Bible-believing Christians still see the matter. A little over forty years later, it is a behavior amounting to an identity. In their book *The Homosexual Agenda: Exposing the Principal Threat to Religious Freedom Today*, Christian authors Alan Sears and Craig Osten note that change with horror:

> In 1983, 30 percent of Americans said that they knew someone who was homosexual. By 2000, that figure had skyrocketed to 73 percent. In 1985, only 40 percent of those polled said they were comfortable around individuals who practice homosexual behavior. By 2000, that number had risen to 60 percent. Also in 1985, 90 percent of Americans said they would be upset if their son or daughter announced they were homosexual. By 2000, that figure stood at just 37 percent. Those of us who have dealt with the homosexual agenda issue over the years often stop and ask

ourselves in disbelief: How has 1 or 2 percent of the population achieved so much success in transforming American culture and restricting religious freedom?

The change isn't just a matter of sexual desire. It has become a question of liberty for these believers. Another finding of the CDC study hits even closer to home. Children are becoming sexual shortly after puberty. The study reports that, at the ages of fifteen through seventeen, more than 10 percent of girls and boys practice oral sex, though not vaginal intercourse. Cunnilingus and fellatio have become increasingly popular ways for high school kids to practice both "abstinence" and "safe sex." Christian kids figured it out long ago. When I was in high school, girls would call themselves "technical virgins," a term that still has currency. It means that everything but the vagina has been penetrated. Over drinks, after we'd gone to college, one old friend told me that she'd done it all and then some, but not "that," which she would save for marriage. The problem has become serious enough in Christian circles that Focus on the Family, in its fitness guide, has to point out that oral sex is, in fact, sex. In general, the study makes clear that young people have a lot of sex, that by the time the average man has reached the age of thirty-four, he's had about six partners, that a woman of the same age has had about four.

But it's one thing to see these numbers in the population at large and make inferences to a theoretical Christian population. It's another to come across figures that demonstrate just how these much larger trends play out among a population of people who should be among the most sheltered and protected in society, the students and alumni of some of the most prominent fundamentalist colleges in the United States. In 2005, a firm called Right Ideas, with the cooperation of a dozen or more fundamentalist colleges and universities, conducted a survey of 11,000 students and graduates, asking 105 questions about personal life and beliefs. The survey was then posted on a popular Christian website called SharperIron, where I found it. Very few documents have illuminated so well the reasons for Christian panic over the larger culture.

The respondents were fundamentalists. Two-thirds were male, one-third female. They ranged in age from their late teens through their early thirties. A third of the total number had gone into the ministry after college. Their alma maters were places like Bob Jones University, the best-known fundamentalist school in the country, Maranatha Baptist Bible College, Calvary Baptist Theological Seminary, and Faith Baptist Bible College. Most respondents said they had been saved before the age of twelve. The overwhelming majority, 84 percent, believed that personal faith in Christ represented the only means to salvation. By far the greater number were Republicans, at 87 percent. Most witnessed verbally to people they knew. A third practiced total abstinence in alcohol. In short, as a group, as individuals, they should have been well equipped to withstand the modern sexual onslaught.

At first glance, they were. Only 8 percent of the total had had sex before marriage, a finding far below the CDC study. Only a fifth of them had kissed before marriage. Many in the Bible-believing world make the point that statistics indicating equivalence between believers and nonbelievers in matters of sex, drugs, and other vices don't tell the whole story. If one counts only those people who live as the Bible teaches, the evidence of worldly depravity drops sharply among believers. The respondents to the fundamentalist poll are students and graduates who have been educated by home, church, and community to do just that, and a lot of their answers do bear out the claim that sexual license has less of a hold . . . and yet even here, in the best case scenario, among the most vehement adherents, we find a world at war.

Fourteen percent of respondents had viewed pornography in the last year. Well over half had gone further with a member of the opposite sex than they had wanted. Almost 10 percent had been preoccupied with sexual fantasies about members of the same sex, and roughly the same number had participated in sexual activity with a member of the same sex. The last few questions require statements. What is your vice? What do you feel guilty about? What is your greatest regret?

Here, I found the best evidence for a sexual tension underlying the good intentions of so many fundamentalists. Many vices had to do with a lack of commitment to God, a lack of prayer, an indifference to other people, a litany of completely nonsexual problems. But one vice kept repeating itself over and over, what the respondents called their "thought-life." It rang to my ear like a translation of one of those German conceptual nouns, like *Weltanschauung*, "worldview," or *Lebenswelt*, "life world," but I had never heard the exact term before. Again and again, dozens of times, respondents complained of a thought-life deficit. Often enough, they indicated that their thought-life had developed a kind of sexual virus, as when one described his problem as "my thought-life as a male and my past history of pornography." Quite a few named porn as their vice. Even more had masturbated a lot, and much larger numbers simply called it a problem with lust. It was the same with the question of guilt. Sex topped the list, page after page, and that's not counting those who put "sin" as the source of their guilt. But there was no mistaking the guilt over pornography—"spitting in God's face so many times with porn," as one respondent put it.

THE POWER OF the flesh itself overwhelmed a home-schooled kid named Daniel. I met him at Biola. He was another of Craig's students, and I first encountered him in passing as he handed out leaflets charging two candidates for student government with "cloak-and-dagger" approval of a suspect Spring Banquet. The words on his T-shirt left no doubt about his attitude: "Damn You All." He was a rebel, but Craig considered him one of the most gifted students in the mass communications department.

By the time I sat down with Daniel, several months later, he had lost almost everything that mattered to him. Among other things, thanks to a restraining order, he could no longer set foot on the campus. The order forbade him to go near his ex-girlfriend or any of her family, including her sister, who attended Biola.

He grew up in Phoenix, the eldest of seven siblings. His mother had been in the military and seen some of the world. His father was an electrical engineer, one of those reliable types who had earned two masters degrees and never partied in college. Both were devout Christians, but neither had ever been rigid. His mother, in particular, had lived a pretty wild early life. He told me that he'd inherited a streak of rebellion from her, and she understood him in ways that others couldn't.

When the family moved from a much more relaxed charismatic church to a conservative Baptist congregation, Daniel's rebellious streak became a problem. In the old church, he told me, he'd been the good kid. Everyone loved him. In the new church, he was quickly branded the bad kid. His infractions began with fashion.

"I didn't wear nice clothes to church on Sunday," he said, "because, one, I didn't like to wear nice clothes, and two, I didn't have a lot of nice clothes because I really didn't have anywhere else to wear them."

Disheveled clothes and a propensity for telling inappropriate jokes set off alarm bells with the Baptist elders, but the anxiety didn't really have anything to do with manners. It had to do with sex. The Baptists feared for the daughters of the congregation.

"It was hard," he told me. "I found out once that the fathers of the church were in a Bible study together, and they happened to be the fathers of a lot of the girls my age. At the Bible study, they talked about not letting me date their girls. And I was like, why? Because I wear a black leather trench coat? Because I have black fingernails? It's like, so what? I still worship at my church. That has nothing to do with anything. Or because I told a bad joke once, and it got back to them? Like their daughters hadn't told much worse jokes."

The bad-boy image attracted female interest, but it ultimately got in the way of his sex life. In a pattern that would repeat itself at Biola, Daniel fell for a girl from a particularly conservative family, but the family refused to allow the girl to see him.

At Biola, a few years later, he got the girl. Desire eclipsed all other considerations. But as Daniel told me, and I believed him, it wasn't just about lust. He loved the woman and wanted to marry her. She had been like the conservative Baptist girls back home; she had seen and liked his bad boy act, but unlike the daughters of the Arizona elders, she had been away from family and had been eager herself to rebel.

Even before Daniel met her, Biola was bliss, the honey pot of the Christian social life. He found a fantastic roommate, another wild man named Dan. The two had nicknames for each other—Daniel became Wolf-Dan, the other was He-Dan. He-Dan had a long mane of hair and did Strong Man competitions. "He's huge, absolutely, ridiculously huge and powerfully strong," Daniel told me. "He can lift up VW bugs and tip them over with his bare hands." He-Dan played music, too, working the instrument of his choice so violently that people called him "the piano slayer." He-Dan had a persona that everyone feared, respected, and loved, and he'd picked Wolf-Dan out of a pile to be his roommate.

What most appealed to Daniel about his friend was the nature of his transgressions. He truly broke the rules. Most Biola kids never came close. They considered themselves edgy if they masturbated or looked at pornography. Like He-Dan, Wolf-Dan took it much further. He used obscenities in his conversation. He played pranks and got away with them. In his academic work, he pushed the envelope as far as it would go. "I did a horror film about a bloody cradle," he told me, "and another about a fat kid who hung himself at his own birthday party. At another school, it would have been seen as typical fodder for getting attention. Pure shock value, but at Biola, it was like, oh my God, can you believe he did that film? But it wasn't edgy at all."

Some professors, like Craig, saw through his act. Others just considered him a pain. That worked for Daniel. As long as he could stir things up and stay well liked at the same time, he felt good. "I enjoyed the people at Biola," he said, "because they were easily manipulated and easily impressed."

SHE WAS FROM upstate California, a conservative Christian from a strict household. Like Daniel, she'd been homeschooled. Unlike him, her virtue had been kept under lock and key. She told him that her parents hadn't let her go out very much because "her boobs were too big." Her parents had sent her to Biola because it promised the right values in the safest setting. She hadn't expected to meet anyone like him.

They met in her freshman year, when he was a sophomore. Three weeks after their first kiss, they slept together. He was ready and so was she. "I just got to the point where it was something I wanted," he told me, "and it was something she wanted, and it didn't matter that it was something we'd been taught not to do."

Making the decision to have sex the first time turned out to be the easy part. Having sex in a regular and sustained affair proved to be a much tougher challenge. To avoid paralyzing guilt, both partners had to live in the moment. Nothing could be planned. Lust could not be sanctioned by routine. In practice, that meant no birth control.

"Taking birth control meant an acknowledgment that you are going to do it again and again and again," he told me. "So you don't go out and buy a twenty pack of condoms."

For a full year, they made love without birth control, having sex every other day. In retrospect, they were lucky. She didn't miss her period until the following September. She had become pregnant, but she refused to believe it, and he did, too. Just the same, after she missed that first time, he started wearing a condom.

I asked him how they managed to have sex on a regular basis, going in and out of their dorm rooms, without alerting someone in their vicinity. During my college years, everyone knew when a couple had sex.

"You don't have sex in your dorm room," he told me. "You have sex wherever there's cover. In edit bays and studios and soundrooms and video stations and trash facilities. I eventually got a twelve-passenger van, and those you can hide in church parking lots like they were invisible." A Catholic parking lot gave reliable cover. "The Beatitudes of Our Lord Catholic Church got frequented pretty often. We called it 'going to mass.' My therapist calls it an adolescent sexual mentality. Anywhere and everywhere, we screwed."

They smooched in the lobby, and other students complained. RAs cautioned them about too much public display of affection. They refused to comply, and news quickly reached his girlfriend's family. Her sister attended Biola, too, and she reported back about the progress of the affair, and his girlfriend's mother and father began to agitate against the relationship.

Right around January, three months after they met, the lovers spent a night in a hotel, the first time they had been able to wake up together in each other's arms. In March, he proposed and she accepted. They were engaged, and pretty soon, he rented rooms off campus. One of his roommates was a determined virgin. The other turned out to be gay. In that apartment, things got pretty wild. Daniel's girlfriend moved in with him, for all intents and purposes, and the gay roommate brought home lots of visitors. There were parties with marijuana, mushrooms, and cocaine. When she was a month and a half pregnant, she smoked cocaine-laced marijuana cigarettes. He looked back on that with regret. In the meantime, they'd also borrowed some campus furniture for their apartment. Later, when things went bad, campus safety would consider the furniture stolen.

THEY HAD THEIR first fight in November, one year after they got together, over the Thanksgiving holidays. Her parents didn't want him to come, but he insisted. She wore his engagement ring. At Christmas, the couple went to her parents again, and there was a fight. Her father contributed serious money to the Republican Party. Daniel was a registered Democrat. The 2004 elections had come and gone, but the wounds remained fresh. Their daughter had voted for John Kerry. Her parents blamed that on him, as well as her newfound love of the animated series *South Park*. "They felt that I'd corrupted their daughter," he told me. "Her mom said to me, 'If we'd wanted Amanda to meet a guy like you, we would have sent her to Berkeley.' She meant it as an insult, but it wasn't one to me. I'd love to be considered a Berkeley quality student."

Her parents wrote letters, pleading with her to break it off, asking her not to show the letters to Daniel. Six months pregnant, she still refused to admit that she was going to have a baby. By that time, he knew the truth. He knew the symptoms. He also knew that for him and for her, abortion wasn't an option. In March, she called off the engagement. Shortly after that, he talked her into a pregnancy test.

"She cried for three days," he told me.

It was the eve of Biola's annual film festival, and he had a movie in the competition. Disney executives would be in attendance. Movie industry work might be in the offing. His girlfriend decided to go home for a visit. Daniel stayed at Biola. In retrospect, he saw it as a mistake, maybe the biggest of his life. As soon as she got home, her mother saw that she was pregnant. Daniel didn't know what was said, but his girlfriend returned a different person. Their relationship deteriorated further. She was emotional. She vomited blood. Every night, before going to bed, they prayed. On their last night together, her prayer hinted a warning. "Something felt off," he told me. "It was kind of a prayer for her, not for us, and it didn't address anything. And I said, 'What's going on?' And she said, 'I'm just tired.' And I asked her if she would ever do anything behind my back. And she said no, and I asked if she was sure. And she asked, 'Why aren't you trusting me?'"

The next morning, he sent her an apologetic e-mail. She didn't respond, and never has. As of this writing, they have never exchanged another word, though he saw her once in court. That day at Biola, without his knowledge, with her sister's and his virgin roommate's help, his girlfriend left campus. Within weeks, she had the baby. The child was due the day after Father's Day. That same day, he received a temporary restraining order from a judge. He couldn't go within a hundred yards of his girlfriend or anyone in her family, including the sister, who still attended Biola. He didn't find out till much later that he had a daughter. When he got the news, he and his parents drove to her home in Santa Cruz, and his parents went to the door. His girlfriend told them there was no proof that he had been the father.

When I met him in a Christian coffee shop in La Mirada, near the Biola campus, he still hadn't seen his daughter. He had a few photographs. The night after his parents went to the door of his girlfriend's house, he walked out on the balcony of a hotel and thought about jumping off. He had spent the whole day in prayer, face down on the floor. He didn't eat for five days. Whatever passed his lips, he threw up. "I'd been told all my life, don't do things that will take you from the umbrella of protection. Lying to your parents is a big one. I would rather have told my parents that we were sleeping together than sleep together and lie to their faces about it constantly. And when trust breaks down, you can't trust each other. I told her that I had never lied to her. But she said to me, you lied to your parents. What can I say to that?"

In the end, he's learned a few lessons. One has to do with his theology. While he was enjoying his life and his lust, he was also taking Bible classes, learning the difference between Arminians, who emphasize free will, and Calvinists, who emphasize predestination. At the time, he considered himself an Arminian. Free will determined man's fate. If he ever gets back with the woman he loves, he will definitely be more of a Calvinist. Only predestination could make that happen. "No one in her position would ever choose to get back with me out of free will," he told me. In general, given that he hadn't lost his faith, I foresaw a lot more Calvinism in his future.

He'd also learned something about women, he told me. He'd taken gender classes at Biola and had tended to favor the egalitarian position.

"Equal roles, equal sharing. Now, through my experience, it's shifted again. I think there is a difference between men and women, especially in the home. Maybe not so much in the church, but definitely in the home. I think there's a reason why the man is traditionally head of the home. There are a lot of things that women go through, internally, especially during pregnancy. It's important for the man to be the voice of reason."

Lust had run its course. The woman had returned to the family. The baby hid in the bosom of the faith, waiting for its own turn at the wheel. God's authority had been reasserted, and Daniel had submitted himself.

## chapter 22

## *Submission*

*D*aniel's tale starts with transgression and ends in submission. It's a story right out of the Old Testament. To believe is to submit to the authority of God, who demands it. Submission is the ultimate righteous act. To transgress that authority is a sin and deserving of punishment, as God punished King David for having sex with Bathsheba and murdering her husband.

In the second book of Samuel, chapter 12, verse 11, the prophet Nathan tells David that God will not kill him for his transgression, but the child of his first union with Bathsheba will have to die. The child perishes, King David does penance, and in the wake of his penance, the Lord blesses the fruit of his second union with Bathsheba, a boy named Solomon, who becomes the greatest king of Israel. David submits to God's authority, just as Daniel did, thousands of years later.

To disbelieve is to refuse to submit. To disbelieve amounts to a state of revolt, Lucifer's sin, the ultimate act of evil. King David's father Saul refused to submit, and he was utterly destroyed. In the first book of Samuel, chapter 15, the Lord ordered Saul to wipe out his enemies, the Amalekites, to the last man and burn their goods. Saul disobeyed, sparing the king of the Amalekites and keeping his cattle and sheep for spoils. God sent an enraged and final message to him through the prophet Samuel: "Rebellion is as the sin of witchcraft, and stubbornness is as iniquity and idolatry. Because thou hast rejected the word of the Lord, he hath also rejected thee from being king." Millennia later, the great philosophical difference between Bible-believing Christians and the rest of us resides in our relation to this story.

The act of submission to a higher power engenders a culture in which submission becomes the highest virtue, one that does not take pleasure in outrage and irreverence for its own sake; one that expects and demands a great deal from higher power; one that is comfortable in a state of awe and equally comfortable assaulting a power that doesn't live up to its awesome standards. Such a culture sees society as a mirror of the divine order, with a righteous man submitting to God as the head of every home, a righteous woman submitting to her husband as his partner and second in command, and a heterosexual, married male pastor at the peak of every church, which should be built layer upon layer, wise men like archangels at the top, receding ever further downward to the children and the weaker brothers and sisters. That same divine order applies to the nation, which should be ruled by a heterosexual, married, male president capable of exercising full authority over a Congress made of godly and reliable men of the same sort. This isn't a utopian view of social order. In the eyes of a conservative Christian, it is the only truly desirable social reality.

The refusal to submit annihilates everything else. It is a repeat of the assault of Lucifer and his angels on the gates of heaven. Evil, true evil, begins with disbelief and extends logically to insurrection. So Gandhi, who changed the world with a politics of nonviolent resistance, who championed the poor, the lost, and the sick on the stage of the world, cannot get into this Christian heaven because he failed to do the one thing that would have put those efforts into a proper context. He did not submit to the exclusive authority of the Christian God. Without that submission, his efforts on behalf of fellow human beings take on a completely different character. Each charitable act becomes an argument for the lack of authority of the Christian God. Each gesture of love suggests that there may be goodness that does not stem from his authority. Each sacrifice, including the sacrifice of his life to an assassin's bullet, implies that true justice, true compassion, true knowledge, comes from some other authority, unseen by the eyes of Christians. If the evangelical pastors are to be believed, Gandhi, no matter what good he did for millions, goes down as a human ice pick stabbing the heart of God.

By the same token, Charles "Tex" Watson, one of the Manson murderers, who ordered one of his killers to cut the unborn fetus out of Sharon Tate's body, if his belief is real, rises to the heavens for eternity. His greatest contribution to society may have been an American innovation in the mechanics of slaughter, but he became a born-again Christian in prison. Submission is everything. He lives forever.

As disastrous as his travails in the flesh, Daniel never at that time questioned the existence of God. He and his girlfriend allowed the flesh to rule them for a season, and to this extent, they refused to submit. But their revolt ran its course, and as soon as his life fell apart, Daniel took David's course. He sought relief in the church—in the faith—that framed his universe. He never sought to throw down that universe and replace it with something else. Even when biblical teachings prevented him from using birth control, when another person might have paused to examine the belief system that had contributed so mightily to his woes, disowning the gospel doesn't seem to have occurred to him.

This story contains a clear warning for me. I never got into Daniel's kind of trouble. When I lost my virginity, my girlfriend and I used birth control. Everything was planned. After I lost my virginity, I slept with a handful of women before I fell in love with the woman I married. I puffed a marijuana cigarette once. I barely drank alcohol. I have been a painfully boring goody-goody in so many respects. And yet where it counted, I have committed myself to a far more malevolent line. Daniel lied to his parents and stepped outside of what he called "the umbrella of protection." I set a match to the umbrella. Leaving behind my faith, I became a rebel. In the secular culture, that word may still conjure romance, even virtue. In the culture I left, my rebellion is a meaningless act of self-destruction. I walked away from the Truth. I spat in the face of authority. Allow me to be a little melodramatic. I became a rebel in a culture that executes and burns rebels, and it's only a matter of time before the wall finds my back.

†

WHEN I HEAR the word "submission," I always think of women, and three, in particular, come to mind.

One is a Somali-born Dutch politician who offended Islamists in the Netherlands and had to go into hiding. The other is my first girlfriend, Ellen, a Texas blonde who believed, like I did, that Christ was the son of God. The third is my wife.

I met the first, Ayaan Hirsi Ali, when I worked for *60 Minutes*. Hirsi Ali is a lapsed Muslim. When I met her, she still sat as a member of the Dutch parliament for a center-right party in which she was a rising star. The day we met, she had agreed to do an interview, and the chosen location was the one building where she had no choice but to make public appearances, in parliament itself. Otherwise, she lived in an undisclosed location, surrounded by bodyguards. Her life was in danger. Several months before, she had made a short film with a Dutch director, Theo van Gogh, a descendant of the painter Vincent van Gogh. The film, called *Submission*, had aired on Dutch national television and outraged devout Muslims. The seven-minute piece depicted a series of women in stages of undress, their partially naked bodies covered in Koranic script. One woman faced the camera, her nipples visible, and talked about her life as a victim under Islam, a word that she translated as "submission." Hirsi Ali had fled a traditional Muslim upbringing in Africa and had become an outspoken critic of Islamic traditions regarding women in her adopted country. Her politics earned her death threats, but the movie made her a target of assassination. In 2004, on the streets of Amsterdam, an Islamist shot Van Gogh before stabbing him several times, pinning a document to his body with the bloody knife. The document castigated the makers of *Submission* and promised that Hirsi Ali would be next.

In our interview, Morley Safer asked her if she planned to make a sequel to the first movie, and she told us that she did. He asked her if she would "submit." She replied, "No. Not me."

In this context, the concept of submission becomes wholly negative. The impulse to rebel is completely positive. Violent men are trying to force a principled woman to be silent about the mistreatment of other women. Bible-believing Christians would argue that the usage of the word in Islam, deriving from the Arabic language, has little in common with the Old and New Testament word. The cultural contexts are radically different, among other things. It's simply not fair to compare. And yet the word is the same for both faiths in English, and when I hear it, and when tens of millions of women in the United States hear it, submission sounds like enslavement.

Ellen, the second woman on my list, once had a very different understanding of the word. As a teenage girl, she used it once with me. We sat in her car in her driveway, discussing something to do with the future of our relationship. In a previous conversation, we had talked about sex, and she told me that, if the right guy came along, she might do it, even though she wasn't married. I told her that I would wait until marriage, no matter what. Submission came up in a conversation about the future. We were talking about how it might be to get married, and where we would live, an unserious fantasy, nothing more, and I told her that I didn't want to live in Texas. She told me that she wouldn't mind living in Texas, but if we married and I wanted to leave, she'd probably have to follow biblical teaching and "submit" to my will. I recall being surprised and even a little appalled by it. She had never struck me as the type to submit to anyone. She constantly spoke up in class. She never shied away from saying what she thought. She had played Eliza Doolittle in the school play, and the portrayal owed a lot to her own inner spunk. I liked all of those things. More than that, the thought of invoking scripture to force Ellen to do something against her will struck me as novel. It had never occurred to me before. In the end, I don't know what became of her faith. Last I knew, she had moved to northern Virginia and become a professional in the media business. It's hard for me to imagine that she ever practiced anything like the submission she had mentioned that night in the car.

I know how the third woman, my wife, feels about it. A strong-willed, witty, and intelligent female, she can only laugh. Submission? Like hell! What could I do but fall in love?

THE KEY NEW TESTAMENT verse comes from Paul's letter to the Ephesians, chapter 5, in which he attempts to define a deep mystery: how one shapes a life upon salvation through Christ. Some instructions are very clear.

Don't drink too much. Speak among yourselves in "psalms and hymns and spiritual songs." And then he says this, in verses 21 through 33, lines that are the foundation of all Christian understanding of marriage, and beyond that, a description of the relationship between the church and God, man and woman, body and spirit, the world and heaven. Submit yourselves to one another in fear of God, Paul tells the followers of Jesus. "Wives," he writes, speaking directly, "submit yourselves unto your own husbands, as unto the Lord. For the husband is the head of the wife, even as Christ is the head of the church: and he is the saviour of the body. Therefore as the church is subject unto Christ, so let the wives be to their own husbands in every thing."

Christian women dismiss the notion that these lines from Ephesians refer to a form of modern slavery. Nonbelievers hear the word incorrectly, they say. Read the lines. A good Christian wife submits to her husband as her good Christian husband submits to God. It's a liberated and liberating act of love, they say, a mirror image of the entire cosmic order. In the same way that a man should love God, and submit to God, with all his heart and mind, in the same way that the church submits in every part of its body to Christ, a wife should love and submit to her husband. In return, she is owed the kind of love and respect that God shows her husband, that Christ shows the church. In other words, as strange as it may sound to nonbelieving ears, one woman after another has argued to me that submission is, in fact, freedom.

But is this biblical—or is it merely traditional? Or is it, in fact, simply a lifestyle choice? I went to Odessa, Texas, to see for myself. One part of my personal geography lies in south central Oklahoma, where my mother's family had settled, but another equally important landscape centers on west Texas, in the Permian Basin, home to my father's family. My parents met in Odessa as children and grew up together. I was baptized in the First Presbyterian Church of Odessa. My mother's parents moved there during the 1950s oil boom and opened a dress shop called Batemans. My father's father entered the oil business around the same time, founding a trucking company, Marks Crane & Rigging, that still exists.

When I was growing up, my dad's mother lived in Odessa, as did my Aunt Margaret and Uncle Dick and their children. I spent many summers in Odessa, and the place worked a funny magic on me. The city rested flat on the earth, and at night, on the edge of town, when the sun had vanished from the sky, you couldn't tell the ground from the heavens. A huge blackness swallowed everything, except here and there a few lights, a sensation of disorientation and exhilaration at the same time, as if the world itself had disappeared.

I returned to Odessa because the city's school board had passed a motion allowing a Bible course created by a conservative Christian organization to be taught as an elective. My Aunt Margaret, who still lives in Odessa, told me that one of the conservative Christian board members, Renda Berryhill, had once lived down the street from her. When I mentioned the name of Berryhill to my mother, she immediately recognized the name. That same family had owned a kids' clothing shop on the same street as my grandparents' dress shop. My mother had known Jamie Berryhill, the son, and the husband of the school board member. From Aunt Margaret, I also learned that Jamie and Renda Berryhill had done something that shocked a lot of their friends and acquaintances. A few years back, they had moved into an abandoned hotel on one of the roughest drags in Odessa to serve the needs of troubled women.

That's how I found the ladies of Mission Messiah, who taught me what it means to submit yourself into freedom.

AT THE TIME of my visit, the Berryhills had enrolled sixteen women at Mission Messiah. The women lived, prayed, and worked together in the rooms of a defunct hotel on the side of a mostly deserted strip of urban west Texas, a haunt of prostitutes and drug dealers a few blocks from where Jamie Berryhill's parents had once run the clothing store. In the gap between two eras, Odessa had become a sad, rough place afflicted by oil busts, illegal immigration, and a failed war on drugs. Mission Messiah began as a message from God to Jamie Berryhill, a wealthy local businessman wrecked repeatedly by bad business decisions and crushing debt. Aunt Margaret could still remember the day when the Berryhills had been evicted from their home down her street.

The ladies at Mission Messiah have endured their own calamities and barely survived. They are women who have seen the bottom of the social pit in the small towns and cities of west Texas, places like Pampa, Borger,

Lubbock, Midland. Most have been sexually abused at one time or another. Drugs figure in the résumé, domestic violence, prostitution, various other kinds of criminal activity. These ladies have done prison time, lost their children to social services, lost their husbands, their homes, their livelihoods. A lot of them end up at Mission Messiah on court orders. The hotel on Second Street looks like the end of the line, the last stop before jail or worse.

Miss Tammy, the program's administrative assistant, told me that the principle of submission tops the list of priorities. "For most of the women who come to our program, just learning to submit to authority is a huge step forward," she said. "Most of the time, their problems have come from running up against authority, rather than learning to honor authority." Among other things, the women learn to pray for the leaders of the country, the leaders of the local government, and the leaders of the mission.

I spoke with three of the ladies. Miss Tammy, the administrator of the program, sat at her desk, taking calls and augmenting their answers to my questions. One woman had been at the mission six weeks and hadn't quite come to terms with the rigors of the program. Another had been there three months, and another six. Two of them came from nonreligious backgrounds and had had to struggle with the emphasis on faith. The third, a woman named BJ, came from a devout Baptist family. She was bipolar and taking four different medications when she entered the program. When she started, three months before, she had barely been able to walk or speak. By the time we met, she had gone off her meds and functioned like anyone else. But even BJ had been a little creeped out by Mission Messiah at first.

Another woman, Lisa, had brought her two-year-old son Greggy. Lisa came from Pampa, Texas, a panhandle town where she had cooked the books at an insurance business and received five years' probation. She had been fined $7,500 and still owed $6,000 in restitution for her crime. She also had a coke habit despite rehab. Her probation officer had been a strong Christian and offered her one more chance, this time in a faith setting. She agreed, but had to be dragged kicking and screaming to Mission Messiah. The Christian angle freaked her out. Over the phone, Jamie Berryhill had prayed for her and asked for an Amen. Lisa said, "I guess."

Once at the mission, nothing much improved. "It was scary," Lisa said.

"I felt like I didn't belong, and the devil was telling me, 'Girl, you don't belong.'"

Everything changed when Greggy caught the flu, and his temperature shot to 104. The mission has Motrin on hand, and Lisa wanted to use it, but the volunteer nurses talked her out of it. They told her the fever needed to run its course. Miss Tammy gave her a Bible and told her to focus on the book of Galatians. Lisa wept as she told me this story. "It was three in the morning, and I was scared, so scared. I started reading the book again and again and again. I read it at three in the morning, at five in the morning, and I just felt like God took me in his lap, and I could hold Greggy, and this calm came over me, this peace came over me, and pretty soon, Greggy was asleep, and his fever broke."

Over my shoulder, Miss Tammy said, "Amen."

"I got goose bumps now," Lisa told me. "It was like God took me in hand, Jesus took me in his hand, and said, 'Okay, Lisa, okay.' I was just so concentrating on reading, and I am just going to do this, and all the girls were saying, you can do this, you can do this, and I quit reading, and Greggy was sleeping, and his breathing was calm, and it was just a peace that I had never felt, not any drug, not any man, not my mama, not my daddy, not nobody, has ever made me feel what I felt in that early morning."

The question of the Motrin hadn't quite been settled, though. "I was just lost. My little feller was sick, and that's all I knew. And I did listen, and try, and was willing to try. But that was the longest night, and we went to the emergency room the next day. His fever came back up, and I panicked again, and we went, and he got a big old shot, but that peace, that was real, that was awesome."

THE THIRD OF the women had an even more extraordinary tale, but she wouldn't tell it until the other ladies left the room, and she wouldn't let me use her name. She was forty-one and had four daughters, the progeny of a twenty-year marriage to a member of the Mexican mafia, or so she told me. She had come to Mission Messiah on the heels of a drug charge. Methamphetamine was her drug of choice, and she'd done it for three and a half years before she got hit with a possession charge. She went to jail for ten days, got out, did the drug again, got caught again. This time, she struck a plea bargain and served six months in the county jail in Pampa. While she was inside, social services took her daughter away. There was also a female visitor who would come from time to time and pray with her, and when she'd done her time, she was ready for Mission Messiah.

There was just one problem. She feared men. She feared her father, who'd accepted Christ and asked her forgiveness. She feared Jamie Berryhill, who wanted to give her a new life. She feared God, who, in her eyes, was just another man. And she had her reasons.

From the age of five, she told me, her father had sexually molested her. That stopped when he went to prison on charges of having molested her half-sister. At a later age, she had been molested by one of her mother's boyfriends in the backseat of the family car. When she was fourteen, she married into a life of hell on earth.

Her husband slept with other women, and if she confronted him, she got hurt. "I would go out on the street looking for him, and he would beat me up. He broke my nose. He broke a jawbone. He cracked two of my ribs. He punctured one of my lungs. He used my hair as a mop more times than I'd like to count."

Prison ended her marriage. When her husband went to jail, she left him. Freedom led to a job in a bar, and that led to methamphetamine, which had brought her to Mission Messiah. Coming to the mission was a beginning, but her fear of men meant that she couldn't bear male criticism, not even the slightest tremor of disapproval. She feared that she would be sent back to jail or beaten or worse. The answer, in the end, had been a deliverance. *The* deliverance, the woman told me.

When I first heard this word, I asked Miss Tammy what she meant. Miss Tammy explained. "It's a time that we go in with some real strong spiritual leaders, and they just sit down with these women, and we get talking through these things that have just held them captive their whole lives, working them up to the front, breaking through, and breaking away, through the Lord, and basically denouncing some of the things that have held them. We do believe the word says that the battle is not against flesh and blood, but against the principalities and powers of darkness, and that's what we do. We tell those things to give it up. In a lot of Christian circles, it can be pretty debatable, but I feel like, because it's firmly in the word, it's fine."

She was talking about an exorcism. Deliverance meant exorcism. The woman who feared men had to undergo an exorcism to rid herself of fear of men. Before it happened, Renda Berryhill told the woman to look at the Old Testament book of Numbers, chapter 4, in which Moses and Aaron receive the precise instructions for building the tabernacle of the Ark of the Covenant. The woman read the book, but she didn't understand, she said, and Renda Berryhill told her that verses from Numbers were about purification and cleansing of the tabernacle, and this is what would happen to her in the deliverance. She would be cleansed.

"I was so scared of Mister Jamie," she told me, "because he was my authority, because he's a man, because every authority figure I had hurt me . . . but I'm not afraid of him anymore. I see he's the loving man who loves us all. Part of that was my deliverance. That's one of the results. Freedom from fear of men. One of the hard things in my deliverance, I had to tell God that I forgive him. I couldn't get close to God, because I saw him as a man. He was high, high up in my authority, and I was scared of him."

The deliverance had worked. If it hadn't, Miss Tammy told me, the woman wouldn't be sitting there with me, telling her story.

In this woman's eyes, submission to God had meant freedom from the violence of men. I don't know if her cure lasted. I don't know if Mission Messiah had used the practice of exorcism to give her an even more frightening father figure, one who would obliterate any man who ever touched her. Cosmic terror had, perhaps, trumped the mortal kind. I do know that she believed in her liberation, and it had come about through her surrender to a divine male authority.

of an animal, a deer or a coyote. He certainly hadn't seen a human being at that hour in that completely inappropriate place. Retaining walls rose five or six feet on either side of the concrete ramp. There wasn't much traffic, and he pulled over and stopped. He saw no sign of life. He got on the freeway, found the next exit, and returned to the spot a few times. It was late and he was tired. He went home.

The next morning, he went back to the same spot and had no better luck. The police didn't find the body until later that day. On Monday, Derek went to the police. He had a dent in the car and wanted to find out, if possible, what had happened on the ramp. The police told him. An indigent man suffering from bipolar disorder had been walking up the concrete incline at a very late hour. Derek's car struck him at such an angle that he flew several dozen feet into the weeds on the other side of one of the retaining walls. The man, Tedd McWhinney, died instantly.

"Me and Don have been together ever since," Derek told me. "We've been bonded."

For his part, Don McWhinney called his new friendship with Derek Citizen a divine appointment. Tedd's death had brought Lillie and him together with this young black man, a fellow Christian, a fellow sojourner in the vale of sorrows. One day, they would all know why.

DEREK GREW UP Catholic and took his first communion when he was seven. A little later, to his grandmother's chagrin, he decided to become a Baptist.

When he was twelve, he and his mother moved to Dallas, where she had found a better job. He went to high school in Dallas, college at Oklahoma University in Norman, where he got a master's degree in public relations and criminology. He loved to write and dreamed of starting a criminology magazine one day. At work, he handled calls from clients with mental health issues and referred them to mental health professionals in the insurance company's database.

His extended family had had some luck in the Hurricane Rita disaster. Most of them had been in Dallas for a wedding when the storm hit, so no one was hurt. Most of the property had been spared. His grandmother's tool

## chapter 23

## *Skin*

*A*round two in the morning, a few hours after I had my first dinner with Don and Lillie McWhinney, a man named Derek Citizen drove home from his own Friday night meal in north Texas. Every week, after work, Derek and his colleagues in the mental health department of an insurance company gathered at the same sushi restaurant near the LBJ Freeway. The workweek felt long, and the Friday night meal helped everyone unwind. No one drank much, but the evening went later than usual. Derek liked the company. He lived by himself in the greater Dallas area and didn't have a wife or girlfriend. His mother lived in the area, and they were extremely close, but mothers don't exactly constitute a social life. The two of them had come from Lake Charles, Louisiana, where they had roots. He attended a good, supportive church. He had a job that valued his time and paid him a decent wage. Compared to many of his friends and relatives from Louisiana, who had become refugees in the wake of Hurricane Rita, he had done well for himself.

He had slightly changed his routine that night, taking an alternate route home and using the on ramp to LBJ Freeway. Later, this small fact would torment him. Why that night? Why at all? Halfway up the ramp, he felt the thump of impact. He knew that he'd hit something. He hadn't seen the flash shed had been wiped out, and she complained a bit about that. Otherwise, his Lake Charles people had made out all right. His aunts, uncles, and cousins were still in Dallas on the morning we met at a pancake restaurant just off LBJ Freeway.

I asked him about that night, and he made clear to me that, four months later, it was no easier to talk about. "For some reason, I chose a different direction that night. I don't know what made me go that direction. To this day, I don't understand it, I don't understand why, because I'm into routine, I get comfortable in a routine. All of a sudden, I was out on the highway, and next thing you know, Tedd is struck by my vehicle."

He became emotional. Don said the blessing. "Father, we thank you that your mercies are new and fresh every morning."

Dallas is a mostly segregated city. White and black usually live in different neighborhoods, go to different schools, attend different churches. That had been my experience, and as far as I could tell, it still held true. So I was surprised to find this very unlikely pair, a fairly traditional and avuncular older white man from Denton and a young professional black man from Dallas, forming a bond over an act of unintentional killing committed by one against the child of the other. I asked Derek why he thought the two had become close.

"It's easy," he said. "God's will. God's grace. Two Christian men bonded together by this. That's his purpose. Together, me and Don gonna find that purpose."

Don told me that the detective on the case had given him his first impression of Derek. When Derek learned what had happened, he almost fainted. The detective hadn't wanted to give Don the young man's name, but Don had passed on a message. Tedd's funeral service would be the following morning. Derek and his mother would be welcome.

After the service, the two families met. Don said, "I remember Derek and his mother coming down, and Derek just fell into my arms and wept. And his mother fell into Lillie's arms and wept. And somehow, that was consolation for Lillie and for me. It gave us emotional support. It gave us sympathy and empathy, a realization that this man and this family were deeply saddened by the loss of our son."

Derek had begun to weep. Don started to muse on the meaning of the encounter. "I think this is the way Christians are supposed to act, the way we're supposed to live. Your faith affects the way you live."

"Absolutely," Derek said.

WHEN YOU IMAGINE an evangelical Christian, what does that person look like? Chances are, the face in your mind is white, Southern, and male. He or she will sound a lot more like Don and Lillie McWhinney than Derek Citizen, an irony in light of the fact that those omnipresent Barna polls tell us that, based on church attendance, prayer life, evangelization, and other indices, African Americans consistently rate as the most devoutly Christian people in the country. Black pastors have a standing in their communities that white pastors generally do not. Black churches tend to play a social role in their neighborhoods that white ones don't, as maintainers of community and defenders of justice, though this balance has begun to change in certain parts of the country, in the inner cities, where the black churches have begun to lose influence in their neighborhoods.

In the 1960s, 1970s, and 1980s, black and white Christianity had such divergent paths that it wouldn't have made sense to talk about them as aspects of the same phenomenon. The dire state of race relations in the United States meant that skin color mattered in the pews as it did everywhere else. Typically, at the evangelical end of the spectrum, the Jesus of the black church has always placed a far greater emphasis on social justice, on combating racism and poverty, than on the more theological abstractions, such as the end-times or creationism. The influential pastor of an African American megachurch in south Dallas told me that he believed in the Rapture, but didn't make too much of it. His focus lay on the here and now. His people still had to fight the long war to reclaim pride, jobs, families, and neighborhoods from the legacy of slavery and segregation, which, more than color, had always been the true dividing line between the identities of white and black Protestant churches. The former acted as bastions of identity, without doubt, and gave to many rural and urban whites their most profound sense of right and wrong as well as their culture and learning. But the black churches proved to be arks of survival for an entire people. It would be hard to overestimate the way that

African American Christianity not only nurtured and sustained the spirits of generation upon generation, but formed the instincts and motivations of leaders from W. E. B. Du Bois and Frederick Douglass to Martin Luther King Jr. and Jesse Jackson.

But a change has begun to blur the color line that always divided American Christianity. Three developments, at least, account for something like a rapprochement between white and black believers. It would be hard to rank them in importance, but each weighs heavily in the transformation of the relationship.

First, as I've demonstrated in these pages, the body of evangelical Christianity has made a decisive turn toward social justice in the last decade. Rather than hiding in the bunker defensively and protecting its own, more and more local white churches seek to effect change in their cities and towns. Whether embodied by Rick Warren's trips to Africa, and his statements on poverty, or the efforts made by churches during and after Hurricane Katrina, or the increasing use of Martin Luther King Jr. by white evangelicals as a poster child for the real-world benefits of faith, American Christians have begun to find spiritual truth in areas that black churches long ago embraced as a matter of necessity.

Second, in the culture wars, particularly over questions of gay marriage and the tax status of churches and religious institutions, African American Christians have seen reason to listen to overtures from conservative Christian circles. In the days when abortion dominated discussion, race continued to have a divisive effect. Disproportionate numbers of teen pregnancies occurred in the black population, and still do, making the economics of keeping a baby somewhat different than those among whites. Black pastors viewed the issue in terms of a larger network of social ills and never made it a key cause for their congregations. The vast majority of protestors at abortion clinics, and in the pulpits, have been white-skinned.

Gay marriage, on the other hand, has mobilized the black faithful. Why now, given that portions of scripture are clear on the subject, and that white believers have been vocal about it for years? It may be because homosexuality, which has always been deeply taboo among blacks, now seems unavoidable as a subject for discussion. It may be that marriage and family, which have always represented the great bulwark against disintegration for middle-class and upper-middle-class African Americans, more important even than the church, appear more threatened by homosexuality than by, for instance, abortion, which tended to be more of a poor woman's problem. Among lower-income African Americans, the disproportionate numbers of young black males who die from violence or end up in prison mean that no young man in the community can be spared. Among other things, homosexuality becomes a waste of needed manpower.

Black churches and pastors, along with traditionally conservative Hispanic Catholics, have made common cause with whites in marriage initiatives all over the country. My cousin Scott, who openly acknowledges that he was raised in a racist setting, said that only once in his life did his anxiety about skin color melt away. At a rally to celebrate the passing of a law to protect heterosexual marriage in Texas, he said, he looked around and saw blacks, whites, and Hispanics gathered in common cause and didn't feel himself to be anything but a Christian among fellow Christians. Such moments have occurred all over the country, the mostly unreported diminishment of a color line in the name of a perceived higher good.

And that's the third change. According to a recent study in the *American Sociological Review*, intermarriage rates have decreased between whites and Asians and Hispanics, due, in large part, to the massive growth in immigrant populations. As those latter numbers have increased, more Hispanics and Asians are marrying into their own racial groups. Marriage rates between blacks and whites have increased significantly, however. Blacks still tend to intermarry less than other groups, but they are doing it more often, and mostly to whites. That change mirrors a general rapprochement between the races in the 1990s and the last decades, somewhat masked by the uproar over the racial dimension of Hurricane Katrina. The changes can be seen anecdotally in megachurches, which have increasing numbers of African American members, drawn like whites to those imposing structures that dominate entire exurban and even urban neighborhoods. In a congregation of 10,000 or more on the outskirts of a sun-belt or western American city, or in the middle of New York City, even one that is predominantly white, race, like denomination, like geographical origin, like economic status, matters less.

At the Times Square Church in Manhattan, admittedly serving one of the most eclectic racial populations in the country, the services and the sensibility have a distinctly African American flavor, but the ethnic makeup of the crowd draws from every heritage. One Sunday morning, I spoke with three elderly immigrant women of color: a Nigerian, a Dominican, and a Pakistani. Each of them clutched a Bible to their chest. Each told me they would pray for my soul, that I should be saved. In the Times Square Church, the mixture of race is such a given that it's moot.

In the United States, in general, race has dwindled as a division, yet it still matters enormously.

"We're doing better," Bob Russell told me about Southeast. "But I feel like we've got a long way to go. I'm surprised that it's taken so long for those barriers to come down. There are cultural practices in worship, an attitude toward preachers, that are just different, and it's hard to breach those." He spoke with admiration, even a little envy, of a friend's congregation in Los Angeles. "Boy, they're doing great," he said. "They're probably a third Hispanic, maybe 15 percent black, and the rest are Caucasian, and it's no factor. I feel like we're about fifteen to twenty years from that in the Midwest."

Out of nine elders at Southeast, with its congregation of 18,000, one is black. Four or five of the deacons are black, and more African Americans get added to the membership rolls all the time. Russell says he doesn't think it's about prejudice. To put it in the most practical terms, a service at Southeast lasts about an hour. If they run longer, people start to get antsy, and pastors will hear about it the following week. Everything at Southeast has to be timed so that members can come, worship within a clearly defined framework, and head home.

At Canaan Baptist Church, an African American megachurch housed in what had once been the Southeast facility in Louisville, I attended a service that lasted three to four hours. The music alone flowed in a single, spectacular, gospel epic that began in swinging formality before dissolving into theatrical ecstasy. I enjoyed every second of it. I was hugged and called "brother" more times than I can count. I held hands. I closed my eyes and sang aloud to the repetition of a single refrain over and over. As far as I could tell, I was the only white man in a sanctuary of 5,000 people, but I felt completely welcomed, completely at home, transfixed by a version of redemption that no white church had ever offered me. People in the choir and in the pews collapsed. The voices reared up to the sky and got down in my guts. They went on and on, like a wind, while the pastor, a guest from the Bahamas, spoke of things earthly and eternal, things local and distant, in one breath, the value of the regular pastor, the value of Jesus, the importance and the meaning of the tithe, of evil outside the walls, and evil done in the ranks. I left at the three-and-a-half-hour mark, but I had received the message. I never came closer to doing an altar call than in that church in Kentucky.

If you want to understand why white and black Protestant churches have never melded into one large body of believers, a service like that one answers the question. And it's not just a matter of style or taste. The gospel journey of a black church on Sunday morning travels a separate road than a white church, through a history and suffering all its own, such that it's near impossible to imagine a day when the two will be as one.

IN MY FAITH, race figured significantly. It was a matter of absence. Mine was an extremely white belief, racially speaking.

But once a year, at Highland Park Presbyterian, an African American pastor by the name of E. V. Hill preached a sermon in the sanctuary. In my town, this was a very big deal. Sociology professor James Loewen has identified Highland Park as "sundown town," a place where blacks were actively discouraged from buying homes, and where, as a consequence, less than 0.01 percent of the community is African American. This rings true to me. When I was in seventh grade, the Park Cities successfully beat back racial integration, and the kids in my metal shop cheered when the news was announced. In church, E. V. Hill came as a shock.

Like my father, I had less patience for Sunday morning services, with their sermons and stuffy old hymns, than I did for Sunday school. It was hard for me to sit still in a pew without closing my eyes. But one morning, my mom urged me to come to services, and I've never forgotten the experience. It was the first time that I had ever heard the gospel "shout," in which a black preacher brings the Holy Spirit through the cadence of voice and the pressure of intonation into the presence of believers. We've all experienced the

cliché on television, in the movies, or in political speeches given by everyone from Dr. King to Al Sharpton and Jesse Jackson. The shout cracks like
a whip, summoning the moral attention. That morning, it snapped in front
of my drowsiness like two huge fingers. I don't recall exactly what E. V.
Hill said that morning, but the Highland Park Presbyterian Church youth
minister of that time, Murray Gossett, had memorized his favorite line and
repeated it to me when I paid him a visit years later in Amarillo, Texas. The
Reverend Hill had been reared by people who raised hogs, and he never left
out this piece of his personal biography.

"It's a *long way* from the *hog farm* to *Highland Park*," he would say.

In some ways, it was an even longer distance from Highland Park to
Alford Refrigerated Warehouses, where I worked a summer job in sanitation for five or six years in high school and college. If E. V. Hill introduced
me to a vitality of faith that I had never experienced before, the warehouse
in south Dallas introduced me to a version of my country that I had never
seen before.

In my high school, there had been no black kids and one Asian American, a Vietnamese boy who became our valedictorian. I had one friend of
Hispanic origin, but he was also an anomaly. Alford might have been in the
wrong part of town, but it paid extremely well, better than anything where I
lived. When I took my first job there, chipping ice off the floor of one of the
frozen-food bays, I entered a world that was predominantly African American and Hispanic. Whites held the upper-management jobs. A white guy
named Darrell ran the sanitation crew. He gave me my assignment as a trash
collector with a pair of Hispanic men: Pedro, an illegal immigrant who spoke
no English; and Jaime, gentle, thoughtful, and deeply anxious, a Seventh-
Day Adventist in his late twenties. For my first two summers, Pedro, Jaime,
and I cleaned the detritus off the mile-long main street of what claimed to
be the largest warehouse in the Southwest. They called me Juan-John, or
Johnny Juan. We had a small red tractor that had to be gassed up with diesel
every few hours, and we hooked trash bins to the hitch of the tractor. One
of us drove, the other two clung to the sides of the bins, and we spent the
morning going up and down the street, plucking and shoveling and sorting
out trash left by the long haul truckers. It was hot and filthy work, hundred

degree days. Every now and then, Jaime and I found a dark corner of the air-conditioned peanut bay, and we'd climb up on the sacks of peanuts, eight or nine layers above the floor, and talk about God.

Jaime was devout. He observed Saturday sabbath, like all Seventh-Day Adventists, and didn't drink or smoke or mess around with women, though he longed to be married. He sold a kind of pinball game called a pachinko machine on the side, but he took his day job seriously. His faith urged compassion, but he had a kind nature, too. His friendship with Pedro stands out as the best example in my memory. Everyone knew that Pedro was illegal, and everyone looked the other way, thanks to Jaime, no matter how many times he screwed up. Once, Pedro drove the tractor off the edge of the candy bay, putting it into the shop for a week. Other days, he showed up late or went home too early. He attracted a lot of attention as the stereotypical "lazy wetback," which plenty of people called him, but Jaime always stepped to the defense. One of the Latino foremen, a hard case named Juan, observed Pedro's antics with complete and total disgust. He had no patience for illegals, especially those who couldn't do a job. Though he had no material reason to help Pedro, Jaime stuck by his friend, arguing time and again with Juan, imploring him not to call immigration. Juan respected Jaime, so he never did.

Jaime also had the evangelistic fervor. One day, while we sat on the sacks of peanut bags, he gave me a copy of Ellen G. White's *The Great Controversy*, urging me to read it. He considered the woman a prophet on a par with John the Baptist and believed that, if I read the book, I would think so, too, and want to become an Adventist like him. Very few books in my life have terrified me as much as *The Great Controversy*. I still have the copy that Jaime gave to me. The subtitle of the book is: *Between Christ and Satan: The Conflict of the Ages in the Christian Dispensation*. That may give some idea of the spirit of the work, which is considered heretical and cultish to mainstream fundamentalists and evangelicals alike. But I didn't know anything about the history of the Protestant church in the United States. I didn't know about offshoots like Adventism and Mormonism and couldn't have told you much about the differences between Presbyterians and Methodists—except for predestination. I took everything at face value, believing all non-Catholic Christians to be of one accord. If I believed in Jesus, then I must also listen to Ellen G. White. So I did, and she told me this.

> It is the restraining power of God that prevents mankind from passing fully under the control of Satan. The disobedient and unthankful have great reason for gratitude for God's mercy and long-suffering in holding in check the cruel, malignant power of the evil one. But when men pass the limits of divine forbearance, that restraint is removed. God does not stand toward the sinner as an executioner of the sentence against transgression; but he leaves the rejectors of His mercy to themselves to reap that which they have sown.

Jaime never bullied me with his beliefs, but he was far more convincing, in his way. He would simply look at me with large, woeful eyes—he had the saddest expression, a wan, concerned, burdened look that accepted doom and horror as inevitable and imminent—and said, "I am simply worried for you, Juan John."

ONE OF MY youth ministers theologically disemboweled Ellen G. White—and I long ago lost touch with Jaime, but a piece of that lesson stuck with me. From the perspective of white America, Christianity in this country looks mostly white and a little black, and those two principles work at opposite ends of a clichéd spectrum. In the popular culture, white Christianity most frequently wears the face of either sentimentalized or brutalizing Catholicism or intolerant Protestant Puritanism, by and large negative images. Black Christianity can be summed up in the image of a gospel choir, a completely positive image. But dig beneath the surface, and Christian America has a far more variegated look and feel.

The growth in numbers of Hispanic Protestants tells its own story. In Gonzalez, Louisiana, I met the Reverend Fernando Gutierrez, the pastor of the Hispanic campus of Healing Place Church, which now gets 150 people per weekend for Spanish-language services. At the end of 2005, around Christmas, that number was closer to 90. By 2008, if current trends continue, it will be well over 200, and Gutierrez will have to start thinking about building a new facility. The Spanish campus was established in Gonzalez as a mission ten years ago. Back then, Gutierrez told me, there weren't that many Hispanic people in the area. But an influx of Mexican strawberry pickers over the last decade changed the population. The strawberry pickers didn't go home. They got jobs in the local chemical plants, and then they brought their families.

Gutierrez told me that he doesn't ask anyone to tell him about their immigration status, but he does let them know, in no uncertain terms, where they are. "I basically say, this is a sovereign country, and you've been given the opportunity to be here. It's a tremendous privilege, so respect the laws and speak the language and do what is right. Don't become a statistic of the bad people." A lot of the men in his church have come from rough backgrounds, so every week, he holds a men's group in which he serves as role model and counselor. "A lot of the men who come here, they feel different than they did in Mexico. Over there, they beat their wives, they drink a lot, they don't take care of their home. Over here, they're learning otherwise. They have responsibilities. They're supposed to love their wives and children and sacrifice for them. I tell them being a male is a matter of birth. Being a man is a decision."

The church also provides English classes, and every two weeks, it turns itself into a medical clinic that receives twenty to thirty patients for checkups. In the process, Gutierrez and his small staff are turning a poor, itinerant population into a permanent fixture, and this kind of experience happens all over the country, informing the future of American Christianity more than its past. Immigration and birthrates being what they are, if I were to write this book again in fifty years, it would look far more Asian and Latino than Caucasian and African American.

IT'S TOO EARLY to identify a large movement of black conservative Christians who sympathize more with white conservative evangelical values than with traditional African American progressivism and religiosity. But a handful of black Republican congressmen and a number of large conservative black congregations around the country attest to an increased willingness to break with tradition. La Shawn Barber, a popular conservative Christian blogger, may be as representative as anyone of the new realities.

Barber had a conversion experience to both conservatism and Christianity. "Like most black people," she told me, "I voted for Democrats. That's just what you did. Sometime in my twenties, I started thinking about why I voted for Bill Clinton twice, and if he really represented my interests and what I believe, and this is before I became a Christian. So I started picking apart certain issues, and I realized that Republicans sort of agreed with things I agreed with. So why am I voting for Democrats? Is it just a family tradition? No, I have to vote my conscience. I sort of started leaning right. I hesitated to call myself a conservative, but I eventually adopted that *c* word."

The political change happened as a slow evolution, but Barber's watershed came in the midst of impeachment proceedings against Bill Clinton. "I was a legislative correspondent for a Democrat senator right at the height of impeachment," Barber told me. "And I just didn't want to vote for any more Democrats after that."

The religious transformation occurred in sync with the political change. "At first, I was on the wrong track. I thought if I could be a moral person, that meant I would be a good person. And it took me a while to realize that's not the measure. It's whether you're forgiven. You can't be good enough for God. You have to be forgiven. And he makes you righteous. That's the way I started thinking. And as a conservative Christian, I really couldn't vote for a liberal, so it was a natural progression, an evolution, not one specific moment."

One measure of the change was her stance on abortion. Before she became a conservative Christian, she considered herself pro-choice. Afterward, she took the opposite position. "I consider it to be murder. I'm unequivocal."

I brought up the subject of gay marriage. "I really don't care what two adults are doing," Barber said. "The problem is where it's equated with the civil rights movement. Blacks were second-class citizens, fighting for our rights to be full citizens, and to compare that with a sexual lifestyle, to equate the two, like it's some kind of civil rights movement?" That stance has put her well beyond the pale of progressive black liberal politics that she once embraced as a matter of habit. "I've been called a religious bigot I don't know how many times," she said.

†

IT WOULD BE misleading to suggest that the conversion of La Shawn Barber happened in a political vacuum. Religious conservatives in the Republican Party have been working for years to get a hearing with African Americans, and few have worked with as much zeal as the founder of Wall Builders, David Barton, who makes his usual case with history, original documents, voting patterns, and faith, but with a very particular slant for black audiences.

One summer, in the basement of the King's College in Manhattan, I saw Barton and his wife Cherry woo an audience that included several black pastors. When the speech ended, he received thunderous applause, and it was no wonder. Barton made the people in that room feel as if he had uncovered a huge conspiracy to hide or distort the history of their color and their beliefs. With a treasure trove of period diaries, flyers, letters, and other relics of the American past, Barton launched right into his argument. Any African American Christian who believed that the Democratic Party deserved the unswerving loyalty of the black voter should review the historical record—and consult the Bible.

"Scripture teaches us that the way a people views its own history affects the way that people behaves," he began.

He turned to the New Testament, to the book of Acts, and described a section of oratory by the apostle Stephen. In those chapters, Stephen gives an account of the relationship between God and Israel through the generations: Abraham, Isaac, Jacob. "We call that a providential view of history," he told the crowd. He was moving swiftly, from the Bible to the teaching of history, as if everything in his message dovetailed seamlessly with everything else. "We used to teach history that way. We used to teach history with a purpose. What was God up to? What was he doing? Why did he do it? We don't teach it that way anymore. We teach it as a series of unrelated names and dates and places, and it's lost its purpose. It's also lost its interest. Most of us enjoy biblical history. It's got a purpose. We don't enjoy American history, doesn't have a purpose."

He switched to the subject of textbooks, explaining to the audience that he had written textbook standards for states like Texas and California. But he still wasn't happy with how history was being taught. The Fourth of July, he pointed out, by way of example. Kids today learned only one of the separation clauses in the Declaration of Independence, he told the crowd, and which one? Taxation without representation. Never mind the other twenty-six, four of which, he told them, had to do with objections to activist judges, half of which had to do with objections to slavery, based on Christian conscience. It was a scandal.

He began to talk about the Christian history that "we're" never taught. He brandished a 1761 document, the charter for the very first Protestant missionary society ever started in the American colonies. In 1774, King George III had vetoed the society. "Because we didn't have religious freedom, other founders got involved for religious liberty issues," Barton said. "They got involved so that we could say 'under God' at the pledge, or say a prayer at football games."

From prayer in school, he moved to slavery. Northern colonies began to abolish the institution—in 1773, Rhode Island and Connecticut; in 1774, Massachusetts and Pennsylvania. Then King George III vetoed those laws. "That's where a number of founding fathers say, great, let's not be part of the British Empire, Benjamin Franklin and Benjamin Rush, they got involved to end slavery," Barton says, his words tumbling over each other, a river of polemic flowing from one subject to the next. "The Declaration of Independence has twice as many clauses on the desire to end slavery as it does on taxation without representation."

Using Benjamin Franklin and Benjamin Rush, the founders of the country's first abolitionist society, he moved to the matter of civil disobedience, then to Martin Luther King Jr., then to George W. Bush. He reminded the crowd that King George III had vetoed all the colonial anti-slavery laws in 1774. "This society was formed as an act of civil disobedience against King George III. Let me kind of refresh you on how much you have to believe something to commit civil disobedience. It's not a real active thing that most Christians do these days, but if you have a strong conviction—MLK did—Dr. King did—lot of others—I know a lot of those folks who went down South. Matter of fact, one of the cabinet secretaries under President Bush is happy to pull up his pants leg and show you the dog bites where the police sicced the dogs on him in Alabama. I know a lot of those guys." He meant civil rights activists.

According to Barton, we don't know more about our storied Christian past, and therefore our anti-slavery history, because we've been taught by people like historians Charles and Mary Beard, that the only thing that motivates people is money. This gets him to politics very quickly, and his work as an official for the Republican Party in Texas. He told the crowd that he had looked at a lot of polling data, and one set of figures really jumped out at him. "There are three kinds of Christian voters," he said. "Those who are actually called 'Christian voters,' a person who says, 'I'm religious, I call myself a Christian, and I vote.' Then there are born-again voters, a smaller group, who say, 'I am not only a Christian, I have a personal relationship with Jesus Christ.' And then the smallest group, evangelical Christian voters, who say, 'I have a personal relationship with Jesus Christ, I believe the Bible to be the basis of life, and I pray, read the Bible, and go to church at least once a week.' These evangelical voters are the most serious about their faith. And yet, in the last three elections, 45 percent of those evangelicals, when it came time to vote, said that economic issues were more important than moral issues. There's not a single verse in the Bible that will sustain that position, but for seventy years we've been trained that that's what we're all about."

He lamented to the crowd that this economic view of history had led us to abandon so many of our heroes, particularly in the founding era, and particularly someone like Richard Allen. "He's become a real hero of mine," he said. "He's raised as a slave in Delaware, meets a traveling Methodist evangelist who came across his plantation and preached the gospel. Allen hears the gospel, commits his life to Christ, becomes a zealous Christian, I mean he starts preaching the gospel to everything that moves in that plantation. Pretty soon, he leads his slave master to Christ, and the slave master thinks, 'My Gosh, what am I doing owning slaves?' Gives Richard his freedom, so Richard leaves Delaware, heads up north, comes to Pennsylvania, comes to Philadelphia, a city of 40,000 people, basically a megacity in that day and age, starts pastoring a church of 2,000, basically a megachurch in that day and age, and by the way, all white parishioners. But we don't talk about him."

## chapter 24

# Geist

*M*uch more than history or faith, homosexuality united blacks and whites in a common cause after decades of racial enmity. And yet no other issue divides Christians so completely against themselves. Long before the news broke about the homosexual affair of Ted Haggard, the self-promoting pastor of New Life Church in Colorado, I heard another version of his story in Pennsylvania. Haggard, the former head of the National Association of Evangelicals and a media star of the new movement, had had a longtime relationship with a gay masseur. Right before the midterm elections, the masseur went public. Haggard first dismissed the charges, but then admitted to the relationship. The affair embarrassed his movement and his faith. "I am a deceiver and a liar," he wrote to his congregation. "There is a part of my life that is so repulsive and dark that I've been warring against it all my adult life."

In other words, for Christians, the gay problem isn't an intrusion from the outside. It's internal. Bible-believing Christians everywhere, black, white, Asian, and Latino, wrestle their own impulses in this struggle. Homosexuality sits at their dinner tables, sings in their choirs, competes in sports at their Christian schools, prays in their pews, and stands in their pulpits. The real assault doesn't come from the gay neighbor who moves into the house

And that was just the beginning of a three-hour presentation that Barton has made to black audiences all over the country. It is hard to measure the effect, of course, but in the 2006 midterm elections, black voters in Maryland came very close to putting a conservative African American Republican named Michael Steel into office. A few months earlier, Barton had taken several black pastors on one of his spiritual tours of the U.S. Capitol. Many of them came from Maryland. Others may doubt the connection, but not me. I've seen the man at work.

next door, from the positive representation of gay images on television, or even from a state like Massachusetts, which allows gay marriage. These developments exacerbate the sense of a runaway culture, but they don't account for the visceral sense of panic among so many Christians. The horror starts at home, within four walls, imported by a son or daughter, a closeted father or mother, a conflicted pastor or a deacon in denial.

At the fifty-seventh annual meeting of the Evangelical Theological Society in Valley Forge, Pennsylvania, I met Steve Parelli, a former pastor. He was attending a study group that regularly addresses questions of counseling, psychology, and pastoral care. That year, the group had settled on the theme of homosexuality, and Parelli had come to confront panelists with questions that he himself could not avoid. Each member of the panel came from a different corner of the Christian world, one a theologian, another a conservative pastor, still another a neuropsychologist. But when Parelli began to challenge the panel members from the audience, using their own language of redemption and love, pleading, in a sense, to be allowed back into his own church, I began to see the devilish complexity. Homosexual desire burned in the life of the mind of the evangelical, and no one knew how to put it out.

THE GERMANS HAVE a revealing word for mind: *Geist. Der Geist*, to be exact, taking the article, as all German nouns do, which gives the word a masculine gender. What's telling—and wonderful—about it, to me, is not anything intrinsic to the word itself. It's that *Geist* has so many other meanings that would not seem to be related to "mind," and yet those meanings fold themselves into the word in a way that characterizes an entire approach to thinking. For instance, *Geist* also means "spirit," as in the spirit of an age. It can mean "ghost," as in ghosts and goblins, and, in the land of Martin Luther and Meister Eckehart, it also performs a deep theological function. When German Christians speak of the Holy Spirit or the Holy Ghost, as in "Father, Son, and Holy Ghost," they say *der Heilige Geist*. In this language, the act of thinking envelops faith, death, time, and mind all at once. To use one's mind is also to engage with one's own era, to be haunted by ghosts, and to speak to God. When I moved to Germany, my junior year in college, the nature of the act of thinking changed for me.

When I arrived in what was then West Germany, I had only been outside the frontiers of my own country once, to the Mexican border city of Juarez. At first, the experience depressed me. The city of Marburg, an ancient university town, lay in the valley of the river Lahn, a few dozen kilometers north of Frankfurt, beneath low hills that seemed perpetually wrapped in mist. By the time we got there, fall had turned to winter and the women cloaked themselves in heavy scarves and sweaters. People didn't seem friendly. For the first time, to borrow a phrase from Daniel Wolfley, I found myself outside the national and political "umbrella of protection." My student year abroad coincided with the early years of the Reagan presidency, when his aggressive anti-Soviet politics outraged Europeans. In the Lahn River valley, the *geist* of 1968 had not completely passed away. Revolution could still be discussed with a straight face. The student body was rumored to be one-third communist, and a small percent of those definitely worked as spies for the Communist government of East Germany. During my junior year, hundreds of thousands of West Germans protested the placing of U.S. Pershing II and SS-20 missiles on German soil. Also that year, U.S. troops invaded Grenada. Black spray-painted graffiti on the way to class shrieked *Amis raus!*—"Yanks Out!" The cold war had another six years to go.

I could not have been further away from my Texan and Christian roots. At first, I tried to conform. I engaged with the politics. I boarded a bus to Bonn with a crew of antimissile demonstrators, Demo Notorio, but once the water cannons let fly, I made my way as quickly as possible to a *konditorei* for plum torte and *milchkaffee*. I don't mean to say that my politics changed entirely due to location and circumstance. The change had been coming for a while, but the time and place gave me room to breathe and a different sort of air. My politics shifted decisively to the left in that year. When my parents showed up the following March, I had grown a mustache, donned a beret, and stopped brushing my teeth. I spoke of Nietzsche, a walking cliché from some other decade, far earlier in the century. Slowly but surely, something else was happening to me.

Every day, on my way to class, I would stop to sit in the pews of the Saint Elizabeth Church, the earliest example of Gothic architecture in Germany, and I would absorb the atmosphere of the early fourteenth century. For the first time, I would bow my head and pray to a god who had existed in history. For the first time, my senses filled with that particular aroma that rises from the old churches and cathedrals of Europe, I realized that history itself had existed, and Jesus had been only one part of it. Back home, Jesus had always seemed to occupy one of two places—Bible times and Dallas, Texas. In that church, I began to understand that everything in between had been real, and that the stories of King Arthur and his knights, for instance, had welled out of a specific moment, out of places like Marburg, out of churches like Saint Elizabeth, where Teutonic knights lay buried under tombs carved in armored ideal.

That wasn't all. On the hills above the valleys sat even more remarkable memorials of historic Christianity. In Marburg Castle, which glowed on the other side of the valley, ocher brown in the river mist at night, I discovered my connection to the theologian Martin Luther. In 1529, he and another reformer, Philipp Melanchthon, had met to hammer out an accord over the tenets of a new faith, Protestantism, my faith. The effort was known as the Marburg Colloquy, and I had never heard of it before. I had hardly heard of Luther himself, but in those early months, in the cold and rainy West German autumn, led by a Svengali professor from Atlanta, I began to see who I was, historically, in my beliefs. We traveled to see the Romanesque cathedral at Worms, the place where Martin Luther stood before the holy Roman emperor, Charles V, in 1521 on trial for his beliefs, and uttered words of poetic defiance that instantly locked in my mind, as if I had recited them from infancy: "Here I stand. I cannot do otherwise. God help me. Amen."

I was a Protestant. That meant resistance to authority. That meant the sanctity of private belief. That meant direct contact with God himself. That meant death to tyrants. These notions rushed through my mind, and I can recall feeling them as one enormous sensation, the breath sucked out of my lungs, a joy as loud and uncontainable as a shout. I had spent years learning a Sunday school version of Christianity, a simplified, ahistorical, childish, and deformed Christianity, and now the veil tore and I saw to the core of the faith as it had come down to me. Jesus receded into an immeasurable distance.

A kilometer from the cathedral at Worms, in sight of its towers, we paid a visit to another site that made a less profound impression in that moment. In hindsight, however, it marked yet one more beginning of my new life. We went to the thousand-year-old Jewish graveyard in Worms, the oldest and largest Jewish graveyard on the continent. Before this trip, I had seen the TV series *Holocaust*, which had just played on German television, unsettling the country's sense of its own recent history, and I had seen plenty of World War II movies about the Nazis, but I had no real idea, then, what it meant that these stones had survived to greet me. I had no idea what it meant for my faith, the implications of these abandoned stones, what they would hold for anyone, ever, who decides to follow Jesus. I had no idea what it meant that the Jewish graveyard in Marburg sat behind a locked gate and went mostly untended. A decade later, when I went to Wittenberg, where Luther famously nailed his ninety-five theses to the door of Castle Church in 1517, launching the Protestant religion, I knew much more and wasn't surprised to find the *Judensau* carving on the cornice of the St. Mary's Church, where Luther often preached, a sixteenth-century figure in stone depicting a Jew in the midst of filth and swine. By that time, I knew about Luther's late embrace of anti-Semitism. By that time, too, I had fallen in love with and married a Jewish woman.

In Marburg, in the first half of that college year, my mind came alive with my intellectual heritage as well. I can recall racing up the steps of a medieval path in the old town, up through the cold and wet to the student bookstore to buy thin yellow paperback copies of works by Goethe, Schiller, Nietzsche, Rilke, and Mörike. I read the autobiography of Saint Augustine, the *Confessions* of Rousseau, Tolstoy's *War and Peace*, Dickens's *Our Mutual Friend*, I read John Dos Passos, Emily Brontë, Wolfram von Eschenbach, and Franz Kafka, who would later become so important to me. An English girl named Caroline loaned me a book of essays called *The Disinherited Mind* by a scholar named Erich Heller, and this book seemed to decode a great mystery for me. Where was God, the real God, in this version of history laid out before me in the Lahn River valley? Forget about the preachy, empty, mindless stuff of high school. Where was God? Where were the real gods? Heller told me, in his lovely, mournful prose, that German thinkers back to Goethe, including the philosopher Friedrich Nietzsche, the poets Rilke and Hölderlin, the novelists Kafka and Thomas Mann, had all grappled with this very thing. They had yearned for transcendence in a world in which transcendence slipped like shining water through their fingers. I had been disinherited. This is what I felt. When I mentioned the book to my German professor, the Svengali, he shocked me. Heller had been his *doktor vater*, his doctoral adviser. I wrote to Heller, and he wrote me back, and we corresponded a few times. I didn't learn till much later that he was the Prague-born, gay Jewish son of a family liquidated at Auschwitz by the Nazis. The sorrow in the pages of his books, seemingly abstract, stemmed from the loss of everything. Where was God on this earth? Why have poets? Why think?

Through Heller, Marburg introduced me to the nature of my own century. It gave me, in the darkness of centuries, including my own, a means to see. I can't put it any other way. God may have given me a soul in the eternal moment before my conception. Marburg gave me a mind.

AT DENTON BIBLE Church, I met a young minister named John Brown, an intellectual from a family of farmers in Levelland, Texas, a lover of bookstores, like me, and a former Buddhist who had converted to the faith on the basis of sound and logical arguments made to him by others. We were discussing the intellectual culture of his brand of faith, and he told me that, if I wanted to experience firsthand "the mind of the evangelical," I should attend the annual meeting of the Evangelical Theological Society.

Once a year, divinity school professors and seminary presidents and seminarians gathered to discuss ideas. ETS acted as a gatekeeper of sorts for what got taught in the seminaries as doctrine, keeping out untruth, teasing out the complexities, shoring up sound orthodoxy, and occasionally expelling heretics. During my two conferences, the fifty-seventh and fifty-eighth annual gatherings, there were hundreds of study groups, panel discussions, lectures, exegeses, and debates. Each year, the conference takes on a different theme, which becomes a very rough, very loose compass for people wanting to submit papers. My first year, the theme was "The Early Church," a reference to the *Da Vinci Code* controversy, which had raised questions in the minds of the laity about the historical reality of Jesus and his first followers. Plenty of papers addressed topics like the gospel of Thomas, an apocryphal book of the Bible that had been used to support some of the more controversial assertions about Christ's life. In that lecture, I listened to a professor challenge the usefulness of the apocryphal book and support the decision by the early church fathers to leave it out of the canon.

In room after room, I saw a genuine ferment and disagreement. If John Brown was right, if ETS represented "the mind of the evangelical," that mind boiled with contention. The notion that Bible-believing Christians all hold the same view of life, humanity, and creation gradually faded before a vision of people who agreed on one or two very basic things but diverged everywhere else. I saw two academics give violently opposed readings on dispensationalism, a view of the end-time in which, among other things, God spirits away the believers before Satan takes control of the earth. One professor, Dr. Timothy Weber, gave a bleak history of dispensationalism, questioning its foundations in scripture and charging that it led to an overzealous involvement of Christians in the worldly politics of Israel. His opponent in the debate was Thomas Ice, founder and director of the Pre-Tribulation Research Center in Virginia, a place dedicated to research into dispensationalist views of scripture—in particular, into the fulfillment of biblical prophecy in our own day. Ice argued that no correct reading of scripture could deny dispensationalism and that Christians had been less involved in Israeli politics than was widely reported. There were disagreements over the nature of God, the role of women, the Christianity of George W. Bush, and the centrality of the creation story to the faith.

THE PANEL ON homosexuality consisted of a pastor, a psychologist, and a theologian.

The pastor, a tall, muscular, balding man with a sonorous voice, said, "In homosexuality, as I've observed it, you often find a very strong and intense relationship between the child and the opposite-gender parent and a rather weak or absent relationship with the same-sex parent. The church can play a very significant role by providing one-on-one discipleship between young men and adult same-sex role models, who can model what it means to be a healthy adult male and a healthy adult female."

The pastor mentioned Boy Scouts as a great place to model adult male heterosexual behavior. "There are contexts in which we can provide young men and young women with what it means to be a mature, robust, muscular male or a biblical female, and I think the church needs to take a lead on this."

The psychologist, a slender man with dark wavy hair and a soft, tentative voice, had listened intently, but he commented on these remarks in perplexity. "This may sound completely ignorant. I'm a husband and father of two daughters, and I like football, but having worked in this line for thirty years, I don't know what it means to be a male. I don't know what it means for me to be a male role model to my children, to the people in my church. I realize that it sounds somewhat ignorant, but I'm not quite sure what you're saying. What I opt for are things that I know in scripture, what does it mean to love, what does it mean to serve, and things that are much more overt but that don't seem to be gender-specific."

The pastor replied with rock solid conviction. "Biblically, as a male, I'm charged with two primary tasks. I'm charged with being the provider and being the protector. And attached to that are certain qualities that I need to be demonstrating. As a protector, I need to have a certain muscularity in my faith as well as a certain strength and presence in my home, and as a provider, I need to be able to demonstrate a certain degree of dependability and reliability. For my young kids, two sons and a daughter, one of the great things I can model is loving my wife, and letting them see me in love with my wife, letting them see what it means to be in a committed, covenant relationship with my wife. Also, I can let them see how I take my responsibility as a biblical male seriously, how I take responsibility for being a protector and provider in my home seriously, by being faithful to my wife and God, by modeling my spiritual life before my kids, allowing them to see me to pray, and then doing masculine activities with my boys, whether that be athletic endeavors, or backpacking or camping, or taking my kids to the gym with me, demonstrating what that looks like."

Steve Parelli listened in weariness. He had heard it all before. He raised his hand and argued that homosexual believers should not be excluded from the faith. Theologically, gay people had every right to see themselves in the creation story, not as procreators, but as people who shared a bond of love with each other, and with God. Adam and Eve could be a metaphor for two men or women.

"Interesting," the pastor responded, "but wrong."

A FEW WEEKS later, right before Christmas, I paid a visit to Steve and his partner, Jose Ortiz, at their apartment in the Bronx in New York City. I had introduced myself to Steve after the panel discussion on homosexuality and asked if we could meet. Christmas lights glowed on a small fir, jazz played, and the smell of marinara sauce rose in the kitchen.

I asked Jose and Steve if they still considered themselves to be evangelicals. They started to laugh. "I don't know if the evangelicals would own us," Jose replied.

They told me how they came to faith. Jose grew up in a nominally Catholic Puerto Rican family in Brooklyn. His mother raised him. His father wasn't around. When he was eight, he had his first exposure to evangelicals. Every Sunday, one of his friends went to a small Spanish-speaking church in Williamsburg with his father. "Seeing a kid go to church with his father was really great, and his father was really kind to invite me, and I would attend with them," Jose told me. "When I decided to make a decision about my faith, at the age of twelve, that was my church."

He became vice president of the youth group at his church and took a leadership position with a Christian group at the high school, the Seeker Christian Fellowship. In high school, his nickname was "The Monk." "I used to have this hoody sweater, and on the back of it, it said, 'I love Jesus' and it had my girlfriend's name." Jose laughed. "I brought my Bible to school."

Jose had always considered himself to be different, partially because he was sexually abused as a young kid, once by a neighbor, once by a trusted friend of the family. In his own mind, that difference singled him out from an early age, so he didn't mind being unlike other kids. Normalcy was never an option, and if he was going to stand out, it might as well be for something good and positive. At that point, he'd never had a homosexual experience.

He planned to marry his girlfriend and settle down and lead the whole traditional life. Back then, his best friend, Omar, came to know Christ as his savior through Jose's witness. Omar had been a Jehovah's Witness but he became a born-again Christian and eventually a pastor. Jose and he had remained friends, but the relationship had its tensions.

"Omar doesn't know what to make of us," Steve said.

STEVE PARELLI GREW up in a Baptist home in Syracuse, New York, but Jesus didn't grip his mind until the age of eight, when, one Friday night, a white-haired evangelist came to dinner. At the table, the evangelist told the Parelli family a story about his son, who was about to be married. The evangelist said his son had had a dream about his fiancée, and in the dream, she died and went to heaven. When she got to heaven, she stood at the bottom of a staircase in the presence of Peter the Apostle. On either side of the staircase, bracketing the steps, ran blackboards, and Peter gave her a box of chalk and told her, as she walked up the stairs, to write her sins on the blackboards. "Now, all this is very vivid to me," Steve said. "I'm a second grader, and I'm hearing about blackboard chalk. And here's what happened. The evangelist's son dreamed that his girlfriend kept coming down for more chalk. She kept coming down for more chalk. I remember lying in bed that night and thinking, all that chalk, all that blackboard, and thinking, that could be me."

The next night, a Saturday, when the church pastor asked if anyone wanted to accept Christ, Steve raised his hand. The next morning, at Sunday services, he was baptized. The pastor told the child that somebody had paid the price for his sins, and that was, Jesus Christ. "I really heard it, and I really saw Christ as my substitute," Steve said. In the years after his conversion, Steve said, he became like Jose, a little evangelist, bringing his Bible to school. By the age of thirteen, he'd started buying works of theology with his own money. By the time he was a freshman in college, he was memorizing the book of Galatians in the original Greek and teaching his own divinity school notes at classes at his church. His mind had come alive with the fire of the gospel. As it happened, his body had come alive, too.

†

AT ABOUT THE age of thirteen, Steve went on a weekend wilderness trip with a boys' group at his church, a walk in the Adirondacks followed by a night of camping. Each boy had a tent partner. "As we got into the tent, just at the threshold, I felt a rush, a real rush. I'm going into this tent, and while we're in there, it was hot, and we were lying on top of our sleeping bags, with no clothes on, and it's pitch dark, and he began to talk to me. He really seduced me with his words. It was sexual. I remember him asking about masturbation. He asked me if I'd ever done it in the bathtub or the shower. He told me that I should try it with soap. It wasn't kid talk. He was setting the tone, and I was finding it very stimulating. He said that he wanted to do it with me, and I said no, I wanted to wait for marriage. He said, you're right, if I was a girl. Then he used the words, 'Don't you yearn for it?' That really broke me. Then he mentioned two guys who were older and were also doing things. He said, 'Steve, those two guys, I bet they're doing it right now in their tent.' That did it. He started at my ankle with this real light feather touch, and came up. I was already hard. The talk was just sending me there. When he put his hand on my hard-on, I was in ecstasy. And then he started all over again, down at my ankle. And all I can remember are those light touches. This guy really knew what he was doing."

After that, for the first couple of years of puberty, he was sexually active, but he considered it small-time stuff, mutual masturbation, touching through the clothes in the gym room. At the same time, his faith grew, and he felt called to the ministry. But if he truly wanted to be a pastor, he knew that he would have to give up his sexual habits. He became determined to end the encounters. As his mother had taught him, he would have quiet time with his Bible, and in those moments, he would use scripture to grapple with his sin. "I began to see my homosexuality as something that God had allowed in order for me to depend upon him. I was still young, and I thought, Christ is going to help me."

His efforts paid off for many years, culminating in a trip that he took to Colorado to participate in a national preaching competition, one of the victorious moments in his life. He preached on the subject of America's need for spiritual revival, telling his audience that if the country didn't get revival, its days were numbered. He made reference to Jonah being sent to Nineveh. He won the contest, and the award money paid for his first year at Bible college. That same week, unknown to the people who had listened raptly to his sermon, he achieved another, more personal victory. He spent the entire week in Colorado alone in a room with another guy, a complete stranger. "I remember one night, just praying and praying," he said, "I was on the top bunk, and he was on the bottom, and I really wanted to go down there. But I didn't. I fell asleep. So I won the contest, came home the hero, and I had conquered my sexual desires."

Senior year in high school, everything fell apart. He spent the first half of the year as a missionary on the Caribbean isle of Martinique, and when he came home, he brought a friend, a young man of the island who had never been to the United States. Steve had an infatuation, but his friend didn't share the interest, and that indifference plunged him into depression and prompted him into behavior that still appalls him. One night, while his friend slept, Steve masturbated him in his sleep. The friend woke, furious, and told Steve, in French, that if he somehow picked up a disease from the encounter, Steve would be in a lot of trouble.

"That next morning, I walked all the way to high school," he told me, "and I cried and cried, and I begged for forgiveness."

STEVE AND JOSE met in Manhattan at a therapy group for former gays. When I met them, they had been together eight years. By the time of their first encounter, Jose had dropped out of a ministry in Cleveland, Ohio, moved to New York, and started to work on a degree in school counseling at New York University. He also attended every sexual addiction program that he could find. Steve hadn't yet left his wife and still pastored a fundamentalist congregation in upstate New York. But he'd begun to lose control of his sexual desires and started to go to what is called reparative therapy.

The crisis had hit, at last, after many years in which he and his wife had tried to live with the problem. At the age of forty-two, Steve had been pastoring for two decades. He'd been married to his wife for seventeen years and they had four children. He had met her in Bible college, and before they became engaged, he told her about his sexual desires. During the time they dated, he shared his struggles with her, telling her about sightings of attractive men on buses. After Bible college, he attended seminary in Michigan, and it became clear to him that if he wanted to be a pastor, he needed a wife. One couldn't do the job without an ideal mate, a helpmeet, visible and available to the whole church. But there was never any doubt, he assured me, about his other life. He had told her everything.

The marriage broke down on a vacation in Florida. "I was on a secluded beach with sunbathers. I got to touch this guy's hard-on. That scared me to death. The next day, I told my wife. I should have waited till we got home."

One day, Steve simply left home and the church. His wife kept the house, the children, and his books. She has remained in the faith as a lay preacher, Steve told me, and become an even more committed fundamentalist. At the time of our meeting, Steve hadn't had contact with any of his children. He had missed his daughter's wedding.

JOSE USED PSYCHOLOGY and sociology to struggle with his newly emerging identity. Until he accepted himself, he knew he would never be able to love Steve. His partner, on the other hand, turned to what he knew best. He turned back to scripture, not in devotion this time, but in search of answers. He focused, in particular, on what he called "the clobber passages," gay Christian shop talk for those six or seven points in the Bible where the authors singled out homosexual behavior for attack.

"I've been studying those verses, because I'm an exegete by training," he told me. "That's my love: Hebrew, Greek. I've been studying it all very academically."

That also explained his need to speak up at the ETS study group. As alienated as he was by the attitude toward homosexuality in the room, he also identified with these men who had once been his colleagues and brothers, his fellow disciples in the walk of faith. In his mind, he had never left the faith. I asked him why, after everything, he still believed.

"I had to boil my faith down to the essentials," he said. "Is the resurrection true? That's the only thing that matters. In the end, did Jesus Christ rise from the dead or didn't he? Are those testifying the gospel full of shit or are they speaking to something they witnessed? My answer now is yes. It's historically true. It all happened."

## chapter 25

# *The Castle*

*I*n Marburg, I lost Jesus. I held onto God, but my personal relationship with his son came to an end that year. My salvation literally became history. But my loss of Christ didn't occur in an instant. It took a brutal struggle.

One night, by myself in the French city of Strasbourg, I woke with a fright and fell to the floor of my room in a nameless hotel near the train station. I believed, or so I wrote in my journal, that Satan welled up inside of me in a Dostoyevskian moment. I had been about to embrace him and all his works. I reread this moment in my journal as an adult, and I don't honestly know what to make of it. I don't know anymore what happened in that room. My own words tell me that I woke up in the middle of the night, terrified, and put pen to paper, so afraid of an unnamed assailant that I couldn't turn off the light. It's clear that the assailant had no physical being. Either God or the devil, or both together, had come calling.

The path appeared to part before me. "I can go either of two ways now," I wrote in the wee hours of February 18, 1984, in my bed in the hotel in Strasbourg.

A few weeks before, in a Munich café, after a day spent at the Nazi concentration camp of Dachau, my Svengali professor and his wife chastised me for my approach to "art." I told them that art and creation were very closely linked, that art linked people to the heart of creation. I must have meant the latter word in the Christian sense, and they must have smelled a rotten egg, and so they informed me that I should be careful about making any connection between my work and anything concrete outside of myself. "They told me it's been proven that man has a tendency toward symbolic behavior, toward trying to express the inexpressible, and that art is just a means of trying to encompass that vast section of the universe that is, despite our efforts, impossible to chart."

Within a month of that conversation with my professor, I was backpacking across Europe, an odyssey familiar to a lot of Americans. In my case, the journey became a pilgrimage away from Christ. The university in Marburg gave us six weeks off, and the students in the junior year abroad program scattered in all directions. I took a train to West Berlin and then a plane to Moscow and saw the Kremlin and Red Square and Lenin lying in state. I danced with Russian girls at an all-night disco and saw the emerald domes of the monasteries at Zagorsk. I turned around and followed the compass south from Moscow, by plane and train, to Brindisi, crossing the Adriatic to Athens and the Parthenon, that great pagan shrine to the gods overthrown by Christ.

Then it was on to Istanbul, where I saw the Theodosian walls, built by a Roman emperor in the fourth century A.D., my first real encounter with Roman civilization, and where I first heard the muezzin's call from the minaret beside the Hagia Sofia, the great church of Byzantium, now a mosque, my first real taste of the faith of Islam. From Istanbul, I went to Israel, to Bethlehem, and saw the place where my personal savior had been born, according to tradition. I saw the grotto where Mary and Joseph allegedly hid. There was history everywhere, and yes, I thought, the story of Jesus had happened, but it began to feel less than divine. Christ began to feel less like God and more like the cornerstone of the dilapidated Church of the Holy Sepulchre, a shrine founded by the Empress Helena, mother of the Emperor Constantine, and extremely hard to distinguish from a tourist trap.

In the Judean wilderness, in the hills above the Dead Sea, I fell down old stone steps carved in the side of a valley and broke my arm. My friends had gone. I had no car, and no train ran from the Dead Sea back to Jerusalem. I had to hitchhike while cradling my broken arm in a handkerchief given me by the man who ran the camp at the Dead Sea. A truck full of Palestinians picked me up. They asked me where I came from, I told them Dallas, Texas, and they began to clap their hands and chant, "Bobby! Bobby! Bobby!" a character from the TV show *Dallas*. I was carrying a Cross in My Pocket, the same kind that Julie had given to her boyfriend, but my own popular culture suddenly loomed larger in the Holy Land than the crucifix, binding me loosely to people in another world, a political, social, and economic world that seemed to run fine without the help of Jesus.

I crossed an Israeli checkpoint in that truck of Palestinians, and it triggered a response. At the airport, my backpack was dissected, and the cast on my arm had to be inspected roughly and repeatedly. My passport had East German stamps, and it aroused suspicion. My neighbor on the El Al flight out of Tel Aviv watched me over the top of his newspaper. When I got to Athens, before I could reach the baggage carousel, a man in a suit greeted me by name. One of his colleagues found a foil full of white powder in my backpack. He grinned with satisfaction at me, stuck his finger in the white stuff, and tasted. "Salt!" I cried. It was for use with a boiled egg.

A few minutes later, he found the Cross in My Pocket, and he stopped the search. I was a Christian, he believed. I carried the cross. I was no terrorist, and I didn't appear to be a drug dealer. In that moment, Jesus had intervened, but for the first time, his intervention felt cultural rather than supernatural.

AFTER I WALKED away from Jesus Christ, my life improved dramatically. It would be impossible to list everything here, but the greatest of these wonders would have to be my wife, whom I met several years after Marburg in a writing program at the University of Iowa.

There were other women before her. First, on my path toward Debra, came the Englishwoman, Harriet, who declared to me with a mischievous but sincere grin over beer in a college dive that she practiced Marxism, feminism, hedonism, and atheism and enjoyed each without much effort or sense of guilt. After Harriet came the Southern woman with whom I lost my virginity. She smoked clove cigarettes and loved Eudora Welty. Two more women helped to lift me out of the dark hole of bad hygiene, which had once seemed to me the hallmark of a truly religious sensibility, heedless of worldly considerations.

Debra caught my eye right away, though I had a girlfriend, and she soon got a boyfriend. In Iowa, in the graduate writing program, we became friends, and when it came time to go the next step, in a fit of profound nervousness, I confessed to her right off the bat that I saw destiny at work, only it no longer tasted of my old faith. It was something larger, fixed in human time by our birthdays—she had been born exactly nine months to the day after me.

If we stayed together, I would have to turn my back for good—in the flesh, where it counted—on the things that had meant so much to me just a few years before. But, truthfully, I wasn't thinking too much about God in her company, at least not in the sense of Bibles and prophecies. The cold war had ended by this time. The Berlin wall had fallen, and we had been living for a year in the new Berlin, once divided, now unified. Two years after we moved in together, I proposed to her on the top of steps beside the Hradcany Palace in Prague, in Czechoslovakia, overlooking the spires of the city, above the flow of the Vltava River. Prague had special meaning for Debra. Her father's family had emigrated from Bohemia at the end of the nineteenth century, from the city of Pilsen and surrounding villages, but members of his extended family had gone to law school in Prague, and a few were buried in the large Jewish cemetery in Zelivskeho, also the final resting place of the writer Kafka. Distant relatives had been murdered in the Holocaust, one of them our son's namesake, and her family name was inscribed in a stone wall in the medieval Jewish cemetery of Prague.

On the same trip when I proposed, we went together to visit her relatives and see Dr. Kafka in the new cemetery. And a decade and a half later, when I showed up in Prague for a conference on intelligent design sponsored by an American entity called the Discovery Institute, I sought out the cemetery again.

THE CONFERENCE HAD been the brainchild of Charles Thaxton, a chemist considered to be one of the founders of a philosophical and scientific movement that had begun to make its way onto university campuses and into high school textbooks in the mid-1990s. Before the movement had a name, long before it was even a movement, Thaxton had written one of the first books on the subject back in the 1970s, a critique of Charles Darwin's theories on evolution as they might pertain to the origins of life on earth. As a chemist and as a Christian, Thaxton simply didn't accept that natural selection explained the means by which life emerged on earth. Mainstream science distanced itself from the question of ultimate origins for lack of evidence, but Thaxton suspected that mainstream science had no interest in exploring the possibility of an intelligent and intelligible source at creation. He didn't say so then, but he believed that more evidence supported the intervention of a creator than supported the random workings of natural selection.

Years later, his theories would become part of a corpus of ideas known as intelligent design, ID for short, and he would play an editorial role on an ID textbook called *Of Pandas and People*, which would become a lightning rod in battles over school curricula. A few months before I met him in Prague, he had appeared at public hearings over intelligent design in Topeka, Kansas, where he had maintained that randomness could not explain the very precisely calibrated parameters within which life had formed on earth. The Prague conference had been his brainchild.

Scheduled over two days, it took place in the Congress Center, known in Communist times as the Palace of Culture, a classic piece of late cold war, east bloc architecture. Communist functionaries had met in its halls time and again to enjoy their power in a godless, Darwin-friendly world. To hold a conference challenging Darwin within its walls already felt like a symbolic act of defiance—and appropriate: the first speaker, Dr. Stephen Meier, would devote his opening comments to the persecution of intelligent design scientists back in the United States. By association, they became dissidents, and the American scientific establishment became a dictatorship.

Americans manned the registration tables, but the main hall of the Congress Center was filled with hundreds of Czechs, and a few Hungarian and German speakers. Seven hundred people from eighteen countries attended. Most of the participants appeared to be students in the sciences. I saw a few crosses dangling. A tall, collared, silver-haired dignitary sat beside me,

speaking Austrian-accented German to his neighbor, and I later heard that
he was a high official in the archdiocese of the Roman Catholic Church in
Vienna. I recognized Charles Thaxton from his photograph on the conference website. He moved with speed and purpose in a wheelchair. A missing
leg didn't prevent constant activity.

I noticed someone else, a truly bizarre figure who telegraphed trouble
right away. He snapped belligerent photographs of a pianist playing ragtime
airs on the stage before the conference. The long, brown ponytail, the pale,
jowly face with a five o'clock shadow, and the aggressive way of walking
about, despite a pot belly, as if he had a distinct and hostile mission in the
hall, all suggested subversion. But on top of these, he also wore a black eye
patch, the strap running diagonally down his face, left to right, and this suggested true anarchy. His associate skulked behind, with an emaciated body,
an equally pale face patched with scraps of blond beard. The one with the
eye patch handed the camera to his friend. They glanced at each other in conspiracy and took their seats near me in the front row.

The speakers that day consisted of a roster of Discovery Institute fel-
lows who would each take a piece of the intelligent design puzzle. The
Discovery Institute had been founded in 1990 as part of a campaign by Christians to urge the sciences to be more open to a "theistic" worldview. With
the help of a Czech interpreter, the scientists would present the proofs of
their worldview. Every speaker had a Ph.D., some more than one, and the
high provenance of the degrees could not be denied. The entirely male panel
had been educated at Cambridge and Oxford, Yale and Berkeley, Princeton
and Columbia. Many of them were philosophers of science with sidelines in
some area of biology or physics. One, a Brit, was a mathematician; another,
an American, a research biologist with a doctorate in divinity from Yale;
yet another, a Dutchman, a biophysicist and a specialist in nanotechnology.
Another bit of information, not listed in the biographical materials, emerged
halfway through the conference, prompted by a question. The speakers all
believed in God.

After an introduction, Stephen Meier, the head of the Discovery Institute, opened the conference, officially titled "Darwin and Design: A Challenge for Twenty-First-Century Science."

"Today we will discuss what the most recent scientific evidence can tell us about how life and the universe came to be," he began. "Did life arise from a purely undirected material process, as Darwin and evolutionists have long said, or is there evidence of design, of intelligent design, in the universe and in living things. It's a great privilege to discuss this question freely and openly here in this great city with its long tradition of open inquiry, in valuing debate and dissent. Many of you may know that the idea of intelligent design has become very controversial in the United States and even beyond."

This statement laid the groundwork for a grim message. A period of repression had come, unmistakable in its effects, Meier told the audience. Opinions were being suppressed. Jobs were being lost. Careers were being destroyed. On a screen above the stage appeared the words: "Thought Criminals?"

He told a story about a public television station in New Mexico. The station had planned to air a film called *Unlocking the Mystery of Life* until a group of "angry Darwinian scientists" waged a letter-writing and call-in campaign to suppress the film. The New Mexico station decided not to air it. A Smithsonian publication, *Proceedings of the Biological Society of Washington*, had published a paper by Meier himself, and the editor of the publication, Dr. Richard Sternberg, experienced "severe recriminations in his position as editor and scientist" at the Smithsonian. Sternberg "had been denied access to his office, his samples, and had been threatened with termination in his position as a scientist for allowing an article to be published which made a scientific case for the idea of intelligent design."

Meier went on to say that scientists in the United States had lost research funding, had been denied tenure, had been overlooked for jobs, and even terminated from their teaching positions for questioning Darwinian evolution openly or discussing intelligent design. As a result, the U.S. news media had become fascinated by this debate, but had come down in opposition to intelligent design, relegating it to a species of "warmed-over creationism," based entirely on religion with no scientific evidence to support it. The conference would attempt to challenge that view and answer a few questions: What was ID? Why did people want to "suppress" it? Why did so many people want to "silence debate" on the subject?

Meier pointed out that intelligent design was nothing new. Until the latter half of the nineteenth century, few scientists would have challenged the existence of some kind of creator. Isaac Newton made explicit reference to God in his groundbreaking works on physics. But by the time of Albert Einstein at the start of the twentieth century, God doesn't figure at all, and Darwin had made a vital first step in that direction. He dispensed with the argument for design in the field of biology by offering a mechanism that would conjure the appearance of design without the reality. That mechanism we know as natural selection.

Darwin pointed out that ranchers and farmers changed the characteristics of animals to adapt to the environment in which they lived, breeding the woolliest male and female sheep to create a breed better adapted to cold weather. If human breeders could do it, why not nature itself? So from the very beginning, Meier told his audience, the mechanism of evolution, natural selection, had been understood as a substitute for design, because natural selection made the design argument unnecessary. In the Darwinian view, you have design without a designer.

And this is the deep horror. Christian intellectuals and scientists don't see evolution as merely one theory that can work without God. It's *the* theory that displaces God in the modern world. They see it as the theory that definitively kills God. If you don't need God for the creation of life on earth, then what on earth does one need God for? If God missed creation, then what did he actually do? Scientific theory isn't at stake here. If most Americans still believed that Jesus Christ was the son of God and acted accordingly, there would be no need for this debate. As it is, tens of millions of Christian kids get educated every year in the theory of evolution as a fact of existence, and this theory is seen in Christian circles as an annihilating force, wiping out the generations. There has to be some other credible theory, some other explanation; otherwise, Darwinist reality will supplant theological reality once and for all.

IN ONE OF my favorite novels, Franz Kafka's *The Castle*—like the King James Bible, an indispensable book in my life—the first paragraph of the opening chapter describes how I have come to view the world as an adult.

The protagonist of the work is called K. He has been offered a job in a town with a castle. As the novel opens, he arrives at the town and receives his first impression of the place where he will live and work.

Kafka writes: "It was late evening when K. arrived. The town lay in deep snow. The castle on the hill could not be seen. Fog and darkness rose around it, and not even the smallest light illuminated the shape. K. waited a long time on the wooden bridge that led from the road to the town, looking up at the apparent emptiness."

To me, this image is mysterious and beautiful and terrifying; for all its simplicity, the paragraph places me at the very edge of what words can express about our existence. In my life, in this world in which I find myself, it is always late evening, and I am always just arriving. I can always see just enough before me to make out the road that I have just left, and the place to which I am headed, but not much more. I am always in transit, between the road and the town, never quite leaving the road, never quite arriving home. And yet what lies before me, invisible, is momentous. I can feel the presence of the world, even in the darkness and snow. The castle may not show itself, but it is real, inevitably and indelibly real, just as the world is absolutely real beyond our words and constructions.

But I also know that I will never see the castle. In this life, as I understand it, it will never be daylight and never be summer. The heart of this world will always remain beyond my sight, and I will never get to the gates of the castle until I arrive at my death. To me, this is not a statement of futility or alienation or isolation. It is not despair, and it's not belief. It is an accurate description of what I have found, and what I have found is a world in which expectation is everything, satisfaction almost nothing. And I, as a human being, am always poised in that state.

I hear atheists like Richard Dawkins attempting to dismiss thoughts of God as species childishness, or design theorists positing clear proof of a creator, and both sound to me like failures of imagination. Neither view, scientific or theist, reaches the Castle. Neither can. Yet both positions demand a choice. Both positions exact a price. If I believe like Dawkins, I am damned. If I believe like Meier, I am blind. And if I don't choose, in each case, I am merely a man who can't make up his mind.

†

AFTER MEIER MADE his presentation, he left the podium, and the anarchic man with the ponytail and his associate, the skinny one, leapt from their seats. The eye patch had switched faces. The skinny guy wore it now. They cornered Meier, and I eavesdropped.

At first, I couldn't understand much. They asked him heated questions about mitochondrial DNA, and Meier endeavored to answer. The two interrogators nodded with an air of growing sympathy, and he asked them with a polite collegiality who they might be.

"Pastafarians," the ponytail guy blurted, a little too fast, so I got the impression that he had been bursting for hours to deliver the punch line.

"I'm not familiar with that," Meier said.

"We believe that the world was created by a Flying Spaghetti Monster. He created the mountains, the sky, the trees . . ."

Meier began to nod his head, smiling. "Oh, right, I've heard about this. What's the eye patch?"

"It's the symbol of our religion. The first pastafarians were pirates who gave candy to kids."

Meier looked at his watch. "I'd like to talk to you guys some more."

They understood. They thanked him for his time, and I stepped up. They introduced themselves: Vojtech, the big one, and Mike, the skinny one. I didn't know, until they told me, the real story of the Flying Spaghetti Monster. It was a pseudo-religion, Vojtech said, invented by an American physics graduate named Bobby Henderson to protest the teaching of intelligent design in Kansas schools. Pastafarians got their name by combining the words "pasta" and "Rastafarian," thus commingling the two central features of the invention: its basis in grains and religion. The Flying Spaghetti Monster had its own website, which they loved almost as much as their favorite movie, *Fear and Loathing in Las Vegas*. They had heard about the conference and resolved to make a show of principle. Vojtech was an endocrinologist, Mike a physicist. Both despised religion.

I bring them up, because only three people stood up and challenged the science at the conference, these two young men and one other. Everyone else seemed to agree with the basic premises, and I had the impression that most people had attended in order to share a common vision. Few had come to be convinced. At the Congress Center, seated around me, were people who were already doing research into intelligent design at various central European universities, and it was clear that they feared for their jobs if their institutions found out about their work. It was unlikely that other pastafarians were in attendance.

The next morning, Vojtech, Mike, and I made our way to the question-and-answer session at the Hotel Krystal in a suburb of Prague, just around the corner from the former Marxism-Leninism night school, or so Vojtech informed me after lighting up a joint in an open-air park that lay between the subway and the tram. As the tram carried us up a hill to the Hotel Krystal, Vojtech unzipped his black coat and revealed the image on his T-shirt, George W. Bush within a red circle, a red bar across the face. Above the image ran the words, "No More Bushit." In his view, the speakers had overstated the importance of the evidence for their view and understated the holes in their arguments. They had made their positions appear self-evident and lab-tested, when, in fact, most of their assertions about intelligent design in origins were highly speculative and could never be proven, because no concrete evidence remained from the earliest days of biological life.

In the event, Vojtech sat right in front of Stephen Meier, who tried to ignore him, but as soon as the floor opened to questions, the Czech endocrinologist stood and let the American believer have it.

THE DAY AFTER the conference, feeling jet-lagged and lonely, having retraced my steps to the exact spot where I had proposed to my wife fifteen years before, I got on the subway and went out to the graveyard where Kafka and my wife's relatives were buried. It was a fine, blue-skied October day, golden leaves on the cement moving around in a warm breeze. At the cemetery, I found the gates locked. It was the perfect ending to my rather Kafkaesque visit. A Jewish holiday, Sukkoth or Purim, had shut the place down. I could see the branches of trees rustling in breezes, but there were no people.

My wife's family graves couldn't be seen. I had a memory of their location. They lay far back from the fence line. The names and the dates on the relatively recent stones indicated that they'd had a better twentieth century than some of her relatives. They had survived the Holocaust and died as Czech citizens with Slavicized last names. For a while, I sat on a ledge and sunned myself. My wife's family's names could be found on another piece of stone, on a wall within the confines of the much more ancient Jewish grave-yard in the old ghetto of Prague. On another trip, we had traveled to Pilsen and its environs to find whatever traces remained of the family past. In one village, we visited the house that had belonged to her grandmother's family and seen the family who had moved in after the original inhabitants had been taken to concentration camps. An old relative who had fled the Nazis in 1938 had helped us locate other places, graveyards out in the woods, one of them buried so completely under vines and trees that we almost missed it. The stones had looked like tree stumps.

I remembered that Kafka's grave stood next to the fence line, and I thought, at the very least, I might be able to see it. Sure enough, the oblong tomb bearing his name, Dr. Franz Kafka, occupied a plot near one of the gates. I sat on a warm ledge outside the cemetery gates and became drowsy. Dreamily, I began to entertain a horrible thought. Kafka burned in hell. At first, I tried to banish the thought from my mind, but it wouldn't leave. If Don and Lillie McWhinney were right, if Stephen Meier was right, if the young Reverend Steven Parelli was right, Franz Kafka, one of the great nov-elists in history, a witty and charming and slightly withdrawn man, a favorite of the ladies, though an avoider of marriage, a man whose work had meant so much to me personally, burned in hell for all eternity.

Yes, he was a Jew, and lots of Christians believed that Jews got a special deal in the divine plan, but those only seemed to be Jews who converted to Christianity. That would never be Kafka. I teased out the implications. Many of Kafka's family had been murdered by the Nazis. He himself had died young from a horrible disease. In his imagination, he had created a world in which a person could wake one morning and be transformed into a bug, in which tor-ture consisted of machines writing illegible words on human bodies, in which men were convicted of crimes they never committed, in which travelers were lured to towns where they would be despised and hated. And now, if one ac-cepted even for a moment the legalistic definition of human existence laid out by Calvinist and Arminian Bible-believing Christians, one had to accept that this strange man had landed in the very place that he had described in his books. His imagination had simply captured his own eternity. This is what Don or Lillie might say, or better yet their pastor Tommy Nelson. No redemption for that heathen in the outback, none for that Hegelian in Highland Park, none at all for Franz Kafka.

BUT THE TRULY Kafkaesque moment occurred back at the conference, toward the end of the question-and-answer session. A modestly dressed woman in the row behind me stood up, identified herself as a scientist in crisp, accented English, and began to attack the panelists.

"You cannot say such things," she said, "especially not to an audience of lay people, who have no idea what you are talking about, and this leads me to one major point I would like to make about this conference. I'm a Christian. I believe in God. I believe in creation, so, of course, I'm very positive about the intelligent design argument. But how it's presented here by some of the speakers is really suppressing evidence and information, so with your oversimplified examples, you can maybe impress the public, or impress some people who have no clue what you're talking about, but any scientist would tear apart almost every word you say."

A stunned silence followed her speech. She had called the bluff, this fellow Christian. After the interpreter translated for the Czech audience, the British mathematician thanked her emphatically for the comment. He spoke in a tone soothing, reasonable, and ultimately sympathetic. "I would share your concern at giving any impression of blinding the public with undigested science," he conceded. "And I get the impression that all my colleagues share that view. One of the problems is that this is a highly interdisciplinary kind of discussion. It goes over the boundary of mathematics, physics, and so on. So I tell you how I proceed in my own university. I will not say anything to a public general audience that I have not submitted to my colleagues who are experts and do not share my background beliefs. In other words, I submit what I think to the domain at the highest level of science that I can reach, and I think that's the spirit of true science, because of a fundamental concern to get at the truth of things. I would like to assure you that I respond very much to what you say, because when you are trying to communicate something that really questions a reigning paradigm, like Kepler did so long ago, the question of academic credibility is crucial, and there is a danger of overstating the case, and there is a danger of selective evidence misleading people. But what I would like to say is that is true of both sides of the discussion, and therefore a basic principle in my own procedure is first to gain the respect of colleagues who differ from me completely, who are at the top level of science, and I very often give lectures with them where they take the diametrically opposed point of view."

When the conference ended, one or two of the speakers rushed to meet the dissenting woman, as if she had to be reassured yet again. It had been the one and only serious challenge to anything said at the conference, and the panelists took it seriously at first. I walked up behind her and listened while she explained her position to the Dutch nanotechnology expert. I almost gasped out loud.

She turned out to be a Young Earth creationist, which meant that, as a scientist, a geneticist, to be precise, she believed in a theory so far outside the pale of accepted science that not even the intelligent design people could go along. She believed that the earth had been created approximately 10,000 to 30,000 years ago, as opposed to the generally accepted number of 4 billion years ago, and that the fossil record had been scrambled by a great flood, confusing establishment scientists in their time lines. Moreover, in order to buy that theory, she couldn't believe in the efficacy of carbon-14 dating techniques. In other words, the most vehement critic of the intelligent design conference hadn't come from the comfortable precincts of mainstream science. She came from an even more extreme position. Later, Meier told me it was the fourth time in a month he'd had a heated conversation with a hypersensitive Young Earth creationist. I staggered out of that conference and headed straight for the Jewish cemetery.

## chapter 26

# Habakkuk

*T*<sup>*hat*</sup> was October 2005, a tense season for believers. The conflict between intelligent design theorists and Young Earth creationists mirrored the conflict between Calvinists and Arminians, between Emerging Church and fundamentalist, between gay and straight evangelicals, egalitarians and complementarians, conservatives and liberals—and all of that conflict played itself out in a particularly important way between two watershed political events, the 2004 presidential election and the 2006 midterm elections. Between those two moments, the first an unqualified victory for Bible-believing conservative Christians, the second a disheartening reversal, my narrative runs its course. Over the course of those two years, the war inside the faith became its defining reality.

Ironically, it looked, from the outside, like the opposite of a conflict. In 2004, numbers, voices, and images gave the appearance of a vast and purposeful unity. In that election, 75 percent of those who described themselves as evangelical or born-again voted for George W. Bush. Believers stoked his win, his numbers increasing among Catholics and Jews as well, and commentators wrote of a surge in moral-values voters, as if everyone who had checked that box in the exit polls possessed the same moral DNA. Other results seemed to bear out the interpretation. Same-sex marriage bans passed in eleven states. The marriage issue, used as a campaign cornerstone by the Bush White House, drove millions of normally complacent citizens to the polls, or so said the conservative Christian activists. "The marriage issue was the great iceberg in this election," Robert Knight, the director of the Culture and Family Institute, told the *Washington Post*. "Most people saw only the tip and didn't realize the great mass was affecting races all over the country, right up to the presidential contest."

David Barton, wearing his hat as a Republican Party political strategist, pointed to four issues that converged in 2004 to make what might be called a tipping point. "One, the Judge Roy Moore case," he said, referring to the case of an Alabama state supreme court judge, Roy Moore, who had commissioned a 5,280-pound chunk of granite inscribed with the Ten Commandments to be placed on the grounds of the court. When another judge ordered him to remove the monument, he refused to comply, and the case went all the way to the Supreme Court, which forced him to remove it. He and his "rock" became a conservative Christian cause célèbre. "Most people didn't agree with the way Moore handled it," Barton explained to me, "but they agreed with his right to display the commandments. That was a 77 percent issue across the board, and it's stayed steady at that since then."

Then there was the Lawrence, Texas, battle over sodomy, which pitted two gay men against the state, in a case to decide the legality of their arrest by Houston police officers for having sex together in a private home. In 2003, on grounds of privacy and equal protection under the law, the Supreme Court ruled that all sodomy laws were unconstitutional.

The Pledge of Allegiance case, deciding whether God could be mentioned in the pledge, turned the question of church and state into a third reason to go to the polls, and gay marriage made the fourth.

"Those four things," Barton said. "Suddenly, it's no longer theoretical stuff out there that you argue about at universities. We're now talking, 'My kid can't say God in the pledge,' and 'I can't see the Ten Commandments if I want to,' and 'I can have all this behavior going around me if they agree to it.' I'm just convinced that these were the factors, because of the fact that this is the first cycle in all my years of being involved in politics that judges actually became an issue in the campaign."

In the previous election, in 2000, 14 million fewer evangelical voters had gone to the polls, resulting in a dead heat. In 2004, those numbers jumped significantly, and the Republicans came out on top.

At the Petroleum Club in Midland, Texas, during a boom year, I had lunch with a group of west Texas women, including my Aunt Margaret, who had spent most of their lives around the oil industry. Over steak salads and virgin marys, seated next to tables of oil executives, we chatted about the president, politics, and religion. The oldest of the women had known George W. Bush since he was a young man. Most had been Republicans until recently, all considered themselves to be Christian, but none were evangelicals. Two of the women, however, had evangelical children, and the matter caused tension in their families. The women couldn't bear the rock music at their sons' and daughters' churches. They couldn't bear the hands in the air, or the sermonizing about damnation and hell, or the relentless assaults on homosexuality.

Until the mid-1980s, one of them had been actively involved in grass-roots Republican politics. She saw herself as a typical west Texas conservative who had been impressed with George W. Bush as governor and had voted for him for president in 2000 and 2004. She knew that he had a religious side, but she hadn't seen the overt expression of that faith when he was governor; it hadn't existed back then, she believed, or not to the same degree. She believed, as many Texas conservatives did, that he became a different man in the White House, and in alienating ways.

Her perception had also been colored by the faith of one of her sons. He had left the Presbyterian church in which he had been reared, where she and her husband still attended, and started attending a megachurch with his wife, who had a more fundamentalist bent. Once, after going to service at her son's church, she took him to lunch and let him know what she thought. "I said, listen, I want to tell you, I think that's a lot of bigotry that they're preaching up there. I don't think that's Christianity. When you get down to what is Christianity, most of us can't practice it, it's way too demanding. Concern for the poor, concern for the less fortunate. All of that is absent and what they've got is a reinforcement of cultural prejudices. 'You don't like gays? Well, good, we're going to give you a reason not to like gays. You don't want this? We're going to give you a reason not to want that, and we're going to find it in the Bible.'"

She had been struggling for years with the intrusion of religion into the Republican Party. She recalled that her first political encounter with a more radical version of conservatism had been in San Jacinto, Texas, when Gerald Ford first ran for president in the late 1970s. The head of the state political party put her on the resolutions committee as a sop to the liberal wing, which she considered to be the moderate wing. She was outvoted on every single resolution, she recalled. Someone on the committee stood up and said that he wanted a constitutional amendment against deficit spending, but that was overruled. Republican conventions weren't that well attended back then. "Very few of us really do it, but I did it because I'm interested in my country, and I want to vote and I want to have my say. And I like—I liked, past tense—the Republican Party."

Years after the San Jacinto convention, when George H. W. Bush first ran for president in 1988, she and her husband went to the convention and had a shock. The Reagan years had made quite a change. "The party had gotten bigger and much more conservative. And they were passing resolutions, like getting out of the United Nations, no abortion, no deficit. My goodness. We were astounded that the party that we loved, the party of my parents, who were Republicans all their lives, had gone this way. All of a sudden, we're filling a hall full of these very conservative people. We walked out and said, maybe we are Democrats."

PEOPLE LIKE DAVID BARTON drove her, and people like her, out of the party in Texas, and, increasingly, out of the national party. I have focused attention on Barton for a number of reasons. He's influential and powerful in the evangelical world, and his reach extends far beyond politics into classrooms and courtrooms. Other people wield greater power and just as much influence, and their names are better known. Certainly, politicians have a greater ability to effect actual change. What sets Barton apart is the scope of his work. If one person seems to embody every aspect of the effort to return the Christian faith to the civic center of the national life, he is it. The range of his ambition is also emblematic of everything that is happening now in the body politic of the body of Christ, everything that scares secular people and unnerves and inspires many Christians.

He has been called a reconstructionist and a dominionist by his critics, and therefore labeled a theocrat, a charge that he vehemently denies. A theocracy would require abrogation of the rights and powers of the Constitution, and he would die, he said, before he would let that happen. What he doesn't say is that, within the bounds of the Constitution, many of his goals to bring Christianity back to government can be accomplished. He believes, for instance, that the wall of separation between church and state is a willful misinterpretation of a single line from Thomas Jefferson, enabled and upheld by people as determined to keep faith out of government as he is to return it to its rightful place.

But it would be misleading to imply that Barton's program is the usual mainstream conservatism. He would say that his positions on gay marriage, abortion, the pledge of allegiance, and "activist" judges reflect the views of large majorities across the United States, but his views on the role that faith ought to play in the government would be far more controversial. Where a Republican like the woman earlier, for instance, might reach for political and economic solutions to political and economic problems, Barton emphasizes religious solutions to those same problems, arguing for biblical views on everything from the inheritance tax to foreign policy. He also embodies a truth that every secular American should understand: this movement will far outlast the presidency of George W. Bush.

"There's a good scripture in Ecclesiastes," Barton told me. "Cast your bread on many waters. That's what I do. I work the immediate, the short-term, the long-term. On the one hand, I'm going to bust my tail to get good judges appointed now. In the middle term, I'm going to work my tail off in Senate elections, to make a difference in the kind of people we get."

"At the same time," he said, "part of what we do every summer, we handpick about 120 kids out of law school that some day want to be federal judges . . . and we'll intern them for twelve weeks over the summer. We'll say, look, here's what you get in law school, we know—we teach there— but here's what the Constitution says, here's what history says, here's what precedent has been. You need to know this as well as what you're getting taught in law school. And so now that's twenty years down the road. Even if they graduate this year, it's going to take twenty years' experience before they get put on a federal bench, and that's assuming you get the right president and everything else. At the same time, if we're turning out 120 of these kids every year for the next twenty years, you're going to have a bigger pool to pull from, and that's part of the judicial solution."

Nothing better exemplifies the broad front of his campaign than his Pastors Briefings on Capitol Hill, where he folds history, faith, politics, and the future into a single argument on behalf of Christian government. For Barton, pastors are the key to mobilizing evangelical votes now. One can go door to door, but once a week at least, millions of believers gather in churches around the country and listen to leaders whose credibility with their audiences most politicians could never touch. In the 2004 election, Barton told me, record numbers of pastors got involved in state and national races, and he wants to insure that their participation holds over time.

So, every year, he brings groups of between fifty and a hundred men and women, ministers and their wives, for an overnight trip to Washington, D.C. In the evening, he takes his wards into the past, an evening tour, in the presence of a sponsoring member of Congress, through the echoing halls of the Capitol, down into the vault of the old Supreme Court chambers, into the neoclassical Senate and House rooms, now and then into the Congressional Prayer Room, and on rare occasions into the place where the fifth president of the United States, John Quincy Adams, died, now the Ladies Lounge. The next day, they gather in a room in a House or Senate office building for a strenuous eight hours of information gathering. The roster of speakers testifies to Barton's clout. On my visit, Senators Sam Brownback and Tom Coburn, Representatives Marilyn Musgrave and Walter Jones, head of the White House Office of Public Liaison Tim Goeglein, and Congressional chaplain Barry Black all made appearances. In earlier days, former Senate majority leader Bill Frist and former House majority leader Tom DeLay spoke to the group. It's a Republican affair, for the most part, though if the Democratic Party picks up more evangelical members, Barton says, that could change. As part of my agreement in attending a briefing, I have left the comments of the speakers off the record, but I can say that their presentations reflected substantially the worldview and concerns of Christians echoed throughout this book.

I ATTENDED A briefing for African American pastors, a group of about fifty men and women from all over the country. There were plenty of Democrats in the room.

On the night of the Capitol tour, in the Rotunda, Republican Representative Bobby Jindal of Louisiana, Barton's fan and friend, joined us. Before the tour began, he praised the pastors of his state, and churches around the country, for helping out in the wake of Hurricane Katrina, which had hit his district hard. The tour began. Famous paintings of the era of discovery and settlement encircled us. Barton pulled off his black cowboy boots, revealing bright white socks, and climbed onto the red leather of a bench, the better to project. No matter what one believes, Barton makes a remarkable guide. His enthusiasm has a childlike quality, the son of an aeronautics engineer who designed military hardware, raised on a West Texas ranch, never much of a history student, struck between the eyes by a providential view of the American past and called by God to preach the national destiny to religious and government leaders. More than once, I had a chill up my spine. The pastors demonstrated their own enthusiasm. When the briefing ended the following day, Barton received a standing ovation.

The night before, he had pointed out four paintings on one side of the Rotunda, each of which had been hanging since 1824: Columbus landing in the western world in 1492, the explorer kneeling down in a prayer service; De Soto discovering the Mississippi River in 1541, accompanied by a priest; the baptism of Pocahontas at Jamestown in 1613; and the embarkation of the Pilgrims for America in 1621. "Just notice these four pictures right here," he said. "What you've got, here in the Capitol, are two prayer meetings, a Bible study, and a Baptism. It's not real secular. And that's the way the Capitol is. It is loaded with religious history and religious symbolism."

His wife, Cheryl, handed him a red-jacketed Bible, and he showed us the same page in the same Bible that opened in the painting of the Pilgrims. The Bible in his hand was a copy of the Bible in the painting. It was a Geneva Bible, part of his personal collection. "This particular Bible I hold in my hand," he told us, his voice echoing, "was one of the Pilgrims' Bibles. It's a 1590 Bible, so it's 415 years old."

An audible gasp went through the crowd. Time and again, his point seemed to be that the building in which we stood was a kind of church, and every corner of the church reflected the belief of a people in a sovereign God. In fact, the Capitol had been used for decades in the nineteenth century as a place of worship, long before the opposition between church and state became a feature of the democracy. In the course of the briefing the following day, he would make clear that the spiritual life of the Capitol remained alive and well, with members of Congress in prayer groups and Bible studies, holding each other accountable for casting biblical votes, that is, votes in accordance with an orthodox evangelical view of scripture.

Since 2000, Barton has done seventy-five such tours. During the one I attended, the columns of the Capitol, descended from that classical pre-Christian pagan past of which Barton rarely if ever speaks, seemed to watch our group from the shadows, phantoms outraged by their glaring omission.

I'LL CLOSE WITH three portraits in miniature—three people whom I met in the Capitol. Between them, one may glimpse the difficulty of compressing the Christian political experiment in the United States into a tidy and comforting box.

One was Catherine Flowers, the single, African American mother of a nine-year-old boy. She had been the press secretary for Mitch Landrieu, the lieutenant governor of Louisiana and a Democrat, until Hurricane Katrina chased her out of New Orleans forever. In the storm, she had lost her home, her church, her job, and ultimately her city. She went to Houston and continued to work for the state of Louisiana a while longer, running as liaison between Landrieu and the national press via her cell phone. The performance of her mayor, Ray Nagin, had disgusted her, and she swore to me, a few days before the election, that if voters put him back in, she'd never go back. They did, and she stayed in Houston, where she had already landed an administrative job at another church. She had been impressed by David Barton's presentation, but had the feeling that it was a lot of talk and no follow-through. No one had called her in the aftermath, and that was a mistake, she told me, because she would consider switching parties if someone made the right overture. She no longer had any deep loyalty to the Democratic Party, but she refused to be taken for a ride by Republicans. Despite storm and flight, her Christian faith remained unbroken, though she was a little more cynical about American politics.

The second was Jack Crans, one of three white males, besides Barton and me, on the tour. Crans believed in the larger cause of bringing Christianity back to government and had worked for thirty years in the Chester County Jail as a chaplain and reformer. He also taught a faith-based program for police officers, called Pointman Leadership Institute, and he included among his friends John Ashcroft and former Los Angeles police chief Robert Vernon. He referred to these leaders as "the men who sigh and cry." He meant that, in his view, they had a wounded heart for the devastation that they saw in the criminal justice system in the United States. Jack had labored for years to get more middle-class and upper-middle-class churches involved in prison ministries, but he found the institutions wanting. He had worked for decades to bring a moral code back to police officers and prison wardens, encountering stiff resistance all the way. He also ran a Bible camp in the summers for urban black kids from the blighted, rust-belt city of Coatesville, Pennsylvania. He and his wife lived in a house on the grounds, and everything they owned belonged to the camp.

On the Monday before the 2006 midterm elections, we spent the day together, and we didn't talk much at all about the races. That Sunday morning, before my arrival, he gave the prayer and sermon for a gathering of former members of the honor guard at the Tomb of the Unknown Soldier. That had made an impact on him. Jack believed that men of honor, "men who sigh and cry," must man the walls of the nation again. He believed that such men were hard to find. His sense of mission stemmed from the Old Testament book of Habakkuk, chapter 2, verse 1: "I will stand my watch, and set myself on the rampart, and watch what he will say to me."

## chapter 27

# Burn

*T*he third person I encountered on Barton's spiritual tour of the U.S. Capitol could be one of those soldiers on Habakkuk's rampart. On the morning of September 11, 2001, by chance or divine appointment, Lt. Col. Brian Birdwell stepped out of his office to go to the bathroom. Seconds later, a Boeing 757 jet, American Airlines Flight 77, loaded with 24,000 gallons of fuel, slammed into his office at the Pentagon. He survived with third-degree burns over 90 percent of his body. Everyone else in his office perished. Before rescue workers found him, scalded and soaked in jet fuel, he told me he had waited for what seemed like hours to be called home to the Lord. He had wanted and expected to die, but the Lord had never come, and against his will, he had lived.

"I don't know if there are words in the English language that can give you the gravity and intensity of what this feels like," he told me later. "You're conscious, and you know you're dying, and when you step over that line, you know that, when death comes, there's a peace that comes from knowing, 'I gave my heart to the Lord, I know where I'm going to spend eternity, and I know I'm going to meet the Lord.'"

Lieutenant Colonel Birdwell ended up in a burn unit, which he compared to a modern Golgotha. He compared his experience to the greatest suffering that he had ever imagined. "Because of the astronomical pain thresholds of critical burns, I have a greater appreciation for the pain thresholds associated with crucifixion," he said. "But what was being done to me in that burn unit was for my survival. What was being done to Christ was for his torment and to fulfill scripture. General Shinseki, the chief of staff of the army, came and presented me with the Purple Heart. At Christ's trial, he was adorned with a purple robe to be mocked, as Mark 14 tells us."

He went further. If he had died, he would have been buried in honor, his name memorialized on a tablet of stone for as long as the nation exists. But Christ's sacrifice and death means that "my name is written in a far more important place, in the Lamb's book of life, for all eternity. There is a big difference between the tactical level of day-to-day life that I face and the strategic things that the Lord did for all eternity."

Lieutenant Colonel Birdwell has been a regular speaker at Barton's Pastors Briefings for years. Barton told me that the officer punches home the deeper meanings of the briefing. "Birdwell has a great effect, because the pastors think, 'And I think I've got difficulties? I think I've got problems with my church?' So Birdwell is a good perspective on things. It's also a real good perspective on the war on terror, because it makes it a whole lot more personal than just another $87 billion appropriation for supplemental spending."

In the briefing, Lieutenant Colonel Birdwell tended to emphasize the political dimensions of his ordeal. He stressed the rightness of the war in Iraq, and he connected that effort with the day of the attacks, and his own deliverance. He made clear that he saw the war on terror as a war between good and evil, a form of spiritual warfare. In our conversation, his love and admiration for President Bush was evident. Bush had visited him in the burn unit and had wept at the sight of the soldier.

"The relationship he has with the Lord is the same as I have," he told me, "that relationship with salvation and redemption."

He recounted for me the first occasion of their meeting, pointing out that the last American president to have to visit casualties from an attack in the area around the capital had been Abraham Lincoln, almost 150 years before. "The president comes into the room, he and Mrs. Bush, very genuine, very down-to-earth, very humble. I couldn't speak. The president saluted. I'm prepared for surgery at the time, and I don't have bandages on, I have sterile towels. Once the president leaves, they're going to whisk me off to another scrubbing and a tub and then surgery. When I try to return the salute of the president, I pull my arm from beneath the sterile towel draped over my arm, and he's looking at exposed bone, there's still infection, you're talking about looking at a skinned arm that's blackened, purple muscle, bloody, exposed bone in the hands, wrist, and fingers, elbows, this is a ghastly thing to look at, and the thing that most impresses me is this. I don't think he cried those tears for me. They were the tears of understanding the overwhelming burden of the decisions he's going to have to make to protect the American people. And yet ultimately, as difficult as it was to risk the lives of sons and daughters of the United States in the war on terror, imagine how much more difficult and strategic it was for God the Father to say to the Son, here's your mission, it stinks, get on with it. That's why there is such respect for the president. We love that man."

In the soldier's story, I caught an unsettling glimpse of the state of the Christian nation in the era after 9/11. In our time, the question of authority has assumed a much greater urgency. If the war against terror, for believers, amounts to spiritual warfare between good and evil, right and wrong, then President Bush possesses a holy authority that previous presidents have not had. He therefore commands a deeper strain of loyalty and a far greater freedom of action. This explains, perhaps, the relative silence of evangelical Christians in this country over the question of torture, an issue that I had expected to galvanize the ranks in the pews against government excess. To my surprise, and shock, it never did.

More than that, if Lieutenant Colonel Birdwell can be said to represent the views of many people who share his faith, this war presents an unmistakable earthly reflection of that much greater war, the war between this world and the next, between the kingdom of God, and the kingdom of darkness, between those who believe and those who do not, between the saved and the damned. Another soldier, a high-ranking officer in the Pentagon, General William Boykin, had been reprimanded for making public statements to that effect about the war in Iraq, calling the conflict a form of "spiritual warfare" and claiming that his god was greater than the Muslim god. He had later been promoted to a job in counterintelligence.

I raised the question of spiritual warfare with Lieutenant Colonel Birdwell. In that war, I wondered, who was the enemy, and how did that combat work itself out in a daily walk of faith?

"It's the choice between right and wrong," he replied. "Scripture tells us that God gave dominion of earth, not only to man, to be a steward of the earth, but he gave dominion to Satan, the source of all evil, to the earth as well. He gave man free will to choose between good and evil. And I know that's a simplistic answer, straight out of Genesis, but in many cases, the simplest answer is the right one to the most complex of problems that we face. Choices were made in the Garden of Eden. The Lord knew those choices were going to be made before the Garden was ever created, and it is that spiritual warfare that says, right here are choices in front of you, and you get to make them."

This cosmic interpretation of earthly events constitutes one of the most unnerving aspects of evangelical culture to nonbelievers. To them, the world as described by Lieutenant Colonel Birdwell has no reality. And yet that unreality has played itself in the realm of national and international politics. It seems to have become a guiding force in the most serious questions of state, whether regarding policy toward Israel, Iraq, or stem cell research. A fantasy, a delusion, a belief in the invisible and the supernatural, has overwhelmed the reasonable consideration of cause and effect. That is the fear.

And I have to admit, here and now, despite my sympathy with so much that these people represent for the nation, an indispensable element in its joy and labor, a source of inspiration and hope for millions of working-class and poor people, as well as a moral compass for many among the wealthy and privileged, I share this fear. I share it, not only because of the kinds of faulty decisions that may result from a faith-based politics, but because I know that enormous numbers of Americans will never, ever accept such a politics, just as I know that these conservative Christians have not and will not accept a fully secularized politics. And this realization brings me to the heart of my dread, that an incompatibility in the body politic of such grave proportions will only ever resolve itself through a massive act of violence that will make any talk of spiritual warfare seem quaint indeed. I hear Lieutenant Colonel Birdwell talk, and I think of civil war.

AND THAT THOUGHT brings me back to Don and Lillie McWhinney's question. On June 6, 2006, I paid a visit to Denver, Colorado. The date is more significant than the place. In the book of Revelation, and in American popular culture, thanks to a cryptic mention, the numbers 666 have come to symbolize the Antichrist, also known as the Beast, also known as Satan. On that date, I have no idea what the forces of darkness concocted, but market forces saw at least two sales opportunities.

One was the debut of a movie, the remake of the 1976 Antichrist film *The Omen*, which opened on screens across the country and catered to secular audiences. The other was an event in Christian publishing, the appearance on bookshelves of the next installment in the Left Behind series, this one entitled *The Rapture*. I attended a book signing in the Denver suburb of Littleton, where, in 1999, two teenage boys went on a killing rampage at Columbine High School. The event took place in a Mardel Christian bookstore in another part of town and featured two of the biggest celebrities in the world of evangelical popular culture, Tim LaHaye and Jerry Jenkins.

Long before the producers of *The Omen* chose 666 to launch their movie, Tyndale Press, publisher of the Left Behind books, had seen an unmissable opportunity and named its pub date. That evening, in the store, LaHaye and Jenkins signed books for hundreds of people, the line winding back through the stacks. In a series of eleven previous volumes, the novels retold the biblical account of the end of the world as understood by dispensationalists, from the moment of the Rapture, when believers disappear to be with Christ in the heavens, to the return of Jesus at the end of a seven-year tribulation. In this new series, which started chronologically before the Rapture, LaHaye and Jenkins were taking another stab at the subject.

Fans approached the table laden with books and speaking of their admiration for the writers. LaHaye was in frail health and couldn't sign with his own hand, so his wife, Beverly LaHaye, an evangelical celebrity in her own right, pasted signed stickers on the books, and the author, also a minister and a prominent activist in conservative Christian politics in the 1980s and 1990s, chatted with his fans. Jenkins sat next to LaHaye and signed, too, and it was like watching royalty greet a horde of faithful subjects. People had brought their children, their babies, their stories. LaHaye, who had once been a driving force in conservative Christian politics, asked them when they'd been saved, where they'd been saved, how they'd been saved. People told him about the time they'd seen him preach in this or that church, or how they'd stayed up for night after night, reading the books, or how they had come to accept Christ through the books. Only one dissenter appeared, a grumpy, elderly, self-described gnostic in shorts, suspenders, and a Hawaiian shirt.

"He must be a *Da Vinci Code* fan," Jenkins remarked. A journeyman writer and dispensationalist believer, he had written several nonfiction books before striking it big with the Left Behind series.

I had read half of the first series before doing the *60 Minutes* piece that led to this book. They were poorly written, with stock characters and indifferent dialogue, but the first in the series had an infallible hook in the Rapture. In that moment, when believers disappear, the world is thrown into chaos. Planes lose their pilots and crash to the earth. Cars lose their drivers and hurl into walls. Loved ones vanish from each other's sight. Every child under eleven disappears. Fires, panic, and plague ensue. The publishers have maintained that the books do not distort in any way the biblical teachings of Revelation and are, in fact, a pop culture account of just what the Bible says will happen at the end of time. But it's a premillennial dispensationalist teaching, which means that it is only an interpretation, and one not shared by everyone interviewed in this book.

Dispensationalists like Tim LaHaye and Jerry Jenkins believe that Revelation, along with the books of Daniel and Isaiah and others in the Old Testament, relates a story of the church of Jesus Christ through time, in the form of seven dispensations, the last of which contains a prophecy about the future. It is this form of dispensationalism that places such a heavy emphasis on the return of the Jews to the land of Israel.

For me, as someone who left the faith, as a nonbeliever married to a Jewish woman, as the father of a Jewish child, I see the dispensationalist teaching on Revelation in a far more sinister light, and the Left Behind books clarify my sense of alarm. For me, with all due respect to the people who subscribe to the teaching, I see this entire strain of thinking in Christianity as the articulation of two things: panic about the extinction of the Christian faith on earth—and a death wish for the world.

Dispensationalism, which has been around for about five hundred years, really came into fashion in the late eighteenth and nineteenth centuries, in the era of the French Revolution and the industrial revolution. It wasn't until the modern world erupted and began to threaten the bases for belief in Christ that the need for the world to end came into its own. The turn of the second millennium since Christ has seen a further deepening of the sense of doom, and that makes sense to me. The technological transformation that began in the late eighteenth century has continued at an alarming rate. One hundred years ago, the rapid growth in automation gave us trains, planes, cars, the cinema, the telephone, the telegraph. Right now we live in a period of comparable change, and the transformation is once again being driven by science, based in rational and materialistic beliefs about the nature of reality. The same science that creates the computers used by church worship leaders to design amazing light shows on Sunday mornings, the same science that developed GPS used by missionaries venturing into remote parts of the earth, continues to build its blocks on a reality that doesn't include God or Christ.

At the same time, the last century has left Western civilization with a legacy of tremendous genocidal violence. Blood and change have seeped into the subconscious of the faith, just as they have done everywhere else, and the Left Behind books mix those two forces into a stew with scripture and produce a tale that speaks, beneath the surface, of a real-world obliteration. I think the end-time story cuts both ways. On the one hand, I believe the books' adherents receive a scary chill from the prospect of their own extinction as believers, wiped out not by their enemies, but by time and attrition; the Rapture becomes code for gradual disappearance. And at the same time, readers get to indulge in a revenge fantasy against the nonbelieving world that will preside over their extinction. They get to see the extermination of their enemies without any moral guilt, because God's hand wields the sword.

That will feel like a very serious accusation to Don McWhinney, who enjoyed the books. I don't think that Don would ever consciously wish such a terrible thing to happen to me and mine, and I know that he doesn't consciously believe that his faith will simply disappear from the earth. And yet I don't hear the voice of God contained within his question to me. I hear a reminder of recent history.

BEFORE I ATTENDED the book signing, on 666, I paid a visit to a bare piece of land on a bluff behind Columbine High School. It was a warm, windy, early summer day in Colorado. The front range of the Rocky Mountains lifted its spine to the immediate west. Clouds moved in streaks across a huge sky. School was out for the year. Here and there, people relaxed and played in the park adjacent to the school. It had been seven years since the massacre, and it had taken that long for the community to develop the political will and raise the funds to build a memorial to the victims. In a few weeks, former president Bill Clinton would come to the site for a dedication. I stood at the sign, viewing the design, which would involve trees and a reflecting pool.

After the attack, students had made their way to this spot as evacuees. On my visit, in that wind, by myself, the place had an electric feel. In the massacre, the gunmen had singled out Christians for slaughter. Afterward, a lot of kids had gathered at the home of a Young Life leader who had been in the cafeteria at the time of the attack. The killers had been angry at their treatment by the popular crowd, which had included evangelical kids who were also football players and popular girls. I lingered, and the whole thing became more horrible and sad. I thought of my own child, who would go to high school in just a few years. I could hear the pock of tennis balls on a court on the other side of the bluff. I could feel the sun warming my skin. It seemed impossible, under the circumstances, so much light, such clarity and beauty, and yet a massacre had happened in this bright, breezy, gorgeous world. In the same way, I felt, amid the shining beauties of the American evangelical faith, that there were shadows of cosmic massacres. And the two massacres, worldly and divine, met in the Colorado air. They collided. I had arrived again at my starting point. Would I be left behind?

# chapter 28

## *Eunice*

*I probably* shouldn't answer. Most people don't, not in public. Most people do it in the privacy of their own minds, keeping to themselves the record of the transaction.

But I have published Don and Lillie McWhinney's question. It's only fair, as much as I would like to end this book here and now with a bromide about how every viewpoint is legitimate and we should all just get along. During one of my trips back to Texas, I met an acquaintance of Don's, a staff member of Campus Crusade named Nick Repak. He and I chatted for a while about the effort to evangelize at places like Princeton and Harvard among highly educated, deeply skeptical elites. Nick told me that he enjoyed the company of those nonbelievers as much as he did the company of fellow Christians, if not more. There are a lot of people like that in evangelical Christianity, born missionaries. It's not just that they want to convert the world or feed the hungry or both. It's also that they get easily bored with their fellow Christians.

I told Nick about my effort to use the book as a means to answer the question, and he said, "Great. The key is going to be how *you* answer. You can't just leave it hanging in the air. You can't be wishy-washy. You have to land."

But the landing strip is like one of those places in the Amazon rain forest where missionaries like to park their planes, barely visible through the canopy of trees and surrounded on the ground by men with spears. It's taken me twenty-seven chapters to circle the strip. I will do my best to land.

I HAVE TO begin with Eunice Williams, wife of the Reverend John Williams, author of *The Redeemed Captive Returning to Zion*. At the outset of my story, I wrote about the Deerfield Raid of 1704 and its aftermath, and about the mass grave in the old burying ground. In that account, I mentioned the murder of Williams's wife, Eunice, at the hand of a Mohawk. I want to go back to that moment.

In his account, Williams wrote of his last meeting with his wife. "On the way, we discoursed of the happiness of those who had a right to an house not made with hands, eternal in the heavens; and God for a father and friend; as also, that it was our reasonable duty to submit to the will of God, and to say, 'The will of the Lord be done.' My wife told me her strength of body began to fail, and that I must expect to part with her; saying she hoped God would preserve my life, and the life of some, if not all of our children with us, and commended me under God to take care of them." Then comes the crucial sentence. "*She never spake any discontented word as to what had befallen us, but with suitable expressions justified God in what happened.*"

They separated. The Reverend Williams was taken forward. She struggled behind. He never saw her again. He crossed what is now known as the Green River and climbed to the top of a hill, waiting to get news of her. Down in the valley, in the river, she fell, and her captor bludgeoned her to death. "She never spake any discontented word as to what had befallen us, but with suitable expressions justified God in what happened."

The murder of Eunice Williams has haunted me ever since I read about it, and her husband's judgment on her state of mind increased my sense of unease. On Halloween day, 2006, I drove the two dozen miles from my house to the spot where she was killed. I had read in the local newspaper that one could visit a covered bridge built in the vicinity. The article, about local legends, said that people had seen the image of a woman deep down in the pool beneath the bridge. I drove north of Greenfield, Massachusetts, down a country road to another road that supposedly bore her name. The road wound down a hillside to a yellow barrier, and beyond the barrier, I saw the bridge. Even in the sunshine, it looked a forlorn place. Another person, a woman in blue jeans, meandered on the opposite bank.

The late autumn light felt like a presence in the woods. A last few yellow and brown leaves clung to the trees. Up high, breezes rustled through branches. I parked the car on one side of the barrier and navigated around a leaf-stuffed T-shirt that had fallen off a wooden piling, keeled over beside an empty beer can, someone's idea of a Halloween joke. I crossed the bridge. On my left, green water spilled in translucence across a small dam. On the right, the river foamed into a pool, which I presumed to be the place where Eunice Williams had died and where her ghost supposedly appeared. I had no proof. Nothing in Williams's journal gave a precise location. He himself hadn't seen the murder. But the logistics of the thing seemed apparent. To get to the covered bridge, I had descended a steep incline in my car. It was easy to imagine a sick, grieving woman stumbling through February snow down that same grade under duress. On the far bank, where I stood, the land flattened before rising again. The river made a logical place to finish the business. The body could be floated downstream. It had been found later by Deerfield residents and interred in the burying ground.

Near the spot, a worn metal plaque from the 1920s read: "Eunice Williams, wife of the Reverend John Williams, 'The Redeemed Captive,' was killed at this place on March 1, 1704, during the Deerfield Raid." Across the road, on a stone tablet on the far side, I saw another, older memorial. It looked more like a gravestone, but it wasn't. It quoted Williams: "'The cruel and bloodthirsty savage who took her slew her with his hatchet at one stroke.' Rev. John Williams of Deerfield, the Redeemed Captive, so wrote of his wife Mrs. Eunice Williams, who was killed at this place March 1, 1704." The stone was dated to August 1884. Some sixty years separated the two commemorations. Nothing had been erected since, and I had the strong impression of abandonment. People knew of the Deerfield Raid well enough, and the story of captives, redeemed and unredeemed, had become current again, but her death lay in this place as a forgotten chapter of American history.

I crossed back over the bridge and stopped halfway. I read the graffiti painted on the side of the pumping station and carved into the wood of the bridge railing. On the pumping station cement, someone had written, "To all the wax cats with wack foundations, it had begun." On the railing of the bridge were names and epithets: Drew, Josh, Scorpion, Gook. I made out a Maltese cross and SS style lightning bolt strikes. A rainbow misted out of the green waters, and I had a spiritual whimsy. The rainbow was Eunice, and she lived in redemption.

Or: the rainbow was Eunice, but she had not been redeemed. She never went to heaven. Part of her physical body had stayed in this place and become nature.

More than once, in my travels, Christians said to me that their belief hinged on the Resurrection. If Christ rose from the dead, then everything else must be true. If he didn't, nothing could be. I would put that formula another way. If Eunice Williams's death was final and cosmically meaningless, then so was the death of Christ. If I may believe that God willed and watched her cold-blooded murder and knew it as part of a plan, as he must have willed and watched Auschwitz and Rwanda and Gallipoli, then I may also believe that his son recomposed himself out of death. Unlike Christians, I can't possibly proceed in the opposite direction. I can't start with Christ, because his death happened so long ago, and the records of the event were written by men who had a vested interest in preserving the man as a god. For me, the death of one woman in history will have to be the test.

I would never suggest that her death had no meaning. Her death had a meaning, clearly, to her husband and her children. Her death has a meaning in the annals of New England history. She wasn't some arbitrary victim of random native violence. She perished in Queen Anne's War, a conflict between the French and their Mohawk allies and the British and their colonial allies, and that war had its roots in King Philip's War, a fight that went back to the first appearance of Christian white men and women on the shores of Massachusetts. Those settlers had stolen land from the natives. Eunice's brutal murder came as one consequence of that original sin, committed in the full sanctimony of a divine appointment. In that sense, too, the death of Eunice Williams had a meaning.

But did her death mean something ultimate? Did she die before the eyes of God? Was her murder known to the universe? This is the question.

AROUND THE TIME of Tedd McWhinney's funeral, I had a chance to speak with John Brown, one of Tommy Nelson's younger ministers at Denton Bible Church. We were discussing the impact of grief on a believer's faith, and I remarked that Don and Lillie seemed to have been strengthened rather than weakened by their sadness. John agreed with me and said that it was often the case. Grief rarely destroyed someone's belief. I asked him if he had ever experienced serious doubt.

He nodded. "Once, I was landing by night in the city of Bangkok, and I looked out at all those lights, and I thought, is it really possible that what I believe is true? All those people, all those lights. Can my truth be it?"

He yielded to his God, who exists, by definition, as a diversity in unity, but listening, I felt a tug in the other direction, yielding to the reality of the city over God. The former doesn't disprove the latter, but it is real in a way that the divine never has been, never will be. I never landed in Bangkok, but once over New York, right out of college, I landed by night over field after field of human light, my mouth open in amazement at the feeling of complexity. Down below, people were driving, walking, selling, killing, making love, raising children, despairing, dreaming, believing, disbelieving, everything, in repetition. How was it possible to impose a single truth on so much complexity? There might be gods below, millions of them. But a single redeemer for all, a man who had appeared in history to bring eternal light to all those huddled lanterns on the ground?

IN A BOOK first published in 1983, *The Search for Christian America*, three of the most distinguished evangelical historians in the United States demolish the notion that this country began as a Christian nation or should be seen as one. At the time of publication, David Barton had not yet begun his effort to transform the United States, but authors of the book, Mark Noll, George Marsden, and Nathan Hatch, might be speaking directly to him. They are all Bible-believing Christians, all historians with impeccable credentials, but they disagree vehemently with any attempt to make a direct link between their faith and the identity of the country. That linkage had become especially pronounced in the wake of two events in the 1970s—the 1973 Supreme Court decision legalizing abortion, and the 1976 Bicentennial Celebration, which became an opportunity to rally beleaguered conservative Christian Americans around a new version of the American flag. The 1960s and the first half of the 1970s had seen one devastating faith crisis after another. By 1976, the asking believers had begun to make their counterpunch. David Barton's efforts are the follow-through.

But Marsden, Noll, and Hatch argue that the attempt is misguided. The Puritans, to take the most obvious example, were flawed exemplars of the faith. They made wonderful contributions to American character and culture that cannot and must not be overlooked, but they also used their faith to disinherit the natives and oppress other Christians who held dissimilar views on scripture, Quakers and Baptists, in particular. Their intolerance allowed the Salem witch trials to darken the name of the colonies long before the revolution. The intolerance wasn't an aberration. It was policy.

I cannot attempt here to trace the entire argument, and my intent is not to debunk Barton, but to make clear that serious disagreement exists among Bible-believing Christians on the matter of American identity and history, a reality underscored by the 2006 midterm elections. In my effort to answer a simple question, therefore, I have to set aside the matter of politics. While I believe that secular attempts to erase the Christian past in this country have gone disgracefully far and should be challenged by courts and by public opinion, I completely disapprove of any attempt to turn back the clock and re-create a time and an era that is lost. I believe in the reality of the past, but I do not subscribe to the notion of that past as our destiny. Demographics suggest that, in the future, more Americans will be Catholics and Muslims and Hindus. There will be plenty of Protestants, but they will be Protestants in a land shared by a majority that isn't. Attempts to turn back the clock in such an environment don't smack of faith-based politics. They smack of politics masquerading as faith. And they can only lead to disaster. At best, they will result in an ethnic Christianity on the model of Serbia and Croatia, where the faith becomes a cross on a flag to demarcate a geographical territory. This is the very real danger of the Barton project.

On the Sunday before the 2006 midterm elections, I attended church at Calvary Bible Chapel in York, Pennsylvania. That following Tuesday, Republican senator Rick Santorum, a leader in conservative Christian politics, lost his Senate seat, and House Republican Curt Weldon went down to defeat. Neither in Sunday school at 8:30 nor during the main service at 9:30 did anyone mention the importance of voting biblically or voting at all. The pastor's sermon was about personal salvation, first, last, and always. The only mention of politics that morning appeared in the church events calendar; beside the date, Tuesday, November 7, were the words "Election Day—Vote." At a wonderful lunch cooked by the wife of an associate pastor, we talked about the proofs of the Resurrection. Politics didn't really interest the table. The following day, Monday, November 6, I spent in Coatesville, Pennsylvania, at the Chester County Jail, which has a strong faith-based emphasis for prisoners and employees. I asked my hosts if the elections would change or help or improve or damage anything in their work. Basically, they shrugged. Jack Crans, who ran the programs, told me that he'd never taken a dime of federal money and didn't plan to start. So, no, the elections wouldn't change anything.

And yet the previous week, James Dobson, the leader of Focus on the Family, the most powerful conservative Christian leader in the country, had argued that if the United States didn't turn away from its unrighteousness, God might well remove his umbrella of protection from the country. He implored voters to go to the polls and vote their biblical conscience. He essentially threatened his constituency with divine violence. In Pennsylvania, they were having none of it.

The politics of Christianity wax and wane from state to state, very much bound to time and place, no eternal plan discernible. Despite the defeat of several conservative Christians in the Republican Party, for instance, marriage amendments passed in several states. The Democratic Party sent a few new evangelical members to Congress. There will be more and more religious people in our public life, but they will be less obvious in their political allegiances.

On the third anniversary of the Iraq War, I asked an elder at Southeast Christian Church, a Vietnam veteran, why none of the services or Bible studies had dedicated any time to the subject. If polls were to be believed, three-fourths of evangelicals had supported the war, and just a mile away, there were demonstrations by family members. Headlines and evening newscasts made the anniversary unavoidable. "It's a nonissue," the elder told me. Some members at Southeast had family in the military, and some of them served in Iraq. The church did what it could to support those soldiers and their families. Beyond that, life went on. The war didn't galvanize much emotion, one way or another. Given the initial support for the war, I wondered how that could be.

"We didn't support the war," he told me. "We supported the president, and he supported the war."

It was a crucial distinction for me. If another president, even a Christian, had pushed that policy, it might have gone nowhere. But this president, with this base, had a special connection. When he goes, the politics of faith in the country will be different. Those politics will not go away, they may even become more outspoken, but they will not occur in the form of an intimate link between one man and one constituency. Future generations of conservative Christian Americans will look back and grasp that this was a one-time love affair, rarely to be repeated. One glance at the wholly unsatisfying slate of compromise candidates for 2008 makes that clear.

For me, it's significant that Don and Lillie asked me their question in the heated atmosphere of the Bush presidency, but the more I traveled and researched, the more I saw the roots of the moment burrowing into the previous three or four decades, and the future stretching forward Bush-less into an Awakening, one of those waves of religiosity that are said to transform the country from time to time. But the more I saw, the more I felt that any Awakening would shock and awe Christians more than their secular fellow citizens. America was changing in the presence of an aggressive new version of the faith, but the faith was changing, too, and even more dramatically.

One moment brought this home. My second tour at the annual meeting of the Evangelical Theological Society coincided with a topical theme, "Christianity in the Public Square," which dictated the location, Washington, D.C., two weeks after the midterms. There were speeches about the presidency of George Bush, slavishly pro, angrily con. Steve Parelli gave a presentation. He wasn't in the audience this time. He had applied to be a speaker, presenting a paper. His topic was esoteric: "How Baptist Doctrine May Obligate the Evangelical to View Same-Sex Marriage as Primarily a Civil Matter and a Matter of Individual Conscience." He used the Baptist doctrine of liberty of conscience, as evidenced by Roger Williams in the Massachusetts Bay Colony in the 1630s, as the basis for a plea. For his insistence on practicing his faith according to his own lights, Williams had been expelled from Massachusetts and founded his own colony in Rhode Island. In that colony, freedom of religious conscience reigned supreme. Centuries later, his belief had become Baptist doctrine. Parelli argued that Williams's belief extended to matters of matrimony. Did not freedom of religious conscience extend to that sacred institution? How could Baptists, of all people, deny the right of one of their own to marry before the eyes of God and under the law of the land? Wasn't that the oppression of the Massachusetts Bay Colony all over again?

The room tore him apart. Baptist historians rose and denounced his methodology. Never in all their years had they seen Roger Williams used in such a fashion. Freedom of religious conscience meant just that—*religious* conscience. It could not possibly be extended to cover a practice explicitly condemned by scripture. Williams could never have intended such a thing. When the lecture ended, however, the historians approached him, one by one, and I left those men deep in conversation.

THIS BOOK HAS to end, and I have to answer. Sweet D, my old roommate, once asked me what I had chosen, as if there were only two answers to one question. Don and Lillie asked me if I would be left behind, as if there were only two places to be, here and there. My old Young Life leader, Bobby McCreless, told me that it all came down to truth or lies, as if the first couldn't become a lie, and the second had never turned into truth. The fine old pastor of Southeast, Bob Russell, told me to trust and believe in the question-and-answer room in heaven, and I want to, I want to, but the problem is my inheritance. I was born in the twentieth century, in the relatively safe back half of it. But in the last decade, I saw what the rest had been, and it stunned me. I couldn't imagine a god that presided over a meaning, a redemptive meaning, in the murder by Josef Stalin of 50 million human beings through starvation and repression. I couldn't imagine the God of mercy that ruled over trench warfare or the machetes in Rwanda or the murder of the Jews of Salonika, of Kishinev, of Berlin, and Prague. I don't mean that I can't believe that good could ever coexist with evil or terrible events. I do believe in the possibility and existence of goodness; I've seen it. But the sovereign control of goodness over a temporarily rampant darkness is beyond me.

I understand what that means for the people who asked the questions. If I'm right, and they're wrong, they go nowhere known when they die. If I'm right, then Niki McDonnall's husband and friends were murdered for a delusion in the desert, and she lived to be tormented by an irretrievable past for the rest of her days, Lieutenant Colonel Birdwell survived by sheer chance at the Pentagon, Derek Citizen hit Tedd McWhinney for no rhyme or reason, except perhaps for the fact of a specific highway at a particular time of night. God didn't bring Don McWhinney and Derek together; grief and bewilderment did. If I'm right, the churches of Louisiana mobilized in a purely human effort to help their fellow creatures, a solidarity of skin rather than spirit; the troubled woman at Mission Messiah in west Texas let her son's fever rise so high for no good reason, and the other woman wasn't delivered from demons, but from memory; Craig Detweiler and Joanne Brokaw, two of the most decent and devout people I have ever known, and the best arguments for conversion that I have ever encountered, are delusional; and Steve Parelli and Jose Ortiz suffer from Stockholm syndrome, in love with a way of life, a prison of their own making, that they cannot escape. If God exists, each story here offers hope and redemption. If not, these are tales of superb perseverance in a world of cruelty and absurdity. What choice do they have but to disagree with me?

And these are only the people I've met in the last two to three years. If I'm right, I am also saying that those who were not so lucky, those whom the century laid waste, the mothers and children, the lovers and sinners, the corrupt and the righteous, I am also saying that they did not die as part of a divine plan. They died because monstrous human beings decided that they should, and this is a warning to all other monstrous human beings. The species is watching.

To level this judgment is a huge responsibility. I am afraid of it. And to be honest, I've known moments in my travels when the spirit seemed to alight nearby, and I'm hesitant to dismiss those moments. One morning, in particular, I went to a tiny church in Northampton to attend a prayer service. The church was a recent plant, barely a month old, and I had attended one of the first Sunday services, run by a man and wife, Brent and Leanne, who had just moved into the area from Cambridge. Brent wore an earring, and Leanne wore peasant skirts, and they seemed just about the right people to try and evangelize Hampshire County, which the U.S. Census named as the county with the largest number of lesbian parents in the United States. There were about twelve people in attendance at my first Sunday service; around sixty attend with some regularity now.

At the Sunday service, Brent mentioned that anyone who wanted a quiet time to pray for something specific could come on Wednesday morning and he would join them. I went, but I arrived late. Brent was by himself, standing upright, arms outstretched, lips murmuring ecstatic words too low to be heard. I coughed, surprising and embarrassing him. I was embarrassed, too. It was just the two of us. I sat, and he asked me if there was something I wanted to pray about, and I told him that my friend's wife had been diagnosed with Hodgkin's lymphoma. I was talking about Sweet D. Caroline had received the confirmation on one of my visits. Brent and I put our heads down, and he prayed for a few minutes out loud. He stopped. I guess he was waiting. Finally, he said, "If there's anything you'd like to add, jump right in." I didn't, not out loud. To myself, I prayed that she would get well, and I got out of there. A year later, the cancer went away.

That meant something to me. It would have meant a lot more if it had been my wife instead of Craig's. But even if my own beloved Debra were saved in the wake of a prayer, would it be enough?

The twentieth century, my century, asks its own terrible questions. Bosnia? Hiroshima? Rwanda? Armenia? So many people, and so many Christians, looking away when the Jews of Europe were led to their deaths? So many people, and so many Christians, embracing racist policies all over the world during the era of colonialism, policies that led to murder and catastrophe on a cosmic scale? One species allowed its full, unfettered measure of violence for so long? A god has overseen this nightmare? A god whose divine plan accounts for all the torment, horror, and loss visited upon ourselves by ourselves over the course of this century, and all centuries? And it's not over yet, surely. Someone else, some other nation, is already preparing itself for the next slaughter, in which I do not want to voluntarily, unnecessarily implicate myself. A god who can't stop it has no right to my loyalty or my belief. I can't speak for others. For now, I'm a free man in a free land. I am a man of the twentieth century, and I rest on the authority of the uneasy dead. Leave me behind.